Microsoft .NET XML Web Services

Robert Tabor

201 West 103rd St., Indianapolis, Indiana, 46290 USA

Microsoft .NET XML Web Services

Copyright © 2002 by Sams

International Standard Book Number: 0-672-32088-6

Library of Congress Catalog Card Number: 00-109100

Printed in the United States of America

First Printing: December 2001

04   03   02   01   4   3   2   1

Trademarks

Warning and Disclaimer

ASSOCIATE PUBLISHER
Jeff Koch

ACQUISITIONS EDITOR
Neil Rowe

DEVELOPMENT EDITOR
Kevin Howard

MANAGING EDITOR
Matt Purcell

PROJECT EDITOR
Natalie Harris

COPY EDITOR
Lisa M. Lord

INDEXER
Joy Dean Lee

PROOFREADER
Andrea Dugan

TEAM COORDINATOR
Denni Bannister

MEDIA DEVELOPER
Dan Scherf

INTERIOR DESIGNER
Dan Armstrong

COVER DESIGNER
Aren Howell

PAGE LAYOUT
Ayanna Lacey

Contents at a Glance

Table of Contents

About the Author

Robert Tabor (MCP) has over eight years experience in Microsoft technologies as a software consultant for many well-known companies, such as Ernst & Young, KPMG, Cambridge Technology Partners, Sprint, the American Heart Association, and the Mary Kay Corporation. He has a degree in Management Information Systems from Loyola University of Chicago. Robert provides thought leadership on .NET, SOAP, and Web Services at his site http://www.SOAPWebServices.com.

Dedication

To my loving wife, Beth, and my sons, Conrad and Grant, who unbegrudgingly afforded me this opportunity to pursue a lifelong dream. I could not have accomplished this without your love, encouragement, motivation, and support.

Also, I would like to thank my parents who sowed the seeds for a life of learning and hard work by their example. I thank you especially for the computers, books, education, and other financial sacrifices you made to help me accomplish my goals.

Acknowledgments

I would like to start by thanking David Findley, who has helped in many ways to complete this book. He provided code examples in several of the chapters, supplied technical advice, and through numerous discussions helped me formulate opinions on issues related to .NET and Web Services.

I sincerely thank Jason Bentrum, Barry Bloom, and James Whatley for their friendship and insight into technical writing, as well as many people at the Mary Kay Corporation who offered encouragement throughout this process, including Robert Penn, Gary Hartley, and Bill Brown. Also, I thank my friends Steve Turquette, Conrad Feagin, Chris Armstrong, and Dan Starr for their enthusiasm for this project and for putting a smile on my face every once in a while.

There have been many other people who have had a high degree of influence on me and my career development over the years, and I would like to especially acknowledge Randy Potter for helping me get started years ago by encouraging me to learn Visual Basic and helping me obtain a position at Ernst & Young, LLP in 1995. Additionally, I thank Mike Thomas for his mentoring and friendship, as well as George Santillian, Paul Garret, and Kevin Kidd.

I would like to extend a special thanks to Chris Webb for his initial interest in a Web Services book and to Keith Ballinger, the Product Manager for .NET Web Services at Microsoft, for his ongoing interest and assistance in writing this book. Finally, I thank the Sams Publishing team for their diligent efforts to shape and mold my writing into a book, including my technical editor, John Timney; Lisa Lord, who made my writing intelligible (thereby deserves extra credit); Natalie Harris; and Neil Rowe, for his patience and perseverance in putting up with me while I took forever to finish.

Tell Us What You Think!

As the reader of this book, *you* are our most important critic and commentator. We value your opinion and want to know what we're doing right, what we could do better, what areas you'd like to see us publish in, and any other words of wisdom you're willing to pass our way.

As an Associate Publisher for Sams, I welcome your comments. You can fax, e-mail, or write me directly to let me know what you did or didn't like about this book—as well as what we can do to make our books stronger.

Please note that I cannot help you with technical problems related to the topic of this book, and that due to the high volume of mail I receive, I might not be able to reply to every message.

When you write, please be sure to include this book's title and author as well as your name and phone or fax number. I will carefully review your comments and share them with the author and editors who worked on the book.

Fax:	317-581-4770
E-mail:	feedback@samspublishing.com
Mail:	Jeff Koch
	Sams
	201 West 103rd Street
	Indianapolis, IN 46290 USA

Introduction

In retrospect, I admit that the promise of XML escaped me when I began to read about it in 1997. From a technical perspective, it was definitely attractive: self-describing data, using HTML-like tags, open to all platforms, and so forth. However, from a business perspective, I saw less to be excited about. At that time, there was no "killer app" for XML that revolutionized how we understood technology. In my mind, XML was simply a better way to do what was currently being done with comma- or tab-delimited files.

When I read the SOAP specification in late 1999, I immediately recognized the value of XML when used in the context of a remote procedure call to exchange (typically) non-visual information with any computing platform. This technology would solve many of the problems I had encountered with exchanging information with trading partners. It's not that this was an extremely difficult problem to solve from a technical perspective before SOAP, but rather that each implementation involved a different "by-the-seat-of-your-pants" approach. With the introduction of the SOAP specification, a more standard approach could be agreed on to solve this problem. Additionally, with the accompanying technologies such as the Web Service Description Language, Discovery of Web Services, and others, the adoption of Web Services could thrive.

But more than being a better solution to a technical problem, it is my firm belief that this technology and its future incarnations will allow businesses to interact in ways that were prohibited in the past. New types of businesses will emerge, such as Microsoft .NET My Services, and others we have yet to imagine. New types of partnerships and business relationships will be realized. Different brands and types of devices will be able to communicate with each other seamlessly. In fact, these are some of the tenets of the Microsoft .NET vision.

Obviously, we have only begun to tap into what the Internet is capable of. After all, the Internet is simply a network on a grand scale. It was vogue years ago to refer to the Internet as the "Information Super Highway." The analogy still has a great deal of merit because historically nations with a ubiquitous and healthy road system become major economic powers. In the United States, the Industrial Revolution was made possible by the railways, and the expansion era of the 1940s and '50s was furthered by the infrastructure investment of the U.S. government. In a similar manner, Web Services will fuel the fire of economic expansion in the Internet age, making it easier for companies to exchange information about customers, products, and promotional offers and to form exchanges, partnerships, and affiliations more quickly and efficiently than ever before.

The Microsoft .NET Framework and Visual Studio .NET will help drive this effort to enable businesses to communicate electronically. As you will read in this book, Microsoft's first incarnation of .NET makes XML, SOAP, and Web Services first-class citizens (as Microsoft-ies are fond of saying) of the environment. A colleague recently created a Web Service that enables his company to communicate with a credit card transaction clearinghouse to support a non-typical situation in the business transaction. Having never worked with Visual Studio .NET, he was amazed at how easily he was able to come up to speed on Web Services and create a production-ready .NET Web Service. He kept asking, "Is this all I need to do?", sure that he had missed something because it seemed all too simple.

If it is so simple, why read an entire book on the topic? Although it is true that you can create powerful Web Services quickly by not knowing much more than just the basics about Web Services, you can dig deeper and learn more about the underlying technologies, and learn how to extend your Web Services to offer more functionality to consumers of the services. The goals of this book are twofold: to introduce the fundamental concepts behind Web Services and to explain advanced concepts about building and deploying Web Services for real-world use.

Be forewarned that I have taken a Visual Studio .NET–centered approach to creating the examples in this book. It is my firm belief that when enterprise and corporate developers realize the advantages of using Visual Studio .NET, they will never again return to using Notepad (or some text editor) and the .NET Framework alone. Many of the examples can be modified to use just the .NET Framework, but the steps and ideas presented in this book definitely cater to the Visual Studio .NET developer.

Who This Book Is For

To maximize your experience with this book, you, the reader, should be familiar with development using Visual Basic .NET or C# because a certain fundamental skill level is assumed at the outset. It is also intended for developers who will do most of their development using Visual Studio .NET, as mentioned in the previous section. Finally, you should have an understanding of basic Internet protocols, such as HTTP, and have done some Internet programming, even if it is just simple Active Server Page development. Finally, you should have a basic understanding of object-oriented development because of the nature of .NET languages such as VB .NET and C#.

Conventions Used

As you read the text, you will encounter several elements used to enhance your learning:

NOTE

Notes give you extra information on a topic currently being discussed or point you elsewhere to get extra information about the current topic.

TIP

Tips are used to point out new or different ways to do a task.

CAUTION

Cautions throw up a "red flag" on a topic being discussed. They point out possible trouble spots or pitfalls that you might encounter as you create your Web farm.

The sidebar is used to cover a topic in more detail. Case studies or further instruction often are provided with this element.

You'll notice some typographic conventions used in this book, too. Code listings and code elements, such as classes, objects, and so forth, are formatted in a `monospace computer font`. **`Bold monospace`** lines in code listings and steps indicate text you should type in. *Italics* are used to indicate placeholders and are sometimes used for emphasis or to introduce new terms.

Introducing Web Services

IN THIS CHAPTER

This chapter introduces Web Services from several different perspectives. First, you'll look at current business trends that require data exchange across potentially disparate homogeneous systems. Then you'll review the existing technologies that are available to address these data exchange needs, briefly examining their strengths and weaknesses. I'll introduce Simple Object Access Protocol (SOAP) and Web Services and how they address the shortcomings of existing solutions. Also, I'll briefly explain new specifications and technologies that surround SOAP and provide context to their role in the era of the programmable Web. Finally, I'll introduce ASP.NET Web Services and discuss ways that Web Services can be used in a common n-tier development model.

Why Web Services?

This is a fundamental question: What problem do Web Services solve? What is the need in the marketplace for this technology? Are there other technologies that "fit the bill" for this need? In the first part of this chapter, I'll show the current business and technical climate to paint a picture of the need for a technology such as SOAP and Web Services.

Current e-Business Trends Require Integrating Disparate Distributed Systems

In years past, the lack of a standard communication infrastructure was a barrier to organizations exchanging data with other organizations. Interaction between companies has always existed in some form. However, it was difficult to achieve a high degree of interaction electronically because of the number of different hardware and software platforms, the lack of common protocols, and the number of proprietary data stores. Through the Internet and its accompanying technologies, businesses are finding new ways to cooperate electronically with each other and enjoy higher degrees of business process cohesion. Within your organization, you might see one or more of the following trends beginning to emerge.

Business to Business Integration (B2Bi) Trend

The term *Business to Business* (B2B) came into vogue in the summer of 1999. It seemed every company was tacking this term onto existing corporations and dot-com startups' business plans to find favor with investors. B2B soon became synonymous with procurement auctions. Suppliers would list their goods, both tangible (such as paper and light bulbs) and intangible (storage, shipping, labor, and so on), and they would be sold to the highest bidder. Dozens, if not hundreds, of industry-specific B2B sites currently exist as the middleman between buyers and sellers to create (in theory) a more efficient marketplace for goods and services.

However, procurement auctions did not adequately describe all the different interactions between businesses that could be achieved by using the Internet. A new set of terms began to pop up that described different ways businesses could work together to create a more efficient way of doing business. The most ubiquitous term you'll see is *Business to Business Integration* (B2Bi). Also, the term *trading partner* has gained a high degree of use recently. The idea is that companies can rely on each other as partners to promote and sell each other's products and services to their existing client bases. For example, two trading partners can tightly integrate their systems so that Company A is selling Company B's products. The product's prices and availability are retrieved in real time and displayed on Company A's Web site. When customers come to Company A's Web site, they are actually looking at the price and availability information that Company B has supplied. After the order is placed, Company B is responsible for fulfilling the order and providing customer assistance. Company A may, in fact, have many of these relationships with vendors and never have an inventory or customer service department of its own! This arrangement could represent significant savings. Company A's value to the marketplace could be that it aggregates the best products from many different vendors, or supplies deep discounts based on its volume, or just that it has the most recognizable brand name in the marketplace. Nike outsources most of its operations for creating athletic wear and shoes. However, its value to the marketplace is its designs and strong brand recognition.

Additionally, companies might integrate their systems in many other ways. Corporations can create purchase orders directly into their suppliers' order entry systems by using their own inventory management system or procurement software. Likewise, companies can seamlessly integrate a number of different services such as doctor referral, insurance, pharmacy orders, and patient transfers through the use of open and agreed-upon data exchange standards. There's literally no end to the possibilities. In the past, such tight integration would have been challenging and expensive.

Trend Toward the Virtual Value Chain

The concept of the value chain emerged many years ago as a way for companies to outsource business processes that were not the organization's core competency. Henry Ford used a vertically integrated value chain in the 1930s to design, build, deliver, market, and support his Model T Fords. More recently, companies began to outsource their human resource needs to third-party vendors who essentially "hired" the company's employees, gave them benefits packages, and managed the payroll, taxes, uniforms, and so forth. This concept expanded in many ways and is prevalent today. In fact, almost every company depends on an outsourced organization to contribute value to the organization.

Over time, companies started to rely on third-party outsourcing organizations to perform tasks that were even more critical to product or service delivery. A company might rely on one vendor to take orders, another vendor to manage inventory, and yet another vendor to make sure the product or services were delivered. In these instances, the value chain is virtual: Customer and product data must be exchanged between potentially many different companies to get the product or service from the order to the delivery.

Again, to quickly integrate two or more different systems requires open network and data exchange standards as well as a set of robust tools that allow developers to pull together these disparate systems quickly and easily.

Software as a Service Trend

Microsoft made a shocking statement in the summer of 2000. No longer did it want to be thought of as a software company that sells a product. Instead, it wanted to be a company that supplies software services. Microsoft began to outline how the entire product line would be available in some fashion as a software service. In other words, each application would be licensed as a rental, users would need to be somewhat connected to the Internet to take advantage of all the features of that software, and new updates to the software would be made automatically as you accessed the software over the Internet.

Although Microsoft is probably the best known, it's not the first software company to sell software as a service. Some of the first companies to offer software as a service did so more than 30 years ago. IBM, CSC, and EDS all provided computation, payroll, and other financial services to companies. More recently, a new crop of companies known as application service providers (ASPs) have provided their own software and hosted software from other companies to many clients since the summer of 1999. Applications for e-mail, customer relationship management, and supply chain management are just a few examples of the types of applications that have become available via the ASP model. From the clients' perspective, the ASP model offers them a more inexpensive way to implement and maintain these types of applications than hiring professionals to do these tasks. With professional staffing costs on the rise because of a recent high-tech labor shortage, this method makes sense financially in certain situations. From the ASPs' perspective, they can offer services to many companies, thereby achieving an economy of scale by hiring one staff that can service many companies. Also, they can offer their clients the expertise of professionals who are deeply focused on a particular technology. Such expertise is a luxury many companies cannot afford on their own.

Similar to ASPs are companies that allow clients to outsource certain business activities, such as credit card validation, payment processing, and order fulfillment.

Trend Toward Repackaging Expertise

A new trend is emerging among companies that have developed a high degree of expertise in one or more business processes. For companies that have spent a lot of time and money developing a staff and infrastructure that can efficiently support online order management or order fulfillment, they can choose to repackage their expertise and offer these services to other companies (perhaps even their competitors!). As a result, they create a second company that continues to service the original company, but also repackages that expertise and sells it to other companies who are looking to outsource that particular business function. The most important benefit to the company is that the business process changes from a cost center to a profit center.

Trend of System Integration Within the Distributed Enterprise

Many large organizations have subsidiaries, departments, and divisions that are geographically and technologically dispersed. In most cases, an entire enterprise does not use just one type of hardware/software platform. There are a number of reasons for this: Some platforms are better suited for certain core business tasks, the particular division is not profitable enough to warrant the purchase and development of new hardware and software. Or, the divisions represent companies that had been purchased by the parent company, so the organization decided to leave the divisions' existing information technology (IT) infrastructure in place instead of mandating an expensive transition to systems that integrate better with the parent company and the other divisions. Whatever the case might be, in large (and even not so large) enterprises, multiple systems must be supported and these systems are often required to "talk" to each other.

In the past, integrating disparate systems was challenging. First, the gateway interfaces between two platforms were not always available. When there is no common ground--no common network transport mechanism, no common character codes, and therefore no common way to send data back and forth--it makes integrating these systems a nightmare. The dust has settled somewhat in this arena. However, there is still a need to quickly and easily share data between systems in a way that does not require the two systems to become tightly coupled, but securely shares corporate data within the organization.

Problems with Existing Technologies

Each of the trends I've discussed can be addressed with currently available technologies. Why do we need another technology? Unfortunately, existing technologies have some severe limitations that have thwarted many projects (or at least made them more challenging). Let's take a look at some of the most popular methods of exchanging data in the IT world from two perspectives: how companies format data they want to exchange, and how they transmit that data.

Data Format

In the past, companies have struggled to exchange data because one company prefers to send data in a different format than another company prefers to receive it. Translating the two formats is often difficult because few tools were available to automate this process. The tools that did exist were merely patches on a bad idea--a bad approach to formatting data for transmission in the first place. The following sections are two examples of how the IT world typically formats data and why these formats pose a problem when exchanging data between two companies.

ASCII Comma-Delimited or Columnar-Delimited Files

Although ASCII-based text files are open and used extensively in the IT world, this approach to exchanging data has problems. (By "open," I mean that the format of ASCII-based text files is not proprietary, but published--or, in this case, obvious.) First, there's no standard way to format the files or a way to describe the values in the file. The implementation of ASCII is up to each business partner. Partners exchanging data in ASCII format must then work closely together to build custom loading software to handle each other's file format. Also, ASCII files do not describe relational data or hierarchical data very well, so they are better suited to flat file formats.

Specific File Format

Two companies can exchange data via a specified file format, such as Microsoft Excel or Access files, DB2 databases, or some other "proprietary" format. However, this solution does not "scale" well and requires a great deal of customization to create "bridging software" when you want to bring in a new trading partner who does not accept your file format.

Data Transmission

Companies have also struggled with sending and receiving data to and from their trading partners because the existing approaches were antiquated and error prone. The following sections give just a few examples of how companies have attempted to exchange data and the problems encountered in doing so.

Sneaker Net

Companies can communicate via *sneaker net*, a term used to refer to the data transfer method that consists of someone copying data on to a diskette, and then walking (or mailing or flying) the data over to another computer. In fact, many companies still use this approach! The obvious problem is the time it takes to deliver the data, and the delivery is only as guaranteed as the person you depend on to deliver it.

File Transfer Protocol (FTP)

Companies can transfer data files back and forth to each other by using FTP. This method is popular, but not a highly automated solution. You can ensure guaranteed delivery with tools like IBM's MQ Series. However, this solution depends on files being sent, which is not a dynamic way to exchange data. Custom code must be written for each trading partner to understand and process the data being received. Ultimately, FTP does facilitate file transfer, but sending files is not a tight, object-oriented approach to exchanging data.

What About Electronic Data Interface (EDI)?

EDI has been a proven solution for exchanging information between companies. However, EDI is rigid and complex. As a result, it's expensive to implement, maintain, and deploy to new trading partners. This cost becomes a barrier to small companies who might want to exchange data with large organizations but can't afford the software, hardware, and network connection required to bring them into the EDI fold. What eventually happens is that the larger trading partners rely on EDI, which accounts for 80% of the business. In contrast, smaller companies rely on faxes or telephones as a means of exchanging data, which accounts for 80% of the costs of time and money.

If there were an easier and less expensive way to implement and use EDI, both large and small trading partners could enjoy its benefits.

COM and CORBA/ORB/IIOP

More recently, two technologies emerged to allow

- A more Remote Procedure Call (RPC)–based approach, as opposed to the file-based transmission approach
- A more object-oriented approach to exchanging information
- A less expensive implementation of data exchange (than say, EDI)

The Distributed Component Object Model (DCOM) allowed Microsoft/COM-based applications residing on different computers to communicate with each other as though they were on the same machine. The Internet Inter-ORB Protocol (IIOP)/Object Request Broker (ORB)/Common Object Request Broker Architecture (CORBA) standard accomplished a similar feat for Unix-based applications.

However, these approaches were not without their own special brand of challenges.

Existing Technologies Are Platform Specific

The biggest problem is that DCOM and CORBA are platform specific. To create a system based on DCOM, you must be fairly sure that all your potential business partners can use DCOM as well.

Existing Technologies Do Not Easily Integrate

To get two systems based on different technologies to work together, you must create some type of *bridge*, a mechanism that translates messages from one system's message format so that a different system can understand and act on the requests and responses (see Figure 1.1). These bridges do exist but are less than perfect because of the difficulty involved in mapping all the DCOM functionality, data types, and so forth to CORBA (and vice versa).

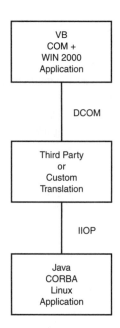

FIGURE 1.1

Bridging DCOM- and CORBA-based systems.

Existing Technologies Pose Security Risks

Most companies use firewalls to protect their networks against potential security problems. Firewalls prevent network communications across certain configurable ports and protocols and also prevent certain types of data, such as binary executables, from being transferred to the company's network. Most companies allow Hypertext Transfer Protocol (HTTP) requests on port 80, and perhaps Simple Mail Transfer Protocol (SMTP) for e-mail, but little else.

However, both DCOM and CORBA require that certain ports be opened on the firewall to accommodate their messages (which are binary, not ASCII text). Hackers can exploit this hole in the firewall and at the very least intercept the messages; the worst-case scenario is that they could bring down the entire system!

Many companies attempt to take the proper precautions, but they readily realize the risks of having systems online that require an opening in the corporate firewall.

What Is Needed

Current e-business trends require integrating disparate distributed systems, and although some technologies address these requirements, they are inappropriate, fiscally or technically challenging (and therefore costly), inflexible, or nonstandard.

To accomplish the needs of today's businesses, developers require a technology that can be integrated across many different types of systems, can interface easily with legacy systems, and does not pose network security risks.

Additionally, it would be an advantage if that technology

- Used existing technologies (protocols, network access, hardware, software) that were inexpensive, easy to implement, easy to maintain, and allowed leverage of knowledge and existing resources.
- Was based on an open standard that was accessible to everyone.
- Inherently guaranteed delivery of messages without expensive software solutions.
- Was human readable (verbose) and understandable to be of more help when trying to debug a problem.

SOAP: An Integration Solution

Since existing technologies aren't ubiquitous in the marketplace, they are not good candidates on which to build a new economy so that any company can offer data and computational services--*inexpensively*--to another company regardless of the hardware or software platform. What is needed is a way to transfer information across platform and company boundaries to provide services to any other business on the Internet. Because of the phenomenon of "Internet Time," the service must be easily integrated into the consuming businesses' existing systems. It would also be helpful if this process of discovery could be automated to some degree. SOAP affords the world of B2B e-commerce these integration advantages.

What Is SOAP?

Simple Object Access Protocol (SOAP) is covered in more depth in Chapter 7, "Examining SOAP," but briefly, it is a specification that defines how messages can be sent between two software systems through the use of eXtensible Markup Language (XML). These messages typically follow a Request/Response pattern (shown in Figure 1.2): One computer makes a method call, and the other computer performs some computation or service and then returns a result to the calling application. There are other ways to use SOAP, but this is probably the most common way it's used at first.

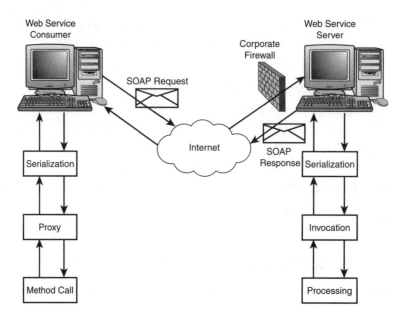

FIGURE 1.2

How SOAP works.

As I've mentioned, SOAP has tremendous advantages over other protocols:

- **SOAP is platform independent:** Because SOAP is just plain XML, it can be used on any platform, meaning that the typical barriers between systems based on RPCs can be eliminated. For example, if you are running a credit card authorization system on a mainframe computer and I have built an e-commerce storefront using ASP.NET, there will be no problem using your services as long as you expose them as Web Services that receive and transmit SOAP. As you can imagine, this advantage opens the doors for more competitive pricing and more diverse business opportunities.

  "So what?" you might exclaim. "I can already do that with EDI." That's true, but you can't do it as quickly, simply, and inexpensively as you can with SOAP and Web Services. SOAP makes it possible for thousands of smaller companies and departments to find new ways of working together on-the-fly.

- **SOAP is easy to integrate into disparate systems:** Because SOAP is just XML, it is easy to integrate a service that resides as a message filter or proxy to send and receive SOAP messages and then translate them into messages specific to any given application or platform.

- **SOAP poses fewer security risks:** SOAP is simply XML, so it can be used on port 80, which is typically configured for HTTP. This feature gives SOAP messages the advantage of being able to go through firewalls without any other ports being opened, which reduces potential security breaches.

Relationship Between SOAP and Web Services

SOAP is a specification that defines the structure of an XML message that can be sent over the network to call and return results from an application. *Web Service* is the term used to describe an application that makes SOAP (or other types of) callable methods available. Web Services are not, however, exclusive to Microsoft! Web Services can be created by any software or operating system vendor and do not necessarily have to use SOAP to send messages. However, so far it seems that SOAP and Web Services are used almost synonymously, and Microsoft has embraced the term quite heartily by naming its implementation of Web Services "ASP.NET Web Services," or if you are among other Microsoft developers, just "Web Services."

Now that you've reviewed Web Services and SOAP and their benefits, take a moment to examine some possible uses of Web Services.

Scenario 1: A Simple Web Service for an Auto Parts Distributor

An auto parts distributor decides to allow its customers to order online using Web Services (see Figure 1.3). It notifies its existing customers, mainly body and repair shops, of this new way to automate placing orders and determine their status. Soon orders from some of its largest customers begin to automatically appear in the order management system. The distributor realizes a significant time savings for the employees who typically answered the phone and took orders or tried to determine whether the customer's order was shipped. It can then reallocate those employees to other efforts to ensure better quality and faster order fulfillment.

Scenario 2: Auto Parts Revisited

The auto parts distributor then decides to submit its Web Services and other contact information to a search engine made especially for companies that conduct business over the Web in this manner (see Figure 1.4). This "search engine" is known as Universal Description, Discovery, and Integration, or UDDI. Soon other companies from around the world begin to query the auto parts distributor's Web Services for pricing and availability information, and many begin to place orders. This is a huge success for the auto parts distributor because without UDDI, these companies might never have realized this company existed.

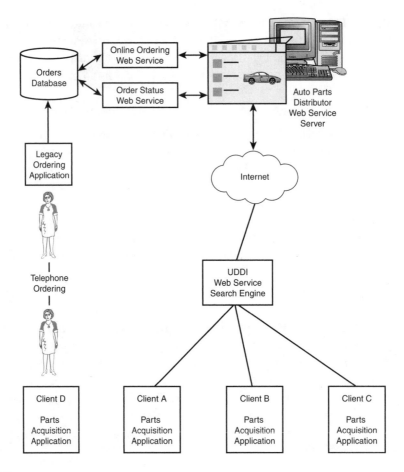

FIGURE 1.3

Auto parts distribution.

Additionally, the distributor signs a deal with a vertical Business to Consumer (B2C) market-place where users can query a database for a given part and find the best price for the part any-where in the world. The vertical B2C marketplace uses information supplied by the Web Services from the chosen company to dynamically create a distinct order form for that company. After the consumer fills out the payment information, the purchase order is completed and sent to the supplier. The auto parts distributor thus finds a new market for its products.

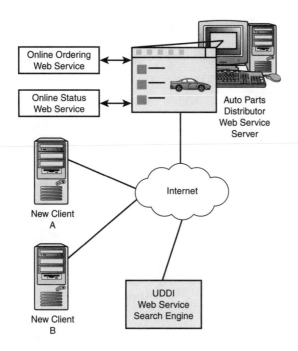

FIGURE 1.4

Auto parts distribution--revisited.

Scenario 3: Futuristic Web Service

In this scenario, suppose that David has an accident. His car is equipped with a "Safety and Security Global Positioning System" (call it an "SSGPS") system that can detect when David's car has been damaged (see Figure 1.5). Immediately, the SSGPS wirelessly contacts its server and sends everything it knows, including the accident location, the severity of the damage, and the driver's information. The SSGPS server locates Web Services that interact with the 911 rescue facility closest to the accident and sends along all pertinent information. The SSGPS awaits confirmation, and then contacts a towing company's Web Service and the driver's insurance company with the information. It also directs the towing company to take the car to a preferred body shop where the car will be assessed by both a claims adjuster and the body shop.

The ambulance assesses the driver's health and, if required, sends his status and diagnostic information to a nearby hospital. In anticipation that David will be taken to an area hospital, the SSGPS sends the driver's pertinent information, including primary physician information, to all area hospitals where it is saved into a queue. The ambulance arrives and the driver's information is pulled from the queue, thereby speeding his entry and treatment. The primary physician's Web Service is called and an attending physician reviews the patient's medical records. The doctor discovers that David is allergic to certain medicines. The doctor uses this information to better treat David.

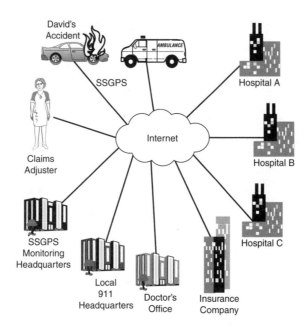

FIGURE 1.5
Web Services of the future.

David's health insurance provider is also contacted by the hospital, and fewer forms need to be manually filled out. The bill is sent electronically to the health insurance provider. The towing company bills the auto insurance company. The claims adjuster is notified on her PDA. She drives to the body shop, reviews the damage, and approves the need for repairs. After negotiating with the body shop, she sends her authorization back. The body shop bills the insurance company via Web Services and that amount is checked against the negotiated amount.

What Is WSDL?

Web Services are a lot like the objects you've created in your applications for years. Your objects have callable methods and properties and are instantiated from a definition called a *class*. Similar to a class is the Web Services Description Language (WSDL), which is an XML document that defines the programmatic interfaces of your Web Service. You can learn about all the methods a Web Service makes available by looking at its WSDL document, just as you can learn about an object's properties and methods by looking at its class. The WSDL also defines the "method signature"--that is, the arguments (and their respective data types) it expects and the values it returns (and its data type).

Although you could access the WSDL, read it, and then code your application to reference the Web Service accordingly, tools such as Visual Studio.NET can automate this process for you.

That explains *how* you learn enough about the Web Service to call it, but how do you find *what* Web Services are even available? There are two pieces to this puzzle: DISCO and UDDI.

What Is DISCO?

DISCO, an abbreviation for Discovery of Web Services, is a specification created to help developers determine how they can find Web Services on a server. A DISCO file contains the uniform resource identifier (URI--similar to a URL except it applies to more than just the location of Web pages) of each Web Service available on that machine. The URI typically points to the WSDL document, which then points to the actual Web Service.

What Is UDDI?

UDDI, an acronym for "Universal Description, Discovery, and Integration," can be thought of as the search engine for Web Services. It is a specification that defines how a business directory can be created that holds a series of references to companies that offer Web Services online; it also stores additional information about the company offering the Web Services, such as its business categorization (for example, SIC code), geographical location, and so forth. When you find a business in the search engine, you'll see information on where to find out more about the company's business processes and Web Services. The directory typically offers a URI representing a DISCO or WSDL file on the company's server.

The idea behind UDDI is that it's a meeting place for companies looking for goods and services and those supplying goods and services and a place where both parties want to conduct business electronically.

Figure 1.6 illustrates the relationship between Web Services and the companion technologies discussed in the preceding sections.

Web Services can be called and the results returned via SOAP. For a potential business partner to learn of a company's Web Service offerings, it must already know that company, its server location, and the URI to its WSDL or DISCO file, or find the company on a UDDI search engine. After the company has been located, the business partner can make financial arrangements and have its software developers create code to consume the Web Service.

UDDI and DISCO have a use within an enterprise too. After all, with so many distributed offices and departments, large companies can best leverage existing code and software services only if they actually know that such software services exist.

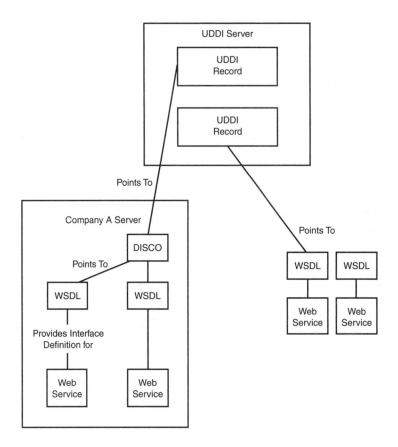

FIGURE 1.6
Relationship between UDDI, DISCO, WSDL, and Web Services.

Now that you've seen the need for SOAP and its fellow technologies and have examined some real-world scenarios of their use, it's time to learn how Microsoft has implemented its vision for creating Web Services.

Microsoft's Implementation of SOAP and Web Services

There have been many SOAP implementations in its first year that use different programming languages and operating systems. Microsoft is no exception. In fact, soon almost every product will use SOAP in some fashion, including Microsoft Office. Until now, there have been three Microsoft implementations of SOAP.

SOAP Toolkit for Visual Studio

In spring 2000, Microsoft released the first version of the SOAP Toolkit for Visual Studio. It was a technology preview to allow developers to get their feet wet in this new technology. With this toolkit, developers could wrap a COM object in a proxy that would send and receive messages in SOAP and would handle instantiating the component when a SOAP message was received via HTTP. A consuming application could then use that proxy to call the methods on the remote Web service (the COM object).

The SOAP Toolkit for Visual Studio was important for several reasons. First, it brought SOAP into the spotlight as a premier technology that developers could not ignore.

Second, it introduced the purpose of proxies in the context of SOAP and Web services (see Figure 1.7). *Proxies* are objects used by the consumer of a Web Service to allow an application to call the Web Service's methods as though they resided on the local machine. The proxy takes the request, bundles it up as a SOAP request, and then sends it to the real Web Service across the network. The proxy is also responsible for retrieving the results of the call to the Web Service, deserializing the SOAP response, and then delivering the result back to the calling application. This architecture hides the gory details of serialization and network communication from the developer. Proxies used in the .NET incarnation of Web Services are called *Web References*.

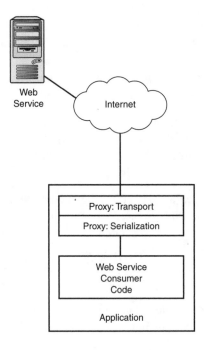

FIGURE 1.7
Purpose of a proxy.

Third, Microsoft's SOAP Toolkit for Visual Studio showed the need for a way to discover the existence and attributes of Web Services. The SOAP Contract Language was introduced, which provided a method for describing a Web Service's inputs and outputs. It later became the SOAP Definition Language (SDL) and finally the Web Service Definition Language. There are nuances that differentiate the three, but in concept they are essentially the same. Discovering the existence of Web Services on a server was made possible by the DISCO specification. Although the SOAP Toolkit cannot be credited with single-handedly ushering in the need for these specifications, it made their purpose more obvious for those who were struggling to understand how all the pieces fit together.

However, it soon became clear that the SOAP Toolkit was not the complete solution Microsoft had in mind to support the concept of Web Services and SOAP. In the summer of 2000, Microsoft released the bomb that its entire organization would again turn on a dime and become a service-oriented company, selling its software on a subscription basis and using technologies such as SOAP to make the messaging work. Microsoft announced it was creating a toolset that would allow developers to do the same for their organizations' applications.

.NET Remoting

Microsoft's second implementation of SOAP is .NET Remoting. It was introduced late in the summer of 2000 with the initial release of the .NET SDK. Remoting allows components to reference each other across application boundaries, whether they run across contexts and AppDomains, across servers, or across the world. It accomplishes this by using hidden proxies that act as the real interface for the object. The proxy resides inside the context of the calling application and is responsible for accepting the call to that object, serializing the method call, and sending it to the appropriate URI. It then accepts the values returned from the object and delivers them to the calling application.

.NET Remoting has multiple extensibility points that allow developers to hook into and intercept the messages sent at various times through the proxies to the remoted object. Additionally, developers can create their own channels for sending the information (if HTTP is undesirable) and use custom formatters (if SOAP is undesirable).

.NET Remoting uses SOAP as the means of serializing method calls and return values. However, applications built using .NET Remoting require that both systems be built on top of the .NET Framework. The purpose, then, for a Remoted application is different than for a Web Service: It accommodates the need for objects to be distributed when using the same platform. This purpose limits the system's ability to be open to all platforms, but Remoting is still a powerful tool when you need the availability and load balancing of a distributed application.

Although it is entirely possible to create Web Services that can be discovered and used over the Internet, the ASP.NET Web Services are more simple and targeted more for this purpose.

ASP.NET Web Services

Microsoft's third implementation of SOAP is ASP.NET Web Services, which was introduced along with .NET Remoting in late summer 2000 with the initial release of the .NET SDK.

ASP.NET Web Services allow developers to easily develop SOAP-based applications that are created in the spirit of Active Server Pages (ASP) applications. Unlike .NET Remoting, ASP.NET Web Services don't require a great degree of understanding how they work to effectively create them. In fact, in Chapter 2, "Creating a Simple Web Services with .NET SDK," you'll see how to create a Web Service that will provide the basis of discussion throughout several chapters in this book. However, if you wanted nothing more than learning how to create a simple ASP.NET Web Service, you need look no further than a few lines of code and a few simple instructions.

Unlike Active Server Pages, ASP.NET Web Services have no visual element associated with them. Instead, they return XML that is formatted to comply with the SOAP specification.

The services you can create fall under the category of "Simple Services," or in other words, services that do not necessarily maintain state, and that provide some information or calculation that can be supplied back to the consuming application that called the Web Service in one single message.

The Benefits of ASP.NET Web Services

ASP.NET makes it easy to provide and consume Web Services for those who are familiar with creating ASP Web pages.

Simple to Build

In Chapter 2, you'll dive in and begin creating ASP.NET Web Services. It could be fairly complex to build all the plumbing required to call and provide Web Services (including creating your own SOAP interpreter, and so forth), but the .NET Framework and Visual Studio.NET hide this complexity from the developer. Software developers can therefore concentrate on the business rules instead of the technical details of sending and receiving SOAP messages.

Simple to Test

The developers of ASP.NET made it simple to test the Web Services you create by offering a simple test harness. This test harness, also known as just the Web Services test page or the WSDLHelpGenerator.aspx, allows you to actually call the Web Service and see the result. This feature could save hours of building custom test harness pages for each of your Web Services. The Web Services test page also describes all the information you need to integrate Web Services into your applications.

Simple to Deploy

Utilities and configuration mechanisms, such as the web.Config file, make deployment of Web Services (and all .NET Web applications) much less complex. Because registration of components isn't required, you can simply copy files into your application's directory, and they are automatically registered and ready to be used. Applications can use the web.Config file to transition your Web Services from development and staging to production environments. Visual Studio.NET has tools that make this process even easier.

How ASP.NET Web Services Differ from BizTalk

BizTalk is a multipurpose technology that includes a repository of schema documents, which define how industries can exchange information using the same structure. It is also the Microsoft software that allows a company to send and receive these documents with its trading partner. If two companies have different schemas for how they exchange data, BizTalk (the tool) has a mapping feature that enables data elements to be mapped from one document to another.

With BizTalk (the tool), a company can also orchestrate business processes as a result of receiving a new document from one of its business partners. For example, XYZ Corp allows its customers to send purchase requests via the Web. XYZ Corp uses BizTalk to receive those messages (via one of several transport mechanisms), and those requests all get placed in a queue. BizTalk grabs these documents from the queue and transforms the XML format of the customers' document to the XML format that the XYZ Corp uses (based on its predefined mappings).

BizTalk's Orchestrator then begins firing off a flurry of requests (see Figure 1.8) to other applications to check the customer's account status, determine his credit limit, check inventory levels for the requested item, reserve inventory, create a purchase order in the accounting system, retrieve the confirmation number, and send status information back to the customer via an XML document with a confirmation number if the process succeeded or an error message explaining what went wrong. If the order is large enough, Orchestrator could even page the sales representative in charge of the customer's account or call the customer via a automated telephony system that confirms the order in a computer monotone voice. Orchestrator might go on to forward the purchase request to the shipping department and to the merchandise picker's wireless handheld PDA to save time. When the picker fulfills the order, a message is sent back to Orchestrator, which in turn sends a status e-mail to the customer letting him know when his order was sent.

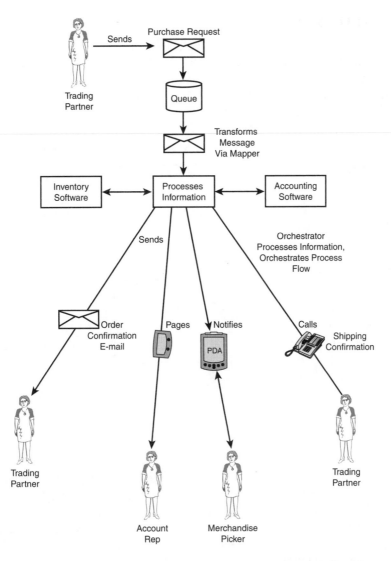

FIGURE 1.8

A complex flow managed by Orchestrator.

This complex scenario, if developed by hand, might take considerable time. The promise of BizTalk is that the time to develop such a system is greatly reduced by using Mapper and Orchestrator. BizTalk Orchestrator uses Microsoft Visio and enables business analysts to design the workflow or the processes. Software developers can then hook up components, script, Web Services, or other programming elements to accomplish what the business analyst has designed.

I've already tipped my hat to answer what exactly is the difference between BizTalk and Web Services. BizTalk sits at a higher level in the "Web Services protocol stack" than does ASP.NET Web Services (see Figure 1.9).

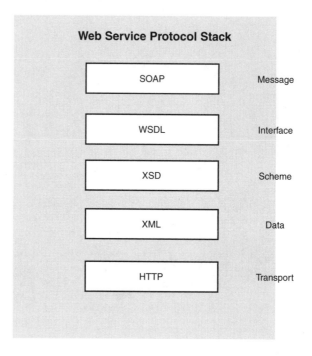

FIGURE 1.9
Web Services protocol stack.

HTTP is used as a transport mechanism to send data from one computer to another. XML is used as a language element that can express data. SOAP uses HTTP and XML to send and make remote procedure calls across a network. Orchestrator groups multiple SOAP calls (as well as other programmatic interfaces) to fulfill a business process such as "process order request" or "create purchase request." It is at a higher level than Web Services and can be used to rapidly aggregate Web Service calls from multiple systems inside and outside an organization.

Before you conclude that BizTalk is a competitor to your own application development efforts, I'd like to suggest that your role in this environment change from one of "gluing applications together" to "creating components and Web Services" that are consumed by BizTalk Orchestrator. Years ago, it was common to think of Visual Basic as this glue. Visual Basic excelled at bringing multiple COM objects into the same application, and as a Rapid

Application Development tool, it enabled you to build applications that integrated these disparate COM objects into one application. The benefit was that the developer could concentrate on developing a business application and avoid writing a lot of the plumbing code associated with using COM. Visual Basic hid much of that for you. BizTalk seeks a similar goal: to hide the plumbing code of tying Web Services, COM objects, and script together. This goal allows you, as the developer, to concentrate on writing the objects Orchestrator uses to fulfill a business process.

ASP.NET Web Services Are Implemented Using ASP.NET

Microsoft promotes ASP.NET, the next generation of Active Server Pages, as the premier way to create Web applications. ASP.NET sits on top of the .NET Framework and, as a result, benefits from significant performance, security, and deployment improvements (see Figure 1.10).

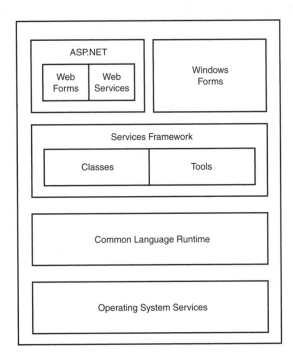

FIGURE 1.10

ASP.NET and the .NET Framework.

First, ASP.NET is not ASP 4.0! In fact, you cannot use VBScript to create ASP.NET Web pages. You must use a language supported by the .NET Framework, such as Visual Basic.NET, C#, "Managed" C++, or JScript.NET, because the Web page is compiled into a dynamic link library (DLL). This is not an ActiveX or COM DLL; rather, it's an Intermediate Language (IL) DLL file that runs exclusively on top of the Common Language Runtime (CLR), an environment that hosts your IL and provides many system services to your application. IL, .NET Framework, and the CLR are beyond the scope of this book. However, as a .NET developer, you will want to learn as much about these concepts and technologies as possible. The key point is that you are no longer dealing with script files that are interpreted and run inside an Internet Server Application Programming Interface (ISAPI) filter, as ASP was.

You've spent a lot of time reviewing ASP.NET Web pages and not Web Services per se. However, the improved speed, scalability, security, and configurability you enjoy while creating ASP.NET Web pages will also be a benefit as you create ASP.NET Web Services.

Where Do Web Services Fit into Your Architecture?

When Web Services debuted, it was clear it could be thought of as purely a middle-tier concern. Figure 1.11 shows the model you are probably most familiar with. Note my symbol for Web Services--it resembles a COM object, but it's modified to reflect that Web Services resides "in the cloud," referring to the Internet (see Figures 1.12 and 1.13). I'll use this symbol throughout the book to illustrate where Web Services sits architecturally when designing a solution.

Typically, a Web Service in the middle tier is accessed by a server, whether it's a component server such as COM+/Microsoft Transaction Server (MTS) or a Web server such as Internet Information Server (IIS). The Web Service returns data to the server, and the server integrates the data into the visual interface (that is, the Web page) and delivers the content to the client (a Web browser).

One plausible server-to-server scenario is a client Web browser making a call to a Web server for a particular page. The requested page is a portal that could contain news stories, weather updates, and stock quotes. The page that resides on the Web server might make calls to other servers that provide Web Services. After all the data from the Web Service providers is collected, the data is inserted into the Web page and returned to the client's Web browser.

Here's another server-to-server possibility with two applications: A purchase request system in Company A connects to an order entry system in Company B via a Web Service. The two applications can communicate via SOAP-based Web Services and expedite the process of ordering and fulfilling those orders. However, two additional scenarios are possible.

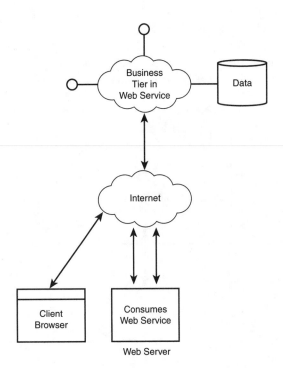

FIGURE 1.11
Web Services on the middle tier.

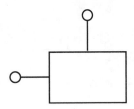

FIGURE 1.12
The symbol for a COM object.

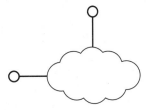

FIGURE 1.13
Modified symbol for Web Service.

Soon many different applications, including Microsoft Office and SQL Server, will host the
.NET Framework runtime (see Figure 1.14). From a practical perspective, that means you can
create code that runs inside these applications and allows for many more options, such as calling and processing the results of Web Services on client computers.

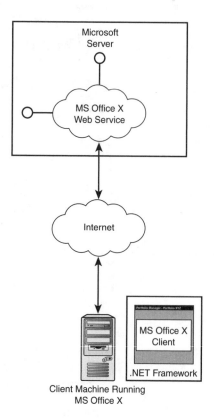

FIGURE 1.14

Server to client--hosted .NET framework.

However, with the arrival of Web Service Behaviors (see Figure 1.15), developers have more flexibility in how they obtain and display data. Web Service Behaviors allow Web Browsers (including Internet Explorer 5.5) to send a request to a Web Service, receive the result, and update the Web page based on the collected information. This method opens up a new possibility for the architecture of your applications by leaving the interface code and graphics on the client while occasionally updating the data it displays. Web Service Behaviors are discussed in more depth in Chapter 21, "Web Service Behaviors."

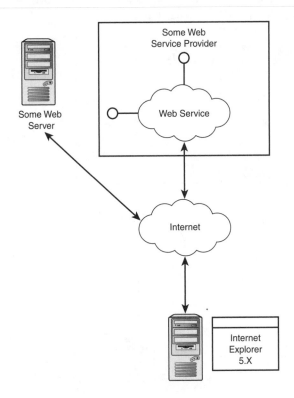

FIGURE 1.15

Server to client--Web Service Behaviors.

In the scenario shown in Figure 1.16, the client initially contacts a Web server for the user interface. Within the interface is code that calls Web Services from around the world; the code gathers and integrates the results of those Web Service calls into the Web page dynamically via Dynamic HTML (DHTML). In this manner, the load on the Web server is greatly reduced. This scenario represents a true separation between the data and the interface.

Finally, it is not very far-fetched to see that an upcoming version of SQL Server might be able to host Web Services and serve up SOAP messages instead of just XML (as it currently does). The model would look something like Figure 1.17.

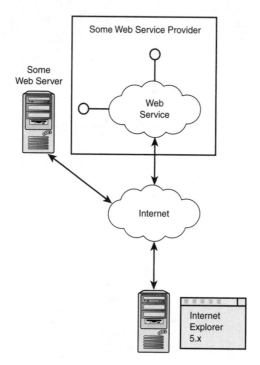

FIGURE 1.16
Web Services called by client.

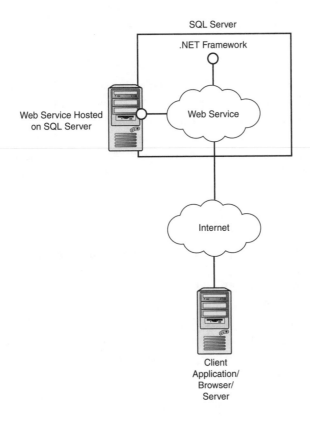

FIGURE 1.17

Web Services on the data access tier.

Selecting a Language

During the course of this book, I will be discussing concepts and showing many code examples of developing ASP.NET Web Services. The first challenge is deciding which programming language to use when developing an ASP.NET Web Service. Developers have several choices (I'll explain why in more depth in Chapter 6, "How ASP.NET Works").

Out of the box, ASP.NET allows you to create ASP.NET Web Services using Visual Basic.NET, "Managed" C++, and a new language called C#. Of these languages, it has become obvious that Visual Basic and C# will be most popular because of their simplicity in comparison with C++. However, you certainly are not limited to just Visual Basic.NET or C#. Microsoft will supply a JScript compiler, and other third-party vendors will create compilers for other languages, such as Smalltalk and even COBOL! Again, I'll reveal the reason for these choices in Chapter 6.

For your purposes in this book (and even the purposes of the .NET SDK's help files), all examples will be in Visual Basic and C#. In the future, it's quite possible that you'll see, as you peruse the want ads, potential employers looking for a .NET developer rather than a VB programmer or a C# programmer. However, for maintenance purposes, individual companies might choose to mandate that all their code will be written in a particular language. The point is that components written in VB are accessible by code in C#, which is accessible by code written in JScript, and so forth. Regardless of the code, they are all reduced to a common denominator: the Intermediate Language.

Selecting a Code Editor

The next challenge is to select a development environment/code editor to help you create a Web Service. Microsoft's Visual Studio.NET has been created to speed your development of Web-based and Windows-based applications. I use Visual Studio.NET in most of this book for the examples because I believe it's how most developers will ultimately choose to create their applications. However, you don't have to use Visual Studio.NET to create or compile .NET applications! Visual Studio.NET helps speed your development by automating development tasks, but for some topics, you'll want to take your time and understand exactly what is going on "under the covers." This knowledge is important in case you ever need to debug a problem.

Microsoft Notepad is always a popular choice for developers. In fact, I used Notepad the first year I developed Active Server Pages (ASP) applications until I switched to Visual InterDev. Unfortunately, Notepad might not be a good choice because you lose the advantage of syntax highlighting. There are several good text editors that allow you to enjoy syntax highlighting for most major programming languages. If you are going to go this route for a while until you can afford a more powerful tool, I recommend UltraEdit or EditPlus as inexpensive text editors that support syntax highlighting for Visual Basic and C#.

Summary

Businesses on the Internet have increasingly complex needs to integrate heterogeneous systems quickly. Multitudinous platforms, software, and hardware combinations thwart such efforts because no standards exist. With the emergence of SOAP and its myriad associated technologies, new and legacy systems can exchange data both inside and outside the enterprise, thereby facilitating dynamic business relationships at Internet speed.

SOAP is a technology that uses industry-accepted standards, such as HTTP and XML, to allow two or more disparate systems to communicate across network boundaries. Other supporting technologies, such as WSDL, DISCO, and UDDI, allow systems to be built around SOAP, making it easier to automatically discover and integrate SOAP Web Services.

One of Microsoft's implementations of SOAP is the topic of this book. ASP.NET Web Services allows developers to quickly create applications that can communicate via SOAP. The new .NET Framework lends a strong infrastructure to ASP.NET Web Services, providing improved performance, better security, and excellent maintainability.

Web Services can be used in many different ways within the context of application architecture. They have most frequently been associated with the middle-tier of a distributed n-tier architecture. However, emerging technologies are opening possibilities for Web Services to become ubiquitous on the presentation and data access tiers, too.

Web Services can be created using any language supported by the .NET Framework, including Visual Basic and C# as well as JScript and other languages that will be supported by third-party vendors. Web Services can be created using a simple text editor. The .NET SDK gives you the rest of the tools necessary to compile, test, and debug your code, but you could potentially enjoy higher productivity by using Visual Studio.NET in your development efforts.

This chapter has given you an overview of many topics that will be covered in greater depth throughout this book. In the next few chapters, you'll dive in and learn how to create and consume simple Web Services using the .NET Framework and the Visual Studio.NET Integrated Development Environment (IDE).

Creating a Simple Web Service with .NET SDK

IN THIS CHAPTER

Chapter 1, "Introducing Web Services," made a business case for Web Services and overviewed Web Services from a technical perspective. In this chapter, you're going to get your hands dirty and create an ASP.NET Web Service. You'll learn how to manually set up an Internet Information Server to create a Web Service application, create and test a simple Web Service, and examine the Web Services Help Page, also known as the DefaultSDLHelpGenerator.aspx, and discover how it knows so much about your Web Service. In the next chapter, you'll create a Web Forms application to consume this Web Service using only the .NET SDK.

What Will Your Web Service Do?

For your first attempt at building a Web Service, I'll keep the functionality simple in order to concentrate on the steps, techniques, and tools you rely on to build a Web Service. The idea for this Web Service came from a cynical project manager at a large consulting firm, who claims that whenever he asks a software developer to provide an estimate of how many hours he needs to perform a given task, he doubles the estimate and adds 10 hours. Realizing that such calculations are the toughest part of his job, I decided to create a Web application that he and other managers can use to reduce their workload and spend more time on important managerial duties (such as organizing his e-mail into tidy Outlook folders and learning how to use his Palm Pilot). The application could be made accessible to others by using a Web Service so that developers can share this feature with their managers.

The Web Service code will be placed in an Internet Information Services (IIS) Virtual Directory. In a moment, you'll examine what actually happens behind the scenes that makes a Web Service file distinct from any other file in IIS, but first, you'll create a sub-Web in IIS.

Setting Up the Environment

If you haven't already done so, you need to install the .NET SDK. The process is rather straightforward: After downloading the executable (search for ".NET Framework SDK" at http://msdn.microsoft.com), simply run it and the installer walks you through the installation process. Therefore, I'll refer you to the .NET SDK instructions provided on Microsoft's Web site if you have any additional questions.

Creating a Web Folder in Internet Information Services 5.0

After you have a successful installation, you'll be ready to create a folder on your hard drive that IIS designates a Virtual Directory. If you are unfamiliar with how to do that, follow these simple steps:

1. Create a directory on your hard drive that will become the Virtual Directory and contain the files necessary for your Web Service. For this example, the following folder was created:

   `g:\pmcalc`

2. Start IIS by navigating to its icon in the Start menu: Start | Programs | Administrative Tools | Internet Services Manager.

3. In the left-hand pane of Internet Information Services , expand the tree until you see the Default Web Site node.

4. Right-click the Default Web Site icon and choose New Virtual Directory from the pop-up menu, as shown in Figure 2.1.

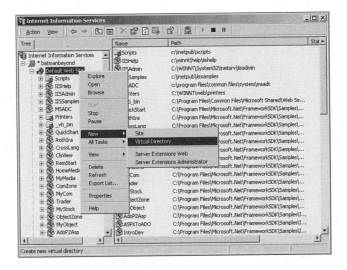

FIGURE 2.1

Creating a Virtual Directory on the default Web site.

5. The Virtual Directory Creation Wizard opens. This wizard walks you through a series of steps to create the Virtual Directory. After reading the introduction (see Figure 2.2), click the Next button.

6. In the first screen, you are asked to supply a Virtual Directory Alias. Type in **pmcalc**, which will be your subdirectory name. Consumers of your Web Service will use this name (that is, `http://localhost/pmcalc/`) to access the Web Service. Click the Next button to continue.

FIGURE 2.2
The Welcome page of the Virtual Directory Creation Wizard.

7. In the next screen, you are asked to supply a Web Site Content Directory, which represents the directory where your Web Service files will be stored on your system. You must either type in the folder name or navigate to the same folder you created in Step 1. Click the Next button to continue.

8. In the next screen, you are asked to select Access Permissions for this Virtual Directory. By default, the Read and Run Scripts entries are selected. There is no need to modify the defaults, so click the Next button to continue.

9. In the last screen you are notified that the procedure finished successfully. Click the Finish button to close the Virtual Directory Creation Wizard.

10. To verify that your new Virtual Directory exists, expand the Default Web Site node and look for the pmcalc child node in the left-hand pane of IIS. If you cannot see it, you might need to right-click on the Default Web Site node and choose "Refresh" from the pop-up menu.

Coding the Web Service

Next, you need to write the code for your Web Service. This code will be saved into a file with the extension .asmx. This extension notifies the ASP.NET engine that the file's contents are intended to be used as a Web Service, as opposed to .aspx files, which are intended to be used as Web pages. I created the following file:

```
G:\pmcalc\pmcalc.asmx
```

You can find further discussion of the importance of the .asmx file extension in Chapter 6, "How ASP.NET Works."

Code Listing

You have two options for the code listing. If you want to use Visual Basic.NET, type the code in Listing 2.1 exactly as it appears. (Alternatively, you can download this listing and all the other code samples in this book from the Sams Web site or from http://www.soapwebser-vices.com/book.)

LISTING 2.1   Visual Basic Listing

```
<%@ WebService Language="VB" Class="pmcalc" %>

Imports System.Web.Services

Class pmcalc
    <WebMethod()>_public function developerEstimate(xintHours As integer) As
integer

        developerEstimate = (xintHours * 2) * 10

    End Function

End Class
```

Or, if you prefer C#, you can type the code in Listing 2.2 exactly as it appears.

LISTING 2.2   C# Listing

```
<%@ WebService Language="C#" Class="pmcalc" %>

using System;
using System.Web.Services;

[WebService()]
public class pmcalc : WebService
    {
    [WebMethod()]
       public double developerEstimate(int xintHours)
        {
        return (xintHours * 2) + 10;
        }
    }
```

In a moment, you'll come back to the code and dissect it to understand exactly what is going on inside the code, but first, taste the fruits of your labor.

Testing the Web Service

Now that you've written the code for your Web Service, you need to test it. Creating a Web Service is analogous to creating a COM component. A component typically has no graphical user interface and, most important, doesn't do anything by itself. It can be exercised only when it is brought to life by a calling application. In some cases, it's not easy to debug a component from the application it was originally intended for, such as an ASP Web application. Therefore, developers have written little test applications, or *test harnesses*, to fully exercise all the component's methods and properties. This rather redundant task ended up being "throw away code" after the component was stable.

Microsoft has removed the necessity of this chore by supplying a built-in test harness in ASP.NET Web Services. Its filename is DefaultWSDLHelpGenerator.aspx, and it appears automatically when you use your browser to request the Web Service.

> **NOTE**
>
> You never actually type the name of the page, DefaultWSDLHelpGenerator.aspx, into the Web browser, nor do you ever see the name of this file anywhere in your browser. The actual page is just a template used by the code that handles Web Service requests to dynamically create a help screen. For the remainder of this chapter, I'll refer to it as the Service Help Page.

Using the Service Help Page to Test Your Web Service

Open your Web browser and navigate to the following URL:

```
http://localhost/pmcalc/pmcalc.asmx
```

You should see the screen shown in Figure 2.3.

Notice that the name of your Web Service (pmcalc) and the name of your Web method (developerEstimate) were displayed. The Service Help Page is able to determine your Web Service's programmatic interfaces and creates a help file/testing harness to test the formula you've implemented.

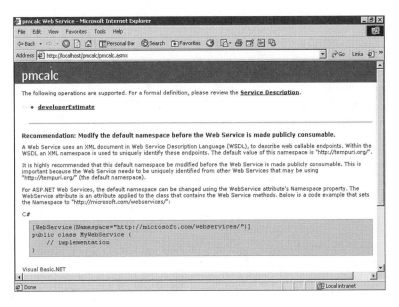

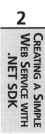

FIGURE 2.3
The Service Help Page's results.

Important

If there was an error during the compilation process caused by a problem in your code, you might see the screen shown in Figure 2.4.

If that happens, double-check the previous steps, especially the code listing, and try to refresh your Web browser. The code must be typed exactly as it appears in Listing 2.1 or 2.2.

Before you actually use the test page to start your Web Service, take a look at several features of this helpful tool. At the top of the page, look at the following line of the generated Service Help Page:

```
For a formal definition, please review its Service Description
```

Select the link under Service Description and view the results, shown in Figure 2.5.

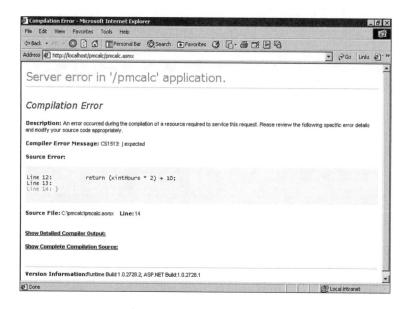

FIGURE 2.4

Error while compiling the Service Help Page.

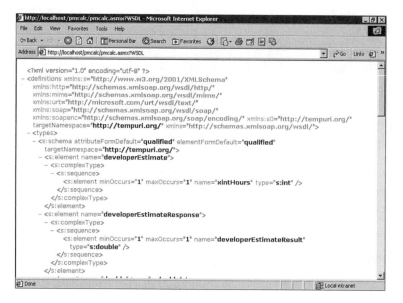

FIGURE 2.5

WSDL file that describes the pmcalc Web Service.

Web Service Description Language (WSDL) is a way of describing your Web Service in an XML format to potential consumers of your Web Service. By using a standardized Web Service description, it tells consumers what methods are available and what values to send and receive from your Web Service. WSDL is discussed in more depth in Chapter 8, "Understanding WSDL," but for now, just remember that the Service Help Page gives you ready access to this information.

This Service Help Page also lists all the Web methods for your Web Service. Click the `developerEstimate` link at the top of the page. You should now see the screen shown in Figure 2.6.

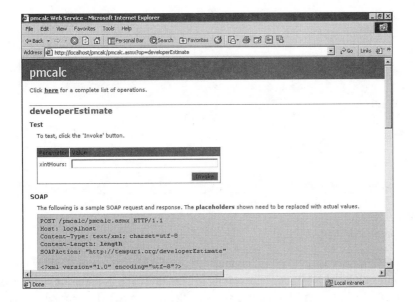

FIGURE 2.6
The developerEstimate test page.

Notice how much it knows about the Web Service! It knows the name, the methods, parameter names for the methods, the data types of those parameters, and the return value types. It learns about the Web Service by examining the associated WSDL file. It also provides sample code to explain how to call the Web Service using three methods: SOAP, HTTP-GET, and HTTP-POST, all legitimate ways of sending a request to your Web Service. Chapter 12, "Three Methods of Calling Web Services," covers these methods and explains why you need them and how to use them to call a Web Service"."

The greatest value of the Service Help Page, however, is that it allows you to actually test your Web Service by invoking it. To test the pmcalc Web Service, enter the number **8** in the xintHours text box and then click the Invoke button. You should see the XML shown in Figure 2.7 returned in a new browser window.

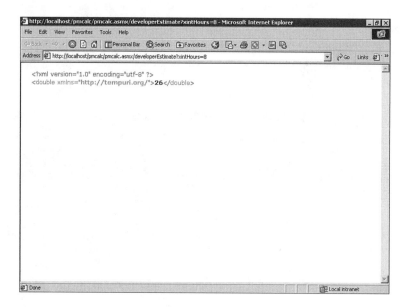

FIGURE 2.7
Results of testing the Web Service.

Notice that the value 26 is returned in the midst of some XML. The astute reader might observe that the returned XML does not resemble SOAP. That's because the Service Help Page uses the HTTP-GET method of calling the Web Service, so SOAP is not returned.

Important

If you made a mistake in the value you submitted to the Web Service (for example, you typed in the word **bob** instead of the number **8**), you might see a screen that looks similar to Figure 2.8.

This *call stack dump* helps you determine the cause of the problem in your Web Service. If this happens, double check the previous steps, especially the code listing and the value you submitted to the Web Service, and try the Invoke button again. The code must be typed exactly as it's shown here, and to start the Web Service, you must enter a value that corresponds to the correct data type (in this example, a numeric value, not a string like bob).

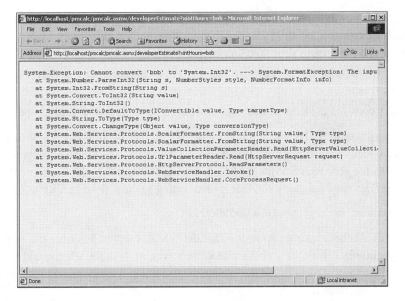

FIGURE 2.8
Call stack dump.

Creating the Web Services Description Language (WSDL) File

The WSDL file is used by all applications that want to communicate with your Web Service to discover your available methods and properties, the parameters and their data types, and the types of returned values. WSDL is explained in more detail in Chapter 8.

Methods of Creating the WSDL File

There are two methods of creating a WSDL file:

- **Create it by hand:** Although it seems ludicrous to select this method, it is an option, nonetheless. With this method, you would use a text editor and the latest version of the WSDL specification to write the XML from scratch. I think you'll prefer one of the next two methods for three reasons: creating the WSDL by hand is time consuming; because of the specification's complexity, this method is error prone; and it's completely unnecessary because you have utilities that can do it instantly and perfectly.

- **Create it by copying the results of the Service Help Page and saving them into a file with the extension .wsdl:** If you recall, the following link on the Service Help Page was generated by accessing your WebService via a Web browser:

  ```
  For a formal XML definition of the Addition WebService, please review its:
  SDL Contract.
  ```

  You can copy the contents of this page and save it in a file called pmcalc.wsdl.

Many times, a physical WSDL file residing on the Web server is not necessary. When your consumers are ready to discover your Web Service's properties and methods, they need only access the URI for your Web Service, adding the string ?WSDL at the end. For example, the Service Help Page displays the WSDL file by navigating to the following URI:

```
http://localhost/pmcalc/pmcalc.asmx?WSDL
```

This is actually a benefit because it ensures that the WSDL file that describes the Web Service is always synchronized with the Web Service's latest version. Imagine what would happen if you changed your .asmx file, but did not update the .wsdl file--your consumers would be confused and likely perturbed.

You might be wondering how the ?WSDL query string works behind the scenes in ASP.NET. Although that topic is covered in more depth in Chapter 6, "How ASP.NET Works." I'll provide a brief explanation to satisfy your curiosity for now. A series of classes in the .NET Framework collectively perform a process called *Reflection*. They are able to look at a class and determine all the properties, methods, data types, and data structures that the class supports. The ASP.NET engine uses Reflection to get this information, and then formats it to comply with the WSDL specification. Finally, it is presented to Internet Explorer, which recognizes that the document is XML based and formats it so that it's easier on the eyes.

NOTE

If you refer to other books or articles on Web sites that were written based on the first beta of the .NET Framework, you might see a reference to a utility called WebServiceUtil.exe. This tool has been somewhat replaced by two new tools (wsdl.exe and disco.exe). However, neither of the new tools can generate a WSDL file. The help file for the wsdl.exe hints that this utility will do it, but currently that functionality does not exist. As I just explained, however, not having a physical WSDL file is not a problem for ASP.NET Web Services because of its ability to generate WSDL on-the-fly.

Examining the Generated WSDL File

Let's take a look at the WSDL file that was generated by the Service Help Page and try to make some sense of it. I'll break up the discussion on the file so that it's clearer. Feel free to view the full file that was generated earlier by the Service Help Page if you want to see how all the sections fit together. Please keep in mind that this is a high-level overview of WSDL, which is dissected further in Chapter 8.

There are five distinct sections in WSDL that are enveloped by a <definitions> tag:

- **The <types> section:** Defines the data types and data structures that will be used by the Web Service. Think of this section as the Web Services version of a type library.

- **The <message> section:** Defines the programmatic interfaces for each method of calling a Web Service (SOAP, HTTP-GET, HTTP-POST) for both a Request (In) and a Response (Out). So, in this section, there are six <message> tags. They refer to items defined in the <types> section to bind the data types that will be sent and received to each of the calling methods.

- **The <portType> section:** Ties together the Request (In) and Response (Out) messages for a given calling method (SOAP, HTTP-GET, HTTP-POST). If your consumers will use SOAP, for example, they need to know how to create a SOAP request and receive a SOAP response. Notice that this section refers to values defined in the <message> section.

- **The <binding> section:** Used differently by each calling method type. Basically, it assigns known standards (HTTP or SOAP) to each <portType>.

- **The <service> section:** Contains all the different bindings that are supported for this Web Service. Most important, it provides the exact URIs for each calling method.

The WSDL is written perfectly for computers, but might seem a little backward to humans who prefer to drill down into the details rather than work from the smallest details (definitions) up to the big picture (how those definitions are used). Doesn't make sense? Don't worry. I'll talk more about WSDL in Chapter 8. In the meantime, I'll answer a more general version of the question in the following section.

What Does Your WSDL Describe About Your Web Service?

First, it gives you three different methods of calling the Web Service: SOAP (the de facto method of Web Service calls), HTTP-POST (sending the parameters in a Web page form), or HTTP-GET (sending the parameters in a Web page's URL query string).

Second, it specifies that there is one Web Service, called developerEstimate, available at the specified URI.

Third, it indicates that there is one input parameter for the `developerEstimate` method called `xintHours` of the integer data type.

This is all the information requesters (whether human or computer) need to know if they want to interact with your Web Service.

Summary

Web Services are simple to create and simple to test. Microsoft automatically provides the Service Help Page that tells you whether you have any compile-time errors and allows you to easily access your Web Service with a Web-based interface to supply arguments to your Web Service.

In this chapter you have created a simple Web Service. You tested it using the Service Help Page and generated a WSDL file that will be essential as consumers begin to access your Web Service. You looked at the generated WSDL file, but will delve into this topic more later in the book.

In the next chapter, you will consume this Web Service and display its results in a Web page.

Consuming a Simple Web Service with .NET SDK

IN THIS CHAPTER

In Chapter 2, "Creating a Simple Web Service with .NET SDK," using little more than a text editor and the .NET SDK's utilities, you created and tested a Web Service. In this chapter, you'll use the same tools to consume the Web Service in a Web Forms application, which is the enhanced version of the Active Server Pages applications you might have created in the past (see Figure 3.1). Your Web Forms application will call your Web Service, gather information, and then synthesize it into a Web page that's delivered to your Web Browser.

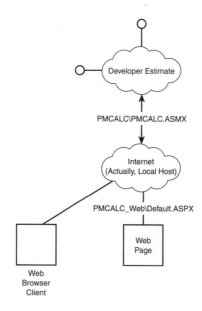

FIGURE 3.1

The basic architecture of your application.

Although you are creating a Web Service and a Web Forms application on the same computer for the purpose of this example, that's probably not how you will create production-quality applications. You will either create Web Services that others can use and access from anywhere, or you will create Web Forms applications (or Windows Forms applications) that use Web Services other organizations have created. To simulate two different Web Servers for this example, you will actually create a new sub-Web in your Default Web Site node in Internet Information Services.

How to Consume a Web Service

To consume a Web Service within your application, you have to know the following:

- The location (URI) of the Web Service's WSDL file. You can find this information in a number of different ways. Someone could supply it to you, you could use DISCO to find it on a particular server, or you could use a UDDI search engine for Web Services. DISCO and UDDI are covered in more detail in Chapters 9, "Understanding DISCO," and 25, "Understanding UDDI."

- After you have the WSDL file, you can create a proxy to the Web Service, which acts as the mediator for all requests and responses to or from the Web Service (see Figure 3.2). The proxy allows you to develop your application as though the Web Service resided locally on your computer. It serializes your method requests into SOAP and then sends the SOAP message to the Web Service via the network. After the Web Service has finished processing your request and returns its results encoded in a SOAP message, the proxy steps into action by intercepting the message, deserializing it, and returning the results to your application. The proxy is important because it hides the gory details of SOAP serialization and network communications.

You will use the wsdl.exe utility that I mentioned in Chapter 2 to create a proxy for your Web Service so that you can use it in your Web Forms application.

Creating a Separate Web Folder in IIS

As I mentioned, you need to create a separate sub-Web in IIS to simulate your Web Service and Web Forms application running on two physically different machines. For this example, you'll create a folder on your hard drive called C:\pmcalc_web and create a sub-Web called pmcalc_web that points to the folder. (For instructions on how to create a sub-Web in IIS, refer to Chapter 2.)

IMPORTANT

This chapter assumes you are using just the .NET Framework that can be downloaded from Microsoft's MSDN site (msdn.microsoft.com). I recommend that you add a PATH statement to your autoexec.bat file in order to use the command line utilities from any directory. This will save you a lot of time rummaging through the folders on your hard drive to find the wsdl.exe, vb.exe, and csc.exe applications, and will save you a great deal of effort to include the proper /out: parameters when defining where you want the code generated or compiled. To add the PATH statement, first locate the correct Program Files directory (contains the wsdl.exe) and the Windows directory (contains vb.exe and csc.exe) for the .NET Framework. You should find the following locations:

```
c:\Program Files\Microsoft.NET\FrameworkSDK\Bin
c:\Windows\Microsoft.NET\Framework\v1.0.2914
```

Therefore, you should add the following PATH statement in your autoexec.bat file:

```
SET PATH=c:\Program Files\Microsoft.NET\FrameworkSDK\Bin;c:\Windows\
Microsoft.NET\Framework\v1.0.2914
```

After you make this change, you must reboot. Now you will be able to use the necessary command line applications from ANY directory on your hard drive.

Using the wsdl.exe to Create Your Proxy

First, open a DOS command-prompt window. Remember to navigate to the folder C:\pmcalc_web in the DOS prompt before running wsdl.exe so that it creates the proxy code in the appropriate folder of your hard drive. If you don't, you might have to search your hard drive to find it! Alternatively, you can use the utility's /out: switch to specify the exact folder where you want the proxy code file created.

To generate a Visual Basic proxy, enter this line:

```
wsdl /language:vb http://localhost/pmcalc/pmcalc.asmx?wsdl
```

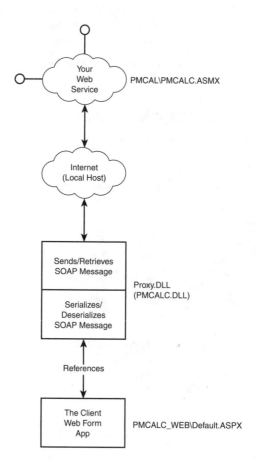

FIGURE 3.2

How the proxy works.

After a few moments, you should see the following confirmation:

```
Microsoft (R) Web Services Description Language Utility
[Microsoft .NET Framework Version 1.0.2728.2]
Copyright (C) Microsoft Corp 2000. All rights reserved.
C:\pmcalc\pmcalc.vb
Writing file 'C:\pmcalc\pmcalc.vb'.
```

To generate a C# proxy, enter this line:

```
C:\pmcalc>wsdl /language:cs http://localhost/pmcalc/pmcalc.asmx?wsdl
```

After a few moments, you should see the following confirmation:

```
Microsoft (R) Web Services Description Language Utility
[Microsoft .NET Framework Version 1.0.2728.2]
Copyright (C) Microsoft Corp 2000. All rights reserved.
C:\pmcalc\pmcalc.cs
Writing file 'C:\pmcalc\pmcalc.cs'.
```

Examining the Generated Proxy Class

The wsdl.exe utility has created the source code for your proxy class. You will compile it into a component in a moment, but first inspect the source code to learn a little bit about how the proxy works. Use your favorite text editor and open the pmcalc.vb (for Visual Basic; see Listing 3.1) or pmcalc.cs (for C#; see Listing 3.2) file.

LISTING 3.1   The pmcalc.vb Proxy File

```
'--------------------------------------------------------------------------
' <autogenerated>
'     This code was generated by a tool.
'     Runtime Version: 1.0.2728.2
'
'     Changes to this file may cause incorrect behavior and will be lost if
'     the code is regenerated.
' </autogenerated>
'--------------------------------------------------------------------------


Option Strict On
Option Explicit On

Imports System
Imports System.Web.Services
Imports System.Web.Services.Protocols
Imports System.Xml.Serialization


'
'This source code was auto-generated by wsdl, Version=1.0.2728.2.
'

<System.Web.Services.WebServiceBindingAttribute(Name:="pmcalcSoap",
[Namespace]:="http://tempuri.org/")> _
Public Class pmcalc
    Inherits System.Web.Services.Protocols.SoapHttpClientProtocol

    Public Sub New()
        MyBase.New
```

LISTING 3.1   Continued

```
        Me.Url = "http://localhost/pmcalc/pmcalc.asmx"
    End Sub


<System.Web.Services.Protocols.SoapDocumentMethodAttribute("http://tempuri.org/
developerEstimate",
Use:=System.Web.Services.Description.SoapBindingUse.Literal,
ParameterStyle:=System.Web.Services.Protocols.SoapParameterStyle.Wrapped)> _
    Public Function developerEstimate(ByVal xintHours As Integer) As Double
        Dim results() As Object = Me.Invoke("developerEstimate", New Object()
{xintHours})
        Return CType(results(0),Double)
    End Function


    Public Function BegindeveloperEstimate(ByVal xintHours As Integer, ByVal
callback As System.AsyncCallback, ByVal asyncState As Object) As
System.IAsyncResult
        Return Me.BeginInvoke("developerEstimate", New Object() {xintHours},
callback, asyncState)
    End Function


    Public Function EnddeveloperEstimate(ByVal asyncResult As
System.IAsyncResult) As Double
        Dim results() As Object = Me.EndInvoke(asyncResult)
        Return CType(results(0),Double)
    End Function
End Class
```

LISTING 3.2   The pmcalc.cs Proxy File

```
//----------------------------------------------------------------------------
-
// <autogenerated>
//     This code was generated by a tool.
//     Runtime Version: 1.0.2728.2
//
//     Changes to this file may cause incorrect behavior and will be lost if
//     the code is regenerated.
// </autogenerated>
//----------------------------------------------------------------------------
-


//
// This source code was auto-generated by wsdl, Version=1.0.2728.2.
//
```

LISTING 3.2   Continued

```
using System.Xml.Serialization;
using System;
using System.Web.Services.Protocols;
using System.Web.Services;


[System.Web.Services.WebServiceBindingAttribute(Name="pmcalcSoap",
Namespace="http://tempuri.org/")]
public class pmcalc : System.Web.Services.Protocols.SoapHttpClientProtocol {

    public pmcalc() {
        this.Url = "http://localhost/pmcalc/pmcalc.asmx";
    }


[System.Web.Services.Protocols.SoapDocumentMethodAttribute("http://tempuri.org/
developerEstimate", Use=System.Web.Services.Description.SoapBindingUse.Literal,
ParameterStyle=System.Web.Services.Protocols.SoapParameterStyle.Wrapped)]
    public System.Double developerEstimate(int xintHours) {
        object[] results = this.Invoke("developerEstimate", new object[]
{xintHours});
        return ((System.Double)(results[0]));
    }

    public System.IAsyncResult BegindeveloperEstimate(int xintHours,
System.AsyncCallback callback, object asyncState) {
        return this.BeginInvoke("developerEstimate", new object[] {xintHours},
callback, asyncState);
    }

    public System.Double EnddeveloperEstimate(System.IAsyncResult asyncResult)
{
        object[] results = this.EndInvoke(asyncResult);
        return ((System.Double)(results[0]));
    }
}
```

Regardless of whether you use C# or Visual Basic.NET, you can see how the wsdl.exe utility performed a great service for you. The class itself inherits from System.Web.Services.Protocols.SoapClientProtocol, and then uses the Me (this) statement to refer to its instance. It then sets properties such as the URL when it is instantiated in the New method. This pmcalc class has three methods. The first is DeveloperEstimate, which you use in your Web Forms application. The next two methods, BeginDeveloperEstimate and

`EndDeveloperEstimate`, allow for asynchronous calls to Web Services (covered in more depth in Chapter 19, "Calling Web Services Asynchronously"). When your Web Forms application calls the `DeveloperEstimate` method, your class calls the `Invoke` method on itself. This call starts the serialization and transportation of your information over the network and also handles deserialization in the response to your call. All this functionality is encapsulated in the `System.Web.Services.Protocols.SoapClientProtocol` class.

Compiling the Proxy

Now that you have the source code for your proxy, you need to compile it into a .NET Assembly. To accomplish this, the .NET Framework supplies you with a Visual Basic compiler (vbc.exe) and a C# compiler (csc.exe).

Before you compile, you'll need to create a folder called \bin as a subfolder in your pmcalc_web folder, as shown here:

```
C:\pmcalc_web\bin
```

To compile the proxy code, you'll need to navigate to the DOS prompt and type the following command for the Visual Basic.NET compiler:

```
vbc.exe /out:bin\pmcalc.dll /target:library
/reference:system.xml.serialization.dll /reference:system.web.services.dll
pmcalc.vb
```

If everything worked correctly, you will see the following message:

```
Microsoft (R) Visual Basic.NET Compiler version 7.00.9030
for Microsoft (R) .NET Framework Common Language Runtime version 1.00.2204.21
Copyright (C) Microsoft Corp 2000. All rights reserved.
```

For the C# compiler, enter this command:

```
csc.exe /out:bin\pmcalc.dll /target:library
/reference:system.xml.serialization.dll /reference:system.web.services.dll
pmcalc.cs
```

If you have typed in the command correctly, you should see the following confirmation message:

```
Microsoft (R) Visual C# Compiler Version 7.00.9030 [CLR version 1.00.2204.21]
Copyright (C) Microsoft Corp 2000. All rights reserved.
```

Chapter 6, "How ASP.NET Works," explains in more detail what the compiler does. Briefly, the compiler does not compile your source code into native machine-level code. Instead, it creates an assembly (.dll file) containing Intermediate Language that's later compiled into machine language code by a "Just In Time" compiler specific to your operating system and computer chip.

Creating the Web Service Consumer

Now that you have created your proxy, you need to create an ASP.NET Web Forms page to call your Web Service and display the results to the user's Web browser.

1. Open your favorite text editor, and type in one of the following blocks of code:

VB Code Listing

```
<html>
<head>
<title>Developer Estimate</title>

<script language=vb runat=server>

    sub btnGo_Click(Sender as Object, E as EventArgs)

        dim wsPMCalc as new Pmcalc
        dim intHours as integer

        intHours = txtDeveloperEstimate.text.toInt32

        lblResult.text = wsPMCalc.DeveloperEstimate(intHours).toString

    end sub

</script>
</head>

<body>
<form runat=server>

  <p align="center"><b>Developer Time Estimate for Project
Managers</b></p>
  <p>Enter Developers Estimate: <asp:textbox id=txtDeveloperEstimate
size=5 runat=server />
  <asp:button id= btnGo text=Go runat=server onClick=btnGo_Click /></p>
  <p>Modified Projected Estimate: <asp:Label id=lblResult runat=server
/></p>

</form>
</body>
</html>
```

C# Code Listing

```html
<html>
<head>
<title>Developer Estimate</title>

<script language=CSharp runat=server>

    public void btnGo_Click(Object Sender, System.EventArgs E) {

        Pmcalc wsPMCalc = new Pmcalc();
        Int32 intHours;

        intHours = txtDeveloperEstimate.Text.ToInt32();

        lblResult.Text = wsPMCalc.DeveloperEstimate(intHours).ToString();

    }

</script>
</head>

<body>
<form runat=server>

  <p align="center"><b>Developer Time Estimate for Project
Managers</b></p>
  <p>Enter Developers Estimate: <asp:textbox id=txtDeveloperEstimate
size=5 runat=server />
  <asp:button id= btnGo text=Go runat=server onClick=btnGo_Click /></p>
  <p>Modified Projected Estimate: <asp:Label id=lblResult runat=server
/></p>

</form>
</body>
</html>
```

2. Save the file as

```
c:\pmcalc_web\default.aspx
```

Examining Your Web Page Code

Before you continue, spend a moment to look at the code. No matter which language you chose to use, there are two things I want to point out. First, notice that you are not using typical HTML form fields. Instead, you are using ASP.NET server-side controls. When these tags are processed on the server, the ASP.NET Web Forms HTTP Handler interprets and renders them as HTML. These Server Side controls give you a high degree of programmability when creating your Web Forms applications.

Second, notice that you have a method called btnGo_Click, which is an event handler that fires when the user clicks the Go button. This "post-back" and event-based programming model is a little different from the "classic" ASP pages you might have created in the past.

After the user fires the btnGo_Click event, a call to the Web Service is made (via the proxy). Notice how your code to reference and call the Web Service treats it as though it were an object residing on your physical system. This is the value of the proxy: to make method calls transparent to the user-programmer.

Testing the Web Service Consumer

Now it is time to test what you've created.

1. Open your Web browser to

   http://localhost/pmcalc_web/default.aspx

   You should see the screen shown in Figure 3.3.

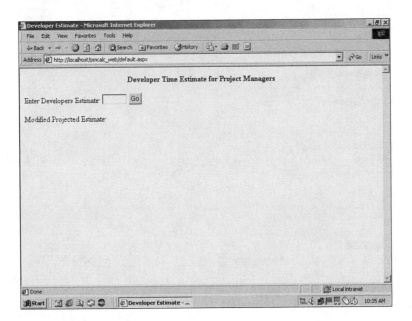

FIGURE 3.3

Testing your Web Service.

2. Enter the value 8 and click the Go button.

NOTE

The first time you run your Web Service and your Web Forms application, a .NET Just In Time Compiler specific to your operating system, processor, and so forth compiles the assembly into real machine-level instruction code. This might take a few moments, so be patient. After the compilation is done, it doesn't have to be compiled again, and you will benefit from the ASP.NET caching feature, thus enjoying a tremendous performance benefit over traditional Active Server Page applications.

Examining the Results

If everything worked correctly, you should see the screen shown in Figure 3.4.

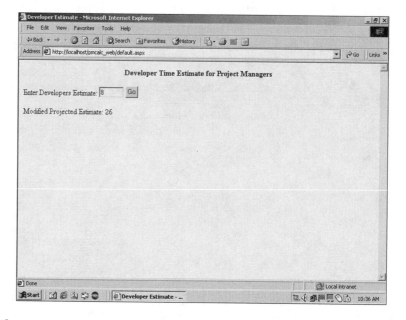

FIGURE 3.4

Results of consuming your Web Service

You can see that the Web Service successfully returned your result and that it was consumed by your Web page.

> **NOTE**
>
> If you see anything other than the result in Figure 3.4, you could have mistyped some code. Double-check your code against the previous code listings. It is imperative that you pay attention to capitalization in C#! If you are convinced you typed the code correctly, you might want to check your configuration. For other suggestions, refer to Chapter 10, "Exceptions and Error Handling."

Summary

In this chapter, you have learned how to create and compile the proxy code that wsdl.exe generates for you. The proxy is an important component of consuming Web Services because it encapsulates the serialization/deserialization of SOAP messages and the communication mechanism to transport and receive your messages over the network. After examining the generated proxy code, I for one am grateful to the ASP.NET Web Services team for relieving me of that burden.

You looked briefly at the steps required to compile your proxy class, including the process and benefit of compilation in the .NET Framework.

Finally, you created an ASP.NET Web Forms application that called the Web Service you created from Chapter 2 (via your proxy) and displayed its results in your Web Page.

From here, you might want to try the following:

- Add error-handling code (refer to Chapter 10).
- Learn more about the inner workings of ASP.NET (refer to Chapter 6).
- See how easy it is to create and consume Web Services using the Visual Studio IDE (refer to Chapter 4, "Creating a Simple Web Service in Visual Studio.NET," and Chapter 5, "Consuming a Simple Web Service in Visual Studio.NET").
- Extend your Web Service by adorning it with various settings (refer to Chapter 13, "Web Service Attributes and Properties").

3

CONSUMING A
SIMPLE WEB SERVICE
WITH .NET SDK

Creating a Simple Web Service in Visual Studio.NET

IN THIS CHAPTER

If you worked through the examples in Chapters 2, "Creating a Simple Web Service with .NET SDK," and 3, "Consuming a Simple Web Service with .NET SDK," by using the .NET Framework's tools, you were probably impressed by how the WSDL.exe and the Web Service test page tools automated several tasks for you. However, the Visual Studio.NET Integrated Development Environment (IDE) makes creating Web Services even easier. In this chapter, you will create the same Web Service created in Chapter 2 (although you'll give it a new name to distinguish it from the one created earlier) and then review which steps in the process Visual Studio.NET completed for you.

Creating a New Visual Studio.NET Web Services Project

To create a new project in Visual Studio.NET, follow these steps:

1. Start Visual Studio.NET, and choose File/New/Project from the menu.

2. The New Project dialog box appears, as shown in Figure 4.1.

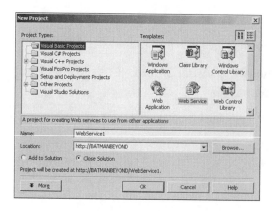

FIGURE 4.1
The New Project dialog box.

In the left pane, Project Types, select Visual Basic Projects or Visual C# Projects, depending on which language you're using. In the right pane, Templates, select ASP.NET Web Service.

3. In the Name field, enter **Chapter4VB** (or **Chapter4CSharp**). You'll notice that the text at the bottom of the dialog box changes to one of the following:

```
Project will be created at http://localhost/Chapter4VB
```

```
Project will be created at http://localhost/Chapter4CSharp
```

Or, depending on how your machine is configured, it could change to one of the following (just substitute your machine name for the text *YOURMACHINENAME*):

```
Project will be created at http://YOURMACHINENAME/Chapter4VB

Project will be created at http://YOURMACHINENAME/Chapter4CSharp
```

This message confirms the location of the project. In the Location field, you could change the server name and/or the folder that you want to save this project into. However, in this book, we'll assume that you are always developing on your own machine.

4. Click the OK button. Visual Studio creates a new Web Folder named Chapter4VB (or Chapter4CSharp), loads the template, and creates a folder on your hard drive for the project files. When it is finished, you'll see the screen shown in Figure 4.2.

> **NOTE**
>
> The Visual Studio.NET installation program checks to make sure you have Internet Information Services installed, along with the FrontPage extensions. If you do not have them installed, it gives you detailed instructions on how to do it. This is not a requirement: You can continue installing Visual Studio.NET without these pieces of software, but the consequence is that you will be unable to create ASP.NET Web Form applications or ASP.NET Web Services applications on your own machine. Instead, you will be required to create applications that reside on other boxes in your network or on the Internet. This book assumes you will be creating the exercises on your local machine (localhost).

5. By default, the Web Service designer opens for the Service1.asmx page that is created by default when you create a new Web Service project. You'll use the Web Service designer window in Chapter 16, "Using the Web Services Designer in Visual Studio.NET." For now, click the View Code button in the Solution Explorer pane to view the source code (see Figure 4.3).

6. A new tabbed window filled with code is now displayed in the main area. At the top of its tab, it has the name "Service1.asmx.vb" or "Service1.asmx.cs." This is the Code Behind page for the Web Service, containing the code that you'll modify for your new Web Service. In the code window (near the bottom) you'll see the following commented sections of code:

For Visual Basic.NET code:

```
' WEB SERVICE EXAMPLE
' The HelloWorld() example service returns the string Hello World
' To build, uncomment the following lines then save and build the project
```

```
' To test, right-click the Web Service's .asmx file and select View in
Browser
'
' Public Function <WebMethod> HelloWorld() As String
'     HelloWorld = "Hello World"
' End Function
```

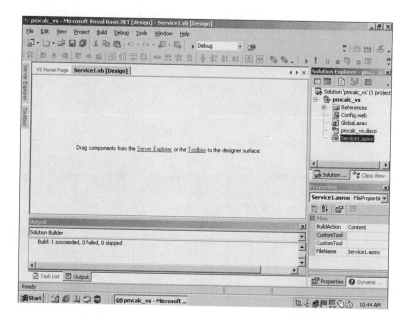

FIGURE 4.2

Result of creating a new Web Services project.

For C# code:

```
//WEB SERVICE EXAMPLE
//The HelloWorld() example service returns the string Hello World
//To build, uncomment the following lines then save and build the project
//To test, right-click the Web Service's .asmx file and select View in
Browser
//
//[WebMethod]
//public string HelloWorld()
//{
//    return "Hello World";
//}
```

This code is provided as a "head start" on developing a Web Service.

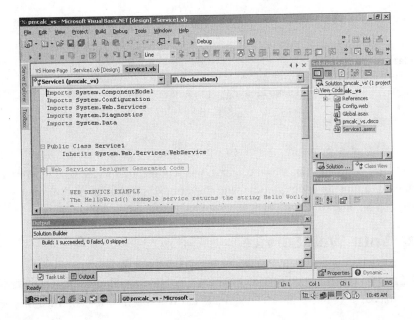

FIGURE 4.3

The result of clicking the View Code button in Solution Explorer.

7. Type in one of the following code blocks under the Web Service Example section:

For Visual Basic.NET code:

```
<WebMethod()>_ Public Function CalculateEstimate(ByVal xlngHours As
Long) As Long
    CalculateEstimate = (xlngHours * 2) + 10
End Function
```

For C# code:

```
[WebMethod()]
public int CalculateEstimate(int xintHours)
    {
    return (xintHours * 2) + 10;
    }
```

You'll notice that while you're typing the example, the IntelliSense pop-up window shows various options.

8. Click the Save button on the button bar, or choose File/Save All from the menu

9. Choose Build | Build Solution from the menu. The following output is displayed in the Output pane:

4

CREATING A SIMPLE
WEB SERVICE IN
VISUAL STUDIO.NET

```
------ Build started: Project: Chapter4VB, Configuration: Debug .NET ------

Preparing resources...
Updating references...
Performing main compilation...
Building satellite assemblies...

------------------- Done -------------------

    Build: 1 succeeded, 0 failed, 0 skipped
```

This is an important step! If you forget it, you will get unexpected results. For those of you used to running in design time with Visual Basic or creating ASP script pages, this step takes some getting used to.

Testing Your Web Service

You've already witnessed the power of the Web Service test page (the DefaultWSDLHelpGenerator.aspx page) from working with the .NET Framework in Chapter 2. Visual Studio.NET uses this page to allow you to easily test and review information about your Web Service as well.

1. Right-click the Service1.asmx file in Solution Explorer, and choose View in Browser from the pop-up menu (see Figure 4.4).

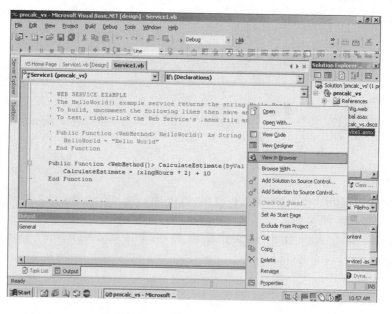

FIGURE 4.4

Solution Explorer's context menu.

A Browse tab appears in the main workspace, and you should see the page shown in Figure 4.5.

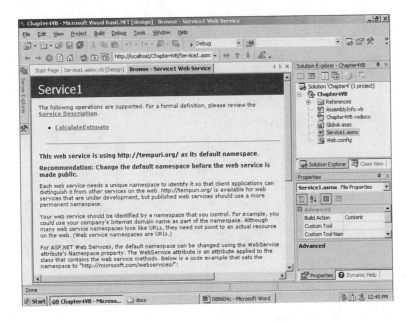

FIGURE 4.5

Preview tab displaying the Web Service's test page.

2. Click the CalculateEstimate hyperlink near the top of the page to load the test page specific to the CalculateEstimate Web method (see Figure 4.6). Each Web method has its own test page.

3. To test the Web Service, enter **8** in the xlngHours field, and then click the Invoke button. Another tab appears that displays the result of the Web Service (see Figure 4.7).

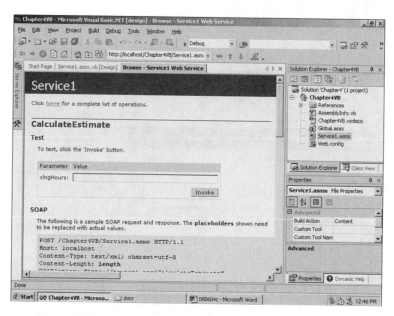

FIGURE 4.6

The test page for the CalculateEstimate *Web method.*

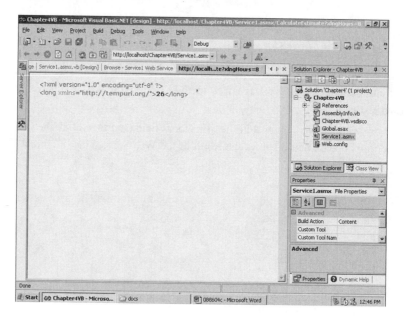

FIGURE 4.7

Results of the test page.

Reviewing Visual Studio.NET's Advantages

After having created a Web Service with the .NET SDK, you probably noticed that Visual Studio.NET automated many of the tedious development chores. Take a moment to review exactly what Visual Studio did to lighten your load:

- Visual Studio.NET created a new sub-Web in Internet Information Services as well as the associated folder on your hard drive.

- All you had to write was the method itself. You didn't have to write any of the class heading information. Also, you were even given a basic template in the form of a "HelloWorld" method with instructions on how to use and test it.

- Visual Studio uses syntax highlighting and IntelliSense pop-up windows to give you that extra reassurance you are typing the correct code. The byproduct is more accurate code that takes fewer attempts to be compiled. My Visual Studio.NET application compiled the second time I tried. My .NET Framework example took 10 tries to get the code and compiler syntax correct.

- You didn't have to create the WSDL document. Visual Studio created it for you automatically based on the methods and parameters created in your class.

- Visual Studio offered easy access to the test harness. Simply right-click on the Web Service and choose View in Browser. The results show up in the IDE's Browse tab.

- Visual Studio automatically supplied other files, such as a .vsdisco file, so that your Web Service can be discovered. You'll learn more about DISCO and discovery later in Chapters 9, "Understanding DISCO," and 25, "Understanding Universal Description, Discovery, and Integration."

Summary

Web Services can be created quickly using the Visual Studio.NET IDE. It automates many of the tedious tasks performed in Chapter 2, thereby making development much quicker.

In the next chapter, you will consume this Web Service into a Web Forms project using the Visual Studio.NET IDE and observe how it makes consuming a Web Service easier as well.

4

CREATING A SIMPLE
WEB SERVICE IN
VISUAL STUDIO.NET

Consuming a Web Service in Visual Studio.NET

IN THIS CHAPTER

Now that you've created a Web Service, you will create a Web Forms application using Visual Studio.NET's rapid application development features that consumes the Web Service created in Chapter 4, "Creating a Simple Web Service in Visual Studio.NET." You'll also observe how the Integrated Development Environment (IDE) makes your task easier than it was in Chapter 3, "Consuming a Simple Web Service with .NET SDK," when you consumed a Web Service using just the .NET Framework.

Creating a Web Forms Application

A Web Service can be consumed (or rather, used) by any type of application running on virtually any computer running almost any software. This shifts the focus from the best protocol to use (DCOM versus CORBA, for instance) to the best tool for taking advantage of the standard protocol (SOAP). Microsoft has created a compelling experience for the developer who wants to create and use Web Services, as is demonstrated in the following steps. It masks the complexity of:

- Finding a Web Service on the Internet/intranet
- Determining the programmatic interface for a Web Service
- Creating a proxy class that wraps the call, serialization of the method call, transmission, and deserialization of the return values from the Web Service behind a simple point-and-click/drag-and-drop interface

To follow along in this chapter, please perform the following steps:

1. Start Visual Studio.NET and choose File/New/Project to open the New Project dialog box.

2. In the left pane, Project Types, select Visual Basic Projects or Visual C# Projects, depending on which language you're using. In the right pane, Templates, select ASP.NET Web Application.

3. In the Name field, enter **Chapter5VB** (for Visual Basic.NET) or **Chapter5CSharp** (for C#). Notice that the text at the bottom of the dialog box changes to one of the following (just substitute your machine name for the text *YOURMACHINENAME* or *localhost*, depending on your machine's configuration) to confirm the location of your project:

   `Project will be created at http://YOURMACHINENAME/Chapter5VB`

   `Project will be created at http://YOURMACHINENAME/Chapter5CSharp`

4. Click the OK button. Visual Studio creates a new Web folder named Chapter5VB (or Chapter5CSharp), loads the template, and creates a folder on your hard drive for the project files.

When it is finished, you'll see the screen shown in Figure 5.1. By default, it loads a Web Form named WebForm1.aspx into the IDE's main area. Typically, you should rename this file, but you don't need to do that in this chapter.

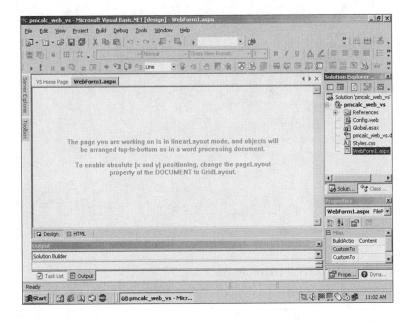

FIGURE 5.1
The Web Forms application in the IDE.

5. On the right-hand side of the screen is the Solution Explorer pane. Locate the project node (typically the top node is the Solution, and its child is the Project node) and right-click it. Choose Add Web Reference on the pop-up menu to open the Add Web Reference dialog box (see Figure 5.2).

6. In the left-hand pane, click the `Web Reference on Local Web Server` hyperlink. The document on the left is a Dynamic Discovery document, which lists all known Web Services (known to Internet Information Services, at least) on your local machine. On the right-hand side are a series of hyperlinks (Linked Reference Groups). Each hyperlink represents one of the entries to the left.

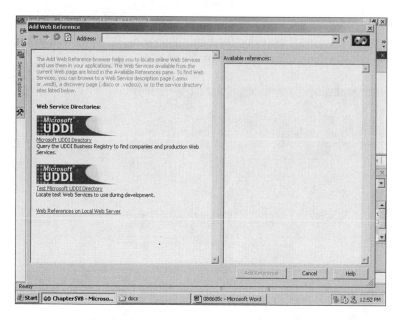

FIGURE 5.2
The initial state of the Add Web Reference Dialog Window

NOTE

A Dynamic Discovery document is an XML file that contains a reference to each of the Web Services on your local machine (or any other machine that has the .NET Framework installed). It enables you to locate the Web Services that a particular server or company supports. The Dynamic Discovery document contains a link to a DISCO file, which contains a reference to the documents that describe aspects of a given Web Service using XML. These two files, along with the WSDL (Web Service Description Language), allow you to find and discover everything you need to know about a Web Service so that the entire process can be automated with a tool such as Visual Studio.NET. These concepts are explained in more depth in Chapter 9, "Understanding DISCO."

---

7. Select the Chapter4VB (or Chapter4CSharp) entry on the right. The DISCO file for the Web Service is displayed in the section on the left, and in the Available References section on the right, you'll see two links (View Contract and View Documentation), shown in Figure 5.3. When you click these links, you see the automatically generated WSDL file and the test page, respectively. At the top of the Add Web Reference dialog box is a set of buttons you can use to go back, forward, stop, and refresh, and an address bar that works much like Internet Explorer.

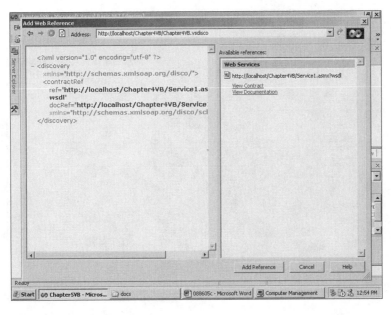

FIGURE 5.3
Viewing a DISCO file in the Add Web Reference dialog box.

8. Click the Add Reference button. The Add Web Reference dialog box closes, and Solution Explorer will refresh to display the new Web References node with a child node called localhost or the name of your server (see Figure 5.4).

NOTE

When you create a Web reference, Visual Studio.NET is secretly building the proxy class that will encapsulate opening an HTTP connection to the network, serializing your method call into SOAP, and sending the SOAP message to the location you selected when creating the Web reference. When the data returns from the Web Service, the proxy class will deserialize the SOAP message into a set of objects to be evaluated and manipulated by your code. The proxy class is the key to making Web Services work so easily from your client.

To view and modify the proxy class, click the View All Files icon in Solution Explorer (second from the last icon), and expand the Web References node, the localhost child node, and the Service1.wsdl file (or the WSDL file you created a reference to). Select the Service1.vb (or Service1.cs) file, and click the View Code button in Solution Explorer (the first button from the left). The proxy class is displayed in the main window. This class provides methods for the initialization, the call, and the asynchronous Begin and End calls to the Web Service (explained in Chapter 19, "Calling Web Services Asynchronously."

5

CONSUMING A WEB SERVICE IN VISUAL STUDIO.NET

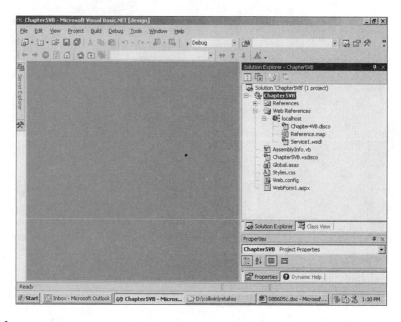

FIGURE 5.4

Solution Explorer with the Web References and localhost nodes displayed.

9. Now you add interface elements from the Toolbox pane to display the results of your Web Service. Make sure the WebForm1.aspx design tab is selected in the IDE's main area. Place your mouse over the Toolbox tab on the far left side, and the pane will scroll into view. Click the Web Forms button to see all the items you can drag and drop onto the designer window (see Figure 5.5).

10. Drag a TextBox interface element from the Toolbox and drop it onto the designer window.

11. Repeat this step again with a Button and a Label interface element. The screen should look like the one shown in Figure 5.6.

12. Double-click the Button element on the Web Form to open its Code Behind file (see Figure 5.7).

13. Type the code from Listing 5.1 (for Visual Basic.NET) or 5.2 (for C#) into the code window. You need to type only the bold code. The rest of the code is provided as context for determining where to add the code.

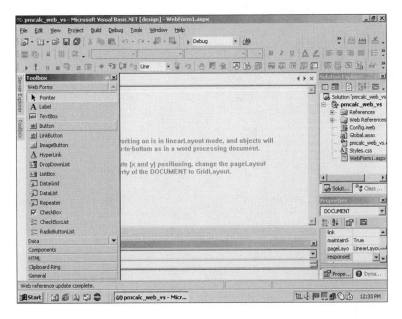

FIGURE 5.5

The Toolbox pane.

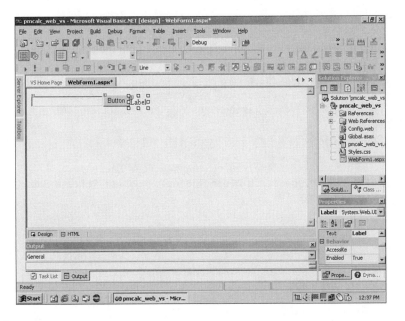

FIGURE 5.6

Placing a Button element on the designer window.

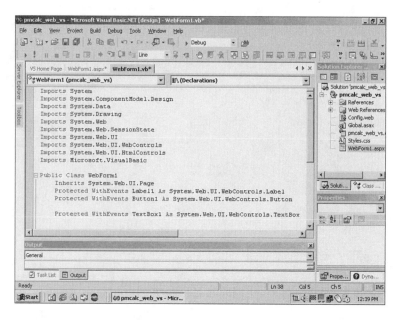

FIGURE 5.7

Result of double-clicking the Button on the Web Form.

LISTING 5.1   WebForm1.aspx.vb in Visual Basic.NET Code

```vb
Public Class WebForm1
    Inherits System.Web.UI.Page
    Protected WithEvents Label1 As System.Web.UI.WebControls.Label
    Protected WithEvents Button1 As System.Web.UI.WebControls.Button
    Protected WithEvents TextBox1 As System.Web.UI.WebControls.TextBox

    #Region " Web Form Designer Generated Code "

        'This call is required by the Web Form Designer.
        <System.Diagnostics.DebuggerStepThrough()> Private Sub
InitializeComponent()

        End Sub

        Private Sub Page_Init(ByVal sender As System.Object, ByVal e As
System.EventArgs) Handles MyBase.Init
            'CODEGEN: This method call is required by the Web Form
Designer
            'Do not modify it using the code editor.
            InitializeComponent()
        End Sub
```

LISTING 5.1 Continued

```
    #End Region

    Private Sub Page_Load(ByVal sender As System.Object, ByVal e As
System.EventArgs) Handles MyBase.Load
        'Put user code to initialize the page here
    End Sub

    Private Sub Button1_Click(ByVal sender As System.Object, ByVal e As
System.EventArgs) Handles Button1.Click
        Dim oWebService As localhost.Service1 = New localhost.Service1()
        Label1.Text = oWebService.CalculateEstimate(CLng(TextBox1.Text))
    End Sub
End Class
```

LISTING 5.2 WebForm1.aspx.cs in C# Code

```
using System;
using System.Collections;
using System.ComponentModel;
using System.Data;
using System.Drawing;
using System.Web;
using System.Web.SessionState;
using System.Web.UI;
using System.Web.UI.WebControls;
using System.Web.UI.HtmlControls;

namespace Chapter5CSharp
{
    /// <summary>
    /// Summary description for WebForm1.
    /// </summary>
    public class WebForm1 : System.Web.UI.Page
    {
        protected System.Web.UI.WebControls.Label Label1;
        protected System.Web.UI.WebControls.TextBox TextBox1;
        protected System.Web.UI.WebControls.Button Button1;

        public WebForm1()
        {
            Page.Init += new System.EventHandler(Page_Init);
        }
```

LISTING 5.2   Continued

```csharp
        private void Page_Load(object sender, System.EventArgs e)
        {
            // Put user code to initialize the page here
        }

        private void Page_Init(object sender, EventArgs e)
        {
            //
            // CODEGEN: This call is required by the ASP.NET Web Form
Designer.
            //
            InitializeComponent();
        }

        #region Web Form Designer generated code
        /// <summary>
        /// Required method for Designer support - do not modify
        /// the contents of this method with the code editor.
        /// </summary>
        private void InitializeComponent()
        {
            this.Button1.Click += new
System.EventHandler(this.Button1_Click);
            this.Load += new System.EventHandler(this.Page_Load);

        }
        #endregion

        private void Button1_Click(object sender, System.EventArgs e)
        {
            localhost.Service1 oWebService = new localhost.Service1();
            Label1.Text =
oWebService.CalculateEstimate(Int32.Parse(TextBox1.Text)).ToString();
        }
    }
}
```

14. Choose Build | Build Solution from the menu. It should return the following test in the Output pane:

```
------ Build started: Project: Chapter5VB, Configuration: Debug .NET -----
-

Preparing resources...
```

```
Updating references...
Performing main compilation...
Building satellite assemblies...



-------------------- Done --------------------

    Build: 1 succeeded, 0 failed, 0 skipped
```

Again, you must remember to do this step each time you make a change in your source code, or the changes will not appear as you test them. Also, if errors occur in your code, the Output pane is replaced with the Task List pane (see Figure 5.8), showing you exactly which lines of code must be changed to successfully compile the source code.

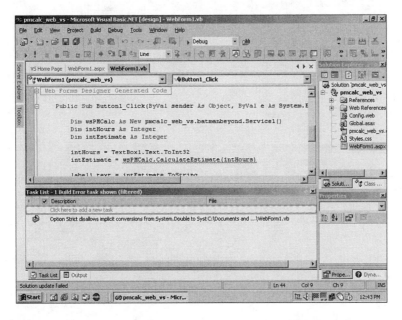

FIGURE 5.8

The Task List pane.

15. Right-click the WebForm1.aspx file in Solution Explorer, and choose View in Browser on the pop-up menu. You should see the screen shown in Figure 5.9.

16. Enter a number in the TextBox element and click the Button element. In a moment, you should see the Label element change to the result of the Web Service (see Figure 5.10).

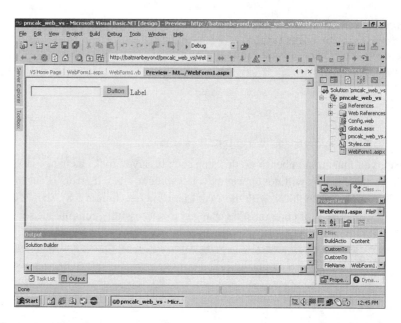

FIGURE 5.9

Seeing a preview of your Web Forms application.

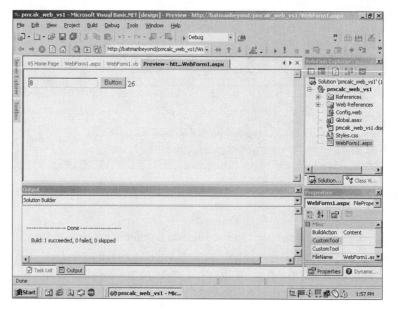

FIGURE 5.10

Results of testing your Web Forms application.

Reviewing Visual Studio.NET's Advantages

Visual Studio.NET performed several tasks for you automatically that made consuming the Web Form application much more simple. Look over the following list to review how Visual Studio simplified matters for you:

- Visual Studio created all the files for you, the folder on the hard drive, and the sub-Web in Internet Information Services.
- You were able to create a Web reference by simply navigating to it in Server Explorer, popping up the context menu on your Web Service, and selecting Add To pmcalc_web_vs. Visual Studio.NET took care of creating and compiling a proxy. This method was much easier than going through the two-step process of creating a proxy, as you did in Chapter 3.
- You could create the Web Forms application by simply dragging and dropping server controls onto the designer window. Also, you were able to code in a Visual Basic event-oriented fashion, by double-clicking the Button element you added to the Web Form and adding code under the `Click` event.
- The Visual Studio.NET IDE offered syntax highlighting and IntelliSense to help guide you as you developed the application. It even knew about your Web Service's methods and parameters through the magic of Web references and proxies.
- You could build, view, and test your Web Forms application within the IDE by simply choosing View in Browser from the pop-up menu on your Web Forms page.

Summary

Consuming Web Services is highly automated and much simplified in Visual Studio. The concepts you have learned in these first five chapters will provide a foundation as you learn how to extend your Web Services in subsequent chapters.

How ASP.NET Works

IN THIS CHAPTER

Up to now, you've simply walked through the steps describing how to create a Web Service, and you could go through your entire Web Service programming career never needing to know what is going on behind the scenes. You might never need to know the relationships between the .NET Framework, Common Language Runtime (CLR), Intermediate Language (IL), and ASP.NET, and you may never wonder about the chain of events that occurs from the time your Web Service is requested until it magically returns a result. However, understanding the internals of Web Services (and the .NET Framework) will not only make you a developer who can write better code and debug tough problems, but it will also provide interesting conversation at parties. As you begin to explore ASP.NET Web Services, it is important to understand some of the fundamentals. You'll briefly examine the "classic" Active Server Pages (ASP) model and its shortcomings as a springboard to learning about the technologies that make up the .NET Framework's support of creating ASP.NET Web Services. You'll also learn the purpose of the Common Language Runtime, the .NET Framework, and the programming models that ASP.NET comprises, and see how requests of your Web pages and Web Services are accepted and processed.

How "Classic" Active Server Pages Work

The first time I saw the term *classic* in reference to ASP and the Component Object Model (COM), I laughed. These were the technologies I depended on every day to create applications as a software consultant, and it appeared I was working on an antiquated, outdated, "classic" technology! Immediately, I was inspired to learn the "new" ASP and the "new" COM because after all, who wants to be caught dead working with "classic" technology?

This is a risky proposition for Microsoft. After all, the Coca-Cola Corporation dropped the "new" Coke in favor of "Classic Coke" because consumers revolted. People just loved the flavor of the original. Let's hope the new ASP tastes better to developers.

In the classic ASP model, the ASP processor was implemented as an Internet Server Application Programming Interface (ISAPI) extension (asp.dll). *ISAPI* is a programming interface that developers can use to extend the functionality of Internet Information Services (IIS). The asp.dll is simply a COM object that supports specific interfaces and types in order to be an ISAPI extension. ISAPI extensions are associated in IIS with certain file types. For ASP, the .asp file type is associated with the asp.dll.

When IIS receives an HTTP-Request, it looks in its Metabase to determine which ISAPI extension is registered to handle this type of file. IIS then routes the HTTP-Request to the appropriate ISAPI extension (that is, the asp.dll).

The asp.dll is then responsible for handling the request (see Figure 6.1). ASP loads the file into memory (if it has not already been cached), parses it, and based on the language directive at the top of the ASP page, loads the appropriate Active Scripting engine. The Active Scripting engine runs the parsed script and the asp.dll sends the results back to the browser in a return string.

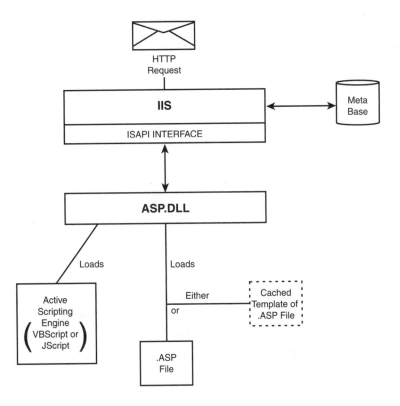

FIGURE 6.1
How "classic" ASP works.

The Problem with Active Server Pages

The classic ASP model served us well, but it had some inherent limitations that could be optimized and covered up for only so long. Some of these limitations and problems--performance issues, maintainability, state management, and use of COM components--are discussed in more detail in the following sections.

Performance

The ASP parser is an incredible piece of software that handles just about everything you can throw at it, whether poorly written or well-formed ASP code. Ultimately, however, even after the code has been parsed and cached into memory, it is still just script that relies on an Active Scripting engine to run it. The IIS 5.0 team has optimized this process, but your pages are script, not compiled code.

Maintainability

The ASP pages were a mixture of HTML and server-side script, such as VBScript or JScript. Additionally, the pages could contain other client-side script, such as VBScript or JavaScript. With these different code sections intermingled throughout the document, the pages could get rather unwieldy. As developers tried to implement more complex business rules in their Web pages, the need for code separation became more evident.

State Management

Managing state was one of the most important features of early ASP because of the home-grown solutions that developers came up with on their own. However, classic ASP's state management was not without its inherent flaws, some of which were compounded by bad coding techniques and improper use by developers. There are four issues with managing state by using the Application and Session objects in classic ASP:

- These objects require that the user's Web browser cookies be turned on. A unique identifier is stored in a cookie that allows the state information to be matched up between the user's request and the cached cookie information.

- If the user does not take action within a set period of time, the cookies expire and the user's data is forever lost.

- Developers stored object references in the Application and Session objects, which caused noticeable memory problems.

- Session state using cookies does not work across a Web farm because each session is created by a single Web server; it's not designed to transfer to multiple servers.

Use of COM Components

When you needed to access data, implement security, send mail, or just about anything outside the scope of VBScript or JScript, you had to reference a COM component to do it. Although this is a viable option that has proved successful, this approach has configuration, deployment, and performance problems. In an ideal world, all these services would be built right into ASP so that relying on them would be more tightly integrated with your application.

The Microsoft.NET Framework

The ASP development team sought a better way to create Web applications that would improve speed, provide more built-in system services, improve state management, and separate the HTML (interface) from the script (business rules). In a nutshell, they were aiming to make it easier to build Web-based applications. Also, they wanted to give developers additional ways to have access to extensibility points within this new ASP framework that would enable more developers (that is, all developers who were not C++ developers) to create functionality similar to ISAPI filters and extensions. The culmination of the ASP team's efforts, and of other teams in Microsoft, led to the larger effort known as the .NET Framework we have today.

Microsoft.NET Framework Architecture

The diagram in Figure 6.2 is a good way to see all the pieces of the .NET Framework. In the following sections, you'll take a brief look at each of the components of this architecture.

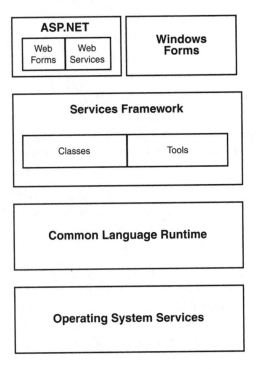

FIGURE 6.2

Microsoft.NET Framework architecture.

At the bottom of this diagram are the services that the operating system makes available. You might already be familiar with the Windows 32-bit Application Programming Interface (API) and the services it provides, such as the ability to draw windows, mouse support, memory management, and the like. On top of that API lies the Common Language Runtime.

Common Language Runtime

The Common Language Runtime (CLR) is the heart of .NET; the foundation on which all the dreams of the programmable Web are resting for Microsoft. It is arguably the most important move forward for Microsoft-based development and constitutes the single greatest paradigm shift yet introduced for the PC. In this section, I'll introduce the CLR and discuss how it is different from and similar to the ASP/COM environment.

Code that runs within the CLR is known as "managed code." Because there is no IL compiler for Visual Basic 6.0 and Visual C++ 6.0 (and probably never will be), the traditional applications you have created in the past are considered to be "unmanaged." The CLR, however, offers some major benefits.

First, the CLR defines a common set of data types across all CLR programming languages, allowing for multi-language integration. This feature makes it possible to create classes in Visual Basic.NET that derive from classes created in C# and vice versa.

Second, the CLR defines a common metadata so that components can be "self-describing." In other words, no separate type-library file or header file is necessary because the class definition, version, and so forth reside within the component or executable file. This metadata is generated from the component's actual source code, so it is never out of sync with the actual executable file.

All parts of the executable, the code, and the metadata combine to create an *assembly* (see Figure 6.3). Actually, assemblies are "logical" DLL files. In other words, an assembly can be one physical DLL file with one or more classes and resources, or an assembly can have multiple DLL files, each with one or more classes and resources.

From the user-programmer's perspective, all the classes appear to be packaged into the same component. There are a number of advantages to this approach, including how you can formulate a security policy around assemblies, control versioning in your components (that is, which version of the dependent component should be used if multiple versions are present on the system), and improve control of the configuration and deployment of your applications.

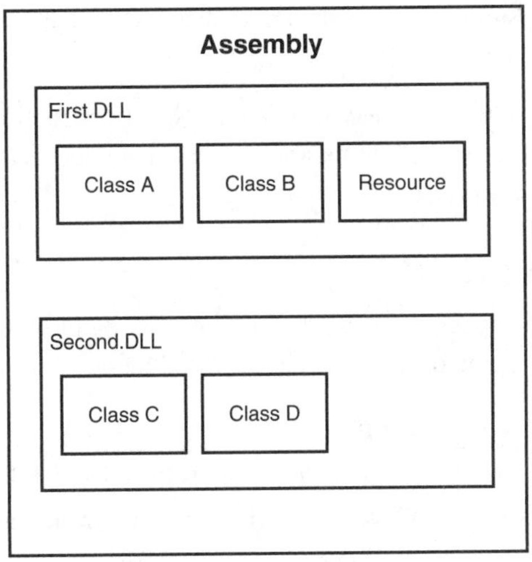

FIGURE 6.3

Assemblies.

The assembly's metadata is actually known as the *manifest*, which includes dependency information, the version of the component, the types that the component supports, and other information. Since assemblies are self-describing, no explicit registration of your components is necessary. You simply copy your assembly into a directory (designated as a \bin directory) and the CLR takes care of managing the registration process. Delete the file, and the CLR takes care of unregistering the assembly. This method is in sharp contrast to the registration (and unregistration) process for COM/COM+ components that required you to create an application in COM+/MTS or use the regsvr32.exe command-line utility.

Third, the CLR provides code-access security, which is, in essence, mini-checkpoints your code must pass through based on the actions it is trying to perform. This security measure ensures that unauthorized users cannot access resources on a machine and that code cannot perform unauthorized actions. If your code must access information or perform actions on the machine it is running on (access files on the hard drive or access the network), it must ask the CLR if it has permission to do that. The CLR at runtime determines the source of the code and where it was obtained from, as well as other information stored in the code's assembly, and grants or denies permission to the code to perform the given task. The CLR also provides role-based security, which is similar to code-access security except that the CLR makes permission judgments based on the privileges of the person using the application.

System administrators, developers, and users can work together to determine which combination of security services to use and at what level to ensure that unauthorized code and unauthorized users do not gain access to sensitive information or are not allowed to perform malicious actions on the computer systems or network. These security policies are stored in an XML file for each configuration.

Fourth, the CLR manages memory, object invocation, object destruction, and garbage collection so that developers can focus on writing applications that address the needs of their business users, not writing base services or plumbing.

Services Framework

On top of the CLR is the Services Framework, a rich collection of class libraries and programming tools for developers. Some of the libraries are listed here:

Library	Purpose
System.Data	Classes that support the ADO.NET architecture
System.IO	Classes that allow reading from and writing to data streams and files
System.Diagnostics	Classes that allow you to debug your application and trace the execution of your code
System.XML	Classes that provide standards-based support for processing XML
System.Security	Classes that provide the underlying structure of the .NET Framework security system (such as permissions)
System.Threading	Classes that enable multithreaded programming

Each of the libraries owns dozens of child classes within its hierarchy, each with potentially dozens of properties, methods, and events. The Services Framework has so many classes, in fact, that it's difficult to digest all the things you can do!

Some tools are also supplied for developers:

Tool Name	Purpose
CorDbg.exe	Runtime debugger to help find and fix bugs
ILDasm.exe	Allows you to view the IL from an assembly
Xsd.exe	XML Schema Definition tool, which converts several different data formats--such as classes and DataSets--from and to XML schemas

Entire volumes could (and will) be written about any of the items in the Services Framework. As you develop Web Services, you will become particularly familiar with the classes in the System.Web.Services tree.

ASP.NET and Windows Forms Application Services

At the next level up on the .NET Framework architecture are the services that allow you to create applications. ASP.NET services include the ability to handle HTTP-Requests that come from Internet Information Services. Windows Forms services handle painting windows and handling events such as button clicks. I'll focus more on ASP.NET services because they support Web Services.

The Application Services for ASP.NET is further divided into Web Forms and Web Services. Web Forms are similar to classic ASP in that they typically have a visual representation in HTML with a programmable element that runs on the Web server. Both adhere to the same ASP.NET application model.

The ASP.NET Application Model

With sophisticated page caching and configurable state management, ASP.NET gives developers much more flexibility in their Web applications. Developers will also enjoy better performance because source code compilation results in speed enhancements.

ASP.NET is much more extensible than classic ASP because of its rich object model (see Figure 6.4). It also allows non-C++ developers to create powerful applications that take advantage of preprocessing Web page requests and responses. For example, you can create an HTTP Module that intercepts a request for a Web page and does some validation, such as "Does this user have rights to call this Web page?" or "Should I reroute the use to a different Web page based on what he asked for?" HTTP Modules are the .NET equivalent of ISAPI filters.

You can also create HTTP Handlers that actually handle different file extensions, so you could create your own type of Web Service with the extension .BOB if you were so inclined. Of course, you would be responsible for writing all the plumbing to handle requests, invoke objects, and so on. This kind of flexibility is now available, and although you might not imagine you would ever want it, over time you will probably come to be thankful such extensibility was built in.

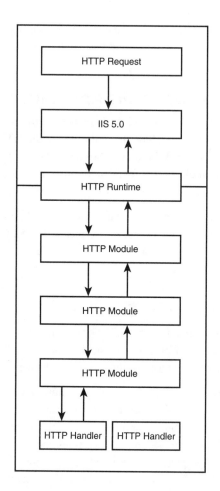

FIGURE 6.4
The ASP.NET application model.

How Do Web Services Work?

As noted earlier, when an HTTP-Request is made for a particular resource on a Web server--
say a classic Active Server Page--IIS checks its Metabase for the appropriate ISAPI extension
to handle the requested file type. For ASP, that ISAPI extension is the asp.dll. ASP parses the
code, executes its commands, and returns values to the client. (I'm speaking in very broad and
general terms.) Similarly, when a request is made for an .aspx (Web Forms) file or .asmx (Web
Services) file, an ISAPI extension called IIS checks its Metabase and determines that the
ASP.NET ISAPI extension, xspisapi.dll, is responsible for handling that request. IIS funnels
the request to the xspisapi.dll. The xspisapi.dll is "unmanaged," so it calls on the xsp.exe, a
"managed" parser/handler, to take over.

This begins a chain of calls that sends the HTTP-Request through many layers of code (called HTTP Modules) until your Web Service or Web Forms file is executed. HTTP Modules are similar to ISAPI filters.

Figure 6.5 gives you a general idea of the layers and the sequence of events in the life of a Web Service's execution.

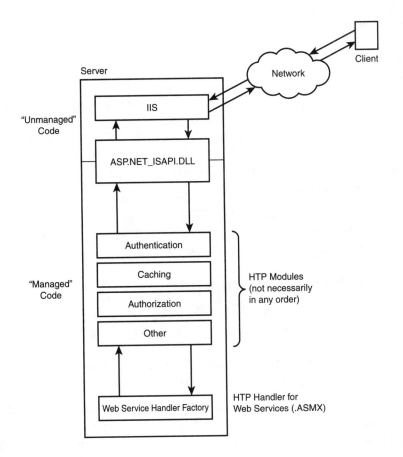

FIGURE 6.5

Events in the life of a Web Service.

The first time your .asmx file is called, it must be compiled to run within the ASP.NET Runtime as managed code. Compilation is covered in more depth in the following section, "Just-In-Time (JIT) Compilation."

After the Web Service has been compiled, the HTTP-Request can then be sent through a "pipeline" to the appropriate HTTP Handler for final processing. The pipeline consists of multiple HTTP Modules that perform various functions on the HTTP-Requests. Out-of-the box modules include functionality for logging, authentication, authorization, and session state. The modules can be replaced by your own code if necessary, and you can add new ones.

Additionally, you can create your own HTTP Handlers to add more flexibility and power. You could create your own custom HTTP Handlers to provide special monitoring and authorization functions as a means of managing your Web Services; however, this topic is outside the scope of this book.

Eventually, the WebServiceHandlerFactory (System.Web.Services.Protocols. WebServiceHandlerFactory class) is called. This class performs several functions, not the least of which is being responsible for deserializing the Simple Object Access Protocol (SOAP) call and then actually running your compiled code to perform the logic you developed in your Web Service. Like most other items in ASP.NET, the Web Services HTTP Handler can be configured as an entry in the web.config file. Configuration issues are discussed at length in Chapter 27, "Securing Web Services."

After your code has finished processing the HTTP-Request, it serializes the return values into a SOAP message and sends it back up the chain of HTTP Modules, and then back to Internet Information Services and the consumer of the Web Service.

Just-In-Time (JIT) Compilation

Your Web Service or Web Forms file must be compiled to run within the CLR. Compilation can be implicit or explicit. Yes, that is correct. Your Web Service (and Web Forms, too) will be compiled into an assembly. (By the way, this is the main reason you must now create ASP.NET Web pages by using Visual Basic.NET or C# instead of VBScript. Only CLR languages can be compiled into CLR assemblies to run within the CLR.)

Although you could explicitly call the appropriate compiler (the vbc.exe for Visual Basic or the csc.exe for C#) to compile your Web Service or Web Forms files, it is easier to allow the file to be compiled implicitly. Implicit compilation occurs when you request the .asmx file via HTTP-SOAP, HTTP-GET, or HTTP-POST. The parser (xsp.exe) determines whether a current version of the assembly resides in memory or on disk. If it can't use an existing version, the parser makes the appropriate call to the respective compiler (as you designated in the Class property of the .asmx page). Again, you could compile it yourself, but Microsoft put a lot of work into making this task painless for the developer.

When your Web Service (or Web Forms page) is implicitly compiled, it is actually compiled twice. On the first pass, it is compiled into Intermediate Language (IL). The IL is not necessarily the most human-readable language you might ever attempt to read. However, you can sort of understand what's going on if you stare at it long enough. Your C#, Visual Basic.NET, or any other third-party language that is created to be CLR compatible (Cobol.NET, JScript.NET, and so on) is compiled into essentially the same IL. Just for fun, you could create a "Hello World" Web Service (like the one supplied in Visual Studio.NET as an example) in both Visual Basic.NET and C#, and then compare the ILs of both Web Services using ILDASM, the Intermediate Language Dis-assembler.

During the compilation's second pass, your Web Service, now an IL assembly, is compiled into machine language. This process is called *Just-In-Time (JIT) compilation* because it does not occur until the assembly is on the target machine. The reason you don't compile it ahead of time is so that the specific "JITter" for your operating system and processor type can be used. As a result, your assembly is compiled into the fastest possible machine language code, optimized and enhanced for your specific configuration. It also enables you to compile once and then run on any number of operating systems. Perhaps the components, Web Services, and Web pages you create today could be sold tomorrow to companies who run purely Linux or Macintosh operating systems. Only time will tell.

Summary

Thanks to the efforts the ASP.NET team put into the .NET Framework, ASP.NET applications offer a greater degree of control, flexibility, and performance than "classic" ASP applications.

The .NET Framework consists of the CLR, the Services Framework, and the Applications Framework. The CLR manages a common data type system, a common metadata structure for describing components, and a common security mechanism, and also manages memory, object invocation, and so forth. The Services Framework is a rich set of libraries and tools developers can use to create applications that work within a managed execution context. The Applications Framework includes tools for developers to create traditional Windows Forms applications and ASP.NET Web Forms and Web Services.

The ASP.NET Application Framework performs many steps automatically, such as implicit compilation and pipeline services (logging and authentication, for example). With HTTP Handlers, you can create additional plug-in functionality. A special HTTP Handler called the WebServiceHandlerFactory is responsible for running your code as well as other critical functions necessary to serve up data to consumers of your Web Service.

Examining SOAP

IN THIS CHAPTER

Although it is entirely possible to create Web Services without ever needing to understand the Simple Object Access Protocol (SOAP) messages exchanged between the provider and the consumer, developers will be better served by understanding their structure and format. As you develop Web Services, you might need to "crack open the code" and watch the actual SOAP messages to test or debug your applications. You could be forced to make some modifications in the SOAP message's structure to conform to that of a trading partner, or perhaps you want to better understand SOAP so you understand the constraints and extensibility of Web Services. In this chapter, you gain a better understanding of SOAP's features and components, its advantages over existing Remote Procedure Calls (RPC) protocols, and why it's proving to be the protocol of choice for the next era of Internet applications. The next several chapters will discuss the SOAP specification and how it applies to the ASP.NET Web Services implementation of the specification. Additionally, you'll examine the technologies that surround SOAP, such as WSDL, DISCO, and UDDI.

A Few Words About the SOAP Specification

Before you begin, it is important you understand that the ASP.NET Web Services implementation of SOAP attempts to make available only those features of SOAP that make sense within the context of Web Services. For example, ASP.NET Web Services, by default, are bound to HTTP. The SOAP specification does not require HTTP, so it can be used with Simple Mail Transfer Protocol (SMTP) and File Transfer Protocol (FTP). Using the SOAP specification's encodingStyle property, you can also modify the payload portion of the SOAP message. You cannot, however, do that with the default implementation of ASP.NET Web Services. Although I'm sure there will be critics of such an omission, consider the following two points.

First, the SOAP specification was created to be flexible enough to support different types of implementations for a wide array of purposes using varied protocols and potentially different rules to interpret the actual XML in the message. The specification is a "one size fits all" proposition. Such flexibility is great for a specification that seeks a long shelf life, but at some point you have to take that specification and build applications that concretely implement it. This is what ASP.NET Web Services attempts to do.

Second, ASP.NET Web Services was created so that it could use the aspects of the SOAP specification that made sense to facilitate a simple implementation of the Web Services concept. You can enjoy the benefits of Web Services without a great deal of knowledge of SOAP or the need to memorize dozens of different attributes, properties, methods, rules, exceptions, and so forth.

For those ambitious developers who feel they have been deprived of functionality they might need for their specific project, I'd like to remind them they are welcome to extend the implementation of Web Services by overriding the .NET Framework classes. However, that is outside the scope of this book.

What Is SOAP?

Simply put, SOAP is a message format that allows two software systems to communicate regardless of what software and hardware platform the two participating computers are using. It accomplishes this task through the use of industry standards such as HTTP and eXtensible Markup Language (XML). The communication typically (but not necessarily) takes the form of a request for information and then the response to that request.

In Figure 7.1, Computer A requests a stock price from Computer B via a SOAP message that explains which stock Computer A is interested in. Computer B receives the request, interprets the SOAP message, and looks up the request in its database. Computer B creates a SOAP response including the price of the requested stock and sends it back to Computer A. Computer A receives the SOAP message, interprets it, and then represents it onscreen to the human user. SOAP facilitates this sharing of data by standardizing the format and structure of the message passed between the computers.

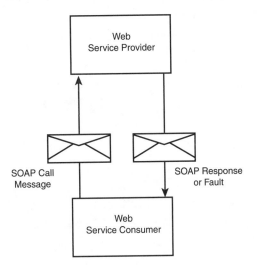

FIGURE 7.1

SOAP's request/response nature.

The word *simple* in *SOAP* is a relative term. In this case, it's simple in is relation to other protocols that exist for this purpose, including Distributed Component Object Model (DCOM) and IIOP/ORB/CORBA, both of which also enable communication between software systems, but do so in a rather unfriendly (in other words, non–industry standard) way. The term *protocol* denotes a standard that two parties can agree on. For the purposes of this book, the protocol is a specification that defines how messages are formatted so that both parties (that is, software systems) can communicate with each other. Without the protocol, the software systems would be free to send and receive messages any way they want to, but doing so would be counterproductive because the systems would not understand each other.

The words *object access* in SOAP might be a little misleading because *procedures* are accessed, not necessarily objects. When we think of objects, we typically think of object-oriented programming's (OOP) definition of an object—that an object is a representation in code of something in the real or abstract world. Dogs, pencils, data access, and the like fall into this definition. Therefore, an object contains more than just a bunch of unrelated procedures thrown into the same package together. Objects have methods and properties that define their actions and attributes, respectively. Objects come to life when an instance of the object is created in a computer's memory based on a class definition. Those objects remain in the computer's memory as long as they are needed and released from memory when they are no longer needed. During their lifetime, they can maintain state (that is, information about the dog, pencil, or data access is maintained in memory).

Although you can use SOAP to access an object's methods and properties, SOAP has nothing to do with OOP per se. The SOAP specification does not require that a procedure must be part of a class definition; it could be a Web page that statically or dynamically returns values that are formatted according to the SOAP specification. The procedure does not have to be related to other procedures that reside on the same server or in the same "package." SOAP does not define how a class is instantiated and does not require that state be maintained between procedure calls. SOAP is simply a message format that facilitates an RPC between two computers.

> **NOTE**
>
> A small distinction, but an important one: As you create ASP.NET Web Services, you are actually implementing your methods as members of a class. This process more closely adheres to what the spirit of SOAP is as an object-oriented method call, as opposed to a more procedural approach of returning data from a function encoded as a SOAP message.

SOAP is simply a specification, a definition of how requests and responses must be formatted so that two applications supporting SOAP can communicate with each other. SOAP does nothing by itself. Each platform or software vendor must decide how best to implement the SOAP specification to get the most value from it. SOAP has meaning only within the context of carrying out communication between two software systems that support the specification. There are a number of specifications dealing with how to call procedures remotely, each with inherent advantages and disadvantages, and they are covered in the following section.

One feature of SOAP that makes it stand out from other RPC mechanisms is that the SOAP specification was developed by many different major organizations, such as Microsoft, IBM, and Lotus. Other major organizations, such as the Object Modeling Group (OMG), Sun, and Oracle are supporting this standard as well. The first specification was submitted to the World Wide Web Consortium (or W3C, a governing body for Internet standards) in September 1999. A second version (1.1, the current one as of this writing) was submitted early in 2000. The most notable change between version 1 and 1.1 was the move from an HTTP-centered protocol to an all-inclusive standard. This standard enabled other protocols, such as SMTP and FTP, to use SOAP messages.

However, because SOAP was born from an HTTP-based protocol mindset, its strength continues to be the request/response format you are accustomed to on the Internet. That is not to say that messages could not be sent via e-mail and queued until another process on the server checks the mailbox, responds to the request, and sends an e-mail to the original requestor or multiple requestors. Additionally, FTP could be used to upload, process, and download the results of a procedure call. Again, although possible, I don't foresee that implementation of SOAP being used as often as the HTTP request/response method.

SOAP and XML

Several existing specifications are similar to SOAP, and they all have one aim in mind: to facilitate Remote Procedure Calls (RPC). The RPC is a technology that enables an application to call a procedure (function, method, or whatever you call it) that physically resides in code somewhere else. That "somewhere else" could be across the room or across the world, across a LAN, a WAN, or the Internet.

SOAP utilizes XML to express RPC calls and therefore can take advantage of the benefits of XML, as well as its surrounding technologies. In the "Components of a SOAP Message" section later in this chapter, you'll examine the parts of a SOAP message and see how it uses XML schemas and namespaces; you'll also learn how it can be processed and modified by using eXtensible Stylesheet Language Transformations (XSLT) and parsed by using the Microsoft XML Document Object Model (MSXML) or the Simple API for XML (SAX). You have a great deal of flexibility in how you process incoming and outgoing messages and what you can do to those messages.

One problem with relying on XML is that many of the related technologies (such as XML schemas) are still under consideration by the W3C as "drafts." These specifications are near the "recommendation" phase, however, so any changes at this point will have little impact on the SOAP specification. If SOAP does change, the existing tools that hide SOAP's implementation details (such as ASP.NET Web Services) will more than likely handle this transition, too.

Also, because SOAP's essence is XML, SOAP is, therefore, just plain text—a huge difference from protocols that have a binary format (IIOP/ORB/CORBA and DCOM). This difference could be a good thing or a bad thing, depending on how you view it. Other RPC mechanisms have binary formats that make it difficult to crack them open and inspect them. Any platform that can open an ANSI text file, however, can open a SOAP message or file, quite an advantage if you need to read the contents of messages being sent back and forth in the RPC. It's not such an advantage, though, if you like your messages to be compact and travel quickly across the network.

Because XML is the way SOAP chooses to express RPC calls, those calls are easy to read from both a human and a computer perspective. Even a novice developer can read SOAP documents and determine exactly what is being called, what parameters are being sent, and so on. This feature could be helpful in two scenarios. First, viewing the SOAP messages enhances your ability to debug problem situations. Sometimes it's difficult to determine whether a bug is the result of the sender making the call in the wrong way or the receiver interpreting that call incorrectly. By being able to "sniff" incoming and outgoing messages between the two systems and reading the SOAP document, developers can pinpoint where the problem lies.

In the second scenario, the developer wants to quickly create a filter that reads the SOAP message and adds to it, changes it, or just monitors it. From a computer's perspective, SOAP is just plain text, and its specification is open. It's not a proprietary binary format that makes it difficult to understand, so a developer can easily create an interface (or rather, a proxy) to allow the system to handle SOAP.

> **NOTE**
>
> Although it's obvious, there's one caveat to using SOAP: Both the caller and the receiver must understand SOAP. However, there should be no great difficulty in accomplishing that. As I've stated, SOAP messages are simply XML in ASCII text, and as such can be used on virtually any platform using any software tool.

The beauty of SOAP is that because it is just creating XML in a specific way (according to the SOAP specification), absolutely any programming language or scripting language that can concatenate strings, accept strings, and return strings from procedures can provide and consume SOAP Web Services. Admittedly, some development environments (such as Visual Studio .NET) offer components, utilities, or class libraries that make dealing with SOAP easier, but that does not mean that development is impossible in other environments. On the Internet, I've already seen dozens of different implementations of SOAP in every conceivable language, even research languages I've never heard of before. With its roots in XML, SOAP is the perfect way to communicate between applications because there is no affinity for one programming language, platform, computer type, or network.

Not only can SOAP be implemented in any programming language, but it does not require any new hardware or software to be used in your current environment. You can use the same Web servers and Web server software, if you like. Although you might realize productivity gains if you have a toolset or development environment that allows you to develop SOAP-based interfaces and applications more quickly and with a more shallow learning curve, those items are not necessary to enjoy the benefits of SOAP in your current systems with your current hardware.

One feature that differentiates SOAP from other protocols created to accommodate RPC is that it has been submitted to the W3C to be designated a standard means of communicating between applications over the Internet. This designation is significant because no one company will "own" SOAP, so it will not be proprietary or change on the whim of a company that wants to sell new tools. It will not be a licensed technology (like Java) and, therefore, will not be cost prohibitive to use. Admittedly, Microsoft and IBM have spent a great deal of time developing the specification submitted to the W3C, but they do not "own" it. Input will be solicited and changes made from many large and small companies as the standard evolves, much like modifications to HTML over the years.

As a result of being open and an Internet standard, SOAP has garnered a lot of attention from vendors. In fact, SOAP support now has become expected among tools that enable business-to-business integration.

Because SOAP is XML, it can be transmitted on any port to complement any number of other protocols. I often mention SOAP being sent over HTTP using port 80, but it's not limited to port 80 (it can be sent across *any* port) or to HTTP (it can be sent via SMTP, FTP, or any other conceivable protocol, including proprietary protocols your company might want to develop). Although it is easy to understand how SOAP is used in the request/response manner HTTP accommodates, in other situations you might want an application that supports queued calls and takes advantage of SMTP and FTP. I don't explore this situation in depth in this book, but remember that it's possible to use SOAP in that way.

What's important to remember is that because SOAP is just plain text and can be transported over HTTP via port 80, you gain the benefit of offering Web Services to the world without requiring your system administrator to open "holes" (data ports) in your firewall. Corporate firewalls typically allow access through port 80 so that users can view Web pages, but all other ports are closed to prevent unauthorized and potentially malicious use of the company's networks. Being able to use port 80 is an important benefit over other RPC technologies that require other ports to be opened for them to function properly. Opening other ports to accommodate these technologies is more of a security risk.

I've recently read criticism of SOAP from those who are concerned it poses new potential security problems. Their argument is that firewalls will be called on to do more sophisticated checks on the format and content of SOAP messages. However, new extensions to the HTTP protocol have been proposed that will simplify administration of firewalls (using the M-POST verb) to verify that the requested message in HTTP is the message requested in the SOAP body. Security is always a concern, but there is no way to maliciously design a SOAP message that does something other than what the developer of the Web Service originally designed it for.

SOAP Versus Other RPC Technologies

Several RPC technologies have emerged over the past decade, most notably DCOM and IIOP/ORB/CORBA. These technologies are popular and solid; however, support for them usually divides down the lines of Microsoft (DCOM) versus Unix/Java (IIOP/ORB/CORBA). Neither technology has gained ubiquity throughout the industry, which is a problem because the two technologies do not interface with each other directly. A translation layer must be created to allow systems that speak DCOM and systems that speak IIOP/ORB/CORBA to interact. Although these technologies are not covered in detail, this section outlines some of their limitations and explains how SOAP provides a solution to these limitations.

One problem with DCOM and IIOP/ORB/CORBA is that when implementing either one, you are tied to a single vendor. From a CORBA perspective, there might be different vendors that provide ORB tools, but they do not operate out of the box with each other (much less with DCOM) without a lot of tweaking. This extra effort might be acceptable in small to medium organizations, but it could prove to be a roadblock in large organizations where interdepartment communication is a factor. If one department chooses a particular technology, it has inadvertently committed the entire organization to using the exact same technology throughout or expending a great deal of effort and money to create a bridge between it and the other systems in the company. As a side note, some have suggested the use of SOAP to solve this dilemma. Each system would need to implement a proxy through which it could send and receive SOAP messages and translate those messages as it deems fit.

DCOM and IIOP/ORB/CORBA rely heavily on a predictable environment. When you can control all the servers that will communicate via these technologies as well as the network between them, you can use DCOM and IIOP/ORB/CORBA more successfully. For your purposes, when building Web Services that can be consumed by anyone using any platform, this simply will not do. You cannot control the network or the consuming server, and you will not always be able to diagnose the software on the other side of the endpoint.

Also, DCOM and IIOP/ORB/CORBA have a reputation of being relatively hard to build, especially when compared with the rather open and text-based approach of SOAP. Although I have not focused on IIOP/ORB/CORBA, I can attest to the complexity involved in building DCOM-based applications. From a theory standpoint, DCOM is masking a lot of complexity from the developer. However, it is generally agreed that a certain level of understanding of what goes on behind the scenes is necessary to be an adequate COM developer (or at least to pass the technical interview). From a practical standpoint, building DCOM applications means the developer must be ever mindful of a number of "gotcha's." Even more complex than building DCOM-based applications is actually implementing them, especially in high-volume environments that require multiple servers. I'm not saying it's impossible, just that it is harder than it should be.

I do not want to dismiss these technologies. It is generally believed (although I have not personally seen actual performance statistics for this blanket claim) that DCOM and IIOP/ORB/CORBA still have the advantage over SOAP when you are building a system that primarily involves server-to-server communication within the same organization—at least from a performance standpoint. These situations demand high speed, do not require the openness of a Web Service, and are run in an environment where all the variables can be controlled (for example, in the server room). In an enterprise, SOAP might actually have the advantage of being open (thereby encouraging cross-system compatibility), discoverable (thereby encouraging reuse), and self-documenting (further encouraging reuse). Each enterprise must evaluate performance against openness individually based on the goals and risk of each (again, assuming there is a performance gain).

However, when there's a need to communicate with different software systems across an unstable network such as the Internet, SOAP fills the bill nicely. Perhaps someday when bandwidth is less an issue and servers become even faster, the lag associated with a verbose SOAP message will diminish, and SOAP will then be the RPC of choice both inside and outside the enterprise.

SOAP's Benefits and "Drawbacks"

SOAP is the RPC of choice for Web Services for the following reasons:

- SOAP provides cross-platform interoperability between software systems by taking advantage of the ubiquity of standards such as ASCII and XML.

- SOAP can be sent via HTTP on port 80, as well as other protocols and ports, which makes it ideal for transporting RPC calls and responses through firewalls. This is the biggest disadvantage of the other technologies, which require potentially dangerous holes to be created in a corporation's firewall.

- SOAP messages are descriptive of each data element in the message's payload, which makes it easier to diagnose problems that could arise.

Admittedly, SOAP's goals are not as lofty as other RPC technologies. There are several features SOAP does not address, but for good reason. SOAP allows each platform to address the following features in the way it deems best:

- **Object invocation:** The SOAP specification does not attempt to define how instances of objects are created.

- **Garbage collection:** The SOAP specification does not try to define how objects are destroyed after they are no longer needed, nor does it define how the objects are to be removed from memory.

- **Security:** It's true that the SOAP specification doesn't discuss security, but other protocols, such as Secure Socket Layer (SSL), can be used to fill the bill. Instead of reinventing the wheel, SOAP chose to rely on other technologies in this area.

- **Authentication:** Again, there is no mention of this feature in the SOAP specification. Plenty of technologies can accomplish authentication, and you can implement a homegrown solution to address this task.

Now that you've reviewed SOAP from a theoretical standpoint, the remainder of the chapter dissects a SOAP message and uncovers the nuances of its design.

Components of a SOAP Message

If you're interested in reading the entire SOAP specification, I'll refer you to Microsoft's site or the W3C's site (see Appendix A, "SOAP, Web Services, and .NET Links on the Internet," for a list of URLs). This section focuses on the SOAP features that ASP.NET Web Services uses.

Just like a Web page, a SOAP message has several major sections, each serving a special purpose. There are three major sections to a SOAP message:

- **SOAP envelope:** This container for the header and body can contain XML namespace declarations, attributes, and potentially other information (that must follow the body of the SOAP message).

- **SOAP header:** This section contains optional information that a consumer may or may not be required to understand.

- **SOAP body:** This section contains the actual method call or response data (depending on the context of the situation).

Figure 7.2 illustrates the composition of a SOAP message. The following sections explain the major sections of a SOAP message in more detail.

SOAP Envelope

You can think of the SOAP envelope in several ways. First and foremost, the SOAP envelope is the XML contained in the SOAP message, which includes the SOAP header and SOAP body as well as additional subelements you can define. The envelope is therefore referred to as the

XML payload. To send a message using a protocol, the intended recipient's addressing information is added to conform to the protocol's standard. This information ensures—you hope—that the message gets to the correct recipient.

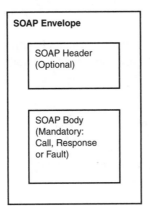

FIGURE 7.2
The structure of a SOAP message.

SOAP Header

The first element you might see in a SOAP envelope is the header. It is optional, but its purpose is to include additional information that is not part of the method call but might be important to your application. Think of the SOAP header as a type of metadata that gives context to the method call or the Web Service response. For example, you could include account information (server ID, login, client ID, and so forth) here to notify the Web Service about the client who is using the service. The server could use it for billing or logging purposes, for authentication, and so forth. Another possible use for the SOAP header is transactions. The message header could contain information to synchronize the partners in a two-phase commit scenario.

The following is a sample SOAP message with a header:

```
<SOAP-ENV:Envelope
  xmlns:SOAP-ENV="http://schemas.cmlsoap.org/soap/envelope/">

  <SOAP-ENV:Header>

    <ACCT:AccountID
      xmlns:ACCT="urn:schemas-myurl-com:accountid"
      SOAP-ENV:root="1">
      T120769
    </ACCT>
  </SOAP-ENV:Header>
```

```
<SOAP-ENV:Body>

  <!-- The rest of the SOAP body goes here -->

</SOAP-ENV:Body>
</SOAP-ENV:Envelope>
```

In this example, you pass in T120769 as the account identifier (AccountID) and reference a fictitious schema as the namespace for this element. If this were a method call, you could take this information and credit or debit the account, or at least log which of your customers made this request.

There are several rules to keep in mind when dealing with SOAP headers:

- Although the header element is optional, if present it must be the first element to follow the opening envelope tag (or rather the root <SOAP-ENV:Envelope>). Here is an example of a bad SOAP header that breaks this rule:

```
<SOAP-ENV:Envelope
  xmlns:SOAP-ENV="http://schemas.cmlsoap.org/soap/envelope/">

  <SOAP-ENV:Body>

    <!--This is a bad example because the header comes after the body! -->

  </SOAP-ENV:Body>

  <SOAP-ENV:Header>

    <ACCT:AccountID
      xmlns:ACCT="urn:schemas-myurl-com:accountid"
      SOAP-ENV:root="1">
      T120769
    </ACCT>
  </SOAP-ENV:Header>

</SOAP-ENV:Envelope>
```

The ASP.NET Web Services implementation always places the SOAP header in the right spot so that you cannot violate this rule.

- The header element must adhere to the SOAP specification unless it is modified by the SOAP-ENV:encodingStyle attribute. Because you can't modify the encodingStyle attribute using the .NET Framework classes, you can't violate this rule either.

- Header subelements must be namespace qualified, but ASP.NET Web Services takes care of this rule for you.

- The header can contain the `SOAP-ENV:mustUnderstand` attribute, which is used when you want to require that the consumer of the SOAP message understand the value being passed.

Modifying the SOAP Header with Web Services

Of course, ASP.NET Web Services protects you from having to know all the rules and semantics of the SOAP specification. In addition, ASP.NET Web Services allows you to specify whether the SOAP header should be sent only on the request message, only on the response message, or on both the request and response. These details are discussed at length in Chapter 22, "Manipulating SOAP Headers in Web Services."

Next you'll delve into the many different facets of the SOAP body (see Figure 7.3). Depending on the nature of the SOAP message (whether it is a method call or a response to that call), the contents of the body change. The body's contents also change when an error or exception occurs (referred to as a *fault*).

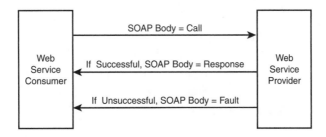

FIGURE 7.3
The flow of SOAP messages.

SOAP Body: Call

The call is responsible for specifying the method name to be executed and all the parameters that must be passed to the method for it to execute correctly. To do this, the first child node beneath the `Body` node is the actual name of the method. Then the method's parameters are children nodes beneath the method node's name. The following example should make this more obvious:

```
<SOAP-ENV:Envelope
  xmlns:xsi="http://www.w3.org/1999/XMLSchema/instance"
  xmlns:SOAP-ENV="http://schemas.xmlsoap.org/soap/envelope/">
  <SOAP-ENV:Body xmlns:MyMethod="urn:some-uri-com:MyMethod">
    <MyMethod:CalculateNumbers>
      <lFirstNumber xsi:type="long">500</lFirstNumber>
      <lSecondNumber xsi:type="long">350</lFirstNumber>
```

```
        </MyMethod>
      </SOAP-ENV:Body>
  </SOAP-ENV:Envelope>
```

First, notice that I created namespaces called SOAP-ENV and MyMethod. Although this is not necessary, it's a good practice to use namespaces to prevent naming collisions. The crux is the SOAP-ENV:Body tag. Notice that the first child node of the Body tag is the name of my method, called CalculateNumber. Under that node are two additional nodes, lFirstNumber and lSecondNumber. These are the method parameters. Inside the tag of each method parameter node elements are attributes called type, which defines the data type of the data being passed into my method. You should check this attribute on the Web Service consumer to ensure that the correct data type is being sent.

As a point of reference, this might correspond in Visual Basic to the following method signature:

```
Public Function <WebMethod> CalculateNumber(lFirstNumber as long, lSecondNumber
as long) as long
```

Or the following C# method signature:

```
[WebMethod]
Public long CalculateNumber(long lFirstNumber, long lSecondNumber)
```

SOAP Body: Response

After the Web Service provider receives, interprets, and processes the method call, it sends a response or fault message. Assuming that the processing was successful, the response to the previous example might be the following:

```
<SOAP-ENV:Envelope
  xmlns:SOAP-ENV="http://shcemas.xmlsoap.org/soap/envelope/">
  <SOAP-ENV:Body xmlns:MyMethod=urn:some-uri-com:MyMethod">
    <MyMethod:CalculateNumbersResponse>
      <value>850</value>
    </MyMethod:CalculateNumbersResponse>
  </SOAP-ENV:Body>
</SOAP-ENV:Envelope>
```

In this case, the Response value is encoded inside the SOAP-ENV:Body tag as the first child node. Notice that the child node has the term "Response" appended to designate it as a response:

```
    <MyMethod:CalculateNumbersResponse>
```

Adding "response" to the method name is a common convention, not a requirement.

Additionally, notice that the actual value is a child node of the `CalculateNumbersResponse` node. The name of the element node (`value`) does not matter.

```
<value>850</value>
```

SOAP Body: Fault

Again, after the Web Service provider receives, interprets, and processes the method call, it sends a response or fault message. If the processing was unsuccessful, the response to the previous example might be the following:

```
<SOAP-ENV:Envelope
  xmlns:SOAP-ENV="http://schemas.xmlsoap.org/soap/envelope/">
    <SOAP-ENV:Body>
      <SOAP-ENV:Fault>
        <faultcode>SOAP-ENV:Server</faultcode>
        <faultstring>Server Error</faultstring>
        <detail xmlns:MyMethod="urn:some-uri-com:MyMethod">
          <MyMethod:MyErrorMessage>The numbers were out of the range I
➥expected</MyMethod:MyErrorMessage>
          <MyMethod:ErrorCode>9999</MyMethod:ErrorCode>
        </detail>
      </SOAP-ENV:Fault>
    </SOAP-ENV:Body>
</SOAP-ENV:Envelope>
```

Notice the `faultcode`, `faultstring`, and `detail` subelement nodes under the parent `<SOAP-ENV:Fault>` node. There are four possible fault subelements:

`faultcode`	Has one of four values that can be used programmatically to ascertain the nature of the problem: `VersionMistmatch`, `MustUnderstand`, `Client`, and `Server`. See the SOAP Specification section 4.4.1, "SOAP Fault Codes," for more details.
`faultstring`	A human-readable explanation of the fault.
`faultactor`	Indicates the source of the fault and is used when the source was not the ultimate destination of the SOAP message.
`detail`	Used to carry application-specific information about the fault. It must be present if the fault happened as a result of processing the body. For example, if your application didn't like the values passed in, then a `detail` section must be included. If the SOAP message was in the wrong form, though, this node is not used.

The `detail` node is important because it can be used to add custom error information. In the previous example, I added a friendly error message and a custom error number that can be used to pinpoint the source of the problem:

```
<detail xmlns:MyMethod="urn:some-uri-com:MyMethod">
   <MyMethod:MyErrorMessage>The numbers were out of the range I
►expected</MyMethod:MyErrorMessage>
      <MyMethod:ErrorCode>9999</MyMethod:ErrorCode>
   </detail>
```

There are many more rules to throwing and processing SOAP faults. However, they fall outside the scope and intent of this chapter. Please refer to the SOAP 1.1 specification or *Understanding SOAP* by Scribner and Stiver (published by Sams).

Supported Data Types

The SOAP specification enables many different data types and data structures to be passed in the SOAP message. First, it defers to the XML schema specification's `Structure` and `DataType` definitions, which include simple types (for example, integers, strings, longs) and enumerations, as well as structures defined by the SOAP specification, including `Structs`, `Arrays` (including multidimensional arrays, varying or partially transmitted arrays, and sparse arrays), and generic compound types, which resemble a "typical" XML document and will probably be used when you pass objects and ASP.NET DataSets via Web Services. Listing 7.1 is an example of a generic compound type that has information about a customer, the customer's ship-to location, and ordering information.

LISTING 7.1   Example of a Generic Compound Type

```
<xyz:Purchase Order>
  <CustomerName>Jason Bentrum</CustomerName>
  <ShipTo>
    <Street>123 E. Main St.</Street>
    <City>Frisco</City>
    <State>TX</State>
    <Zip>75111</Zip>
  </ShipTo>
  <PurchaseLineItems>
    <Order>
      <Product>Foo Bars</Product>
      <Price>3.00</Price>
    </Order>
    <Order>
      <Product>Bizquirk 10 oz.</Product>
      <Price>4.00</Price>
    </Order>
  </PurchaseLineItems>
</xyz:PurchaseOrder>
```

What does this discussion about data types mean to you? Probably very little because the ASP.NET Web Services classes take care of serializing your data for you and making decisions about how best to represent your data in the SOAP message. The SOAP specification spends nearly 10 printed pages (almost a third of the entire document) outlining the rules surrounding all the data types. I chose not to spend too much time on this topic, but if you thirst for more knowledge on data types, again I encourage you to drink from the fountain of the aforementioned SOAP 1.1 specification or the *Understanding* SOAP book.

Single-Reference Versus Multi-Reference Accessors

Before you leave the topic of data types and structures, there is an important feature you often see when dealing with SOAP (and WSDL). A *single-reference accessor* is a piece of data referred to only once in the SOAP message. Listing 7.2 shows a simple example.

LISTING 7.2 A Single-Reference Accessor

```
<xyz:Purchase Order>
  <CustomerName>Jason Bentrum</CustomerName>
  <ShipTo>
    <Street>123 E. Main St.</Street>
    <City>Frisco</City>
    <State>TX</State>
    <Zip>75111</Zip>
  </ShipTo>
  <PurchaseLineItems>
    <Order>
      <Product>Foo Bars</Product>
      <RetailPrice>3.00</RetailPrice>
      <Manufacturer>Vandalay Industries</Manufacturer>
      <SalePrice>2.50</SalePrice>
      <Category>Snack</Category>
      <Quantity>3</Quantity>
    </Order>
    <Order>
      <Product>Bizquirk 10 oz.</Product>
      <RetailPrice>4.00</RetailPrice>
      <Manufacturer>Kramerica Industries</Manufacturer>
      <SalePrice>3.75</SalePrice>
      <Category>Baking</Category>
      <Quantity>5</Quantity>
    </Order>
  </PurchaseLineItems>
</xyz:PurchaseOrder>
```

The product information for Foo Bars and Bizquirk is used only once in this document. However, when transmitting a large amount of data, such as a dataset, chances are some of the data will repeat itself. What if you had 50 or 1,000 orders sent via a SOAP message? Would you want to represent the product's information 50 or 1,000 times in your SOAP message? That repetition would make for an extremely large SOAP message being sent across a potentially low-bandwidth wire. Instead, you can use multi-reference accessors. Listing 7.3 shows a simple example.

LISTING 7.3 A Multi-Reference Accessor

```
<xyz:Purchase Order>
  <CustomerName>Jason Bentrum</CustomerName>
  <ShipTo>
    <Street>123 E. Main St.</Street>
    <City>Frisco</City>
    <State>TX</State>
    <Zip>75111</Zip>
  </ShipTo>
  <PurchaseLineItems>
    <Order>
      <SelectedProduct href="#1002" />
      <Quantity>3</Quantity>
    </Order>
    <Order>
      <SelectedProduct href="#1001" />
      <Quantity>5</Quantity>
    </Order>
  </PurchaseLineItems>
</xyz:PurchaseOrder>
<xyz:Purchase Order>
  <CustomerName>David Findley</CustomerName>
  <ShipTo>
    <Street>345 S. Elm St.</Street>
    <City>Plano</City>
    <State>TX</State>
    <Zip>75000</Zip>
  </ShipTo>
  <PurchaseLineItems>
    <Order>
      <SelectedProduct href="#1002" />
      <Quantity>5</Quantity>
    </Order>
    <Order>
      <SelectedProduct href="#1001" />
      <Quantity>6</Quantity>
```

LISTING 7.3   Continued

```
    </Order>
  </PurchaseLineItems>
</xyz:PurchaseOrder>
.
.
.
<Product id="1001">
      <Product>Bizquirk 10 oz.</Product>
      <RetailPrice>4.00</RetailPrice>
      <Manufacturer>Kramerica Industries</Manufacturer>
      <SalePrice>3.75</SalePrice>
      <Category>Baking</Category>
</Product>
<Product id="1002">
      <Product>Foo Bars</Product>
      <RetailPrice>3.00</RetailPrice>
      <Manufacturer>Vandalay Industries</Manufacturer>
      <SalePrice>2.50</SalePrice>
      <Category>Snack</Category>
  </Product>
```

7

EXAMINING
SOAP

As you can see, the `<Product>` node data would have to be repeated for each customer's order if you didn't reference all the product's information by simply using the `href="#1001"` statement in the `<SelectedProduct>` node. Over the course of two orders, there is a substantial amount of space saved. Imagine if hundreds of orders were returned in the SOAP message!

Summary

SOAP is a specification that defines how to integrate heterogeneous information systems by exchanging messages based on industry-standard protocols. It excels over its predecessors by being more conducive to transmission over the Internet via HTTP. It also has the advantage in an enterprise because of its interoperability with disparate software and hardware systems.

SOAP messages have several different parts. The SOAP envelope is the package that holds the elements of the SOAP message together. It contains a SOAP body and an optional SOAP header.

The SOAP header element can be used to send metadata along with the SOAP message. Its intent is to give context to the method call or the method response. It can be used to send along payment, authentication, or transactional information.

The SOAP body takes on three different forms, based on the context of the situation. When a SOAP method call takes place, the method name and parameters are passed in the body. When a SOAP response occurs, the calculation or returned value is returned in the body. If an exception occurs, the consumer is made aware by means of the SOAP fault, which consists of a series of fault subelements that specify the nature of the problem.

SOAP has many different ways to send data and can use techniques such as multi-reference accessors to reduce the potential size of SOAP messages.

You will view many SOAP messages throughout the remainder of this book to see how the .NET Framework works behind the scenes with each different scenario or nuance that's introduced. This is one of the best ways to understand how your Web Services are behaving and one of the distinct advantages to developing Web Services (as opposed to using the other RPC mechanisms discussed in this chapter).

Understanding WSDL

IN THIS CHAPTER

After you have created your Web Services and are "ready for business," you'll need some way to explain to potential users how to programmatically call these services. At a minimum, your users will want to know what parameters they should expect to pass (that is, the parameter's intent and its data type or format) and what they should expect to get in return from your Web Service (such as data type, format, and so on). They will certainly want to know the Web Service's actual address and how to access the Web Service (for example, if it supports HTTP-SOAP, HTTP-POST, and HTTP-GET).

There are a number of ways to get this information to your users. You could post a Web page with your telephone number so that people could call you for a one-on-one explanation of how to use the service, but that would quickly get tiresome. Or, the Web page could supply a reference that lists the inputs and outputs. Although this is certainly a viable option, there are two potential shortcomings. First, it does not lend itself to automatic discovery of the Web Service, meaning an automated way for the Web Service consumer to programmatically discover the service's inputs and outputs. Second, even if the consumer figured out how to programmatically parse a particular Web Service's accompanying reference document, it would not be consistent for all publishers of Web Services.

As you may have guessed, SOAP has no built-in mechanism for this level of description. Web Services, therefore, are not self-describing. They require an additional file to describe the Web Service's methods, parameters, and data types, which is the purpose of the Web Service Description Language (WSDL).

Although it's not a requirement, a WSDL document gives potential users of your Web Service all they need to know to access the Web Service, including location, parameter information, and protocol support. If your user's development environment supports automated discovery of your Web Service (as Visual Studio .NET does), your user can point at your Web Service's WSDL file, which builds a proxy to make calling your Web Service simple. A WSDL document is a convenience that saves many hours of development, a benefit that should lead to wider adoption of its use.

This chapter explains WSDL, its purpose, and its nuances. The goal is to understand the purpose of WSDL, understand the major sections of a WSDL document, distinguish between "concrete" and "abstract" descriptions of Web Services, and explain why these descriptions are important when used in WSDL.

The Genealogy of WSDL

There have been several iterations of the WSDL specification. The first was the SOAP Contract Language (SCL), followed by the SOAP Definition Language (SDL). There were small improvements from SCL to SDL, mostly in the intent of the language; that is, the *contract* in SCL implied an enforceable permanent relationship. In the world of Web Services, however, no such guarantees could exist. A "contract" would bind the Web Service developer/maintainer to the original interface no matter what, but a "definition," as in SDL, could change over time.

Presumably, if the definition changes, the tools used to develop against the Web Service would automatically update the client's proxy to the Web Service, allowing for a seamless transition to the new version of the Web Service's definition. Let me caution you that this functionality does not yet exist, but is implied (in fact, this is a characteristic of the DISCO specification, discussed in Chapter 9, "Understanding DISCO"). If this change should happen, you can be assured that at the very least, your application will raise errors the next time it attempts to access the Web Service.

As the specification was evolving, it became necessary to separate the intent of the definition language document from SOAP, thereby making the specification usable no matter what underlying protocol your Web Service supported. This opened the door for HTTP-GET and HTTP-POST as viable mechanisms for accessing Web Services, in addition to SOAP. It also leaves open the door for future protocols when they become available. This openness to new protocols is the idea behind bindings in the WSDL, and is the major differentiator between it and its predecessors. Additionally, WSDL enables you to abstractly define elements in the document to minimize the document's potential size.

How the WSDL Works

When potential clients want to use the Web Service, they are pointed to the WSDL document's URI manually or through some automated mechanism (such as UDDI or DISCO). Typically, the software developer does not use a Web browser to access the WSDL file and manually create the code to access your Web Service, although this is certainly possible. Instead, developers point their IDE to a WSDL file or use a utility that accesses the WSDL file, and then create code to access the Web Service, according to the WSDL specification. This code is called the *Web Service proxy* (see Figure 8.1). It gives the programmer an easy way to interface with your Web Service by encapsulating the complexity of constructing the appropriate call and sending it to the network.

From that point on, there is (in theory) no need for the WSDL file because the Web Service description is encoded in the user's proxy code. However, at times you might need to revisit the WSDL file. For example, if the Web Service's interface has changed, it might require an additional parameter to supply a response. Or perhaps the location of the Web Service has changed to a different server, making it necessary to find the Web Service's WSDL file again and create a new proxy. Ideally, this would happen automatically, but that automation may be far in the future.

8

UNDERSTANDING
WSDL

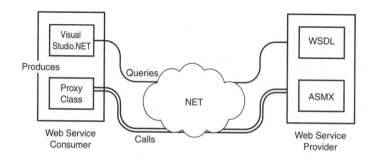

FIGURE 8.1
Using the WSDL to create a proxy for the Web Service.

The WSDL file, then, must always be a complete and accurate description of the actual Web Service it purports to describe. If it's not, consumers might not be able to successfully access the Web Service.

The Sections of the WSDL File

In its most basic form, a WSDL file uses XML to describe all aspects of a Web Service, including the Web Service method's parameters, its return type, and the network bindings and protocols that can be used to communicate with it. The WSDL file has five major sections, plus the <definitions> element that wraps them together. These major sections are explained in more depth in the following sections.

The Types Section

The Types section of the WSDL document defines which data types are used in the Web Service and where to find the definitions for those types. In many cases, this section refers to the XML Schema Definition (XSD) type definitions. It gives all Web Service consumers and providers a level playing field by setting the ground rules of the definition of a long, an integer, a string, and so forth. A Types section might define MyInput1 as an integer, but not just *any* integer: an XSD integer (as opposed to a custom-defined integer). When the remainder of the document refers to MyInput1, this definition can be referenced.

The Messages Section

The Messages section abstractly defines the incoming and outgoing messages by grouping together the parts (basically, parameters and data types as explicitly defined in the Types section) for that particular message. For example, a SOAP message sent as a Web Service request might be described like this:

```
<message name="MyWebServiceSoapIn">
  <part name="parameters" element="s0:MyInput1"/>
  <part name="parameters" element="s0:MyInput2"/>
  <part name="parameters" element="s0:MyInput3"/>
  <part name="parameters" element="s0:MyInput4"/>
</message>
```

This description, an example of an abstract definition, enables the remainder of the document to reference the collection of parameters as `MyWebServiceSoapIn`.It allows a degree of reuse in the document, thereby potentially making the document smaller. (For an already small document, however, this type of abstraction actually makes the document larger.)

The PortTypes Section

The PortTypes section creates an abstract definition that combines the protocol (SOAP, `HTTP-GET`, `HTTP-POST`) with the operations (or the function names) it supports and the messages used by those operations, as defined in the Messages section. Again, this combination of elements in a PortType definition is a form of reuse and another example of an abstract definition. In the remainder of the document, this combination of a protocol, a message, and an operation can be identified by a name. See Figure 8.2 for a visual representation of the relationship between PortTypes and the other sections of the WSDL document.

8

UNDERSTANDING
WSDL

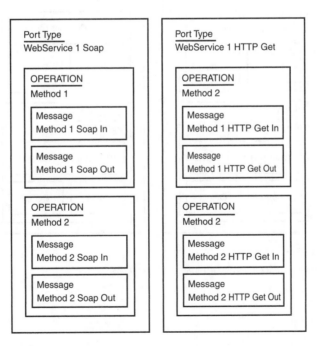

FIGURE 8.2

PortTypes: Relating protocols, operations, and messages.

The Bindings Section

Bindings create a concrete relationship protocol (SOAP, HTTP-GET, HTTP-POST) with a data format for a particular port type. This section is where the PortType points to an actual URI for the transport mechanism (SOAP) or to the appropriate HTTP verb (GET or POST). Also, it's where you tell the Web Service clients *how* to package the information they will be sending and receiving for a particular operation (method call). For example, if they are using HTTP-GET to access MyWebService, they must use URL encoding (that is, the query string) to send the message, and they should expect return values formatted in mimeXML. See Figure 8.3 for a visual representation of the relationship between the Bindings section and the other sections of the WSDL document. (This complex section is covered in greater detail in "Examining the Bindings Section," later in this chapter.)

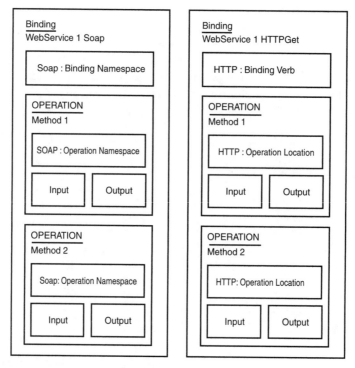

FIGURE 8.3

Bindings: Relating protocols, data formats, PortTypes, and operations.

The Services Section

Services bring together all the different ports with their concrete locations that are all considered part of the same service. In other words, the Services section tells your users that they can use different protocols to access the Web Service. It supplies the addresses to use when accessing each Web Service. See Figure 8.4 for a visual representation of how the Services section relates to the other sections of a WSDL file.

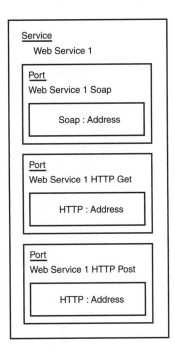

FIGURE 8.4
Services: Relating bindings and URIs.

Examining the WSDL File

Now let's examine the WSDL file that Visual Studio .NET (or the wsdl.exe utility) produced in Chapters 4, "Creating a Simple Web Service in Visual Studio .NET," and 5, "Consuming a Simple Web Service in Visual Studio .NET." Instead of just dumping the entire WSDL file into your lap, the following sections separate the file into its major sections and offer a brief commentary on each section.

Keep in mind that you are merely looking at the .NET framework's *implementation* of the WSDL specification. It's an accurate implementation, but it does not use each and every feature of the WSDL. For a comprehensive understanding of WSDL, please refer to the specification, which is available at `http://msdn.microsoft.com/xml/general/wsdl.asp`.

The `<definitions>` Element

The following code is an example of using the `<definitions>` element:

```
<?xml version="1.0"?>
<definitions xmlns:s="http://www.w3.org/2000/10/XMLSchema"
xmlns:http="http://schemas.xmlsoap.org/wsdl/http/"
xmlns:mime="http://schemas.xmlsoap.org/wsdl/mime/"
xmlns:urt="http://microsoft.com/urt/wsdl/text/"
xmlns:soapenc="http://schemas.xmlsoap.org/soap/encoding/"
xmlns:soap="http://schemas.xmlsoap.org/wsdl/soap/"
xmlns:s0="http://tempuri.org/" targetNamespace="http://tempuri.org/"
xmlns="http://schemas.xmlsoap.org/wsdl/">
```

The `<definitions>` element primarily wraps all the other WSDL sections together and establishes the namespaces for the most commonly used protocols, data types, schemas, and so forth that are used in the remainder of the document. Remember, a *namespace* is just a qualifier used to remove ambiguity and avoid naming collisions. The URI for the namespace is not necessarily used to find any special definitions or processing instructions for the document's parser.

Examining the Types Section

The following code snippet shows an example of the Types section in a WSDL document:

```
  <types>
    <s:schema attributeFormDefault="qualified" elementFormDefault="qualified"
targetNamespace="http://tempuri.org/">

      <s:element name="developerEstimate">
        <s:complexType>
          <s:sequence>
            <s:element name="xintHours" type="s:int"/>
          </s:sequence>
        </s:complexType>
      </s:element>

      <s:element name="developerEstimateResponse">
        <s:complexType>
          <s:sequence>
            <s:element name="developerEstimateResult" type="s:int"/>
          </s:sequence>
```

```
        </s:complexType>
      </s:element>

      <s:element name="int" type="s:int"/>

    </s:schema>
  </types>
```

The Types section defines the data elements used in the remainder of the document in an XSD format, as indicated by the s: namespace qualifier that resolves to the XSD URI. The basics of this format are discussed in the following paragraphs. For more detailed information on the XML Schema Definition specification, visit http://www.w3c.org/xml/schema.

The <s:schema /> element has several attributes. In the preceding example, the attributeFormDefault and elementFormDefault attributes are set to "qualified", indicating that throughout the document, both elements and attributes must be namespace-qualified. The targetNamespace indicates that as the elements are defined, they should be referenced by the namespace "http://tempuri.org/", which is shortened to s0 as defined in the <Definitions> element at the beginning of the WSDL document. So in the remainder of the document, developerEstimate is referenced as s0:developerEstimate.

There are two data elements defined as complex types (developerEstimate and developerEstimateResponse) and one data element defined as a simple type (int). The main distinction between complex and simple types are their child elements and subnodes: simple types have neither. Therefore, because the developerEstimate element has a child element called xintHours (the name of the input parameter for this Web Service), it is defined as a complex type. The element int is a simple type because it has no child element or attribute subnodes.

The child elements <s:complexType> and <s:sequence> are simply part of defining a complex type, allowing a number of child elements to be added in a specific sequential order. In this case, the developerEstimate is composed of only one value, the xintHours value. If you had multiple input parameters to your Web Service, they would appear as siblings to the xintHours element.

One last point before continuing: You might be wondering how developerEstimate and developerEstimateResponse got added to the document when they were not part of the original Web Service you created in Chapters 4 and 5. The .NET framework's created them automatically to describe the group of inputs (developerEstimate) and outputs (developerEstimateResponse) that you defined in the Web Service. These types are now used in the Messages section of the WSDL document.

Examining the Messages Section

The following code snippet shows an example of the Messages section:

```
<message name="developerEstimateSoapIn">
  <part name="parameters" element="s0:developerEstimate"/>
</message>
<message name="developerEstimateSoapOut">
  <part name="parameters" element="s0:developerEstimateResponse"/>
</message>
<message name="developerEstimateHttpGetIn">
  <part name="xintHours" type="s:string"/>
</message>
<message name="developerEstimateHttpGetOut">
  <part name="Body" element="s0:int"/>
</message>
<message name="developerEstimateHttpPostIn">
  <part name="xintHours" type="s:string"/>
</message>
<message name="developerEstimateHttpPostOut">
  <part name="Body" element="s0:int"/>
</message>
```

There are six <message> tags, each one defining an input and output message for the protocol types made available in the Web Service (HTTP-GET, HTTP-POST, and SOAP). Once again, the .NET framework's performs some naming magic by concatenating the name of the Web Service, the protocol, and its direction. Notice that the developerEstimateSoapIn and the developerEstimateSoapOut messages use the complex types defined in the previous Types section. The Get and Post versions of the message use the simple types as defined in the XML Schema Definition (s:string and s0:int).

The messages defined here are used in the PortTypes section, discussed in the following section. When referenced, they adhere to the targetNamespace attribute of the <schema /> element (that is, "http://tempuri.org/" or, as defined in the <definitions> element, s0).

Examining the PortTypes Section

The following code snippet shows an example of the PortTypes section:

```
<portType name="pmcalcSoap">
  <operation name="developerEstimate">
    <input message="s0:developerEstimateSoapIn"/>
    <output message="s0:developerEstimateSoapOut"/>
  </operation>
</portType>
```

```xml
<portType name="pmcalcHttpGet">
  <operation name="developerEstimate">
    <input message="s0:developerEstimateHttpGetIn"/>
    <output message="s0:developerEstimateHttpGetOut"/>
  </operation>
</portType>
<portType name="pmcalcHttpPost">
  <operation name="developerEstimate">
    <input message="s0:developerEstimateHttpPostIn"/>
    <output message="s0:developerEstimateHttpPostOut"/>
  </operation>
</portType>
```

The PortTypes section serves the purpose of associating an operation name (the actual method name of the Web Service) and the input and output messages as defined in the previous Messages section. Three `<portType>` elements are defined in the preceding example, corresponding to the three protocols that can be used to access the Web Service (HTTP-GET, HTTP-POST, and SOAP). These `<portType>` elements are used in the Bindings and Services sections (described in the following sections).

Examining the Bindings Section

The following code snippet is an example of the Bindings section:

```xml
<binding name="pmcalcSoap" type="s0:pmcalcSoap">
  <soap:binding
      transport="http://schemas.xmlsoap.org/soap/http"
      style="document"/>
  <operation name="developerEstimate">
    <soap:operation
      soapAction="http://tempuri.org/developerEstimate"
      style="document"/>
    <input>
      <soap:body use="literal"/>
    </input>
    <output>
      <soap:body use="literal"/>
    </output>
  </operation>
</binding>

<binding name="pmcalcHttpGet" type="s0:pmcalcHttpGet">
  <http:binding verb="GET"/>
  <operation name="developerEstimate">
    <http:operation location="/developerEstimate"/>
```

```
      <input>
        <http:urlEncoded/>
      </input>
      <output>
        <mime:mimeXml part="Body"/>
      </output>
    </operation>
  </binding>

  <binding name="pmcalcHttpPost" type="s0:pmcalcHttpPost">
    <http:binding verb="POST"/>
    <operation name="developerEstimate">
      <http:operation location="/developerEstimate"/>
      <input>
        <mime:content
            type="application/x-www-form-urlencoded"/>
      </input>
      <output>
        <mime:mimeXml part="Body"/>
      </output>
    </operation>
  </binding>
```

The Bindings section serves to associate a `<portType>` element, a protocol, the operation name, and the actual message content's format (for example, SOAP, mimeXML, or urlEncoded). By describing the protocol and the message content's format, the Bindings section deals with the concrete facts of how to interact with the Web Service. For this reason, it is one of the most important sections of the document.

The Bindings section is heavily dependent on the protocol binding extension (SOAP or HTTP), which is discussed later in the section "Binding Extensions."

Examining the Services Section

The following code snippet displays the final section of a WSDL document, the Services section:

```
  <service name="pmcalc">
    <port name="pmcalcSoap" binding="s0:pmcalcSoap">
      <soap:address location="http://superman/wsdltest/pmcalc.asmx"/>
    </port>
    <port name="pmcalcHttpGet" binding="s0:pmcalcHttpGet">
      <http:address location="http://superman/wsdltest/pmcalc.asmx"/>
    </port>
```

```
        <port name="pmcalcHttpPost" binding="s0:pmcalcHttpPost">
          <http:address location="http://superman/wsdltest/pmcalc.asmx"/>
        </port>
      </service>
</definitions>
```

This final section of the WSDL associates the bindings from the previous section with an actual concrete URI. It also serves the purpose of tying together all the different bindings into essentially the same service, called "pmcalc" in this example.

Binding Extensions

The Bindings section of the WSDL document is different for the SOAP and the HTTP-based protocols. This is because WSDL defines three binding extensions (SOAP, HTTP, and MIME) that enable the Bindings section of the WSDL document to have protocol-specific information used for calling the Web Service with a particular protocol. For example, the SOAP binding has information about the format of the SOAP message's body (whether encoded or not). The HTTP binding contains information about the verb (GET or POST) and the way the data should be packaged when sent or interpreted when received.

Essentially, binding extensions give the WSDL document some flexibility in allowing different types of information to be discovered, based on the needs of the particular protocol. Again, for a thorough examination of WSDL, please consult the specification at the URL listed earlier in the chapter.

The Future of WSDL

WSDL has gone through several iterations and has yet to be commented on by a standards organization, such as the W3C, but two things lead to thinking that WSDL is stable and "ready for prime time." First, it has a good degree of abstraction that allows it enough flexibility to be used regardless of the protocol used or the type of Web Service. Second, many major tool vendors, including IBM, Ariba, Oracle, and Microsoft, are developing their first-generation tool sets for Web Services and must have some closure on the de facto method for describing Web Services.

As the abstract for the WSDL specification notes, there is room for future enhancement to include features that enable multiple Web Services to be associated and sequenced to perform higher level workflow-type services and for brokering services from multiple vendors that essentially provide the same type of service.

Summary

The Web Service Description Language is a document that uses an XML syntax to tell a potential Web Service consumer how to interact with one or more Web Services. It provides a reference for the names or the Web Services, the URIs, the protocols, the input parameters, the output parameters, their data types, and so forth of the messages the Web Service receives and sends. Web Services are not inherently self-describing, so they require this "third-party" mechanism to explain to the consumer how to interface with them.

The WSDL document resides both logically and physically separate from the Web Service. Although it can be created by hand, it is preferable to use Visual Studio .NET or the wsdl.exe utility to create it for you to remove the possibility of a mistake. One small mistake in the WSDL file can affect the success of all potential consumers of the Web Service.

A WSDL file is typically used once during the development of a client application that uses the Web Service to create a proxy file, and is not referred to again until needed (typically a relocation or an interface change in the Web Service). The WSDL document is composed of five sections. Some of these sections are abstract and used to define attributes of the Web Service, such as data type definitions and messages, and other sections are concrete and reference the abstract items with actual information, such as the name of the Web Service and its location.

Understanding DISCO

IN THIS CHAPTER

Almost immediately after the SOAP specification was released and developers began to digest the concept of Web Services, a unified cry came forth: "How will people find my Web Service?" DISCO (and the UDDI specification discussed in Chapter 25, "Understanding UDDI") was created as an attempt to solidify a process by which consumers of Web Services could locate and programmatically interrogate services at a given URL.

Visual Studio .NET handles creating and managing DISCO and dynamic discovery documents for your applications and server. The IDE automatically adds a .vsdisco file to every ASP.NET application you create—even ASP.NET Web Forms, in case you want to add a Web Service to the project in the future. Additionally, Visual Studio .NET relies heavily on dynamic discovery and DISCO files as you attempt to create Web references to a Web Service on your local Web server, a corporate intranet server, or a Web server across the world.

This chapter explains the concept of discovery and its formal process, and discusses the content and purpose of DISCO files and the concept of dynamic discovery. Finally, you'll see how to modify dynamic discovery files that provide granular control over the visibility of the Web Services on your servers.

What Is Discovery?

In a nutshell, *discovery* is the process of locating a Web Service and interrogating it. After the discovery process is complete, a developer or consuming software application should know the Web Service's exact location (its URI), its capabilities, and how to interface with it. There are several aspects to discovery, but from a programmatic standpoint, discovery typically starts with a .disco file, which is an XML document that contains links to other resources that describe the Web Service. The DISCO file typically points to a WSDL source (or some other description file) that in turn points to the actual Web Service (see Figure 9.1).

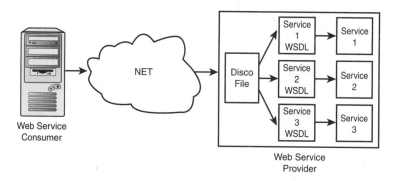

FIGURE 9.1

DISCO files contain links to all (or a subset of) Web Services' WSDL files hosted on a Web server or within a subdirectory of a Web server.

Admittedly, DISCO is not an acronym; it's a shortened version of "Discovery of Web Services." DISCO is a specification that defines how these roadmaps to Web Services should be formatted in XML, but also defines how a potential Web Service consumer should go about locating and processing the actual DISCO document, given a URI.

DISCO documents—and, therefore, the entire process of discovery—are optional. In other words, if you have a private Web Service intended for a small number of potential clients, you do not have to publish a DISCO document on your Web Server. Not having a DISCO document is one way to prevent unwanted consumers from using your Web Service. DISCO is more appropriate when you want to share your Web Service with a potentially large audience and want the world to find it simply by navigating to your Web site's home page (as explained in the following section).

Why Do You Need DISCO?

DISCO enables potential trading partners to learn about the Web Services of a given company by merely navigating to the company's Web site. Any HTML Web page can include a tag that points to a DISCO file. For example, you could include this HTML snippet at the top of each page on your Web site:

```
<head>
<link type="text/xml" rel="alternate" href="default.vsdisco" />
</head>
```

This link tag alerts DISCO client applications that the DISCO file resides elsewhere on the Web server. This doesn't happen magically, by the way; the DISCO client, like the Add Web Reference command in Visual Studio .NET, must know how to look for this tag, and take the appropriate action based on the `href` attribute. In this manner, any company can potentially find a trading partner's Web Services by locating the DISCO file. (In Chapter 25, you'll learn how a UDDI registry can point to a DISCO file, which then points to a trading partner's Web Services.) DISCO is, therefore, an important mechanism in finding and interrogating the Web Services of a given company.

Highlights from the DISCO Specification

As discussed, DISCO is a specification that seeks to facilitate a programmatic method for finding Web Services. Note that discovery documents can point to other discovery documents as well as WSDL files or other descriptive documents yet to be thought of. DISCO was created in this manner to be flexible. There are two parts to the specification: the discovery algorithm and the format of a DISCO document.

9

UNDERSTANDING
DISCO

Discovery Algorithm

In an effort to standardize the process of locating a discovery document on a Web Server, the specification's developers have created a pseudo-code outline to guide developers of client applications that might need to support this functionality. Based on the HTTP Content-Type of a given URI and the actual content of the document at the URI endpoint, the discovery algorithm indicates whether the document contains a DISCO document, points to a DISCO document, or does not contain a DISCO document.

Format of a DISCO Document

The second part of the specification includes a description of the DISCO document's format. Consider the following example of a DISCO document:

```
<?xml version="1.0" encoding="utf-8" ?>
  <discovery xmlns="http://schemas.xmlsoap.org/disco/">
  <contractRef ref="http://www.technicallead.com/jobs/Service1.asmx?wsdl"
       docRef="http://www.technicallead.com/jobs/Service1.asmx"
       xmlns="http://schemas.xmlsoap.org/disco/scl/" />
  <disco:discoveryRef ref="member\default.vsdisco" />
  </discovery>
```

This sample document points to two resources:

- An absolute reference WSDL file located on a Web server; this reference is contained in the XML element `<wsdl:contractRef>`.

- A relative reference to another DISCO file on the current Web server; this reference is contained in the XML element `<disco:discoveryRef>`.

Let's examine these references more closely. First, a DISCO document usually refers to four different types of items. Each of these references, described in the following list, appears between the `<disco:discovery>`...`</disco:discovery>` element:

- **contractRef**   Contains an attribute (`ref`) that refers to a WSDL or other contract or description file. It can also contain a `docRef` attribute, which refers to a human-readable document for more details, as shown in this example:

  ```
  <contractRef ref="http://www.technicallead.com/jobs/Service1.asmx?wsdl"
       docRef="http://www.technicallead.com/jobs/Service1.asmx"
       xmlns="http://schemas.xmlsoap.org/disco/scl/" />
  ```

- **discoveryRef**   Contains an attribute (`ref`) that refers to other DISCO documents, which can point to more resources (WSDL documents or DISCO documents, for example). This is most often seen when a DISCO document is generated via a dynamic discovery document at the root Web (see "What Is Dynamic Discovery?" later in this chapter).

- **schemaRef**   Contains an attribute (`ref`) that points to an XML schema (.xsd) document and an optional attribute (`targetNamespace`) that indicates the schema's namespace, as shown here:

```
<schema:schemaRef ref="mySchema.xsd"
    targetNamespace="http://www.technicallead.com/myScema.xsd" />
```

- **Soap**   Contains an attribute (address) that is the location (URI) of a Web Service that has been defined in a WSDL document. It is provided as a lightweight alternative for locating the Web Service. It is not used in ASP.NET Web Services, however.

Another type of discovery that can assist in locating and interrogating Web Services is called dynamic discovery.

What Is Dynamic Discovery?

Dynamic discovery documents enable potential consumers to discover all the Web Services on your Web server with almost no effort on your part. When the dynamic discovery document is requested, the .NET Framework looks through the subdirectories underneath the root Web and finds all the Web Services. This feature could be a huge convenience: You do not have to create a discovery document for each Web Service you publish on your Web Server; just allow dynamic discovery to do it automatically for you. The following is the dynamic discovery document from the root Web of my local Web server:

```
<?xml version="1.0" ?>
<dynamicDiscovery xmlns="urn:schemas-dynamicdiscovery:disco.2000-03-17">
<exclude path="_vti_cnf" />
<exclude path="_vti_pvt" />
<exclude path="_vti_log" />
<exclude path="_vti_script" />
<exclude path="_vti_txt" />
</dynamicDiscovery>
```

This document was generated automatically, and each project created using Visual Studio .NET will have a similar .vsdisco file. The only caveat is that the Web server must have the .NET Framework installed on it. Also, if you are not using Visual Studio .NET, you will have to create this document by hand.

To view the results of the dynamic discovery document and the discovery process, simply open your Web browser to `http://localhost/default.vsdisco`. You will see a DISCO document that looks similar to this:

```
<?xml version="1.0" encoding="utf-8" ?>
   <discovery xmlns="http://schemas.xmlsoap.org/disco/">
   <discoveryRef ref="http://localhost/articles/articles.vsdisco" />
   <discoveryRef ref="http://localhost/ecommerce/ecommerce.vsdisco" />
   <discoveryRef ref="http://localhost/jobs/jobs.vsdisco" />
</discovery>
```

The consumer never sees the contents of the dynamic discovery document, only a DISCO document that was composed dynamically based on the .NET Web Services on that server and exclusions in the dynamic discovery document. A tool such as Visual Studio .NET reads the dynamically produced DISCO document, allowing the consumer-programmer to further navigate to another .vsdisco file that points to a WSDL document for the Web Service the consumer wants to bind to (that is, create a proxy for). This is how the Add Web Reference command works in Visual Studio .NET.

The dynamic discovery document can be used in different ways, depending on your objective. The default approach used by Visual Studio .NET is to create the dynamic discovery document and place it in the root Web of the Web site. Then, create dynamic discovery documents in each of the subdirectories that have Web Services. This method allows your potential consumers to start the discovery process at the root Web or in a subdirectory. This is the most flexible way for consumers to find the Web Service they are looking for, but could permit too much access if you do not want to allow users to see all the Web Services on the server. If you want less exposure of your Web Services, you can simply remove discovery documents at the root of the Web server, or modify the discovery document to exclude certain Web Services from being made available by using the `<exclude />` element. This technique is sometimes referred to as "security via obscurity."

For example, `www.TechnicalLead.com` (hypothetically) hosts a number of Web Services in different areas of the site, which consumer-developers could consume in their own sites. The site publishes three "families" of Web Services, as well as a Web Service that allows the consumer to search for documents on the site. These services can be used to browse through recently published articles, query the availability of a product line, purchase products from an e-commerce store, and query and post job listings. The site has the following directory structure:

http://www.TechnicalLead.com (root web)

/articles (contains three Web Services for querying and searching for articles)

/ecommerce (contains five Web Services for querying and purchasing products)

/jobs (contains four Web Services for querying and posting job listings)

As the owner of this site, you could have Visual Studio .NET create a dynamic discovery document in the root Web that would display the 12 available Web Services to prospective consumers. Then you would also allow Visual Studio .NET to create a dynamic discovery document for each of the site's subdirectories (articles, ecommerce, and jobs) that returns a list of Web Services in those directories.

However, suppose you have certain Web Services or directories on this site that you do not want the .NET Framework to make available to everyone via the dynamic discovery process.

For example, the articles Web Service includes article submissions that are currently under consideration for publication, so to prevent "intellectual theft," you want to make those articles available only to your co-author and your publisher.In this case, you would simply add an entry for those directories in the document with the `<exclude />` element. In the following discovery document, the articles subdirectory was excluded to hide its Web Services from being discovered:

```
<?xml version="1.0" ?>
<dynamicDiscovery xmlns="urn:schemas-dynamicdiscovery:disco.2000-03-17">
<exclude path="_vti_cnf" />
<exclude path="_vti_pvt" />
<exclude path="_vti_log" />
<exclude path="_vti_script" />
<exclude path="_vti_txt" />
<exclude path="articles" />
</dynamicDiscovery>
```

(Additionally, for the preceding example, you would probably want to authenticate the user of the Web Service to ensure that she is a co-author or publisher.)

In this document, six subdirectories are excluded, including any directories under them. By using `<exclude />` for the articles subdirectory, Web Service consumers can no longer dynamically locate the three Web Services in the articles subfolder. However, all other subdirectories and the root Web can be interrogated by the dynamic discovery mechanism when requested by the consumer.

Add Web Reference: A DISCO Consumer

Probably the best example available of how the DISCO file is used by client applications is the Add Web Reference command in Visual Studio .NET. By using this command, the developer can type in a URI and see all the Web Services available there. It could be a single Web Service (.asmx) file or a DISCO document that could include dozens, or even hundreds, of Web Services residing on a Web server. Figure 9.2 is an example of what you might see when you use the Add Web Reference command to view the Web Services on your local machine.

After a Web Service or DISCO document has been located, the Add Web Reference command requests the WSDL document (either as a file as linked by the `<wsdl:contractRef />` element in the DISCO document, or dynamically by using the .asmx HTTP Handler's ability to create a WSDL document on-the-fly). From the WSDL, a proxy class is generated, and the developer can communicate with the Web Service via the proxy. However, the DISCO document is instrumental in helping developers actually find the Web Service they are looking for.

9

UNDERSTANDING
DISCO

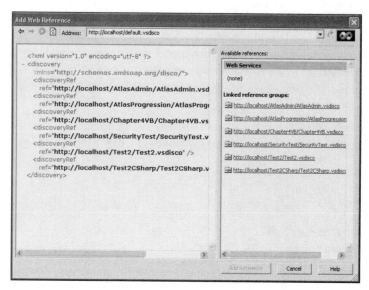

FIGURE 9.2

Results of the Add Web Reference command in the discovery process.

Summary

DISCO, a nickname for "Discovery of Web Services," is a specification outlining an XML document that lists the available Web Services on a Web server. The specification also outlines in pseudo-code how to interpret and use the DISCO file from a client application, such as an Integrated Development Environment. An example of using a DISCO document can be seen in Visual Studio .NET calling the Add Web Reference command.

Another type of DISCO document, the dynamic discovery document, provides instructions to the Web server to look for Web Services within its subdirectories and report them back to the client. This document gives Web Service providers an easy way to allow their clients to go to the root Web or a particular subdirectory on a Web server and locate all the Web Services. By using this feature, the Web Service provider does not have to create a DISCO file for each Web Service.

Exceptions and Error Handling

IN THIS CHAPTER

A friend of mine is fond of saying "Development is easy as long as you ignore what could go wrong." How true. When developing Web Services, keep in mind that consumers depend on those services to be available at all times. They also expect the Web Services to handle anything they send to it (at least, anything within the bounds of the WSDL contract). When the Web Service can't do that, consumers expect that the Web Service provider will dutifully report the errors as SOAP faults, as defined in the SOAP specification. Your consumers will give you bonus points if your Web Service reports as much information in the SOAP fault section as possible so that they can make educated decisions about what to do next. Therefore, "ignoring what could go wrong" is not an option. The Web Services should be able to gracefully handle exceptions and/or report errors correctly.

In this chapter, you'll examine handling exceptions from the perspective of both the provider and consumer of the Web Service. As you will learn, there are responsibilities and design considerations for both roles.

Exception-Handling Methods

As an exception is encountered in your Web Service, you can do one of the following:

- **Ignore it (and hope it goes away).** In this case, you are allowing the .NET Framework to handle the exception. Fortunately, ASP.NET Web Services rewards the inexperienced programmer and nicely wraps up the error in a SOAP fault message. The following code lines are a SOAP request message from a simple division Web Service method that divides one number by another. In this case it divides 3 by 0, but I chose not to handle the inevitable error that would occur.

```xml
<?xml version="1.0" encoding="utf-8"?>
<soap:Envelope xmlns:soap="http://schemas.xmlsoap.org/soap/envelope/"
xmlns:xsi="http://www.w3.org/2001/XMLSchema-instance"
xmlns:xsd="http://www.w3.org/2001/XMLSchema">
  <soap:Body>
    <IgnoreDivision xmlns="http://tempuri.org/">
      <i>3</i>
      <j>0</j>
    </IgnoreDivision>
  </soap:Body>
</soap:Envelope>
```

  As a result, a `DivideByZeroException` is thrown by the .NET Framework, but this exception is wrapped in a SOAP fault element, filling in the fault code and the fault string. (These elements are explained in the next section, "Throwing SOAP Exceptions.")

The following code lines show the SOAP message that is sent back to the consumer of the division Web Service:

```
<?xml version="1.0" encoding="utf-8"?>
<soap:Envelope xmlns:soap="http://schemas.xmlsoap.org/soap/envelope/">
  <soap:Body>
    <soap:Fault>
      <faultcode>soap:Server</faultcode>
      <faultstring>System.Web.Services.Protocols.SoapException: Server was
unable to process request. ---&gt; System.DivideByZeroException: Attempted
to divide by zero.
   at Chapter10CSharp.IgnoreService.IgnoreDivision(Int32 i, Int32 j) in
e:\inetpub\wwwroot\chapter10csharp\ignoreservice.asmx.cs:line
43</faultstring>
      <detail />
    </soap:Fault>
  </soap:Body>
</soap:Envelope>
```

- **Handle the exception and hide it from the consumer.** In this case, you never return a SOAP fault message to the client. This method is the equivalent of ones you might have created within a COM component that returned True if the method was completed successfully or False if it failed. Alternatively, you might have created a method on a COM component that returned some sort of error code you devised. Many developers take this approach as they create Web Services. Although it's a viable approach, it circumvents SOAP's built-in ability to give the consumer specific details on why the call to the Web Service was unsuccessful. Being a proponent of using a technology as it was intended to be used, I don't create home-grown versions of (in this case) exception handling and reporting. Your opinion may differ, and that's fine.

  However, you might want to consider this before you start building your Web Services to use this approach. Web Services are documented and discoverable by their WSDL and DISCO files. The WSDL file in particular is important because its intent is to supply consumers with everything they need to know about how to interact with the Web Service. However, if you plan on using some home-grown method of handling exceptions and reporting a "custom" error code, there's no way to express that in WSDL. You would need to have an actual conversation with the consumer developers on what they should expect in the case of an exception, which makes your Web Service less than discoverable.

10

EXCEPTIONS AND ERROR HANDLING

- **Handle the exception and raise it to the consumer, providing as much detail and context as possible.** This is the preferable approach when handling exceptions. With this approach, you have some options, described in the following list:

  - **Throw a regular exception.** As you saw in the division Web Service example, I was a careless programmer who didn't handle the possibility of a `DivideByZero` exception. However, the .NET Framework saved me from myself, and not only threw a `DivideByZeroException`, but also converted it to a SOAP exception, which serialized into a SOAP fault and was returned to the client. Even though the .NET Framework raised the exception in this case, a regular old exception was thrown, nonetheless. I could have checked for this and thrown it myself if I had done a sanity check on the denominator of the division method's equation.

Do you think that the client can then check for a `DivideByZeroException`? The following lines are a snippet of code from a Web Forms consumer that attempts to learn how the .NET Framework handles this situation. I call the division Web Service attempting to divide 3 by 0, and then try to catch the error several times. The first attempt is to catch any `DivideByZeroExceptions` that may have occurred. The second attempt is to catch any SOAP exceptions. Finally, the code attempts to catch anything that might have avoided the first two traps.

```
try
{
    double dReturn = myIgnoreService.IgnoreDivision(3, 0);
    Response.Write(dReturn.ToString());
}
catch(System.DivideByZeroException de)
{
    Response.Write("Error Message: " + de.Message );
}
catch(System.Web.Services.Protocols.SoapException se)
{
    Response.Write("SOAP Error Message: " + se.Message );
}
catch
{
    Response.Write("Catch-all used");
}
```

So which exception do you think actually traps the error thrown in the preceding code? If you placed your money on the second `catch` statement of `catch(System.Web.Services.Protocols.SoapExceptions se)`, you'd be the lucky winner. The exception is transformed into a SOAP exception and is no longer recognized as a `DivideByZeroException`. To learn the exact nature of the error (that it was a `DivideByZeroException`), you have to examine the fault string more closely.

```
<?xml version="1.0" encoding="utf-8"?>
<soap:Envelope xmlns:soap="http://schemas.xmlsoap.org/soap/envelope/">
  <soap:Body>
    <soap:Fault>
      <faultcode>soap:Server</faultcode>
      <faultstring>System.Web.Services.Protocols.SoapException: Server was
unable to process request. ---&gt; System.DivideByZeroException: Attempted
to divide by zero.
   at Chapter10CSharp.IgnoreService.IgnoreDivision(Int32 i, Int32 j) in
e:\inetpub\wwwroot\chapter10csharp\ignoreservice.asmx.cs:line
43</faultstring>
      <detail />
    </soap:Fault>
  </soap:Body>
</soap:Envelope>
```

- **Throw a SOAP exception, but leave out detail.** This option produces the same results as the previous one. Here you would trap the DivideByZeroException within the Web Service; however, you would then raise a SOAP exception with minimal information about the nature of the problem. Once again, the consumer would have to dig through the fault string returned in the SOAP fault message to determine exactly what went wrong.

- **Throw a SOAP exception, and fill in as much detail as possible.** This option is preferable because you give the consumer some insight into the exact error that occurred. As you might expect, the .NET Framework supports a number of properties that you can fill in to better express the exception that was handled. The next section outlines the possibilities you have when you fully utilize the SoapException object.

Throwing SOAP Exceptions

The SoapException object allows you to write and read many properties that provide rich context and explanation on the exact nature of the problem that was encountered. It is provided as a wrapper around the SOAP specification's SOAP fault message. Table 10.1 lists the properties that can be written to by the Web Service server or read by the Web Service consumer.

TABLE 10.1   Properties of the *SoapException* Object

Property	Details
Message	This property can be set to the exception message or to any custom message you want to send to the client.
Code	The general source of the exception, whether a SOAP version mismatch, a client or server problem, or a MustUnderstand attribute, was not handled correctly. (See Table 10.2 for more information about the Code property.)

TABLE 10.1   Continued

Property	Details
Detail	The Detail property is intended for supplying application-specific error details related to the Body element of the SOAP request. According to the SOAP specification, if an error occurs because the Body element of the SOAP request meant the client request could not be processed, the Detail property must be set. This would happen if a Web Service call was made incorrectly or if too many or too few parameters, or parameters of the wrong data type, were set. If an error occurred in the SOAP request's header entries, you must throw a SoapHeaderException so that the error details are returned in the SOAP header. If the error was not caused by processing the Body element, the Detail property should not be set.
OtherElements	You can send additional information about the exception (not related to the Body element, as specified in the Detail property entry) by creating one or more instances of XML nodes, setting their InnerText properties, and then setting them equal to this property. The OtherElements property is a great spot for the original information caught in exception handling on the server. The client can then reference this property in a similar fashion. See the following section "An Exception Example" for more information.
Actor	The URL of the Web Service method that threw the exception.

Furthermore, the Code object returns a constant that represents the general source of the Exception. Table 10.2 has a list of the constants that are supported.

TABLE 10.2   Fault Code Constants Used in the Code Object

Constant	Details
VersionMismatchFaultCode	A SOAP fault code representing an invalid namespace for a SOAP envelope was found while processing the SOAP message.
MustUnderstandFaultCode	A SOAP fault code representing a SOAP element marked with the MustUnderstand attribute was not processed.
ClientFaultCode	Indicates that a SOAP fault code representing a client call was not formatted correctly or did not contain the appropriate information.

TABLE 10.2 Continued

Constant	Details
ServerFaultCode	Specifies a SOAP fault code representing an error that occurred while processing a client call on the server, where the problem was not caused by the message contents.

Additionally, the Code object has a Name property that allows you to determine which of the constants in Table 10.2 were sent by the server.

An Exception Example

To further illustrate how to throw SOAP exceptions, I have created the following example. You'll see this same example later in the chapter to learn more about handling exceptions from the consumer's perspective. The following Web Service has two Web methods:

- **Foo()** This Web Service merely raises a SOAP exception, setting only the Message property and the Code object.
- **Bar()** This Web Service sets the Message and Code properties, but also sets the Actor and OtherElements properties.

This example uses a new Web Service project called Chapter10VB (or Chapter10CSharp for the C# version) and has renamed the default Service1.asmx Web Service as SoapExceptionSample.asmx. In the Code Behind module for this ASP.NET Web Service page, type the code with bold formatting in Listings 10.1 and 10.2. (Some code was generated by Visual Studio.NET and should not be modified. It's provided as context to help you determine where the lines of code should be entered.)

LISTING 10.1 SoapExceptionSample.asmx.vb in VB.NET Code

```
Imports System.Web.Services
Imports System.Web.Services.Protocols
Imports System.Xml

Public Class SoapExceptionSample
    Inherits System.Web.Services.WebService

#Region " Web Services Designer Generated Code "

    Public Sub New()
        MyBase.New()
```

LISTING 10.1   Continued

```
        'This call is required by the Web Services Designer.
        InitializeComponent()

        'Add your own initialization code after the InitializeComponent() call

    End Sub

    'Required by the Web Services Designer
    Private components As System.ComponentModel.Container

    'NOTE: The following procedure is required by the Web Services Designer
    'It can be modified using the Web Services Designer.
    'Do not modify it using the code editor.
    <System.Diagnostics.DebuggerStepThrough()> Private Sub
InitializeComponent()
        components = New System.ComponentModel.Container()
    End Sub

    Protected Overloads Overrides Sub Dispose(ByVal disposing As Boolean)
        'CODEGEN: This procedure is required by the Web Services Designer
        'Do not modify it using the code editor.
    End Sub

#End Region

<WebMethod()> Public Sub Foo()
        Throw New SoapException("What a bogus SOAP call!", _
            SoapException.ServerFaultCode)
    End Sub

    <WebMethod()> Public Sub Bar()
        Dim doc As New XmlDocument()
        Dim nodes(0) as XmlNode
        nodes(0) = doc.CreateNode(XmlNodeType.Element, _
            "EmergencyWebServiceException", "http://ews.org")
        nodes(0) = doc.InnerText = "This is a test of the " & _
            "emergency exception Web Service.  This is only a " & _
            "test. Had this been an actual exception, you " & _
            "would have received an XML serialized polymorphic " & _
            "derived exception class"
        Throw New SoapException("A special message from your " & _
            "Web Service provider!", SoapException.ServerFaultCode, _
            Context.Request.Url.AbsoluteUri, Nothing, nodes)
    End Sub
End Class
```

LISTING 10.2 SoapExceptionSample.asmx.cs in C# Code

```csharp
using System;
using System.Collections;
using System.ComponentModel;
using System.Data;
using System.Diagnostics;
using System.Web;
using System.Web.Services;
using System.Web.Services.Protocols;
using System.Xml;

namespace CSharpWebSamples
{
    /// <summary>
    /// Summary description for SoapExceptionSample.
    /// </summary>
    public class SoapExceptionSample : System.Web.Services.WebService
    {
        public SoapExceptionSample()
        {
            //CODEGEN: This call is required by the ASP.NET Web Services
Designer
            InitializeComponent();
        }

        #region Component Designer generated code
        /// <summary>
        /// Required method for Designer support - do not modify
        /// the contents of this method with the code editor.
        /// </summary>
        private void InitializeComponent()
        {
        }
        #endregion

        /// <summary>
        /// Clean up any resources being used.
        /// </summary>
        protected override void Dispose( bool disposing )
        {
        }

        [WebMethod]
        public void Foo()
        {
```

LISTING 10.2 Continued

```
        throw new SoapException("What a bogus SOAP call!",
SoapException.ServerFaultCode);
    }

    [WebMethod]
    public void Bar()
    {
        XmlDocument doc = new XmlDocument();

        XmlNode[] nodes = new XmlNode[1];
        nodes[0] = doc.CreateNode(XmlNodeType.Element,
"EmergencyWebServiceException", "http://ews.org");
        nodes[0].InnerText = "This is a test of the emergency exception Web
Service. This is only a test. Had this been an actual exception, you would have
received an XML serialized polymorphic derived exception class";

        throw new SoapException("A special message from your Web Service
provider!", SoapException.ServerFaultCode, Context.Request.Url.AbsoluteUri,
null, nodes);
    }
  }
}
```

The Foo() Web method sets the Message property to "What a bogus SOAP call!" and sets the ServerFaultCode for the returned value. The Bar() Web method does even more, by defining the Actor property, which is set to Context.Request.Url.AbsoluteUri, and defining the OtherElements property as a series of XML nodes that provide more detail about the nature of the exception that was created. Notice that throwing a SOAP exception is as easy as using the Throw statement and then sending in one of many combinations of parameters in the constructor of that class. The .NET Framework handles packaging all the parameters to the constructor as a SOAP fault message.

Testing these Web methods in the default Web Service test page (http://localhost/Chapter10VB/SoapExceptionSample.asmx or http://localhost/Chapter10CSharp/SoapExceptionSample.asmx) does little good: After all, the HTTP Handler for ASP.NET does not serialize the exceptions into SOAP exceptions. If you have not turned off your Internet Explorer's Show Friendly HTTP Error Messages setting, your Web Service simply dies and returns a 500 internal server error. However, if you turn off the Show Friendly HTTP Error Messages setting, you'll see the error in a non-SOAP formatted manner:

```
System.Web.Services.Protocols.SoapException: A special message from your Web
Service provider!
   at Chapter10CSharp.SoapExceptionSample.Bar() in
e:\inetpub\wwwroot\Chapter10CSharp\SoapExceptionSample.asmx.cs:line 56
```

To modify your browser's Show Friendly HTTP Error Messages settings, choose Tools, Internet Options on the menu bar. In the dialog box, select the Advanced tab and scroll down to nearly the end of the Browsing section of options. Otherwise, Internet Explorer hides the underlying error message from you. This display setting is a nice feature for users who want to be protected from the ugliness of error messages, but an annoyance for developers.

To truly test these Web methods and work with SOAP exceptions on the client, you need to create a consumer. Of course, that gives you the opportunity to move on to learning about consuming Web Services and exception handling from the client perspective.

Handling Exceptions in the ASP.NET Client

Just as the Web Service provider has responsibilities when handling exceptions, the consumer should assume some of the responsibility for handling exceptions returned from a Web Service. As you'll see in a moment, not doing so can result in a catastrophic failure of your application to perform correctly. (Translation: Your users will be subject to some very ugly error messages.) But when exceptions are handled correctly, you can learn much about why a Web Service failed and take appropriate action, based on your requirements, on what to do next.

To start, you compile the Web Service created in the previous section and add a Web Reference within the same project. To do that, right-click on the project and choose Add Web Reference from the pop-up menu. When the Add Web Reference dialog box appears, navigate to the DISCO file for your Web Service and click the Add Reference button at the bottom of the dialog box. For more information on adding a Web Reference, please refer to Chapter 5, "Consuming a Web Service in Visual Studio.NET".

After the project has a Web Reference, you can add a new Web Form to the project (ExceptionWebForm.aspx) and drag two buttons from the Toolbox to the Web Form's designer window. When finished, the designer window looks like the one in Figure 10.1.

To add code, you double-click each button to access its respective Click event. Enter the following code, based on your language preference (Listing 10.3 for VB.NET and Listing 10.4 for C#).

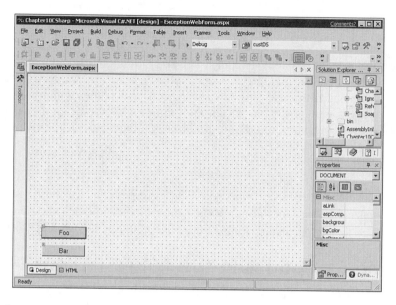

FIGURE 10.1

The Web Form's designer window.

LISTING 10.3   ExceptionWebForm.aspx.vb in VB.NET Code

```vb
Imports System.Xml

Public Class ExceptionWebForm
    Inherits System.Web.UI.Page
    Protected WithEvents Button1 As System.Web.UI.WebControls.Button
    Protected WithEvents Button2 As System.Web.UI.WebControls.Button


    Protected myWebService As Chapter10VB.SoapExceptionSample = New
Chapter10VB.SoapExceptionSample()


#Region " Web Form Designer Generated Code "

    'This call is required by the Web Form Designer.
    <System.Diagnostics.DebuggerStepThrough()> Private Sub
InitializeComponent()

    End Sub

    Private Sub Page_Init(ByVal sender As System.Object, ByVal e As
System.EventArgs) Handles MyBase.Init
```

LISTING 10.3   Continued

```
        'CODEGEN: This method call is required by the Web Form Designer
        'Do not modify it using the code editor.
        InitializeComponent()
    End Sub

#End Region

    Private Sub Page_Load(ByVal sender As System.Object, ByVal e As
System.EventArgs) Handles MyBase.Load
        'Put user code to initialize the page here
    End Sub

    Private Sub Button1_Click(ByVal sender As System.Object, ByVal e As
System.EventArgs) Handles Button1.Click

        myWebService.Foo()

    End Sub


    Private Sub Button2_Click(ByVal sender As System.Object, ByVal e As
System.EventArgs) Handles Button2.Click

        Try
            myWebService.Bar()
        Catch se As System.Web.Services.Protocols.SoapException

            Response.Write("Message: " & se.Message)
            Response.Write("<br>Actor: " & se.Actor)
            Response.Write("<br>Client Fault Code:" & se.Code.Name)

            Dim nodes(0) As XmlNode
            nodes(0) = se.OtherElements(0)

            Response.Write("<p>(Other Elements) Node Name:" & nodes(0).Name)
            Response.Write("<br>(Other Elements) Node Namespace URI: " &
nodes(0).NamespaceURI)
            Response.Write("<br>(Other Elements) Node Inner Text: " &
nodes(0).InnerText)

        End Try

    End Sub
End Class
```

10

**EXCEPTIONS AND
ERROR HANDLING**

LISTING 10.4   ExceptionWebForm.aspx.cs in C# Code

```csharp
using System;
using System.Collections;
using System.ComponentModel;
using System.Data;
using System.Drawing;
using System.Web;
using System.Web.SessionState;
using System.Web.UI;
using System.Web.UI.WebControls;
using System.Web.UI.HtmlControls;
using System.Xml;

namespace Chapter10CSharp
{
    /// <summary>
    /// Summary description for ExceptionWebForm.
    /// </summary>
    public class ExceptionWebForm : System.Web.UI.Page
    {
        protected System.Web.UI.WebControls.Button Button2;
        protected System.Web.UI.WebControls.Button Button1;
        protected Chapter10CSharp.localhost.SoapExceptionSample myWebService =
new Chapter10CSharp.localhost.SoapExceptionSample();


        public ExceptionWebForm()
        {
            Page.Init += new System.EventHandler(Page_Init);
        }

        private void Page_Load(object sender, System.EventArgs e)
        {
            // Put user code to initialize the page here
        }

        private void Page_Init(object sender, EventArgs e)
        {
            //
            // CODEGEN: This call is required by the ASP.NET Web Form Designer.
            //
            InitializeComponent();
        }

        #region Web Form Designer generated code
        /// <summary>
```

LISTING 10.4   Continued

```
    /// Required method for Designer support - do not modify
    /// the contents of this method with the code editor.
    /// </summary>
    private void InitializeComponent()
    {
        this.Button2.Click += new System.EventHandler(this.Button2_Click);
        this.Button1.Click += new System.EventHandler(this.Button1_Click);
        this.Load += new System.EventHandler(this.Page_Load);

    }
    #endregion

    private void Button1_Click(object sender, System.EventArgs e)
    {
        myWebService.Foo();
    }

    private void Button2_Click(object sender, System.EventArgs e)
    {
        try
        {
            myWebService.Bar();
        }
        catch(System.Web.Services.Protocols.SoapException se)
        {

            Response.Write("Message: " + se.Message);
            Response.Write("<br>Actor: " + se.Actor);
            Response.Write("<br>Client Fault Code:" + se.Code.Name);

            XmlNode[] nodes = new XmlNode[1];

            nodes[0] = se.OtherElements[0];

            Response.Write("<p>(Other Elements) Node Name:" +
nodes[0].Name);
            Response.Write("<br>(Other Elements) Node Namespace URI: " +
nodes[0].NamespaceURI);
            Response.Write("<br>(Other Elements) Node Inner Text: " +
nodes[0].InnerText);
        }
    }
}
```

These listings show an example of how *not* to handle exceptions (`Button1_Click` event) and an example of how to handle and discover more about the exception (`Button2_Click` event). The `Button1_Click` event simply has one line of code that calls the `Foo()` Web method. However, there is no `Try...Catch` block around it, so when the Web Service throws the exception and it travels via a SOAP message across the Internet, the ASP.NET Web Form cannot handle the error. When testing this function of the Web Form, you will see a screen similar to Figure 10.2.

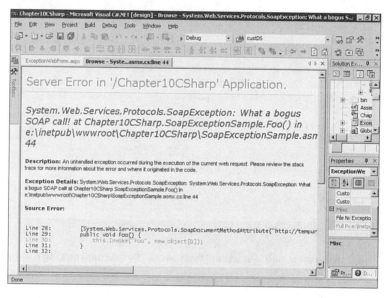

FIGURE 10.2

Result of the `Button1_Click` event calling the `Foo()` Web method.

However, by adding a `Try...Catch` statement around the `Bar()` Web method call in the `Button2_Click` event, you can see how the SOAP fault gets deserialized back into a `SoapException` object that enables the Web Service to dissect each property it makes available. When testing this function of the Web Form, you will see a screen similar to Figure 10.3.

In this case, all the values of the `SoapException` object are simply displayed onscreen. If this had been a serious Web Service, I would have looked for certain problems and tried to correct them before re-sending my request to the Web Service. Or, in the case of the `ClientFaultCode` or `MustUnderstandFaultCode` constants, that could mean that the Web Service's interface has changed since I originally developed against it, so it might be time to re-examine the WSDL for that Web Service to see what has changed. (To do that, you could open the project for the client of the Web Service in Visual Studio.NET, navigate to the Web Reference in Solution Explorer, right-click the localhost node, and choose Refresh Web References from the pop-up menu.) In either case, the rich object model for the SOAP exception becomes a valuable tool for determining what should happen next after an exception is encountered.

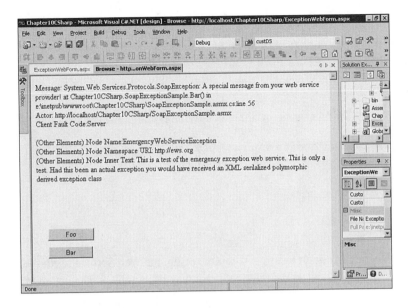

FIGURE 10.3
Result of the Button2_Click event calling the Bar() Web method.

Examining the SOAP Behind the Exception

When I was learning ASP.NET Web Services, I found it extremely helpful to watch the underlying SOAP messages exchanged between the provider and consumer. In Chapter 24, "Using SOAP Extensions," you'll create a SOAP extension that you can apply to your Web Services to monitor the underlying SOAP messages. The following code examples monitor the SOAP messages for both the Foo() and Bar() Web Services by attaching a SOAP extension to the Web Methods and examining their output. This is the SOAP extension output from the Foo() Web Service:

Request

```
<?xml version="1.0" encoding="utf-8"?>
<soap:Envelope xmlns:soap="http://schemas.xmlsoap.org/soap/envelope/"
xmlns:xsi="http://www.w3.org/2001/XMLSchema-instance"
xmlns:xsd="http://www.w3.org/2001/XMLSchema">
  <soap:Body>
    <Foo xmlns="http://tempuri.org/" />
  </soap:Body>
</soap:Envelope>
```

Response

```
<?xml version="1.0" encoding="utf-8"?>
<soap:Envelope xmlns:soap="http://schemas.xmlsoap.org/soap/envelope/">
  <soap:Body>
    <soap:Fault>
      <faultcode>soap:Server</faultcode>
      <faultstring>System.Web.Services.Protocols.SoapException: What a bogus
SOAP call!
   at Chapter10CSharp.SoapExceptionSample.Foo() in
e:\inetpub\wwwroot\chapter10csharp\soapexceptionsample.asmx.cs:line
44</faultstring>
      <detail />
    </soap:Fault>
  </soap:Body>
</soap:Envelope>
```

As you can see, a SOAP fault message is returned from the Web Service for the Foo() Web method. All that is sent back is the fault code that was set as well as the custom message.

The following is the SOAP extension output from the Bar() Web Service:

Request

```
<?xml version="1.0" encoding="utf-8"?>
<soap:Envelope xmlns:soap="http://schemas.xmlsoap.org/soap/envelope/"
xmlns:xsi="http://www.w3.org/2001/XMLSchema-instance"
xmlns:xsd="http://www.w3.org/2001/XMLSchema">
  <soap:Body>
    <Bar xmlns="http://tempuri.org/" />
  </soap:Body>
</soap:Envelope>
```

Response

```
<?xml version="1.0" encoding="utf-8"?>
<soap:Envelope xmlns:soap="http://schemas.xmlsoap.org/soap/envelope/">
  <soap:Body>
    <soap:Fault>
      <faultcode>soap:Server</faultcode>
      <faultstring>System.Web.Services.Protocols.SoapException: A special
message from your Web Service provider!
   at Chapter10CSharp.SoapExceptionSample.Bar() in
e:\inetpub\wwwroot\chapter10csharp\soapexceptionsample.asmx.cs:line
56</faultstring>
```

```
<faultactor>http://localhost/Chapter10CSharp/SoapExceptionSample.asmx</faultact
or>
      <detail />
      <EmergencyWebServiceException xmlns="http://ews.org">This is a test of
the emergency exception Web Service. This is only a test. Had this been an
actual exception, you would have received an XML serialized polymorphic derived
exception class</EmergencyWebServiceException>
    </soap:Fault>
  </soap:Body>
</soap:Envelope>
```

As was to be expected, the `Bar()` Web method's SOAP fault also included the `FaultActor` and an additional node called `EmergencyWebServiceException`, which was added by using the `OtherElements` property of the `SoapException` object. This is how it is manifested in the serialized version of the SOAP message.

Summary

ASP.NET Web Services supports as much or as little exception handling as you need. Without any exception handling, your Web Services still return at least a SOAP fault message with a fault string (or rather a message) that describes the problem. However, you can greatly increase your consumer's knowledge of the problem by populating other properties of the `SoapException` object as it is thrown by your Web Service.

When consuming Web Services, it is important to place a `Try...Catch` statement around the Web Service call because it's too risky to assume that your call to a Web Service will return with no problems. Additionally, it's wise to inspect the `SoapException` properties returned from the Web Service and take the appropriate action based on the nature of the problem, such as logging the exception, reporting a "friendly" version of the error to the end user, or attempting to call the Web Service again with different data values.

Accessing ASP.NET Objects via Web Services

IN THIS CHAPTER

You may be familiar with the Application and Session objects if you have developed ASP-based applications in the past. They are (in)famous for their ability to create ad hoc variables that can store information on the server to maintain application state or state for a given user's session within the application. Developers found uses for Application and Session variables (such as storing object references) that caused great turmoil for Webmasters. The overuse and misuse of the Application and Session objects has left a bad taste in the mouths of many developers, but these features of ASP.NET have been greatly enhanced and deserve another look.

There were other intrinsic objects in Active Server Pages 2.0 and 3.0, such as the Request object that obtained values sent in the GET or POST methods for a given Web page to your ASP page (including cookies), and the Response object, which allowed you to write data to the output buffer while the ASP page was processing on the server.

ASP.NET supplies intrinsic objects that enable you to access authenticated user information, server information, caching mechanisms, application tracing for debugging purposes, and more. Because Web Services are implemented as ASP.NET applications, the Web Services you create have access to all this information. In some cases, these intrinsic objects might not be as helpful. For example, the Response and Request objects are less important for SOAP calls to the Web Service than HTTP GET- and POST-based calls to the Web Services.

By inheriting from the System.Web.Services.WebService class, your Web methods can take advantage of the built-in ASP.NET intrinsic objects, including the Application and Session objects as well as a Context object that gives you access to the other intrinsic objects. The Context object represents an instance of the objects that were created to enable the current user to the use the ASP.NET Web Service. It encapsulates all the functionality for a single specific HTTP request and is your gateway to much of the magic in this chapter.

Inheriting from the WebService Class

Inheriting from the System.Web.Services.WebService class is simple. In fact, Visual Studio .NET creates the statement for you when you create a new ASP.NET Web Service project:

For C# code:

```
public class TheNameOfYourClass : System.Web.Services.WebService
```

For VB .NET code:

```
Public Class TheNameOfYourClass
    Inherits WebService
```

The rest of this chapter offers several examples you can use as a basis for further exploration in using the Application and Context objects. I would highly recommend that you take a few minutes and review the methods and properties in the help file for the `HttpApplicationState` and `HttpContext` objects to familiarize yourself with all the information that's accessible for your applications.

The `Context` and `Application` Example

This example shows a handful of the `Context` and `Application` properties you can use in your applications. To follow along, please perform the following steps:

1. In Visual Studio .NET, choose File | New on the menu to open the New Project dialog box.

2. Select your language in the Project Types list box on the left (Visual Basic Projects or Visual C# Projects), and then select ASP.NET Web Service in the Templates list box on the right.

3. In the Name text box, type **Chapter11VB** if you are creating this project using VB.NET, or type **Chapter11CSharp** if you are using C#.

4. Accept the default location in the Location field.

5. Click the OK button. Visual Studio .NET will create a new project based on the language and template you selected.

6. In Solution Explorer, rename Service1.asmx as ContextApplicationSample.asmx by right-clicking the file, and then choosing Rename on the pop-up menu. Type the new name of the file in the text box with Service1.asmx highlighted, and press Enter on your keyboard to accept the name change.

7. Click the Show All Files icon at the top of the Solution Explorer window to display all the hidden files, including the Code Behind file for the ContextApplicationSample.asmx.

8. The ContextApplicationSample.asmx file should now have a little + sign next to it, indicating that files are hidden beneath it. Click the + sign to reveal the ContextApplicationSample.asmx.vb (for VB .NET) or ContextApplicationSample.asmx.cs (for C#).

9. Select the ContextApplicationSample.asmx.vb or ContextApplicationSample.asmx.cs file in Solution Explorer, and then click the View Code button at the top of the Solution Explorer window to display the Code Behind file in the main area of Visual Studio .NET. This is how you'll edit the Code Behind file. As you can see, Visual Studio .NET has already generated code in this file for you.

10. Type the code formatted in bold in Listing 11.1 for C# or Listing 11.2 for VB .NET into the Code Behind file that is currently open. As is the convention throughout this book, the code not formatted in bold type is included as context to assist you in determining where your code should be entered.

The `GetServerInfo` Web method in the following listings takes in a string parameter used to evaluate which information to display. Based on that parameter, the code returns the appropriate `Context` or `Application` property value(s).

For the `Application` object, you need to set some values as `Application`-level variables that are accessible to all users of the Web Service. Next, the code in the example gets a collection of all `Application`-level variables and iterates through the array of key names while grabbing their values from the `Application` object and returning them to the Web Service consumer.

LISTING 11.1   ContextApplicationSample.asmx.cs in C# Code

```csharp
using System;
using System.Collections;
using System.ComponentModel;
using System.Data;
using System.Diagnostics;
using System.Web;
using System.Web.Services;

namespace Chapter11CSharp
{
    /// <summary>
    /// Summary description for ContextApplicationSample.
    /// </summary>
    public class ContextApplicationSample : System.Web.Services.WebService
    {
        public ContextApplicationSample()
        {
            //CODEGEN: This call is required by the ASP.NET
            //Web Services Designer
            InitializeComponent();
        }

        #region Component Designer generated code
        /// <summary>
        /// Required method for Designer support - do not modify
        /// the contents of this method with the code editor.
        /// </summary>
        private void InitializeComponent()
        {
        }
        #endregion

        /// <summary>
        /// Clean up any resources being used.
        /// </summary>
        public override void Dispose()
```

LISTING 11.1   Continued

```csharp
    {
     }

    [WebMethod]
    public string GetServerInfo(string sInfo)
    {
        string sVal = "";
        switch (sInfo)
        {
            case "user":
                sVal = Context.User.Identity.IsAuthenticated.ToString();
                break;
            case "time":
                sVal = Context.Timestamp.TimeOfDay.ToString();
                break;
            case "server":
                sVal = Context.Server.MachineName.ToString();
                break;
            case "url":
                sVal = Context.Request.Url.Port.ToString();
                break;
            case "application":
                // Setting values using the Application object
                Application.Add("SomeValue", "Rimmer");
                Application.Add("SomeOtherValue", "Lister");

                // Retrieving all the values
                HttpApplicationState myAppContents;

                myAppContents = Application.Contents;

                string[] myKeys = new string[myAppContents.Count];
                myKeys = myAppContents.AllKeys;

                // loop through keys and print out values
                for (int index = 0; index < myKeys.Length; index++)
                {
                    sVal = sVal + myKeys[index] + " = " +
                        Application.Get(index) + "<BR>";
                }
                break;
        }
        return sVal;
    }
  }
}
```

LISTING 11.2   ContextApplicationSample.asmx.vb in VB .NET Code

```
Imports System.Web.Services
Imports System.Web

Public Class ContextApplicationSample
    Inherits System.Web.Services.WebService

#Region " Web Services Designer Generated Code "

    Public Sub New()
        MyBase.New()

        'This call is required by the Web Services Designer.
        InitializeComponent()

        'Add your own initialization code
        'after the InitializeComponent() call

    End Sub

    'Required by the Web Services Designer
    Private components As System.ComponentModel.Container

    'NOTE: The following procedure is required by the Web
    'Services Designer
    'It can be modified using the Web Services Designer.
    'Do not modify it using the code editor.
    <System.Diagnostics.DebuggerStepThrough()> _
    Private Sub InitializeComponent()
        components = New System.ComponentModel.Container()
    End Sub

    Overloads Overrides Sub Dispose()
        'CODEGEN: This procedure is required by the Web Services Designer
        'Do not modify it using the code editor.
    End Sub

#End Region

    <WebMethod()> Public Function GetServerInfo(ByVal sInfo As String) _
                    As String

        Dim sVal As String
```

LISTING 11.2 Continued

```
Select Case sInfo
    Case "user"
        sVal = Context.User.Identity.IsAuthenticated.ToString

    Case "time"
        sVal = Context.Timestamp.TimeOfDay.ToString

    Case "server"
        sVal = Context.Server.MachineName.ToString

    Case "url"
        sVal = Context.Request.Url.Port.ToString

    Case "application"

        ' Setting values using the Application object
        Application.Add("SomeValue", "Rimmer")
        Application.Add("SomeOtherValue", "Lister")

        ' Retrieving all the values
        Dim myAppContents As HttpApplicationState
        myAppContents = Application.Contents

        Dim myKeys() As String
        myKeys = myAppContents.AllKeys

        ' loop through keys and print out values
        Dim index As Integer
        For index = 0 To myKeys.Length - 1
            sVal = sVal & myKeys(index).ToString() & _
                " = " & Application.Get(index).ToString() & _
                "<BR>"
        Next

    End Select

    GetServerInfo = sVal

End Function

End Class
```

To continue, follow these steps:

1. Compile the Web Service by choosing Build | Build Solution on the menu. If there were any problems during the build, make sure you typed the code exactly as it appears in the code listing. And remember, many names are case sensitive in .NET.

2. Create a Web Reference in the same project to the Web Service that was just created. To do this, right-click the Chapter11VB (or Chapter11CSharp) project file in Solution Explorer, and choose Add Web Reference on the pop-up menu. The Add Web Reference dialog box opens.

3. In this dialog box, click the `Web References on Local Web Server` link in the lower-left area. After a moment, the Available References list box will refresh. Click the Chapter11VB (or Chapter11CSharp) entry to refresh the Available References list again.

4. In the Available References list, select ContextApplicationSample.asmx, and click the Add Reference button at the bottom. The dialog box closes, and the new Web Reference is displayed in Solution Explorer. (A `localhost` entry will appear under Web References in Solution Explorer. Click the + next to it to see the WSDL file named ContextApplicationSample.wsdl, and then expand this file to see the proxy class named ContextApplicationSample.vb.)

For the most part, these listings are a random smattering of property values from several of the intrinsic objects you have access to through the `Context` object. Many of the method and property calls are obvious by their usage, but again, I recommend that you take a few minutes to review the methods and properties in the .NET Framework SDK's Class Library help file for the `HttpApplicationState` and `HttpContext` objects, if you want an exhaustive reference of all the tools at your disposal.

The final case, "application," is a more involved example that shows the `Application` object hard at work. Two values are set as `Application` variables, using the `Application` object. Next, you create an instance of an `HttpApplicationState` object that copies all the values from the intrinsic `Application` object. This is a gratuitous use of the `HttpApplicationState` object, just to illustrate how you can create an instance of this object and manipulate the values it holds, without affecting the actual `Application` object it copies from. Next, you get a collection of all the keys (or names in the name/value pairs that are created when you add an `Application` variable) and loop through them, concatenating a string that displays the name and value of the `Application` variable. Several different approaches are used to access the values in this example. You can probably imagine a cleaner use of these objects, but again, these listings are for illustration purposes only.

> **NOTE**
>
> Although these listings illustrated the `Application` object, I could just as easily have used the `Session` object (as long as the client in an ASP.NET Web Service or a Web Form and cookies were acceptable). The obvious difference would be the scope of the values in the `Session` object, which would be a single user as opposed to the entire application. Before attempting to use the `Session` object, however, review the `EnableSession` attribute explained in greater detail in Chapter 13, "Web Service Attributes and Properties."

Despite the fact that you can use the `Session` object in your Web Services, I would caution you to think long and hard before using it. If you are of the opinion that the `Session` object is the best thing to come along since sliced bread, I agree that it's been useful when developing Web pages in ASP 2.0 and 3.0 and even has many uses in ASP.NET. Therefore, there are two architectural questions. First, "Should Web Services be stateful?" and second, "Using the current technology, should you create Web Services that have dependencies and must be called in a particular order to work correctly?"

The problem with state management in Web Services is that it implies that the Web Service consumer will be able to make multiple calls to several Web Services, which may or may not require them to be called in a certain order. My concern is that no current specification seeks to define the orchestration of Web Services to indicate dependencies or contingencies. Without a mechanism (specification and technology) in place to manage the order and dependencies and to have a contingency plan with groups of Web Services, relying on `Session` objects to provide state management and building your family of Web Services to be called in a specific order might be a risky architectural decision. You risk your consumer calling the Web Services out of order, getting a timeout on the `Session` object, or any number of issues that come up when managing state on the server. If the Web Service consumer manages state, and each Web Service call is autonomous, there's reduced cohesion between the services (an object-oriented design heuristic). With less coupling comes a focus on making each Web Service a separate working entity—basically, there would be fewer working parts to break. Universal Description, Discovery, and Integration (UDDI), which is discussed in Chapter 25, "Understanding UDDI," will address some of these issues (namely orchestration) in UDDI Phase 2 or 3.

You might be devising a homegrown authentication mechanism, using the `Session` object to keep track of a particular client's use of your family of Web Services and to enable that client to log in just once. Although this is definitely possible, it would be preferable to use Passport authentication or use Secure Socket Layer (SSL) and SOAP headers to pass authentication information from the client to your Web Service.

Creating the Context Application Sample Client

Now that you have seen how to create the sample Web Service ContextApplicationSample.asmx, you need to create a client to test it out. To do that, follow these steps:

1. Right-click the Chapter11VB (or Chapter11CSharp) project file in Solution Explorer, and choose Add | Add Web Form on the pop-up menu to open the Add New Item dialog box.

2. In the Add New Item dialog box, change the name of the new ASP.NET Web Form to **ContextApplicationSampleClient.aspx**.

3. Click the Open button. The Add New Item dialog box closes, and the new file is displayed in Solution Explorer. Also, in the main area of the IDE, the Web Form Designer appears for the new ContextApplicationSampleClient.aspx Web Form.

4. Place the following six HTML controls on the designer surface, and set their values accordingly, as shown here:

HTML Control	ID	Other Settings
Label	divValue	Text = "" (blank)
Button	btnUser	Label = "User"
Button	btnTime	Label = "Time"
Button	btnServer	Label = "Server"
Button	btnUrl	Label = "Url"
Button	btnApplication	Label = "Application"

When you're finished, the designer surface should look similar to the one shown in Figure 11.1.

5. Double-click each of the buttons on the Web Form designer to access the Code Behind module for this page (ContextApplicationSampleClient.aspx.cs for C# or ContextApplicationSampleClient.aspx.vb for VB .NET). By doing this, Visual Studio .NET creates the appropriate event handlers in the Code Behind module.

6. Type the code formatted in bold in Listing 11.3 for C# or Listing 11.4 for VB .NET into the Code Behind file that is currently open. The code not formatted in bold is included to help you determine where to enter your code.

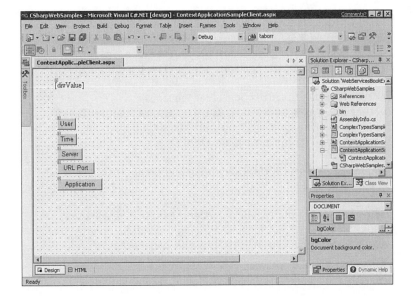

FIGURE 11.1
Designer surface for the ContextApplicationSampleClient.aspx Web Form.

LISTING 11.3   ContextApplicationSampleClient.aspx.cs in C# Code

```csharp
using System;
using System.Collections;
using System.ComponentModel;
using System.Data;
using System.Drawing;
using System.Web;
using System.Web.SessionState;
using System.Web.UI;
using System.Web.UI.WebControls;
using System.Web.UI.HtmlControls;

namespace Chapter11CSharp
{
    /// <summary>
    /// Summary description for ContextApplicationSampleClient.
    /// </summary>
    public class ContextApplicationSampleClient : System.Web.UI.Page
    {
        protected System.Web.UI.WebControls.Label divValue;
        protected System.Web.UI.WebControls.Button btnUser;
        protected System.Web.UI.WebControls.Button btnTime;
```

LISTING 11.3   Continued

```csharp
protected System.Web.UI.WebControls.Button btnApplication;
protected System.Web.UI.WebControls.Button btnServer;
protected System.Web.UI.WebControls.Button btnUrl;

protected localhost.ContextApplicationSample
    myExample = new localhost.ContextApplicationSample();

public ContextApplicationSampleClient()
{
    Page.Init += new System.EventHandler(Page_Init);
}

private void Page_Load(object sender, System.EventArgs e)
{
    // Put user code to initialize the page here
}

private void Page_Init(object sender, EventArgs e)
{
//
// CODEGEN: This call is required by the ASP.NET
// Windows Form Designer.
//
    InitializeComponent();
}

#region Web Form Designer generated code
/// <summary>
/// Required method for Designer support - do not modify
/// the contents of this method with the code editor.
/// </summary>
private void InitializeComponent()
{
    this.btnUser.Click += new
            System.EventHandler(this.btnUser_Click);
    this.btnTime.Click += new
            System.EventHandler(this.btnTime_Click);
    this.btnApplication.Click += new
            System.EventHandler(this.btnApplication_Click);
    this.btnUrl.Click += new
            System.EventHandler(this.btnUrl_Click);
    this.Load += new
            System.EventHandler(this.Page_Load);
}
#endregion
```

LISTING 11.3   Continued

```csharp
        private void btnUser_Click(object sender, System.EventArgs e)
        {
            divValue.Text = myExample.GetServerInfo("user").ToString();
        }

        private void btnTime_Click(object sender, System.EventArgs e)
        {
            divValue.Text = myExample.GetServerInfo("time").ToString();
        }

        private void btnServer_Click(object sender, System.EventArgs e)
        {
            divValue.Text = myExample.GetServerInfo("server").ToString();
        }

        private void btnApplication_Click(object sender, System.EventArgs e)
        {
            divValue.Text = myExample.GetServerInfo("application").ToString();
        }

        private void btnUrl_Click(object sender, System.EventArgs e)
        {
            divValue.Text = myExample.GetServerInfo("url").ToString();
        }
    }
}
```

LISTING 11.4   ContextApplicationSampleClient.aspx.vb in VB .NET Code

```vbnet
Public Class ContextApplicationSampleClient
    Inherits System.Web.UI.Page
    Protected WithEvents btnUser As System.Web.UI.WebControls.Button
    Protected WithEvents btnTime As System.Web.UI.WebControls.Button
    Protected WithEvents btnServer As System.Web.UI.WebControls.Button
    Protected WithEvents btnUrl As System.Web.UI.WebControls.Button
    Protected WithEvents divValue As System.Web.UI.WebControls.Label
    Protected WithEvents btnApplication As System.Web.UI.WebControls.Button

    Protected myExample As New localhost.ContextApplicationSample()

#Region " Web Form Designer Generated Code "

    'This call is required by the Web Form Designer.
    <System.Diagnostics.DebuggerStepThroughAttribute()> Private Sub
InitializeComponent()
```

LISTING 11.4 Continued

```
    End Sub

    Protected Sub Page_Init(ByVal Sender As System.Object, _
            ByVal e As System.EventArgs) Handles MyBase.Init
        'CODEGEN: This method call is required by the Web Form Designer
        'Do not modify it using the code editor.
        InitializeComponent()
    End Sub

#End Region

    Private Sub Page_Load(ByVal sender As System.Object, _
            ByVal e As System.EventArgs) Handles MyBase.Load
        'Put user code to initialize the page here
    End Sub

    Private Sub btnUser_Click(ByVal sender As System.Object, _
            ByVal e As System.EventArgs) Handles btnUser.Click
        divValue.Text = myExample.GetServerInfo("user").ToString
    End Sub

    Private Sub btnTime_Click(ByVal sender As System.Object, _
            ByVal e As System.EventArgs) Handles btnTime.Click
        divValue.Text = myExample.GetServerInfo("time").ToString
    End Sub

    Private Sub btnServer_Click(ByVal sender As System.Object, ByVal e As
System.EventArgs) Handles btnServer.Click
        divValue.Text = myExample.GetServerInfo("server").ToString
    End Sub

    Private Sub btnUrl_Click(ByVal sender As System.Object, _
            ByVal e As System.EventArgs) Handles btnUrl.Click
        divValue.Text = myExample.GetServerInfo("url").ToString
    End Sub

    Private Sub btnApplication_Click(ByVal sender As System.Object, _
            ByVal e As System.EventArgs) Handles btnApplication.Click
        divValue.Text = myExample.GetServerInfo("application").ToString
    End Sub

End Class
```

Viewing the Results of the Client

After you have finished, you should be able to click the buttons and, in a few moments, see various properties of the server and this instance of the Web Service application. To continue with this example, follow these steps:

1. Compile the code by choosing Build | Build Solution on the menu. If any problems occurred during the build, make sure that you typed the code exactly as it appears in the code listing (keep in mind that many things are case sensitive in .NET).

2. Right-click the ContextApplicationSampleClient.aspx file, and choose View in Browser. You should see the screen pictured in Figure 11.2.

3. Click the different buttons to see the values returned from the Web Service.

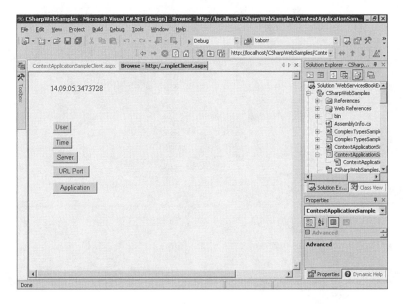

FIGURE 11.2
Results of the example.

Summary

ASP.NET Web Services gives you a fairly straightforward mechanism for accessing information pertinent to the Application and Context objects of the current HTTP request your application is processing.

Using the Session object has some advantages in terms of state management. However, its use brings up the larger architectural issue of creating Web Services that have interdependencies without a current specification or tool to safely support this type of behavior.

In this chapter, you created a sample application that accessed several objects intrinsic to ASP.NET Web Services and displayed their values by consuming the Web Service. You can use this example as a basis for a tool to monitor the health or settings of other servers in your environment.

Three Methods of Calling Web Services

IN THIS CHAPTER

When you created the Web Service in Chapter 2, "Creating a Simple Web Service with .NET SDK," or in Chapter 4, "Creating a Simple Web Service in Visual Studio.NET," you might have been a little puzzled to see that there were actually three ways to call the Web Service. Although it's generally accepted that the primary method of calling a Web Service is sending a SOAP request message via HTTP and receiving a SOAP response message (or SOAP fault), ASP.NET Web Services also allows two additional means by which you can access the Web Service. By default, you can also call the Web Service via the `HTTP-GET` and `HTTP-POST` methods. Ultimately, that means your consumers can access your Web Services via any Web browser, by using the `MSXML` object's XMLHTTP methods or by using an older technology that doesn't understand SOAP but can send HTTP messages to your Web Service.

This short chapter is here to simply discuss how to call Web Services using `HTTP-GET` and `HTTP-POST`. It explains why you would allow this type of access and demonstrates how to exclude calls to your Web Services via `GET` and `POST` requests. This chapter also briefly covers the limitations of calling your Web Service via `GET` and `POST`.

Web Service Help Page and `HTTP-GET`

When you used the Web Service help page, as illustrated in Figure 12.1, you unwittingly tested your Web Service via `HTTP-GET`. You can tell that because the Web browser's location field has a query string appended to the URL. The XML that was returned from the `HTTP-GET` request was not formatted as SOAP, but did have enough information so that you could tell what the values were. Because the XML result was not a SOAP message, several important items are implied. First, any Web Service implementation that relies on SOAP-specific mechanisms, such as SOAP headers, will not work when called via `HTTP-GET` or `POST`. Second, if your Web Service allows XML to be passed into it (discussed in Chapter 14, "Passing Complex Data Types and Structures"), it might not work very well using `HTTP-GET` or `POST`. Sure, you could concentrate all the XML together on the query string, or put it into a hidden form field and then post it, but this implementation is a little messy—especially if you're trying to test it in your Web Service help page.

Given that the .NET Framework offers an eloquent way to call a Web Service without resorting to `HTTP-GET` or `POST`, you're probably wondering why *anyone* would ever want to use anything but SOAP. Conceivably, you might have a trading partner who needs the data returned from a Web Service to be in a specific (non-SOAP) format, or one who is unfamiliar with (and unwilling to learn) SOAP or possibly looking for a low-overhead method of retrieving the data, whether programmatically or manually. These situations are possible, but a more likely situation is that you're building solutions that enlist older technologies that can work with `GET` and `POST` and parse through XML or, at the very least, ASCII text.

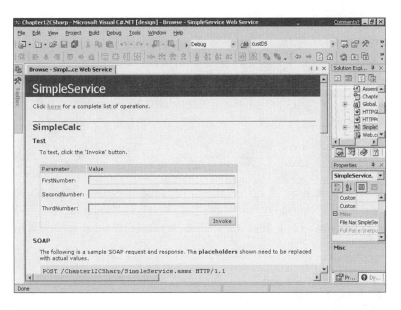

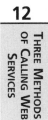

FIGURE 12.1

The Web Service help page via HTTP-GET.

To see how to call a Web Service using HTTP-GET and HTTP-POST, take a look at a simple Web Service called SimpleService.asmx with a single Web method: SimpleCalc. This method takes three integer values and performs a simple calculation. You'll call this Web Service using an HTML Web page via HTTP-GET and POST later in the chapter.

To follow along, please perform the following steps:

1. In Visual Studio.NET, choose File | New on the menu to open the New Project dialog box.

2. Select your language in the Project Types list box on the left (Visual Basic Projects or Visual C# Projects), and then select ASP.NET Web Service in the Templates list box on the right.

3. In the Name text box, type **Chapter12VB**, if you are using VB.NET, or **Chapter12CSharp**, if you are using C#.

4. Accept the default location in the Location field.

5. Click the OK button. Visual Studio.NET will create a new project based on the language and template you selected.

6. In Solution Explorer, rename Service1.asmx as SimpleService.asmx by right-clicking the file, and then choosing Rename from the pop-up menu. Type the new name of the file in the text box where the Service1.asmx filename is highlighted. Press Enter on your keyboard to accept the name change.

7. Click the Show All Files icon at the top of the Solution Explorer pane to display all the hidden files, including the Code Behind file for the SimpleService.asmx.

8. Click the + sign next to the SimpleService.asmx file to reveal the SimpleService.asmx.vb (for VB.NET) or SimpleService.asmx.cs (for C#) file.

9. Select the SimpleService.asmx.vb or SimpleService.cs file in Solution Explorer, and then click the View Code button at the top of the Solution Explorer pane to display the Code Behind file in the main display area of Visual Studio.NET. This is where you edit the Code Behind file. As you can see, Visual Studio.NET has already generated code for you.

10. Type the code in Listing 12.1 (for VB.NET) or Listing 12.2 (for C#) in the Code Behind file that is currently open. Type only the code with bold formatting in the listings. As is the convention throughout this book, the other code is included as context to help you determine where to enter your code.

LISTING 12.1   SimpleService.asmx.vb in VB.NET Code

```
Imports System.Web.Services

Public Class SimpleService
    Inherits System.Web.Services.WebService

#Region " Web Services Designer Generated Code "

    Public Sub New()
        MyBase.New()

        'This call is required by the Web Services Designer.
        InitializeComponent()

        'Add your own initialization code after the InitializeComponent() call

    End Sub

    'Required by the Web Services Designer
    Private components As System.ComponentModel.Container

    'NOTE: The following procedure is required by the Web Services Designer
    'It can be modified using the Web Services Designer.
    'Do not modify it using the code editor.
    <System.Diagnostics.DebuggerStepThrough()> Private Sub
InitializeComponent()
        components = New System.ComponentModel.Container()
    End Sub
```

LISTING 12.1 Continued

```
    Protected Overloads Overrides Sub Dispose(ByVal disposing As Boolean)
        'CODEGEN: This procedure is required by the Web Services Designer
        'Do not modify it using the code editor.
    End Sub

#End Region

    <WebMethod()> Public Function SimpleCalc(ByVal FirstNumber As Integer,
ByVal SecondNumber As Integer, ByVal ThirdNumber As Integer) As Integer
        SimpleCalc = FirstNumber * SecondNumber + ThirdNumber
    End Function
End Class
```

LISTING 12.2 SimpleWebService.asmx.cs in C# Code

```
using System;
using System.Collections;
using System.ComponentModel;
using System.Data;
using System.Diagnostics;
using System.Web;
using System.Web.Services;

namespace Chapter12CSharp
{
    /// <summary>
    /// Summary description for SimpleService.
    /// </summary>
    public class SimpleService : System.Web.Services.WebService
    {
        public SimpleService()
        {
            //CODEGEN: This call is required by the ASP.NET Web Services
Designer
            InitializeComponent();
        }

        #region Component Designer generated code
        /// <summary>
        /// Required method for Designer support - do not modify
        /// the contents of this method with the code editor.
        /// </summary>
```

LISTING 12.2   Continued

```
        private void InitializeComponent()
        {
        }
        #endregion

        /// <summary>
        /// Clean up any resources being used.
        /// </summary>
        protected override void Dispose( bool disposing )
        {
        }

        [WebMethod]
        public int SimpleCalc(int FirstNumber, int SecondNumber, int
ThirdNumber)
        {
            return FirstNumber * SecondNumber + ThirdNumber;
        }
    }
}
```

Compile the Web Service by choosing Build/Build on the menu item. If there were any problems during the build, make sure you typed the code exactly as it appears in the code listing, and remember that many things are case sensitive in .NET.

The purpose of this Web Service is to give you a simple Web Service that you can use to examine how to call it via HTTP GET and POST.

Calling a Web Service Using HTTP-GET

The following HTML code example, called HTTPGET.htm, shows how to call the SimpleCalc Web Service using HTTP-GET (see Listing 12.3). The values in this example are hard-coded, but you could easily replace them on-the-fly by using JavaScript, if necessary. Note that the parameters in QueryString must have the same name as the input parameters for the Web Service, or this example will not work.

Use these steps to continue following along:

1. Create a Web Reference in the same project as the Web Service you just created. To do that, right-click the Chapter12VB (or Chapter12CSharp) project file in Solution Explorer, and choose Add Web Reference from the pop-up menu to open the Add Web Reference dialog box.

2. Click the `Web References on Local Web Server` link at the bottom of the dialog box on the left side. After the Available References list box refreshes its contents, select the Chapter12VB (or Chapter12CSharp) entry. This refreshes the Available References list again.

3. In the Available References list, select SimpleService.asmx, and click the Add Reference button at the bottom of the dialog box. The dialog box closes, and the new Web Reference is displayed in Solution Explorer. (A localhost entry will appear under Web References in Solution Explorer. Click the + sign next to this entry to see the WSDL file named SimpleService.wsdl. Expand this WSDL file to see the proxy class named SimpleService.vb or SimpleService.cs.)

4. Right-click the Chapter14VB (or Chapter14CSharp) project file, and choose Add | Add HTML Page from the pop-up menu to open the Add New Item dialog box.

5. In the Add New Item dialog box, change the name of the new HTML page to HTTPGET.htm.

6. Click the Open button. The Add New Item dialog box closes, and the new file is displayed in Solution Explorer. In the IDE's main area, the HTML Designer appears for the new HTTPGET.htm Web page.

7. Select the HTML tab at the bottom of the HTML Designer to display the page's HTML code. Add the `<A HREF>` tag formatted in bold in Listing 12.3.

LISTING 12.3   HTTPGET.htm HTML Code Listing

```
<!DOCTYPE HTML PUBLIC "-//W3C//DTD HTML 4.0 Transitional//EN">
<html>
    <head>
        <title>HTTPGET</title>
        <meta name="vs_defaultClientScript" content="JavaScript">
        <meta name="vs_targetSchema"
content="http://schemas.microsoft.com/intellisense/ie5">
        <meta name="GENERATOR" content="Microsoft Visual Studio.NET 7.0">
        <meta name="ProgId" content="VisualStudio.HTML">
        <meta name="Originator" content="Microsoft Visual Studio.NET 7.0">
    </head>
    <body MS_POSITIONING="GridLayout">
        <a
href="http://localhost/Chapter12CSharp/SimpleService.asmx/SimpleCalc?FirstNumbe
r=3&SecondNumber=4&ThirdNumber=5">
            Click here</a> to perform the HTTP GET on the SimpleCalc Web
Service.
    </BODY>
</HTML>
```

12

THREE METHODS OF CALLING WEB SERVICES

Continue with the following steps:

1. Save your changes by clicking the Save icon on the toolbar.

2. Right-click the HTTPGET.htm file in Solution Explorer, and choose View in Browser from the pop-up menu. This loads the browser into the main area of Visual Studio.NET with the HTTPGET.htm page displayed.

This Web Service requires multiple parameters to be passed into it, so those parameters were added by using the normal query string syntax for multiple name/value pairs.

When you click the link, the result is a non-SOAP XML document that simply holds the return value, as shown here:

```
<?xml version="1.0" encoding="utf-8" ?>
<int xmlns="http://tempuri.org/">17</int>
```

As the Web Service Help Page points out, the full HTTP message would look something like this:

```
GET
/Chapter12CSharp/SimpleService.asmx/SimpleCalc?FirstNumber=string&SecondNumber=
string&ThirdNumber=string HTTP/1.1
Host: localhost
```

You might need to know this information if you are supplying instructions on how to call the Web Service to someone else who is not SOAP enabled.

Calling a Web Service Using HTTP-POST

Listing 12.4 shows how to call the SimpleCalc Web Service by using HTTP-POST. This example, named HTTPPOST.htm, is an HTML form with three input boxes. Each of the input boxes must be named exactly the same as the input parameters to the Web Service.

Use these steps if you are following along:

1. Right-click the Chapter14VB (or Chapter14CSharp) project file, and choose Add | Add HTML Page from the pop-up menu to open the Add New Item dialog box.

2. Change the name of the new HTML page to HTTPGET.htm.

3. Click the Open button. The Add New Item dialog box closes, and the new file is displayed in Solution Explorer. Also, in the IDE's main area, the HTML Designer appears for the new HTTPPOST.htm Web page.

4. Select the HTML tab at the bottom of the HTML Designer to display the page's HTML code. Add the <A HREF> tag (the code formatted in bold) in Listing 12.4.

LISTING 12.4   HTTPPOST.htm HTML Listing

```
<!DOCTYPE HTML PUBLIC "-//W3C//DTD HTML 4.0 Transitional//EN">
<html>
    <head>
        <title>HTTPGET</title>
        <meta name="vs_defaultClientScript" content="JavaScript">
        <meta name="vs_targetSchema"
content="http://schemas.microsoft.com/intellisense/ie5">
        <meta name="GENERATOR" content="Microsoft Visual Studio.NET 7.0">
        <meta name="ProgId" content="VisualStudio.HTML">
        <meta name="Originator" content="Microsoft Visual Studio.NET 7.0">
    </head>
    <body MS_POSITIONING="GridLayout"><form method="post"
action="http://localhost/Chapter12CSharp/SimpleService.asmx/SimpleCalc">
<p>FirstNumber: <INPUT id="FirstNumber" type="text"
name="FirstNumber"></p>
<p>SecondNumber: <INPUT id="SecondNumber" type="text"
name="SecondNumber"></p>
<p>ThirdNumber: <INPUT id="ThirdNumber" type="text"
name="ThirdNumber"></p>
<P> </P>
<p><INPUT type="submit" value="Submit"></p>
</form>
</BODY>
</HTML>
```

5. Save your changes by clicking the Save icon on the toolbar.

6. Right-click the HTTPPOST.htm file in Solution Explorer, and choose View in Browser from the pop-up menu. This will load the browser into the main area of Visual Studio.NET with the HTTPPOST.htm page displayed.

After entering numeric values in the text boxes and clicking the Submit button, you should get a result similar to the HTTP-GET result shown earlier:

```
<?xml version="1.0" encoding="utf-8" ?>
<int xmlns="http://tempuri.org/">17</int>
```

As the Web Service help page illustrates for you, the full HTTP message would look something like this:

```
POST /Chapter12CSharp/SimpleService.asmx/SimpleCalc HTTP/1.1
Host: localhost
Content-Type: application/x-www-form-urlencoded
Content-Length: length

FirstNumber=string&SecondNumber=string&ThirdNumber=string
```

Again, this information can be useful if you are supplying instructions on how to call the Web Service via POST to someone else who is not SOAP enabled.

Using the MSXML XMLHTTP Object

The Microsoft XML (MSXML) component supports an object that enables you to call and retrieve information from any URI that returns XML. This approach was common when interacting with trading partners before the advent of tools that supported SOAP and Web Services. After the XML is returned from across the Web, it can be loaded into the MSXML DOM (Document Object Model) and easily processed. Listing 12.5 is an excerpt from a Visual Basic 6.0 application that shows how to call the SimpleCalc service by using the MSXML XMLHTTP object.

LISTING 12.5   Using the MSXML *XMLHTTP* Object in Visual Basic 6.0

```
Dim objXMLDom As MSXML2.DOMDocument
Dim oXML_http As MSXML2.ServerXMLHTTP
Dim Full_URL As String
Dim iCounter As Integer
Dim strXML As String

Set oXML_http = New MSXML2.ServerXMLHTTP
Set objXMLDom = New MSXML2.DOMDocument

Full_URL =
"http://localhost/Chapter12CSharp/SimpleService.asmx/SimpleCalc?FirstNumber=3&S
econdNumber=4&ThirdNumber=5"

oXML_http.setTimeouts 5000, 5000, 15000, 15000
oXML_http.Open "GET", Full_URL, False
oXML_http.send

strXML = oXML_http.responseText
objXMLDom.loadXML strXML

' Do something meaningful with the XMLDOM now
```

Obviously, the hard-coded QueryString on the URL prevents this from being a real-world example, but you can dynamically generate the QueryString parameters on-the-fly with the programmatic logic of your application.

Summary

ASP.NET Web Services gives you some flexibility in how your consumers can call your Web Services. This flexible approach accommodates Web Service consumers who might be dealing with older technology that doesn't work with SOAP, or consumers who do not want to incur the overhead associated with adapting their applications to SOAP.

Depending on the implementation of the Web Service, it might not be possible to call it using HTTP-GET or POST. Factors that preclude using these two methods include Web Services that use SOAP headers, Web Services that take complex data types, such as datasets or XML, as input parameters, or Web Services with other restrictions that demand the flexibility and structure of SOAP.

Web Service Attributes and Properties

IN THIS CHAPTER

In this chapter, you'll be exploring in more depth concepts that were introduced in previous chapters, such as ASP.NET Web Service processing directives, Web Service and Web method attributes, and their respective properties. These syntactic elements are the essence of ASP.NET Web Services and provide much of their functionality and flexibility. This chapter adheres to a strict format of discussing each of the properties, providing a brief example, and listing reasons you would choose to use that code element in your Web Service.

Processing Directives

When you create ASP.NET files (whether .aspx or .asmx), Visual Studio .NET generates at least two files you should be aware of. For example, when you add a new Web Service to your project called "MyNewWebService," these two files are created:

- MyNewWebService.asmx
- MyNewWebService.asmx.vb (or MyNewWebService.asmx.cs if you are using C#)

The primary .asmx file is what gets called in your application. Based on the information in its processing directive, it points to a Code Behind file (the .vb or .cs file represented in Visual Studio .NET's Solution Explorer as a child node of the .asmx file) that contains the Web Service's actual implementation code. A *processing directive* is a line in code that tells the .NET Framework the following:

- The coding language
- The Code Behind file that packages the actual implementation for the Web Service
- The class in the Code Behind file that contains the Web Methods for this Web Service

The .vb or .cs file appears as a child node of the .asmx file in Solution Explorer, as depicted in Figure 13.1. To see this .vb or .cs file, you must click on the + sign next to the .asmx file. This file is the Code Behind module for the Web Service (or the ASP.NET Web Form, as the case may be).

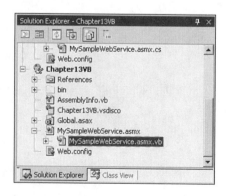

FIGURE 13.1

Solution Explorer and the Code Behind files.

However, you might not see this Code Behind file unless you click the View All Files button at the top of the Solution Explorer window, as shown in Figure 13.2.

View All Files

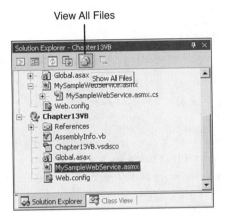

FIGURE 13.2

Solution Explorer's View All Files button.

The concept of the Code Behind file has a clearer function in ASP.NET Web Forms than in ASP.NET Web Services. In a Web Form, it enables you to separate the HTML and other graphical elements that compose a Web Form from the server-side events that take place when a user interacts with the Web Form. In ASP 3.0 and earlier versions, combining these elements posed an aesthetic and a performance problem: The code looked messy when a bunch of <%= %> directives had to be inserted in the midst of HTML code. Some developers used Response.Write to send HTML, saved as long strings in variables, to the output stream. There were also performance concerns as a result of context switching to insert dynamic elements (from, say, an ADO Recordset) into the HTML. Code Behind allows a cleaner separation, with one file handling only visual elements and the other file handling server-side logic to create dynamic Web pages.

On the Web Services side, the use of Code Behind has fewer obvious advantages, but Web Services still have a visual element associated with them—at least during design time. In Chapter 16, "Using the Web Services Designer in Visual Studio .NET," you'll see how Code Behind makes it easier to use the designer surface for dragging and dropping references to resources from Solution Explorer; in this case, Code Behind makes Web Service development a little more RAD-like (that is, Rapid Application Development).

As you create Web Services in Visual Studio .NET, the processing directives generated for Web Services will resemble the following code listings. The only problem is that you cannot view this file in Visual Studio .NET. You'll have to find the file in your file system, and then open it in Notepad or another text viewer to see the contents of the processing directive. The following code is a result of creating a Web Service project in Visual Studio .NET, closing the project, and then opening the MySampleWebService.asmx file in Notepad.

VB Version of MySampleWebService.asmx:

```
<%@ WebService Language="c#" Codebehind="MySampleWebService.asmx.cs"

    Class="Chapter13CSharp.Service1" %>
```

C# Version of MySampleWebService.asmx:

```
<%@ WebService Language="vb" Codebehind="MySampleWebService.asmx.vb"

    Class="Chapter13VB.Service1" %>
```

Language Property

To call the engine that compiles your .asmx file into an assembly, the HTTP Handler must know which language your .asmx file is using so that it can call the appropriate parser. The Language property of the page can be set to any supported .NET language (not just C# or VB).

CodeBehind Property

The CodeBehind property points to the file that contains the Code Behind implementation.

Class Property

The Class property defines for the ASP.NET Web Service execution engine which classes in your .asmx file should be made available at the URI. Your .asmx file can have multiple classes defined in it. However, only one of those classes can be made available as a Web Service (the one marked with the Class property at the top of the .asmx file). In that designated class, you can have one or many methods that are "Web methods." However, the methods in the designated class are the only ones allowed to have the WebMethod attribute associated with them.

Truth be told, you probably won't interact with processing directives much unless you are creating your ASP.NET Web Services from scratch without the aid of Visual Studio .NET. The next two sections of this chapter are much more pertinent to developers because they can be configured through the Visual Studio .NET IDE.

The WebService Attribute

An *attribute* is a keyword that defines the behavior of a class or its members. Attributes can be created for use in classes, methods, interfaces, assemblies, and a number of other items as defined in the AttributeTargets enumeration. You can use attributes to provide some extra information about a particular code element. For example, you use the WebMethod attribute (discussed later in this chapter) to tell the code responsible for running your Web Service which functions in the file should be made available as Web Services. You can even create your own attributes for your application to read and interpret, although this topic is outside the scope of this book.

Within the Code Behind file itself, the class designated in the processing directive section of the .asmx file is the class exposed publicly as a Web Service. You can adorn that class with the `WebService` attribute, using it to specify the namespace, which defaults to `http://tempuri.org`, and description text for the Web Service. There's a caveat, however. When you create a Web Service using Visual Studio .NET, no `Web Service` attribute is supplied by default, so you need to add it in just about every serious Web Service you create. The following code lines are excerpts from a Web Service to illustrate the use of the `WebService` attribute properties:

VB .NET Code Listing:

```
<WebService(Namespace:="http://www.technicallead.com", Description:="This is a
sample description.", Name:="NewName")>
```

C# Code Listing:

```
[WebService(Namespace="http://www.technicallead.com", Description="This is a
sample description.", Name="NewName")]
```

> **NOTE**
>
> The properties of the `WebService` attribute are separated with a comma.

Namespace **Property**

In its general use, the `Namespace` property addresses the potential problem of ambiguity between two or more XML documents (from different sources) that happen to use the same names to define different elements. The same applies to SOAP messages that have XML content. When prefixed by a unique URI, the chance of collisions diminishes significantly. By default, ASP.NET Web Services use a temporary namespace: `"http://tempuri.org/"`. It is highly recommended (and you are reminded by Microsoft in the Web Services help screen) to change it to your own URI. Don't have one? Well, typically a URI is a URL (like your company's URL), but could be any address that uniquely identifies it from another entity that might be using the XML in your Web Service.

If you forget to change the `Namespace` property, the Web Services help screen goes out of its way to remind you by displaying the following text:

```
This web service is using http://tempuri.org/ as its default namespace.

Recommendation: Change the default namespace before the web service is
made public.
```

```
Each web service needs a unique namespace to identify it so that client
applications can distinguish it from other services on the web.
http://tempuri.org/ is available for web services that are under development,
but published web services should use a more permanent namespace.

Your web service should be identified by a namespace that you control.
For example, you could use your company's Internet domain name as part of the
namespace. Although many web service namespaces look like URLs, they need not
point to an actual resource on the web. (Web service namespaces are URIs.)
```

However, in my humble opinion, it doesn't make much sense to state in the Web Service help file that you should change the namespace, but not enforce that change in the Web Service project template. Of course, Microsoft gives you this flexibility to reduce your burden at design time, but ultimately it might cause more headaches at runtime.

Description Property

A descriptive message is displayed to prospective consumers of the Web Service when description documents (WSDL files) for the Web Service are generated, such as the Service Description and the Service help page. The following figures show how setting the Description property changes what you see in the Web Services help file. Figure 13.3 shows the screen before setting the Description property, and Figure 13.4 shows it after.

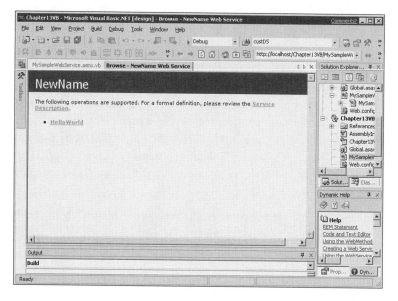

FIGURE 13.3

Before setting the Description property.

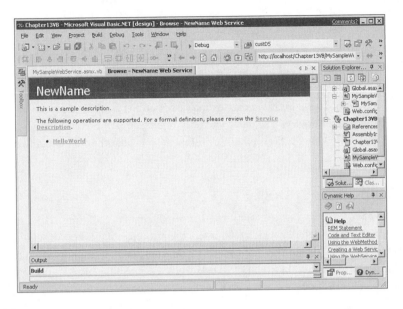

FIGURE 13.4

After setting the Description property.

When you set the `Description` property of the `WebService` attribute, the `<documentation>` element (a child of the `Service` element) is added to the WSDL file for the Web Service, as the following WSDL excerpt shows:

```
...
<documentation>This is a sample description.</documentation>
...
```

Name Property

Setting the `Name` property changes the name of the Web Service in the WSDL from the `ClassName` (which is actually derived from the ASP.NET Web Service filename when you create it) to another name of your choosing. This property affects two aspects of your Web Service. First, it affects the name you see when you test the Web Service in the help page. Second, and more important, it is used as the XML-qualified name in the WSDL that represents the namespace you set. Consider the following WSDL excerpt generated as a result of the `WebService` attribute shown previously:

```
...
<portType name="NewNameSoap"> ... </portType>
...
<binding name="NewNameSoap" type="s0:NewNameSoap"> ... </binding>
...
<port name="NewNameSoap" binding="s0:NewNameSoap"> ... </port>
...
```

The `WebMethod` Attribute

Adorning a public method with the `WebMethod` attribute makes the method accessible as part of the Web Service. Private methods and private classes cannot be Web methods or Web Services. It is possible to have multiple Web methods within a single Web Service. However, a single Code Behind file cannot have multiple classes that are Web Services because the .asmx file's Web Service processing directive can designate only one class as the Web Service. The properties covered in the following sections enable developers to extend the function and utility of their Web methods.

`BufferResponse` Property

The `BufferResponse` property of the `WebMethod` attribute enables buffering responses for a Web Service method. By default, ASP.NET buffers the entire response before sending it to the client (`BufferResponse:=True`). The efficient buffering mechanism helps improve performance by minimizing communication between the worker process (responsible for generating the information) and the IIS process (responsible for sending the information).

Why, then, would you want to set the `BufferResponse` property to false? Perhaps you do not want the response's entire contents in memory at once if you are sending back a large ADO.NET DataSet to the consumer. When `BufferResponse` is set to false, as shown in the following code line, ASP.NET buffers the response in chunks of 16KB, and reduces the amount of memory consumed in this process.

```
<WebMethod(BufferResponse:=False)>
```

`CacheDuration` Property

The `CacheDuration` property enables caching the results for a Web Service method. Caching is a great feature to use—when it makes sense. ASP.NET caches the results for each unique parameter set. For example, if your Web Service returns an ADO.NET DataSet based on the ID for a given record in the database, you could save the round-trip of querying your data source from your Web Service's server by simply setting this value. The value of this property specifies how many seconds ASP.NET should cache the results. Unless otherwise specified, the default value is zero, which disables the caching feature. The following snippet illustrates the use of the `CacheDuration` property:

```
<WebMethod(CacheDuration:=60)>
```

Description Property

You use the Description property to describe the purpose of your Web Service; this description then appears on the Web Service's help page. Using the following setting for this property gives you the results shown in Figure 13.5:

```
<WebMethod(Description:="This is the generic HelloWorld description.")>
```

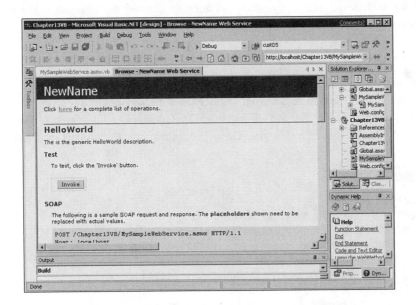

FIGURE 13.5

The Description *property for the Web method displayed in the Web Service's help page.*

This property also sets the WSDL's description property for the method, as follows:

```
<portType name="NewNameSoap">
    <operation name="HelloWorld">
        <documentation>
            The is the generic HelloWorld description.
        </documentation>
        <input message="s0:HelloWorldSoapIn" />
        <output message="s0:HelloWorldSoapOut" />
    </operation>
</portType>
```

13

WEB SERVICE ATTRIBUTES AND PROPERTIES

EnableSession Property

The `EnableSession` property enables session state for a Web Service method. If this property is set to true, the Web Service can access the session state collection directly from `HttpContext.Current.Session` or with the `WebService.Session` property (if it inherits from the `WebService` base class). By default, this property is false.

Sessions and Web Services, and my strong opinions about using the `EnableSession` property, are discussed in Chapter 11, "Accessing ASP.NET Objects via Web Services."

MessageName Property

The `MessageName` property is an interesting feature. It enables you to overload methods in your class, but still allows them to be accessed uniquely as Web Services by supplying an alternative name (or alias) to each one. The WSDL and the SOAP messages refer to `MessageName` instead of the actual name of the method in your class. The following code snippets should illustrate this point clearly.

VB .NET Code Listing:

```
Public Class Service1
    Inherits System.Web.Services.WebService
    <WebMethod(MessageName:="AppendTwoStrings")> _
    Public Function ConcatenateStrings(ByVal sStringOne As String, _
        ByVal sStringTwo As String) As String
        ConcatenateStrings= sStringOne & sStringTwo
    End Function
    <WebMethod(MessageName:="AppendThreeStrings")> _
    Public Function ConcatenateStrings(ByVal sStringOne As String, _
        ByVal sStringTwo As String, ByVal sStringThree as String) As String
        ConcatenateStrings = sStringOne & sStringTwo & sStringThree
    End Function
End Class
```

C# Code Listing:

```
public class Service1 : System.Web.Services.WebService
{
    [WebMethod(MessageName="AppendTwoStrings")]
    public string ConcatenateStrings(string sStringOne, string sStringTwo)
    {
        return sStringOne + sStringTwo;
    }
    [WebMethod(MessageName="AppendThreeStrings")]
    public string ConcatenateStrings(string sStringOne,
        string sStringTwo, string sStringThree)
```

```
    {
        return sStringOne + sStringTwo + sStringThree;
    }
```

TransactionOption Property

The `TransactionOption` property of the `WebMethod` attribute enables the Web Service method to participate as the root object of a transaction. Even though you can set the `TransactionOption` property to any of the values in the `TransactionOption` enumeration, a Web Service method has only two possible behaviors: It does not participate in a transaction (`Disabled`, `NotSupported`, `Supported`), or it creates a new transaction (`Required`, `RequiresNew`). Chapter 18, "Using Transactions in Web Services," discusses in more depth how Web Services fit into a transactional model.

Summary

The processing directives statement in an .asmx file points the ASP.NET HTTP Handler for Web Services to the appropriate file and class where the actual Web Service implementation is located. Also, as the Code Behind file is compiled, it specifies which compiler should be used, the VB .NET or the C# compiler.

The `WebService` attribute adorns classes that implement Web Services and allows the developer to add the namespace, a description, and an alternative name that will be used in the WSDL. By default, the `Namespace` property is set to a temporary one, and should be changed to a unique URI to help avoid potential name collisions between two or more XML documents (in this case, SOAP messages).

The `WebMethod` attribute adorns the actual class methods that are called as Web Services, so that developers can set a range of options, including descriptions, timeouts, and use of transactions.

Although they work behind the scenes, processing directives and attributes offer developers a rich model for customizing their Web Services to suit different needs. The use of attributes can make the purpose and the use of your Web Service clearer. As you saw in this chapter, the attributes and properties you set are used by Visual Studio .NET and the .NET Framework to create documentation, discovery information, and important implementation details about the Web Service.

Passing Complex Data Types and Structures

IN THIS CHAPTER

Before long, you will want to send more than just simple string and numerical values to and from your Web Services. The ASP.NET Web Services handler shields the developer from much of the complexity in passing and retrieving complex values such as arrays, objects, arrays of objects, XML, and so forth. When publishing Web Services you've created with complex data, .NET takes care of creating WSDL that accurately describes the data structure it will accept or return. When consuming Web Services that contain complex data descriptions in their WSDL, the .NET Framework uses the WSDL from a Web Service to create classes that represent the data to be sent and retrieved from the Web Service.

Some of the concepts in this chapter will help you understand how ADO.NET DataSets are transferred using Web Services in the next chapter.

The SOAP Specification and Data Types

The SOAP specification outlines a tremendous amount of detail on how to send a properly formatted SOAP message to accommodate just about any data type and any data structure. In fact, if you were to print the entire specification, Section 5, "SOAP Encoding," would account for almost half (15 of 33 pages) of the document. The specification explains the details of how to encode simple types, enumerations, arrays of bytes, compound types, `PartiallyTransmitted` arrays, `Sparse` arrays, and more.

However, if you are developing Microsoft .NET Web Services and inspect the actual SOAP created by the .NET Framework classes, you'll notice two things: One, it won't interest you very much, and secondly, it varies slightly from the SOAP specification by having a simpler format. For example, .NET Framework does not use accessors to decrease the total size of the SOAP message. You can think of SOAP *accessors* as variables that are used instead of the actual original values in a message. Whenever that value is to appear in the SOAP message, it's substituted for the variable name. The variable is defined at the bottom of the SOAP message with the actual value it represents. This can be done once at the bottom of the document, and in some cases produces a much smaller SOAP message if that value is used often in the message. Also, the type information is not encoded into the actual SOAP message, and data types are not explicitly defined in the SOAP message itself. Instead, the XML Schema Definition (XSD) within the WSDL defines the data types and the client's proxy converts the data elements in the SOAP message to their appropriate data type as defined by the WSDL (more about this in a moment). Most of this happens behind the scenes as a result of the diligent work of the .NET Framework development team.

Because XSD defines data types for Web Services (and is then embedded in the WSDL), XSD must be flexible enough to accommodate the data types found in most programming languages. For two disparate systems to communicate data, there must be an agreement on what a particular data type is. However, there are subtle differences that prevent direct mapping between languages. For instance, a Visual Basic.NET integer type might be different than a Java integer type. The XSD language specification explicitly defines each data type. The following list shows the mapping between a Common Language Runtime (CLR) data type (which Visual Basic.NET and C# use) and an XSD data type.

CLR Data Type	XSD Data Type
Boolean	Boolean
Double	Double
Decimal	Decimal
Single	Float
Int32	Int
Int64	Long
Int16	Short
String	String
DateTime	TimeInstant

However, complex structures such as arrays and classes, must be supported as well, which is why the rest of this chapter focuses on those structures.

Understanding Classes, XSD, WSDL, and Proxies

Before continuing, it is important to understand the "big picture" of the relationship between creating complex types, such as arrays and classes, and how their type information is described by WSDL and eventually used when you create a Web Reference. Figure 14.1 illustrates this relationship.

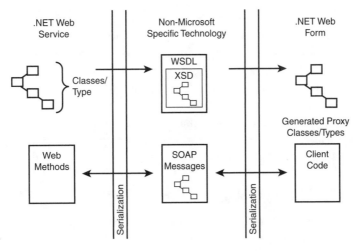

FIGURE 14.1

WSDL describes complex data types using XSD classes to serialize and deserialize the descriptions used when proxies are created.

The left-hand side of Figure 14.1 represents .NET Web Services. Say that your Web Service defines several classes that are instanced and populated by the Web methods in your service. On the right-hand side of Figure 14.1, you see the consumer for those Web Services, a Web page also created by using the .NET Framework. A developer creates a Web Reference, which performs several important tasks. The Visual Studio.NET Server Explorer communicates with the Web Server via DISCO and locates all available Web Services on the server. The developer selects one of those Web Services and creates a Web Reference to it. When this occurs, a series of .NET Framework classes on the server begin to perform the process of *reflection* on the data types and class structures and translate that information into a serialized XML format called *XML Schema Definition* (XSD). .NET uses the reflection process to inspect and discover the methods, properties, and data types used in a given class. It is a large topic fundamental to your understanding of the .NET Framework, but is beyond the scope of this book.

The XSD is then embedded into the WSDL file in the Types section of that document. When using Visual Studio.NET, these XSD/Reflection classes are used behind the scenes to convert classes to XSD and to convert XSD back to classes (explained in just a moment). If you're using just the .NET Framework SDK, it comes with the XSD.exe utility, which performs these functions as well.

After the WSDL file for the Web Service is created and complete--with the XSD for all the data types and structures defined in the file--the WSDL is sent to the Web Service consumer. The consumer's version of Visual Studio.NET then breaks apart the WSDL file and constructs classes (called a proxy) that the developer can use to code with, as though the Web Service code were in the same project the developer is currently working on. The .NET Framework's XSD classes take care of deconstructing the XSD and building classes in the proxy. Visual Studio.NET also creates a hard-coded URI for the Web Service and other assorted functions.

You might be wondering if this process goes against the whole purpose of SOAP, WSDL, and DISCO. The idea behind these three approaches is that they are open and non–Microsoft specific. That is what the middle area in Figure 14.1 represents: non-Microsoft technologies used merely to convey descriptions and data. The format is not Microsoft specific, but is interpreted by Microsoft technologies to perform meaningful tasks. Each development tool vendor has the responsibility of supplying developers with similar tools that can encode and decode documents and data in this manner. The Microsoft .NET Framework and Visual Studio.NET teams just make this task extremely easy for their developers.

Passing .NET Structures over Web Services

The example used in this section illustrates how to send objects via Web Services. Later in the chapter, you'll inspect the actual SOAP messages that are sent to view how the data is being encoded, serialized, and sent to the client.

This example uses the following three classes and properties:

- **CustomersInfo class**

  FirstName property

  LastName property

  EmailAddress property

- **OrderInfo class**

  OrderID property

  Items property (which contains an array of PartInfo objects)

- **PartInfo class**

  PartID property

  PartDescription property

Allow me to jump ahead to make a quick point: Once you've built the Web Service in this chapter, you'll be able to look at the WSDL file. If you inspect the WSDL file, you'll see an example of how the XSD describes objects, arrays, and arrays of objects in the WSDL file. For example, OrderInfo has an Items property, which contains an array of PartInfo objects. Notice how this relationship is modeled in the Types section of the WSDL file via the .NET Framework XSD and Reflection classes (the bold formatting is used to highlight the Items property's reference to the PartInfo definition and the PartInfo definition itself):

```
<s:complexType name="OrderInfo">
    <s:sequence>
        <s:element minOccurs="1" maxOccurs="1" name="OrderID" type="s:int" />
        <s:element minOccurs="1" maxOccurs="1" name="Items" nillable="true">
            <s:complexType>
                <s:sequence>
                    <s:element minOccurs="0" maxOccurs="unbounded"
name="PartInfo" nillable="true" type="s0:PartInfo" />
                </s:sequence>
            </s:complexType>
        </s:element>
    </s:sequence>
</s:complexType>

<s:complexType name="PartInfo">
    <s:sequence>
        <s:element minOccurs="1" maxOccurs="1" name="PartID" type="s:int" />
        <s:element minOccurs="1" maxOccurs="1" name="PartDescription"
nillable="true" type="s:string" />
    </s:sequence>
</s:complexType>
```

If you were to create a Web Reference to this Web Service, the .NET Framework would interpret the XSD and create classes that represented the exact structure of the classes in the Web Service (OrderInfo, PartInfo, and so forth). It would even create the relationship between the two main objects (OrderInfo and PartInfo via the Items property) correctly and allow you to use these objects without worrying that they came from a Web Service.

The client calls the GetCustomers() Web method on the Page_Load event. This method returns an array of CustomerInfo objects, and then iterates through the CustomerInfo objects, calling the GetOrders() Web Method for each one. The GetOrders() method returns an array of OrderInfo objects and the code iterates through each object displaying the order information. When it gets to the PartInfo method, it iterates through each part and displays its information.

Obviously, you would not hard-code customer information into your Web Service methods. This example is presented to illustrate the technique and power of passing objects and arrays via Web Services and to show the actual SOAP messages created when the objects and arrays are serialized by the .NET Framework's SOAP architecture. In the next chapter, you'll learn how to pass ADO.NET DataSets via Web Services, which is usually the more common method for passing data to a client for display. However, this chapter sets the stage for ADO.NET DataSets via Web Services.

To follow along, please perform the following steps:

1. In Visual Studio.NET, choose File | New Project from the menu to open the New Project dialog box.

2. Select your language in the Project Types list box on the left (Visual Basic Projects or Visual C# Projects). Then select ASP.NET Web Service in the Templates list box on the right.

3. In the Name text box, type **Chapter14VB** if you are creating this project using VB.NET, or type **Chapter14CSharp** if you are using C#.

4. Accept the default location in the Location field.

5. Click the OK button. Visual Studio.NET will create a new project based on the language and template you selected.

6. In the Solution Explorer, rename Service1.asmx to ComplexTypesSample.asmx by right-clicking the file and then selecting Rename from the pop-up menu. Type the new name of the file in the text box that has the Service1.asmx filename highlighted. Press Enter on your keyboard to accept the name change.

7. Click the Show All Files icon at the top of the Solution Explorer window to display all the files that are hidden, including the Code Behind file for ComplexTypesSample.asmx.

8. The ComplexTypesSample.asmx file should now have a + sign next to it, indicating that files are hidden beneath it. Click the + to reveal ComplexTypesSample.asmx.vb (for the VB.NET version) or ComplexTypesSample.asmx.cs (for the C# version).

9. Select the ComplexTypesSample.asmx.vb or ComplexTypesSample.asmx.cs file in Solution Explorer and then click the View Code button at the top to display the Code Behind file in the main area of Visual Studio.NET. This is where you edit the Code Behind file. As you can see, Visual Studio.NET has already generated code in this file for you.

10. Enter the code in Listing 14.1 for C# and Listing 14.2 for VB.NET in the Code Behind file that's currently open. Type in only the code that is bold text in the listings. As is the convention throughout this book, the other code in the listing (not in bold type) is included as context to help you determine where your code should be entered.

11. The code for this file is separated into several listings so that each section of the code can be explained more clearly. At the appropriate times, you'll be instructed to add more code to this file.

LISTING 14.1   ComplexTypesSample.asmx.cs in C# Code

```csharp
using System;
using System.Collections;
using System.ComponentModel;
using System.Data;
using System.Diagnostics;
using System.Web;
using System.Web.Services;

namespace Chapter14CSharp
{
    public class CustomerInfo
    {
        public string FirstName;
        public string LastName;
        public string EmailAddress;
    }
    public class PartInfo
    {
        public int PartID;
        public string PartDescription;
    }
    public class OrderInfo
    {
        public int OrderID;
        public PartInfo[] Items;
    }
```

LISTING 14.2 ComplexTypesSample.asmx.vb in VB.NET Code

```vbnet
Imports System.Web.Services

Public Class CustomerInfo
    Public FirstName As String
    Public LastName As String
    Public EmailAddress As String
End Class

Public Class PartInfo
    Public PartID As Integer
    Public PartDescription As String
End Class

Public Class OrderInfo
    Public OrderID As Integer
    Public Items() As PartInfo
End Class
```

In the preceding listings, the code simply creates the classes and defines their properties. Notice that the OrderInfo class defines an Items property, which contains an array of PartInfo classes. This illustrates how to create a class that contains a collection (array) of other classes.

Continue to add code to this file, using Listing 14.3 for C# and Listing 14.4 for VB.NET.

LISTING 14.3 ComplexTypesSample.asmx.cs in C# Code

```csharp
    /// <summary>
    /// Summary description for ComplexTypesSample.
    /// </summary>
    public class ComplexTypesSample : System.Web.Services.WebService
    {
        public ComplexTypesSample()
        {
            //CODEGEN: This call is required by the ASP.NET Web Services
Designer
            InitializeComponent();
        }
        #region Component Designer generated code
        /// <summary>
        /// Required method for Designer support - do not modify
        /// the contents of this method with the code editor.
```

LISTING 14.3   Continued

```csharp
        /// </summary>
        private void InitializeComponent()
        {
        }
    #endregion

    /// <summary>
    /// Clean up any resources being used.
    /// </summary>
    public override void Dispose()
    {
    }


    [
    WebMethod
    ]
    public CustomerInfo[] GetCustomers()
    {
        CustomerInfo[] customers = new CustomerInfo[2];
        customers[0] = new CustomerInfo();
        customers[0].FirstName = "David";
        customers[0].LastName = "Findley";
        customers[0].EmailAddress = "david@technicallead.com";

        customers[1] = new CustomerInfo();
        customers[1].FirstName = "Bob";
        customers[1].LastName = "Tabor";
        customers[1].EmailAddress = "bob@technicallead.com";

        return customers;
    }
```

LISTING 14.4   ComplexTypesSample.asmx.vb in VB.NET Code

```vbnet
Public Class ComplexTypesSample
    Inherits System.Web.Services.WebService

#Region " Web Services Designer Generated Code "

    Public Sub New()
        MyBase.New()

        'This call is required by the Web Services Designer.
        InitializeComponent()
```

14

LISTING 14.4 Continued

```
        'Add your own initialization code after the InitializeComponent() call

    End Sub


    'Required by the Web Services Designer
    Private components As System.ComponentModel.Container

    'NOTE: The following procedure is required by the Web Services Designer
    'It can be modified using the Web Services Designer.
    'Do not modify it using the code editor.
    <System.Diagnostics.DebuggerStepThrough()> Private Sub
InitializeComponent()
        components = New System.ComponentModel.Container()
    End Sub


    Protected Overloads Overrides Sub Dispose(ByVal disposing As Boolean)
        'CODEGEN: This procedure is required by the Web Services Designer
        'Do not modify it using the code editor.
    End Sub

#End Region

    <WebMethod()> Public Function GetCustomers() As CustomerInfo()
        Dim customers(1) As CustomerInfo
        customers(0) = New CustomerInfo()
        customers(0).FirstName = "David"
        customers(0).LastName = "Findley"
        customers(0).EmailAddress = "david@technicallead.com"

        customers(1) = New CustomerInfo()
        customers(1).FirstName = "Bob"
        customers(1).LastName = "Tabor"
        customers(1).EmailAddress = "bob@technicallead.com"

        GetCustomers = customers
    End Function
```

In the preceding listings, you are creating a Web method that returns an array of CustomerInfo classes. This method manually creates two instances of the CustomerInfo class that the customers[] collection will reference. You then set the properties for each of the instances of that class.

Continue to add code to this file, using Listing 14.5 for C# and Listing 14.6 for VB.NET.

LISTING 14.5 ComplexTypesSample.asmx.cs in C# Code

```csharp
[
WebMethod
]
public OrderInfo[] GetOrders(CustomerInfo customer)
{
    OrderInfo[] orders = null;

    switch (customer.EmailAddress)
    {
    case "david@technicallead.com":
        orders = new OrderInfo[2];
        orders[0] = new OrderInfo();
        orders[0].OrderID = 1;
        orders[0].Items = new PartInfo[1];
        orders[0].Items[0] = new PartInfo();
        orders[0].Items[0].PartID = 1;
        orders[0].Items[0].PartDescription = "Managing Microsoft .NET
Web Farms";

        orders[1] = new OrderInfo();
        orders[1].OrderID = 2;
        orders[1].Items = new PartInfo[1];
        orders[1].Items[0] = new PartInfo();
        orders[1].Items[0].PartID = 2;
        orders[1].Items[0].PartDescription = "Microsoft .NET Web
Services";
        break;

    case "bob@technicallead.com":
        orders = new OrderInfo[1];
        orders[0] = new OrderInfo();
        orders[0].OrderID = 3;
        orders[0].Items = new PartInfo[2];
        orders[0].Items[0] = new PartInfo();
        orders[0].Items[0].PartID = 1;
        orders[0].Items[0].PartDescription = "Managing Microsoft .NET
Web Farms";
        orders[0].Items[1] = new PartInfo();
        orders[0].Items[1].PartID = 2;
        orders[0].Items[1].PartDescription = "Microsoft .NET Web
Services";
        break;
    }
    return orders;
    }
  }
}
```

LISTING 14.6   ComplexTypesSample.asmx.vb in VB.NET Code

```
    <WebMethod()> Public Function GetOrders(ByVal customer As CustomerInfo) As
OrderInfo()
        Dim orders() As OrderInfo
        Select Case customer.EmailAddress
            Case "david@technicallead.com"
                ReDim orders(1)
                orders(0) = New OrderInfo()
                orders(0).OrderID = 1
                ReDim orders(0).Items(0)
                orders(0).Items(0) = New PartInfo()
                orders(0).Items(0).PartID = 1
                orders(0).Items(0).PartDescription = "Managing Microsoft .NET" & _
"Web Farms"

                orders(1) = New OrderInfo()
                orders(1).OrderID = 2
                ReDim orders(1).Items(0)
                orders(1).Items(0) = New PartInfo()
                orders(1).Items(0).PartID = 2
                orders(1).Items(0).PartDescription = "Microsoft .NET Web" & _
"Services"
            Case "bob@technicallead.com"
                ReDim orders(0)
                orders(0) = New OrderInfo()
                orders(0).OrderID = 3
                ReDim orders(0).Items(1)
                orders(0).Items(0) = New PartInfo()
                orders(0).Items(0).PartID = 1
                orders(0).Items(0).PartDescription = "Managing Microsoft .NET" & _
"Web Farms"
                orders(0).Items(1) = New PartInfo()
                orders(0).Items(1).PartID = 2
                orders(0).Items(1).PartDescription = "Microsoft .NET Web" & _
"Services"
        End Select

        GetOrders = orders
    End Function
End Class
```

The preceding listings create another Web method. This class method is slightly more complicated than the previous one. It returns an array of OrderInfo classes (referred to as orders[])
and proceeds to populate each of the orders based on the customer.EmailAddress that was
sent to the Web method as a parameter. Each order contains an Items property, which contains

an array of `PartInfo` objects. The code then illustrates setting the `PartInfo` properties of each of the items in the array, and returning the `orders[]` array back to the Web Service consumer.

Creating the Web Service Client

Now it is time to create a Web Service consumer that will use the Web methods you saw in the previous section. If you are following along on this project, perform these next steps:

1. Compile the Web Service by choosing Build | Build Solution from the menu. If there were any problems during the build, make sure you typed the code exactly as it appears in the listings. Remember that many code elements are case sensitive in .NET.

2. Create a Web Reference within the same project to the Web Service that was just created. To do this, right-click the Chapter14VB (or Chapter14CSharp) project file in Solution Explorer and select the Add Web Reference item from the pop-up menu. The Add Web Reference dialog box opens.

3. In this dialog box, click the Web References on Local Web Server link at the bottom of the window on the left-hand side. After a moment, the Available References list box will refresh. Select the Chapter14VB (or Chapter14CSharp) entry to refresh the Available References list again.

4. In the Available References list, select ComplexTypesSample.asmx and click the Add Reference button at the bottom of the dialog box. After a moment, the dialog box closes and Solution Explorer will refresh with the new Web Reference added. (A localhost entry will appear under Web References in Solution Explorer. You can expand it more to see the WSDL file named ComplexTypesSample.wsdl by clicking the + sign next to localhost. You can expand it once more to see the proxy class named ComplexTypesSample.vb by clicking the + sign next to the WSDL file.)

Next, you will create an ASP.NET Web Form that will send and retrieve values from the Web Service you just built:

1. Right-click the Chapter14VB (or Chapter14CSharp) project file, and choose Add | Add Web Form from the pop-up menu to open the Add New Item dialog box.

2. In the Add New Item dialog box, change the name of the new ASP.NET Web Form to ComplexTypesSampleClient.aspx.

3. Click the Open button. The Add New Item dialog box closes, and after a moment, the Solution Explorer window will refresh, displaying the addition of the new file. Also, in the main area of the IDE, the Web Form Designer appears for the new ComplexTypesSampleClient.aspx Web Form.

4. Place a `Label` control from the Toolbox and set its `ID` property to `divOutput` in the Properties window.

5. Double-click the Web Form Designer to access the Code Behind module for this page (ComplexTypesSampleClient.aspx.cs for C# or ComplexTypesSampleClient.aspx.vb for VB.NET). A code window will appear in the main area of the IDE.

6. Enter the code in Listing 14.7 for C# and Listing 14.8 for VB.NET in the Code Behind file that's currently open. Type in only the code that is bold text in the listings. As is the convention throughout this book, the other code in the listings (not in bold type) is included as context to help you determine where your code should be entered.

Most of the "action" for this client happens in the Page_Load event. As the page loads, you access the Web Service to get each of the customers by calling the GetCustomers() Web method. The code iterates through the array of CustomerInfo objects that are returned and then some of the information is formatted and inserted into the divOutput label. Next, the GetOrders() Web method is called and the code iterates through each OrderInfo object and the related array of PartInfo classes that are returned. The information is then formatted and inserted into the divOutput label.

LISTING 14.7   ComplexTypesSampleClient.aspx.cs in C# Code

```csharp
using System;
using System.Collections;
using System.ComponentModel;
using System.Data;
using System.Drawing;
using System.Web;
using System.Web.SessionState;
using System.Web.UI;
using System.Web.UI.WebControls;
using System.Web.UI.HtmlControls;

namespace Chapter14CSharp
{
    /// <summary>
    /// Summary description for ComplexTypesSampleClient.
    /// </summary>
    public class ComplexTypesSampleClient : System.Web.UI.Page
    {
        protected System.Web.UI.WebControls.Label divOutput;

        public ComplexTypesSampleClient()
        {
            Page.Init += new System.EventHandler(Page_Init);
        }
```

LISTING 14.7 Continued

```
        private void Page_Load(object sender, System.EventArgs e)
        {
            // Call the web service to get the customer information
            localhost.ComplexTypesSample ctsample = new
localhost.ComplexTypesSample();
            localhost.CustomerInfo[] customers = ctsample.GetCustomers();

            for (int i=0; i<customers.Length; i++)
            {
                localhost.CustomerInfo customer = customers[i];
                divOutput.Controls.Add(new LiteralControl(
                        "<B>" + customer.FirstName + " " + customer.LastName +
"</B> <I>(" + customer.EmailAddress + ")</I><BR>"
                        ));

                // call the web service and get the orders for a particular
customer
                localhost.OrderInfo[] orders = ctsample.GetOrders(customer);
                for (int oi=0; oi<orders.Length; oi++)
                {
                    localhost.OrderInfo order = orders[oi];
                    divOutput.Controls.Add(new LiteralControl("Order: " +
order.OrderID + "<BR>"));

                    for (int pi=0; pi<order.Items.Length; pi++)
                    {
                        localhost.PartInfo part = order.Items[pi];
                        divOutput.Controls.Add(new
LiteralControl(part.PartDescription + "<BR>"));
                    }
                }

                divOutput.Controls.Add(new LiteralControl("<BR><HR>"));
            }
        }

        private void Page_Init(object sender, EventArgs e)
        {
            //
            // CODEGEN: This call is required by the ASP.NET Windows Form
Designer.
            //
            InitializeComponent();
        }
```

LISTING 14.7 Continued

```csharp
#region Web Form Designer generated code
    /// <summary>
    /// Required method for Designer support - do not modify
    /// the contents of this method with the code editor.
    /// </summary>
    private void InitializeComponent()
    {
        this.Load += new System.EventHandler(this.Page_Load);
    }
#endregion
    }
}
```

LISTING 14.8 ComplexTypesSampleClient.aspx.vb in VB.NET Code

```vbnet
Imports System.Web.UI

Public Class ComplexTypesSampleClient
    Inherits System.Web.UI.Page

    Protected divOutput As System.Web.UI.WebControls.Label

#Region " Web Form Designer Generated Code "

    'This call is required by the Web Form Designer.
    <System.Diagnostics.DebuggerStepThrough()> Private Sub
InitializeComponent()

    End Sub

    Private Sub Page_Init(ByVal sender As System.Object, ByVal e As
System.EventArgs) Handles MyBase.Init
        'CODEGEN: This method call is required by the Web Form Designer
        'Do not modify it using the code editor.
        InitializeComponent()
    End Sub

#End Region

    Private Sub Page_Load(ByVal sender As System.Object, ByVal e As
System.EventArgs) Handles MyBase.Load
        ' Call the web service to get the customer information
        Dim ctsample As New localhost.ComplexTypesSample()
```

LISTING 14.8 Continued

```vbnet
        Dim customers() As localhost.CustomerInfo
        customers = ctsample.GetCustomers()

        Dim i As Integer
        For i = 0 To customers.Length - 1
            Dim customer As localhost.CustomerInfo
            customer = customers(i)
            divOutput.Controls.Add(New LiteralControl("<B>" + _
customer.FirstName + " " + customer.LastName + "</B> <I>(" + _
customer.EmailAddress + ")</I><BR>"))

            ' call the web service and get the orders for a particular customer
            Dim orders() As localhost.OrderInfo
            orders = ctsample.GetOrders(customer)

            Dim oi As Integer
            For oi = 0 To orders.Length - 1
                Dim order As localhost.OrderInfo
                order = orders(oi)
                divOutput.Controls.Add(New LiteralControl("Order: " + _
order.OrderID.ToString + "<BR>"))

                Dim pi As Integer
                For pi = 0 To order.Items.Length - 1
                    Dim part As localhost.PartInfo
                    part = order.Items(pi)
                    divOutput.Controls.Add(New _
LiteralControl(part.PartDescription + "<BR>"))
                Next
            Next

            divOutput.Controls.Add(New LiteralControl("<BR><HR>"))
        Next
    End Sub

End Class
```

14

To continue, follow these steps:

1. Compile the code by choosing Build | Build from the menu. If there were any problems during the build, make sure you typed the code exactly as it appears in the listings. Remember that many things are case sensitive in .NET.

2. Right-click the ComplexTypeSampleClient.aspx file, and select View In Browser. You should see the screen in Figure 14.2.

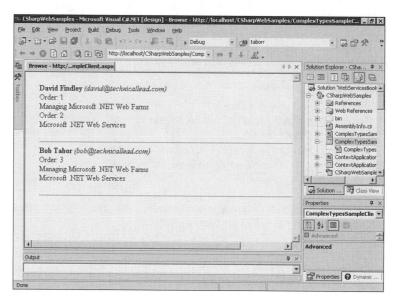

FIGURE 14.2

Results of the Complex Types sample client.

If you use a SOAP extension to watch the SOAP messages as they are sent back and forth between the client and the Web Service, you can gain insight into how this example worked. (You'll learn more about SOAP extensions in Chapter 24, "Using SOAP Extensions.")

The SOAP message is the request for the `GetCustomers()` method:

```xml
<?xml version="1.0" encoding="utf-8"?>
<soap:Envelope xmlns:soap="http://schemas.xmlsoap.org/soap/envelope/"
xmlns:xsi="http://www.w3.org/2001/XMLSchema-instance"
xmlns:xsd="http://www.w3.org/2001/XMLSchema">
  <soap:Body>
    <GetCustomers xmlns="http://tempuri.org/" />
  </soap:Body>
</soap:Envelope>
```

The `GetCustomers()` method returns an XML envelope that contains what can be compared to an array of `CustomerInfo` objects:

```xml
<?xml version="1.0" encoding="utf-8"?>
<soap:Envelope xmlns:soap="http://schemas.xmlsoap.org/soap/envelope/"
xmlns:xsi="http://www.w3.org/2001/XMLSchema-instance"
xmlns:xsd="http://www.w3.org/2001/XMLSchema">
  <soap:Body>
    <GetCustomersResponse xmlns="http://tempuri.org/">
      <GetCustomersResult>
```

```
    <CustomerInfo>
      <FirstName>David</FirstName>
      <LastName>Findley</LastName>
      <EmailAddress>david@technicallead.com</EmailAddress>
    </CustomerInfo>
    <CustomerInfo>
      <FirstName>Bob</FirstName>
      <LastName>Tabor</LastName>
      <EmailAddress>bob@technicallead.com</EmailAddress>
    </CustomerInfo>
      </GetCustomersResult>
    </GetCustomersResponse>
  </soap:Body>
</soap:Envelope>
```

Notice that there is nothing "magical" about the SOAP or the array of CustomerInfo objects. It is simple XML. Most of the power comes from how the proxy on the client interprets this XML, creates two instances of the CustomerInfo object, and hydrates those objects with all this data.

As the consumer begins to iterate through the array of CustomerInfo objects, it calls the GetOrders Web method, passing in an instance of the CustomerInfo object for the current customer:

```
<?xml version="1.0" encoding="utf-8"?>
<soap:Envelope xmlns:soap="http://schemas.xmlsoap.org/soap/envelope/"
xmlns:xsi="http://www.w3.org/2001/XMLSchema-instance"
xmlns:xsd="http://www.w3.org/2001/XMLSchema">
  <soap:Body>
    <GetOrders xmlns="http://tempuri.org/">
      <customer>
        <FirstName>David</FirstName>
        <LastName>Findley</LastName>
        <EmailAddress>david@technicallead.com</EmailAddress>
      </customer>
    </GetOrders>
  </soap:Body>
</soap:Envelope>
```

Again, although an object is being sent via a Web Service request, simple XML is actually being transmitted. The .NET Framework XSD classes turn this XML into an object based on the CustomerInfo class definition. Finally, the GetOrders Web method returns an array of OrderInfo objects, each with an array of PartInfo objects.

```
<?xml version="1.0" encoding="utf-8"?>
<soap:Envelope xmlns:soap="http://schemas.xmlsoap.org/soap/envelope/"
xmlns:xsi="http://www.w3.org/2001/XMLSchema-instance"
```

14

PASSING COMPLEX
DATA TYPES AND
STRUCTURES

```
xmlns:xsd="http://www.w3.org/2001/XMLSchema">
  <soap:Body>
    <GetOrdersResponse xmlns="http://tempuri.org/">
      <GetOrdersResult>
        <OrderInfo>
          <OrderID>1</OrderID>
          <Items>
            <PartInfo>
              <PartID>1</PartID>
              <PartDescription>Managing Microsoft .NET Web
Farms</PartDescription>
            </PartInfo>
          </Items>
        </OrderInfo>
        <OrderInfo>
          <OrderID>2</OrderID>
          <Items>
            <PartInfo>
              <PartID>2</PartID>
              <PartDescription>Microsoft .NET Web Services</PartDescription>
            </PartInfo>
          </Items>
        </OrderInfo>
      </GetOrdersResult>
    </GetOrdersResponse>
  </soap:Body>
</soap:Envelope>
```

Admittedly, the preceding SOAP message is a little more complex because the data therein describes a complex data structure. However, it is still relatively easy to understand (and the indention levels help you see the simplicity of the message).

The message of this exercise is clear: Passing complex structures and data types is made simple as a result of the .NET Framework and Visual Studio.NET.

Passing XML via Web Services

As strange as it might sound, you can send entire XML documents or individual nodes via Web Services. Why would you want to do this? You might need to allow consumers to pass unknown or undefined XML structures to your Web Service, and then perform some parsing on that XML document (such as XSLT, XPath, and so forth) . This method becomes a "variant" of Web Services, enabling your consumers to send individual values, entire classes, or whatever they dream up to the Web Service. Listings 14.9 and 14.10 consist of three methods in the XmlSample class that illustrate how to work with XML in Web Services. Here's a brief description of the methods used in the listings:

- **GetXmlNode**   Creates and returns an XML node via the Web Service.

- **GetXmlNodeInAClass**   Creates an instance of a class, adds an XML node to one of its members, and then sends it back via the Web Service.

- **AggregateDocuments**   Accepts two XML documents as parameters, adds them together, and then returns them via the Web Service.

This example is provided without a Web Form client to call it and without detailed instructions on how to build it. The purpose is to show you what's possible, but because I don't recommend this approach (see the discussion after the listings), I'm not going to facilitate your use of this technique. If you absolutely must try it on your own, you can use the instructions from earlier in the chapter to build it.

LISTING 14.9   Code Listing for XmlSample.asmx.cs in C#

```csharp
using System;
using System.Collections;
using System.ComponentModel;
using System.Data;
using System.Diagnostics;
using System.Web;
using System.Web.Services;
using System.Xml;
using System.Xml.Xsl;
using System.Xml.Serialization;

namespace CSharpWebSamples
{

    public class AuthorInfo
    {
        public string FirstName;
        public string LastName;
        public string EmailAddress;
        public XmlNode EmbeddedMessage;
    }

    /// <summary>
    /// Summary description for XmlSample.
    /// </summary>
    ///
    public class XmlSample : System.Web.Services.WebService
    {
        public XmlSample()
        {
```

LISTING 14.9   Continued

```
        //CODEGEN: This call is required by the ASP.NET Web Services
Designer
        InitializeComponent();
    }

    #region Component Designer generated code
    /// <summary>
    /// Required method for Designer support - do not modify
    /// the contents of this method with the code editor.
    /// </summary>
    private void InitializeComponent()
    {
    }
    #endregion

    /// <summary>
    /// Clean up any resources being used.
    /// </summary>
    public override void Dispose()
    {
    }

    [
        WebMethod
    ]
    public XmlNode GetXmlNode()
    {
        XmlDocument doc = new XmlDocument();
        XmlNode oNode = doc.CreateElement("Message");
        oNode.InnerText = "Hello, World";

        return oNode;
    }

    [
        WebMethod
    ]
    public AuthorInfo GetXmlNodeInAClass()
    {
        XmlDocument doc = new XmlDocument();
        XmlNode oNode = doc.CreateElement("Message");
        oNode.InnerText = "Hello, World";
```

LISTING 14.9   Continued

```
            AuthorInfo info = new AuthorInfo();
            info.FirstName = "David";
            info.LastName = "David";
            info.EmailAddress = "david@technicallead.com";
            info.EmbeddedMessage = oNode;

            return info;
        }

        [
        WebMethod
        ]
        public XmlNode AggregateDocuments(string name, XmlNode one, XmlNode
two)
        {
            XmlDocument doc = new XmlDocument();
            XmlNode oNode = doc.CreateElement(name);
            oNode.AppendChild(one);
            oNode.AppendChild(two);
            return doc;
        }
    }
}
```

LISTING 14.10   Code Listing for XmlSample.asmx.vb in VB.NET

```
Imports System.Web.Services
Imports System.Xml

Public Class AuthorInfo
    Public FirstName As String
    Public LastName As String
    Public EmailAddress As String
    Public EmbeddedMessage As XmlNode
End Class

Public Class XmlSample
    Inherits System.Web.Services.WebService

#Region " Web Services Designer Generated Code "

    Public Sub New()
        MyBase.New()
```

LISTING 14.10 Continued

```
        'This call is required by the Web Services Designer.
        InitializeComponent()

        'Add your own initialization code after the InitializeComponent() call

    End Sub


    'Required by the Web Services Designer
    Private components As System.ComponentModel.Container

    'NOTE: The following procedure is required by the Web Services Designer
    'It can be modified using the Web Services Designer.
    'Do not modify it using the code editor.
    <System.Diagnostics.DebuggerStepThrough()> Private Sub
InitializeComponent()
        components = New System.ComponentModel.Container()
    End Sub

    Protected Overloads Overrides Sub Dispose(ByVal disposing As Boolean)
        'CODEGEN: This procedure is required by the Web Services Designer
        'Do not modify it using the code editor.
    End Sub

#End Region

    <WebMethod()> Public Function GetXmlNode() As XmlNode
        Dim doc As New XmlDocument()
        Dim oNode As XmlNode
        oNode = doc.CreateElement("Message")
        oNode.InnerText = "Hello, World"
        GetXmlNode = oNode
    End Function

    <WebMethod()> Public Function GetXmlNodeInAClass() As AuthorInfo
        Dim doc As New XmlDocument()
        Dim oNode As XmlNode
        oNode = doc.CreateElement("Message")
        oNode.InnerText = "Hello, World"

        Dim info As New AuthorInfo()
        info.FirstName = "David"
        info.LastName = "Findley"
        info.EmailAddress = "david@technicallead.com"
        info.EmbeddedMessage = oNode
```

14

PASSING COMPLEX
DATA TYPES AND
STRUCTURES

LISTING 14.10   Continued

```
        GetXmlNodeInAClass = info
    End Function

    <WebMethod()> Public Function AggregateDocuments(ByVal name As String, _
ByVal one As XmlNode, ByVal two As XmlNode) As XmlNode
        Dim doc As New XmlDocument()
        Dim oNode As XmlNode
        oNode = doc.CreateElement(name)
        oNode.AppendChild(one)
        oNode.AppendChild(two)
        AggregateDocuments = doc
    End Function
End Class
```

The most interesting (if not academic) aspect of these examples is looking at the WSDL and SOAP messages that are produced. First, look at how the XMLNode object is defined for the GetXmlNode method in the WDSL file:

```
<s:element name="GetXmlNodeResponse">
    <s:complexType>
        <s:sequence>
            <s:element minOccurs="1" maxOccurs="1" name="GetXmlNodeResult"
nillable="true">
                <s:complexType mixed="true">
                    <s:sequence>
                        <s:any />
                    </s:sequence>
                </s:complexType>
            </s:element>
        </s:sequence>
    </s:complexType>
</s:element>
```

The term "any" is used when describing a data type of XMLNode, indicating that the Web Service will literally accept anything you pass it.

You might be thinking that you have found a loophole in Web Services--that you can create your Web Services to accept XMLNodes or XMLDocuments (or strings, for that matter). Then, if your client isn't careful and passes a parameter of the wrong type to your Web Service, you can handle it gracefully within your Web Service instead of it being bounced back automatically to your client because it's the wrong type. (You might want to refer back to Chapter 10, "Exceptions and Error Handling," to review some of the details on this subject.) Although it's true that XML is the variant of Web Services, as stated earlier, this "loophole" method is considered bad form. In this case, you would be circumventing the whole purpose of WSDL: to allow a client-side proxy to be created that is strongly typed and "early bound" to the Web Service's data. I recommend that you trust clients of your Web Service to thoroughly test their code, to perform validation before they send values to your Web Service, and to dutifully handle exceptions returned from your Web Service. Of course, I won't be the one who gets calls from Web Service clients when they fail to implement your Web Service correctly. Therefore, you'll have to judge for yourself how "idiot-proof" you want to make your Web Service.

The following SOAP message is returned from the `GetXmlNode` Web method:

```
<?xml version="1.0" encoding="utf-8" ?>
<AnyNode xmlns="http://tempuri.org/">
    <Message xmlns="">Hello, World</Message>
</AnyNode>
```

The actual SOAP message is also interesting because .NET automatically names the `Node` object as `AnyNode`, containing a sole element called `Message` (a name I provided). Contrast this to the following SOAP message from the `GetXMLNodeInAClass` Web method:

```
<?xml version="1.0" encoding="utf-8" ?>
<AuthorInfo xmlns:xsi="http://www.w3.org/2001/XMLSchema-instance"
    xmlns:xsd="http://www.w3.org/2001/XMLSchema"
    xmlns="http://tempuri.org/">
    <FirstName>David</FirstName>
    <LastName>David</LastName>
    <EmailAddress>david@technicallead.com</EmailAddress>
    <EmbeddedMessage>
        <Message xmlns="">Hello, World</Message>
    </EmbeddedMessage>
</AuthorInfo>
```

Summary

.NET Web Services allow you to pass objects of all types and structures to Web Service consumers, and vice versa. The .NET Framework has classes that interpret class structures, including arrays of classes and XML, and that create XSD schemas that represent those classes. The XSD is encoded into WSDL files, and the client of the Web Service uses the WSDL file to create proxy classes that mirror the original classes found in the Web Service. This method allows developers who consume Web Services to concentrate on developing functionality rather than worrying about the minutiae of interpreting the XSD and the WSDL file and creating proxy classes manually.

In this chapter, you created an example illustrating how to pass objects and arrays of objects via Web Services, including catching a sneak peek at the SOAP messages that were passed behind the scenes. Also, you created an example that passed XML via Web Services, illustrating how flexible Web Services can be. Be careful not to overuse XML in your Web Services because it circumvents the process of discovery.

Passing ADO.NET DataSets via Web Services

IN THIS CHAPTER

One of the most highly anticipated uses of Web Services is the ability of trading partners to be able to exchange data. Because most corporate data resides in a relational database, Microsoft needed to develop a data access technology that allows a completely disconnected structure, while still enabling changes to that data to be merged back into the original data source—and at the same time, avoiding the inevitable problems of concurrency, data locking, update collisions, and so forth.

The "programmable Web" is the sweet spot for both Web Services and ADO.NET DataSets. As you will learn in this chapter, DataSets seem to have been developed with Web Services in mind, and Microsoft has made it incredibly easy to pass DataSets to and from Web Services, serializing them into SOAP-based XML messages. After a .NET client application receives these messages, they can be rehydrated and deserialized back into DataSets to benefit from ADO.NET's rich object model. If these messages are consumed by a non-Microsoft application, they can be treated just like any other XML document. The concepts discussed in this chapter represent some of the most important in the book.

A thorough discussion of ADO.NET data access is beyond the scope of this book, so this chapter focuses on the feature of ADO.NET—namely, DataSets—that will help you realize the purpose and promise of Web Services. I'll assume that you have some familiarity with concepts such as connecting to a database, creating command objects, and obtaining Recordsets from your "classic" ADO days. The new ADO.NET objects are explained as they're used in this chapter's examples, but I would encourage you to read the Visual Studio help files (or purchase one of the many upcoming books that focus on ADO.NET).

Web Services, DataSets, and a New Disconnected Architecture

Imagine a scenario in which Company A provides a partner relationship management functionality via Web Services. Imagine also that affiliates use this service to request information about customers and enter updated information about those customers in the data repository (SQL Server or Oracle, for example). Company B is an affiliate whose sales representative is calling Company A's customers to offer them a promotion. A set of data about a customer from Company A's Web Services is exchanged with a client application in Company B's environment. After the sales representative has updated information about the customer including the contact history and has added a sales record, the customer record is sent back to a Web Service in Company A's environment that accepts the changes and writes them back to the data repository.

In another scenario, a disconnected set of data is passed through a series of Web Services and distributed components inside and outside a company's environment to manage and process a series of sales transactions. When the process is completed, the dataset is passed to a data repository that takes each of the data updates, deletions, and additions and writes them to a data repository.

You may be familiar with ActiveX Data Objects (ADO) from creating ASP or Visual Basic 6.0 (and earlier) applications. If you are, then you might have already used ADO Recordsets in a disconnected fashion, sending the object from an MTS/COM+ component to an ASP page and back. The benefit of this method was that it freed up connections to the database while the code processed the data. After the processing was finished, you merged that data back into the database—albeit in a code-intensive manner because you had to write the plumbing to check and handle update collisions. Concurrency issues, such as update collisions, occurred when one instance of an application for User A (or a component, an end user, or other software) requested a record. Then User B (or a component) requested the record and made changes, and those changes were merged back to the database. User A then tries to save her changes to the database and is not aware of the changes User B made. Concurrency issues frequently arise, and there are several standard (and homegrown) solutions for handling these situations.

Microsoft engineered the next generation of the disconnected Recordset, now called a DataSet in ADO.NET, to make this process somewhat easier. Additionally, the DataSet is marshaled across the network as XML/SOAP, so it is efficient and open to many additional non-Microsoft–based clients. Therefore, you could deliver a DataSet to a Linux box running Java (or possibly C# on Linux in the not-too-distant future), which would handle the DataSet as a simple XML document.

Understanding DataSets

DataSets are not a one-to-one mapping of the ADO Recordset. As noted, they are more akin to one type of Recordset: the disconnected Recordset. It is important to note that using the DataSet increases overhead, so if you do not need to pass data in a disconnected manner via Web Services or through distributed components, it would be to your advantage to use the ADO.NET DataReader. The DataReader is best used when you want a fast, "firehose," forward-only method of accessing data from a data source. For example, if you are merely writing data to a Web page, the DataReader is ideal.

The DataSet is significant because it blurs the line between treating data relationally (the traditional tables, rows, and columns approach) and hierarchically (the traditional XML DOM approach). No special commands are needed to serialize a DataSet into XML or to create a DataSet from XML.

The DataSet is very flexible. You can create a DataSet without a data source by creating a blank DataSet object, and then adding tables, columns, and rows of data. (See the section "The DataSetSample Example" later in this chapter for a step-by-step look at this procedure.) Or you could create an XSD (an XML Schema Definition) using the XSD Designer in Visual Studio .NET or Notepad to create it by hand. The resulting XSD can be loaded into the DataSet, which translates it into a tables-and-columns structure. The XSD can be given to a trading partner or used internally as an extensible standard for exchanging a certain type of business data.

Typically, you obtain data from a database such as SQL Server and pass it to a trading partner via your Web Service. To do this, you must accomplish the following steps:

1. A connection to a data source must be made via a *data provider*, which is an implementation of the underlying plumbing needed to connect to a database (or other data source, such as a proprietary file format). Microsoft offers these two data providers (others can be created by database or file format vendors based on the Microsoft specification):

   - The System.Data.SQLClient (formally called the "SQL Server .NET Data Provider") provides an optimized engine for interacting with SQL Server.
   - The System.Data.OleDb (formally called the "OLE DB .NET Data Provider") should be used to access other databases via ODBC.

   Each data provider must provide implementations for the Connection, Command, DataAdapter, and DataReader objects suited for its respective data source, so you must use the correct set of these objects based on the data provider you selected for your application.

2. A data query must be issued to the data source, and the data is then returned from the data source to the DataReader object. This procedure is accomplished in one of two ways:

   - If you are using stored procedures, using a DataCommand is definitely the best choice because it gives you control over setting input and output parameters (through the Parameters object). After the command is issued, the data can be captured into a DataReader object.
   - You can also use a DataAdapter object to issue a query, although its true value is in updating the data source (see the following section, "The DataAdapter Object").

   If you are coding inline SQL (in other words, composing the SQL statements in the source code of your application instead of using a predefined query that resides elsewhere, such as a stored procedure or query), you can use either the DataCommand or the DataAdapter to issue the query statement.

3. You then translate the data from the data source into a usable format. You can use the `DataReader` object if all you need is to navigate one way through the result set, or the `DataSet` object if you need a more flexible mechanism that can be fully navigated and serialized for completely disconnected use.

At a minimum, these steps are necessary to retrieve data from a data source. What about writing data back to the database? The `System.Data` namespace also comes with an object called the `DataAdapter`. It appears to be quite an appealing utility, as it provides a useful way to merge the changes made to a disconnected result set back to the data source.

The DataAdapter Object

The `DataAdapter` object was created to provide a structured method of saving changes made to a DataSet back to the original data source. If you are using the `DataAdapter`'s `Update` method and passing in a DataSet (or a `DataTable` or `DataRow` collection), the `Update` method looks through the DataSet and resolves the updated data, the deleted data, and the inserted data back to the data source. How does it know how to do this? Can it determine where to save changes back to the data source based on the DataSet's original query? Well, yes and no.

Before calling the `Update` method, you must manually or automatically populate the `UpdateCommand`, `InsertCommand`, and `DeleteCommand` properties with SQL statements or stored procedures. If the original `SELECT` query involved multiple tables, you need to supply these statements manually. If, however, your `SELECT` query is simple, such as `SELECT * FROM MyTable`, you can use the `CommandBuilder` to create these statements automatically. (See the section "The DataSetRoundTrip Example" later in this chapter for an example of using this approach.) When the `Update` method is called on the `DataAdapter`, it then looks through the DataSet for changes. Each change is recorded in the DataSet until the `Update` method is called and the DataSet is refreshed.

DataTables and DataRelations of the DataSet

To prepare for the upcoming examples, you should be aware of some other DataSet features. DataSets contain one or more `DataTables`, and a `DataTable` contains the `Columns` (or structure of the data) and the `Rows` (instances of the column collection), much as the ADO Recordset did in the past. Each `DataTable` in a DataSet can come from different data sources and even different data providers! Relational constraints between `DataTables` can then be enforced by creating `DataRelations`. These constraints enable some level of consistency checking while updates, deletes, and insertions are being made to the DataSet. As students of the Web Service, this feature is important because it provides a built-in mechanism to protect the data's integrity in the DataSet while it is disconnected from its original source. The Web Service consumer, or current user of the DataSet, will receive an exception if any insert, update, or delete commands that violate the DataSet's relational constraint are attempted.

Again, I would encourage you to spend some time learning more about DataSets, especially in regards to DataTables, DataRelations, and the other accompanying data objects because these topics are outside the scope of this book.

The DataSetSample Example

Barry (any resemblance to individuals living or dead is purely coincidental) is very passionate about his musical tastes. He publishes his weekly favorites on his Web site for everyone who is interested (and from his perspective, *everyone* cares about his opinions on music—and every other topic, for that matter).

The first example is a Web Service that constructs a DataSet's structure (table and columns) from scratch using code. Then it populates the DataSet with hard-coded data. The DataSet is returned to the Web Service consumer, an ASP.NET Web Form, and is then databound to a DataGrid control for display. This example illustrates the following concepts:

- How to construct a DataSet from scratch without a data source
- How to pass a DataSet via a Web Service
- How to databind a DataGrid to a totally disconnected DataSet

To follow along, please perform the following steps:

1. In Visual Studio .NET, choose File | New | Project from the menu to open the New Project dialog box.
2. Select your language in the Project Types list box on the left (Visual Basic Projects or Visual C# Projects), and then select ASP.NET Web Service in the Templates list box on the right.
3. In the Name text box, type **Chapter15VB** (if you are creating this project using VB .NET) or **Chapter15CSharp** (for C#).
4. Accept the default location in the Location field.
5. Click the OK button. Visual Studio .NET will create a new project based on the language and template you selected.
6. In Solution Explorer, rename Service1.asmx as DataSetSample.asmx by right-clicking the file, and then choosing Rename on the pop-up menu. Type the new name of the file in the text box that has the Service1.asmx filename highlighted, and then press Enter.
7. Click the Show All Files icon at the top of the Solution Explorer window to display all the hidden files, including the Code Behind file for DataSetSample.asmx.
8. Click the + sign next to the DataSetSample.asmx file to reveal the DataSetSample.asmx.vb (for VB .NET) or DataSetSample.asmx.cs (for C#) file.

9. Select the DataSetSample.asmx.vb or DataSetSample.asmx.cs file in Solution Explorer, and then click the View Code button at the top of the Solution Explorer window to display the Code Behind file in the main area of Visual Studio .NET, where you'll edit the Code Behind file. As you can see, Visual Studio .NET has already generated code in this file.

10. Type the code in Listing 15.1 for VB .NET or Listing 15.2 for C# into the Code Behind file that's currently open. Type in only the code formatted in bold in the listings. As is the convention throughout this book, the other code in the listing (not formatted in bold type) is included as context to help you determine where to enter your code.

This example uses two methods. `CreateDataSet`, which is protected within the current namespace, is a help function that handles the dirty work of actually creating the DataSet's structure from scratch. It does this by creating a new instance of the `System.Data.DataSet` object, and then adding a table and creating its columns. The second method, `GetBarrysMediaCollection`, is adorned with the `WebMethodAttribute` and is accessible publicly in the Web Service. This method returns a DataSet that is populated with hard-coded values.

LISTING 15.1 DataSetSample.asmx.vb for VB .NET

```vb
Imports System.Web.Services

Public Class DataSetSample
    Inherits System.Web.Services.WebService

#Region " Web Services Designer Generated Code "

    Public Sub New()
        MyBase.New()

        'This call is required by the Web Services Designer.
        InitializeComponent()

        'Add your own initialization code after the InitializeComponent() call

    End Sub

    'Required by the Web Services Designer
    Private components As System.ComponentModel.Container

    'NOTE: The following procedure is required by the Web Services Designer
    'It can be modified using the Web Services Designer.
    'Do not modify it using the code editor.
    <System.Diagnostics.DebuggerStepThrough()> Private Sub
InitializeComponent()
```

LISTING 15.1   Continued

```
        components = New System.ComponentModel.Container()
    End Sub

    Protected Overloads Overrides Sub Dispose(ByVal disposing As Boolean)
        'CODEGEN: This procedure is required by the Web Services Designer
        'Do not modify it using the code editor.
    End Sub

#End Region


    Protected Function CreateDataSet() As DataSet
        Dim ds As New DataSet("BarrysMediaCollection")
        Dim dt = New DataTable("FavoriteCDs")
        dt.Columns.Add(New DataColumn("Artist", Type.GetType("System.String")))
        dt.Columns.Add(New DataColumn("Album", Type.GetType("System.String")))
        ds.Tables.Add(dt)
        CreateDataSet = ds
    End Function

    <WebMethod()> Public Function GetBarrysMediaCollection() As DataSet
        Dim ds As DataSet = CreateDataSet()
        Dim row As DataRow

        row = ds.Tables(0).NewRow()
        row("Artist") = "Ratt"
        row("Album") = "Ratt & Roll"
        ds.Tables(0).Rows.Add(row)

        row = ds.Tables(0).NewRow()
        row("Artist") = "Warrant"
        row("Album") = "Cherry Pie"
        ds.Tables(0).Rows.Add(row)

        row = ds.Tables(0).NewRow()
        row("Artist") = "Winger"
        row("Album") = "In The Heart Of The Young"
        ds.Tables(0).Rows.Add(row)


        GetBarrysMediaCollection = ds
    End Function

End Class
```

LISTING 15.2   DataSetSample.asmx.cs for C#

```csharp
using System;
using System.Collections;
using System.ComponentModel;
using System.Data;
using System.Diagnostics;
using System.Web;
using System.Web.Services;

namespace Chapter15CSharp
{
    /// <summary>
    /// Summary description for DataSetSample.
    /// </summary>
    public class DataSetSample : System.Web.Services.WebService
    {
        public DataSetSample()
        {
            //CODEGEN: This call is required by the ASP.NET Web Services
Designer
            InitializeComponent();
        }

        #region Component Designer generated code
        /// <summary>
        /// Required method for Designer support - do not modify
        /// the contents of this method with the code editor.
        /// </summary>
        private void InitializeComponent()
        {
        }
        #endregion

        /// <summary>
        /// Clean up any resources being used.
        /// </summary>
        protected override void Dispose( bool disposing )
        {
        }

        protected DataSet CreateDataSet()
        {
            DataSet ds = new DataSet("BarrysMediaCollection");
            DataTable dt = new DataTable("FavoriteCDs");
            dt.Columns.Add(new DataColumn("Artist", typeof(string)));
```

LISTING 15.2   Continued

```
        dt.Columns.Add(new DataColumn("Album", typeof(string)));
        ds.Tables.Add(dt);
        return ds;
    }

    [WebMethod]
    public DataSet GetBarrysMediaCollection()
    {
        DataSet ds = CreateDataSet();
        DataRow row;

        row = ds.Tables[0].NewRow();
        row["Artist"]    = "Ratt";
        row["Album"]     = "Ratt & Roll";
        ds.Tables[0].Rows.Add(row);

        row = ds.Tables[0].NewRow();
        row["Artist"] = "Warrant";
        row["Album"]     = "Cherry Pie";
        ds.Tables[0].Rows.Add(row);

         row = ds.Tables[0].NewRow();
         row["Artist"] = "Winger";
         row["Album"] = "In The Heart Of The Young";
         ds.Tables[0].Rows.Add(row);

        return ds;
    }
  }
}
```

Constructing a DataSet

As mentioned earlier, DataSets are composed of one or more Tables. Even if you have just one table of data, you must still go through the Tables collection as you traverse the DataSet. This is a change from the ADO Recordset, which assumed one Recordset by default, and then allowed you to move to the next Recordset if one existed. After the table is added, new columns must be added by specifying the column name and data type.

After that information is in place, the rows of data can be added to the DataSet. A new instance of a Row is created based on the columns that the row will "belong to." The rows reference the columns and set values, and then are added to the Rows collection.

Finally, the DataSet is returned from the Web Service to the consumer. It is at this point that the DataSet is serialized into XML for transmission via a SOAP package. Based on the tables and columns, an XSD is inferred and the data is serialized accordingly. An alternative is loading an existing XSD in the `CreateDataSet` method, and then using it in the same manner by adding rows to the DataSet.

Now that you have the Web Service finished, you can test it in the Web Service help page. Compile the Web Service by choosing Build | Build Solution from the menu. If there were any problems during the build, make sure you typed the code exactly as it appears in the listing. And remember, many things are case sensitive in .NET.

Building the Client

The next step is to build a client Web Form that can consume the Web Service and display the values in the DataSet. To do that, follow these steps:

1. Create a Web reference in the same project as the Web Service you just created. To do this, right-click the Chapter15VB (or Chapter15CSharp) project file in Solution Explorer, and choose Add Web Reference on the pop-up menu to open the Add Web Reference dialog box.

2. In this dialog box, click the `Web References on Local Web Server` link at the bottom to refresh the Available References list box, and then select the Chapter15VB (or Chapter15CSharp) entry to refresh this list again.

3. In the Available References list, select DataSetSample.asmx, and click the Add Reference button at the bottom. The dialog box closes, and the new Web reference is displayed in Solution Explorer. (A localhost entry will appear under Web References in the Solution Explorer. You can expand it to see the WSDL file named DataSetSample.wsdl, and then expand this file to see the proxy class named DataSetSample.vb.)

4. Add a new ASP.NET Web Form to the project by right-clicking the Chapter15VB (or Chapter15CSharp) project in Solution Explorer and choosing Add Web Form on the pop-up menu to open the Add New Item dialog box.

5. In the Add New Item dialog box, change the name of the new ASP.NET Web Form to DataSetSampleClient.aspx.

6. Click the Open button. The Add New Item dialog box closes, and the new file is displayed in Solution Explorer. Also, in the main area of the IDE, the Web Form Designer appears for the new DataSetSampleClient.aspx Web Form.

7. A design surface for the DataSampleClient.aspx Web Form appears in the main IDE area. Drag and drop a `DataGrid` control from the Toolbox onto this form. Do not set any additional properties for the `DataGrid`.

8. Add a `Label` control from the Toolbox to the DataSampleClient.aspx design surface, and set its `Text` property to `Barry's Favorite CDs`. Figure 15.1 illustrates the design surface after adding the Web controls.

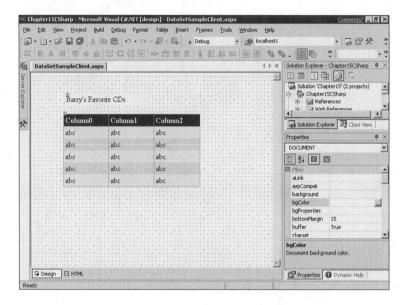

FIGURE 15.1
ASP.NET Web Form's design surface.

9. Double-clicking on the design surface of the Web Form brings up the Code Behind's `Page_Load` event, where you type the code in Listings 15.3 and 15.4. Make sure you enter only the code formatted in bold.

LISTING 15.3 DataSetSampleClient.aspx.vb for VB .NET

```
Public Class DataSetSampleClient
    Inherits System.Web.UI.Page
    Protected WithEvents Label1 As System.Web.UI.WebControls.Label
    Protected WithEvents DataGrid1 As System.Web.UI.WebControls.DataGrid

#Region " Web Form Designer Generated Code "

    'This call is required by the Web Form Designer.
    <System.Diagnostics.DebuggerStepThrough()> Private Sub
InitializeComponent()

    End Sub
```

LISTING 15.3 Continued

```vb
    Private Sub Page_Init(ByVal sender As System.Object, ByVal e As
System.EventArgs) Handles MyBase.Init
        'CODEGEN: This method call is required by the Web Form Designer
        'Do not modify it using the code editor.
        InitializeComponent()
    End Sub

#End Region

    Private Sub Page_Load(ByVal sender As System.Object, ByVal e As
System.EventArgs) Handles MyBase.Load
        If Not IsPostBack Then
            Dim sample As New localhost.DataSetSample()
            Dim ds As DataSet = sample.GetBarrysMediaCollection()
            DataGrid1.DataSource = ds
            DataGrid1.DataBind()
        End If
    End Sub
End Class
```

LISTING 15.4 DataSetSampleClient.aspx.cs for C#

```csharp
using System;
using System.Collections;
using System.ComponentModel;
using System.Data;
using System.Drawing;
using System.Web;
using System.Web.SessionState;
using System.Web.UI;
using System.Web.UI.WebControls;
using System.Web.UI.HtmlControls;

namespace CSharpWebSamples
{
    /// <summary>
    /// Summary description for DataSetSampleClient.
    /// </summary>
    public class DataSetSampleClient : System.Web.UI.Page
    {
        protected System.Web.UI.WebControls.Label Label1;
        protected System.Web.UI.WebControls.DataGrid DataGrid1;
```

LISTING 15.4   Continued

```csharp
public DataSetSampleClient()
{
    Page.Init += new System.EventHandler(Page_Init);
}

private void Page_Load(object sender, System.EventArgs e)
{
    // Put user code to initialize the page here
    if (!IsPostBack)
    {
        localhost.DataSetSample sample = new localhost.DataSetSample();
        DataSet ds = sample.GetBarrysMediaCollection();
        DataGrid1.DataSource = ds;
        DataGrid1.DataBind();
    }
}

private void Page_Init(object sender, EventArgs e)
{
    //
    // CODEGEN: This call is required by the ASP.NET Web Form Designer.
    //
    InitializeComponent();
}

#region Web Form Designer generated code
/// <summary>
/// Required method for Designer support - do not modify
/// the contents of this method with the code editor.
/// </summary>
private void InitializeComponent()
{
    this.Load += new System.EventHandler(this.Page_Load);
}
#endregion
    }
}
```

Next, compile the code by choosing Build | Build Solution from the menu. If there were any problems during the build, make sure you typed the code exactly as it appears in the code listing (remember that many code elements are case sensitive).

Right-click the DataSetSampleClient.aspx file, and choose View In Browser. You should see the screen pictured in Figure 15.2.

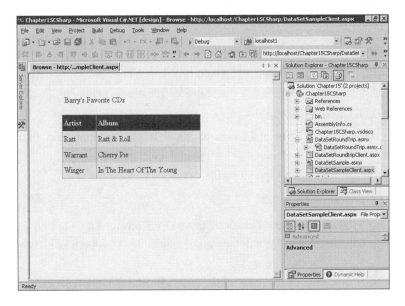

FIGURE 15.2
Results of the DataSetSampleClient example.

Databinding to a DataSet

The meat of the previous code listings is in the Page_Load event, where the call to the Web Service is issued and the DataSet is retrieved. The DataGrid's DataSource property is set to the DataSet, and then the DataGrid's DataBind method is called. At that point, the data in the DataSet is displayed in the grid.

This is a fairly simple example, but it illustrates some important concepts. First, it shows how the .NET Framework hides a lot of the complexity of serializing the DataSet into an XML format, and then deserializing it back to a DataSet that maintains its ability to be used in databinding—or just about any other function the DataSet supports.

The DataSetRoundTrip Example

The second example in this chapter is more involved, and probably comes closer to what you will do in your own Web Services used to share your company's data with a trading partner. This example uses the SQL Server .NET Data Provider to access the Northwind database, which SQL Server installs by default. (It is also installed when using the Microsoft Data Engine, or MSDE, which is provided when installing the .NET Framework examples.) This database represents a fictitious company's customer, sales, and product data. A customer list is shared with a trading partner by querying the database, and the result set is placed into a DataSet. The DataSet is then transported via a Web Service call to a Web Form that traverses the DataSet, writing one record's data to the page. What's more interesting is that the Web Form modifies one of the DataSet's records and passes the DataSet back via another Web Service called SaveCustomers. After the code examples, you'll see a discussion of how changes to the DataSet are maintained and what happens as those changes are written back to the database. This example illustrates the following concepts:

- How to obtain a DataSet from a data source such as SQL Server
- How to use the `DataAdapter` and `CommandBuilder` to quickly implement automatic updates to a DataSet
- How to navigate through a DataSet on the client

To follow along, perform these steps:

1. In Solution Explorer, right-click on the Chapter15VB project (or Chapter15CSharp project), and choose Add Web Form on the pop-up menu to open the Add New Item dialog box.

2. In this dialog box, change the name of the new ASP.NET Web Service to DataSetRoundTrip.asmx.

3. Click the Open button. The Add New Item dialog box closes, and the new file is displayed in Solution Explorer. Also, in the main area of the IDE, the Web Service design surface appears for the new DataSetRoundTrip.asmx Web Form.

4. Double-click the design surface and view the underlying Code Behind file for this Web Service. Next, enter the code in Listing 15.5 or 15.6. Type in only the code formatted in bold in the listings.

LISTING 15.5   DataSetRoundTrip.asmx.vb for VB .NET

```vb
Imports System.Web.Services
Imports System.Data.SqlClient

Public Class DataSetRoundtrip
    Inherits System.Web.Services.WebService

Protected nwindConn as SqlConnection = _
        New SqlConnection("Data Source=localhost;" & _
        "Integrated Security=SSPI;Catalog=northwind")

    Protected custDA As SqlDataAdapter
    Protected custCB As SqlCommandBuilder

#Region " Web Services Designer Generated Code "

    Public Sub New()
        MyBase.New()
```

LISTING 15.5   Continued

```
        'This call is required by the Web Services Designer.
        InitializeComponent()

        'Add your own initialization code after the InitializeComponent() call

        nwindConn.Open()
        custDA = New SqlDataAdapter("SELECT * FROM Customers", nwindConn)
        custCB = New SqlCommandBuilder(custDA)

    End Sub

    'Required by the Web Services Designer
    Private components As System.ComponentModel.Container

    'NOTE: The following procedure is required by the Web Services Designer
    'It can be modified using the Web Services Designer.
    'Do not modify it using the code editor.
    <System.Diagnostics.DebuggerStepThrough()> Private Sub
InitializeComponent()
        components = New System.ComponentModel.Container()
    End Sub

    Protected Overloads Overrides Sub Dispose(ByVal disposing As Boolean)
        'CODEGEN: This procedure is required by the Web Services Designer
        'Do not modify it using the code editor.
    End Sub

#End Region

    <WebMethod()> Public Function GetCustomers() As DataSet
        Dim workDS As DataSet = New DataSet()
        custDA.Fill(workDS, "CustTable")
        GetCustomers = workDS
    End Function

    <WebMethod()> Public Function SaveCustomers(ByVal workDS As DataSet) As
String
        Dim modRows As DataRow() = workDS.Tables(0).Select(Nothing, Nothing, _
                              DataViewRowState.ModifiedCurrent)
         custDA.Update(modRows)
        SaveCustomers = modRows(0).Item(0).ToString
    End Function

End Class
```

LISTING 15.6   DataSetRoundTrip.asmx.cs for C#

```csharp
using System;
using System.Collections;
using System.ComponentModel;
using System.Data;
using System.Diagnostics;
using System.Web;
using System.Web.Services;
using System.Data.SqlClient;

namespace Chapter15CSharp
{
    /// <summary>
    /// Summary description for DataSetRoundTrip.
    /// </summary>
    public class DataSetRoundTrip : System.Web.Services.WebService
    {
        protected SqlConnection nwindConn = new SqlConnection("Data
Source=localhost;Integrated Security=SSPI;Initial Catalog=northwind");
        protected SqlDataAdapter custDA;
        protected SqlCommandBuilder custCB;

        public DataSetRoundTrip()
        {
            //CODEGEN: This call is required by the ASP.NET Web Services
Designer
            InitializeComponent();

            nwindConn.Open();
            custDA = new SqlDataAdapter("SELECT * FROM Customers", nwindConn);
            custCB = new SqlCommandBuilder(custDA);

        }

        #region Component Designer generated code
        /// <summary>
        /// Required method for Designer support - do not modify
        /// the contents of this method with the code editor.
        /// </summary>
        private void InitializeComponent()
        {
        }
        #endregion
```

LISTING 15.6 Continued

```csharp
/// <summary>
/// Clean up any resources being used.
/// </summary>
protected override void Dispose( bool disposing )
{
}

[WebMethod()]
public DataSet GetCustomers()
{
    DataSet workDS = new DataSet();
    custDA.Fill(workDS, "CustTable");
    return workDS;
}

[WebMethod]
public string SaveCustomers(DataSet workDS)
{
    DataRow[] modRows = workDS.Tables[0].Select(null, null,
DataViewRowState.ModifiedCurrent);
    custDA.Update(modRows);
    return modRows[0][0].ToString();
}

    }
}
```

Make sure you compile your Web Service, and then right-click on your project and add a new Web reference to this Web Service by navigating through the Add Web Reference dialog box. Again, for more information on this procedure, please refer to Chapter 5.

Continue by following these steps:

1. Compile the Web Service by choosing Build | Build on the menu. If there were any problems during the build, make sure you typed the code correctly (and remember to check for case-sensitive code elements).

2. Create a Web reference in the same project as the Web Service you just created. To do this, right-click the Chapter15VB (or Chapter15CSharp) project file in Solution Explorer, and choose Add Web Reference to open the Add Web Reference dialog box.

3. In this dialog box, click the Web References on Local Web Server link, and then select the Chapter15VB (or Chapter15CSharp) entry in the Available References list box.

4. After the Available References list is updated, select DataSetRoundTrip.asmx, and click the Add Reference button. The new Web references are then displayed in Solution Explorer. (You can expand the localhost1 entry under Web References in Solution Explorer to see the WSDL file DataSetRoundTrip.wsdl, and then expand this WSDL file to see the DataSetRoundTrip.vb proxy class.)

> **NOTE**
>
> There is one important issue to keep in mind. As you add a second Web Service from the same source (localhost) as an existing Web Service, Visual Studio .NET appends a numerical value starting with 1 and ascending for each subsequent Web Service you add from that same source. I prefer to keep all the proxies under the original source (localhost). To do that, you right-click the WSDL file for the new Web reference (localhost1) and choose Cut on the pop-up menu. Then right-click the original Web reference (localhost), and choose Paste. Delete the new Web reference (localhost1) by right-clicking it and choosing Delete. Finally, open the proxy file, which has the extension .wsdl.vb or .wsdl.cs, and change all references from localhost1 to localhost.

Before stepping through the Web methods, take a look at some significant code elements in the constructor of the DataSetRoundTrip class. This is where you open the connection to the data source, set the DataAdapter's query statement, and use the automatic population of the DataAdapter's UpdateCommand, InsertCommand, and DeleteCommand by using the CommandBuilder. Otherwise, you would need to set these properties manually by using three separate SQL statements or stored procedure references. These statements are placed in the constructor because they are necessary for both the GetCustomers and SaveCustomers Web methods. You could just as easily (although redundantly) have placed these statements in each of those methods.

The GetCustomers Web method fills the DataSet with data as a result of the DataAdapter's query from the constructor. The DataSet is then returned to the consumer of the Web Service.

The SaveCustomers Web method accepts a DataSet as an input parameter and uses the DataTable's Select method to find any Row objects that have been modified. These selected rows are sent to the DataAdapter's Update method, where each row is examined and the InsertCommand, UpdateCommand, or DeleteCommand is issued. Finally, the first column of the first row is returned simply as a sanity check to make sure the changes were actually made.

Building the DataSetRoundTripClient

To test this Web Service, you can create an ASP.NET Web Form client that does the following:

- Obtains the DataSet from the GetCustomers Web method
- Displays some information about the DataSet
- Makes some changes, and then sends the DataSet back to the SaveCustomers Web method
- Displays the result of the SaveCustomers Web method to confirm that the Update method worked

To continue, follow these steps:

1. Right-click the Chapter15VB (or Chapter15CSharp) project file, and choose Add Web Form.
2. In the Add New Item dialog box, change the name of the new ASP.NET Web Form to DataSetRoundTripClient.aspx.
3. Click the Open button. The Add New Item dialog box closes, and the new file is displayed in Solution Explorer. Also, in the main area of the IDE, the Web Form design surface appears for the new DataSetRoundTripClient.aspx Web Form.
4. Double-click the design surface to access the Code Behind module for this page (DataSetRoundTripClient.aspx.cs for C# or DataSetRoundTripClient.aspx.vb for VB .NET). A code window will appear in the main IDE area.
5. Type the code formatted in bold in Listing 15.7 for VB .NET or Listing 15.8 for C# into the Code Behind file that's currently open.

LISTING 15.7   DataSetRoundTripClient.aspx.vb for VB .NET

```
Public Class DataSetRoundtripClient
    Inherits System.Web.UI.Page

    Protected wsCustomers As localhost.DataSetRoundtrip = New
localhost.DataSetRoundtrip()

#Region " Web Form Designer Generated Code "

    'This call is required by the Web Form Designer.
    <System.Diagnostics.DebuggerStepThrough()> Private Sub
InitializeComponent()

    End Sub
```

LISTING 15.7   Continued

```
    Private Sub Page_Init(ByVal sender As System.Object, ByVal e As
System.EventArgs) Handles MyBase.Init
        'CODEGEN: This method call is required by the Web Form Designer
        'Do not modify it using the code editor.
        InitializeComponent()
    End Sub

#End Region

    Private Sub Page_Load(ByVal sender As System.Object, ByVal e As
System.EventArgs) Handles MyBase.Load

        Dim workDS As System.Data.DataSet
        Dim workColumn As System.Data.DataColumn

        workDS = wsCustomers.GetCustomers()

        Dim workRow As System.Data.DataRow = workDS.Tables(0).Rows(0)

        For Each workColumn In workDS.Tables(0).Columns
            Response.Write(workColumn.ColumnName & ": ")

            If TypeOf (workRow(workColumn.ColumnName)) Is DBNull Then
                Response.Write("<br>")
            Else
                Response.Write(workRow(workColumn.ColumnName) & "<br>")
            End If
        Next

        workDS.Tables(0).Rows(0).Item(1) = "Barely Blooms Flowershop"
        workDS.Tables(0).Rows(0).Item(2) = "Stephen Pearcy"

        Dim sValue As String = wsCustomers.SaveCustomers(workDS)

        Response.Write("<p>The return value was: " & sValue)

    End Sub

End Class
```

LISTING 15.8   DataSetRoundTripClient.aspx.cs for C#

```csharp
using System;
using System.Collections;
using System.ComponentModel;
using System.Data;
using System.Drawing;
using System.Web;
using System.Web.SessionState;
using System.Web.UI;
using System.Web.UI.WebControls;
using System.Web.UI.HtmlControls;

namespace Chapter15CSharp
{
    /// <summary>
    /// Summary description for DataSetRoundtripClient.
    /// </summary>
    public class DataSetRoundtripClient : System.Web.UI.Page
    {
        protected localhost.DataSetRoundTrip wsCustomers = new
localhost.DataSetRoundTrip();

        public DataSetRoundtripClient()
        {
            Page.Init += new System.EventHandler(Page_Init);
        }

        private void Page_Load(object sender, System.EventArgs e)
        {
            DataSet workDS;

            workDS = wsCustomers.GetCustomers();

            DataRow workRow = workDS.Tables[0].Rows[0];

            foreach (DataColumn workColumn in workDS.Tables[0].Columns)
            {
                Response.Write(workColumn.ColumnName + ": ");

                if (workRow.IsNull(workColumn.ColumnName))
                {
                    Response.Write("<br>");
                }
                else
                {
```

LISTING 15.8 Continued

```
                    Response.Write(workRow[workColumn.ColumnName] + "<br>");
            }

        }

        workDS.Tables[0].Rows[0][1] = "Barely Blooms Flowershop";
        workDS.Tables[0].Rows[0][2] = "Stephen Pearcy";

        string sValue = wsCustomers.SaveCustomers(workDS);

        Response.Write("<p>The return value was: " + sValue);

    }

    private void Page_Init(object sender, EventArgs e)
    {
        //
        // CODEGEN: This call is required by the ASP.NET Web Form Designer.
        //
        InitializeComponent();
    }

    #region Web Form Designer generated code
    /// <summary>
    /// Required method for Designer support - do not modify
    /// the contents of this method with the code editor.
    /// </summary>
    private void InitializeComponent()
    {
        this.Load += new System.EventHandler(this.Page_Load);
    }
    #endregion
    }
}
```

Next, compile the code by choosing Build | Build Solution on the menu. If any errors happen during the build, make sure you typed the code exactly as it appears in the code listing.

Right-click the ComplexTypeSampleClient.aspx file. and choose View In Browser. You should see the screen pictured in Figure 15.3.

Your data values might be different, depending on the original state of your Northwind database. Because I've run this example several times, I'm sure mine will look different from yours. The next step is to view the records in your database to make sure the Update command actually worked (see Figure 15.4).

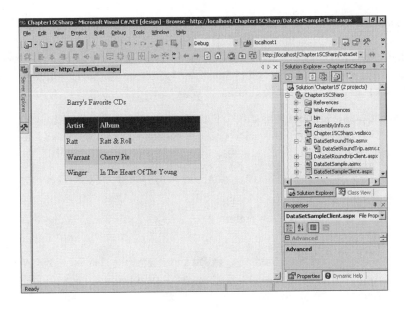

FIGURE 15.3

Results of running the DataSetRoundTrip Web Form.

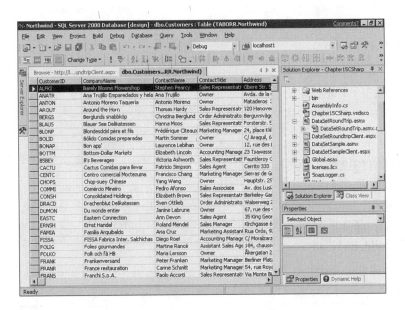

FIGURE 15.4

Results of querying the Customers table in the Northwind database.

All the excitement of this Web Form happens in the Page_Load event. This is where the GetCustomers Web Method retrieves the DataSet (workDS), and then begins looping through and displaying the column name and values for the first row of data. One "gotcha" to watch for is ensuring that a given value is not set to DBNull before attempting to use Response.Write with it. This would cause an error at runtime in your project.

Next, some data in the DataSet is modified. Note that only the ordinal numeric value is used to reference specific items in the Tables and Columns collections. You could also reference them by their names, as shown here:

```
workDS.Tables("CustTable").Rows(0).Item("CompanyName") = "Barely Blooms
Flowershop"
```

Using the collection's names is often preferred because it's a self-documenting method, but the stylistic option is yours.

Finally, the SaveCustomers Web Method is called and returns the DataSet to the Web Service and displays the resulting CustomerID. Something important happens here: As the DataSet gets serialized and sent back to the SaveCustomer Web method, there must be a way for the DataSet to communicate that some of its data has changed. If the DataSet can't articulate this to the DataAdapter, the DataAdapter won't know which rows to update back to the data source. Sure, the DataAdapter could reissue the SELECT command, compare each record, and determine the differences, but that would be an extremely expensive process in terms of code. Instead, this responsibility is delegated to the DataSet. The DataSet keeps track of the changes, and when it is serialized into XML, the changes are represented as DiffGrams. The DataSet keeps the data's original and current versions as well as each row's RowState (Added, Modified, Deleted, Unchanged, Detached), and the resulting DiffGrams reflect each version of the data as well as its RowState (see the section "Understanding DiffGrams" later in this chapter).

Monitoring the Results

To further illustrate what is happening in the previous example, review the SOAP excerpt in Listing 15.9 that was captured as the Web Service was running. This SOAP message is the call to SaveCustomers, which sends the modified DataSet. The entire SOAP message is interesting (although perhaps a little hard to read), but focus in particular on the bold text in the following listing.

LISTING 15.9 SOAP Listing

```
<?xml version="1.0" encoding="utf-8"?>
<soap:Envelope xmlns:soap="http://schemas.xmlsoap.org/soap/envelope/"
xmlns:xsi="http://www.w3.org/2001/XMLSchema-instance"
xmlns:xsd="http://www.w3.org/2001/XMLSchema">
```

LISTING 15.9   Continued

```
<soap:Body>
  <SaveCustomers xmlns="http://tempuri.org/">
    <workDS>
      <xsd:schema id="NewDataSet" targetNamespace="" xmlns=""
xmlns:xsd="http://www.w3.org/2001/XMLSchema" xmlns:msdata="urn:schemas-
microsoft-com:xml-msdata">
        <xsd:element name="NewDataSet" msdata:IsDataSet="true">
          <xsd:complexType>
            <xsd:choice maxOccurs="unbounded">
              <xsd:element name="CustTable">
                <xsd:complexType>
                  <xsd:sequence>
                    <xsd:element name="CustomerID" type="xsd:string"
minOccurs="0" />
                    <xsd:element name="CompanyName" type="xsd:string"
minOccurs="0" />
                    <xsd:element name="ContactName" type="xsd:string"
minOccurs="0" />
                    <xsd:element name="ContactTitle" type="xsd:string"
minOccurs="0" />
                    <xsd:element name="Address" type="xsd:string"
minOccurs="0" />
                    <xsd:element name="City" type="xsd:string" minOccurs="0"
/>
                    <xsd:element name="Region" type="xsd:string"
minOccurs="0" />
                    <xsd:element name="PostalCode" type="xsd:string"
minOccurs="0" />
                    <xsd:element name="Country" type="xsd:string"
minOccurs="0" />
                    <xsd:element name="Phone" type="xsd:string" minOccurs="0"
/>
                    <xsd:element name="Fax" type="xsd:string" minOccurs="0"
/>
                  </xsd:sequence>
                </xsd:complexType>
              </xsd:element>
            </xsd:choice>
          </xsd:complexType>
        </xsd:element>
      </xsd:schema>
      <diffgr:diffgram xmlns:msdata="urn:schemas-microsoft-com:xml-msdata"
xmlns:diffgr="urn:schemas-microsoft-com:xml-diffgram-v1">
        <NewDataSet xmlns="">
          <CustTable diffgr:id="CustTable1" msdata:rowOrder="0"
diffgr:hasChanges="modified">
```

LISTING 15.9   Continued

```
      <CustomerID>ALFKI</CustomerID>
      <CompanyName>Barely Blooms Flowershop</CompanyName>
      <ContactName>Stephen Pearcy</ContactName>
      <ContactTitle>Sales Representative</ContactTitle>
      <Address>Obere Str. 57</Address>
      <City>Berlin</City>
      <PostalCode>12209</PostalCode>
      <Country>Germany</Country>
      <Phone>030-0074321</Phone>
      <Fax>030-0076545</Fax>
    </CustTable>
    <CustTable diffgr:id="CustTable2" msdata:rowOrder="1">
      <CustomerID>ANATR</CustomerID>
      <CompanyName>Ana Trujillo Emparedados y helados</CompanyName>
      <ContactName>Ana Trujillo</ContactName>
      <ContactTitle>Owner</ContactTitle>
      <Address>Avda. de la Constitución 2222</Address>
      <City>México D.F.</City>
      <PostalCode>05021</PostalCode>
      <Country>Mexico</Country>
      <Phone>(5) 555-4729</Phone>
      <Fax>(5) 555-3745</Fax>
    </CustTable>
       .
       .
       .

    <CustTable diffgr:id="CustTable93" msdata:rowOrder="92">
      <CustomerID>WOLZA</CustomerID>
      <CompanyName>Wolski  Zajazd</CompanyName>
      <ContactName>Zbyszek Piestrzeniewicz</ContactName>
      <ContactTitle>Owner</ContactTitle>
      <Address>ul. Filtrowa 68</Address>
      <City>Warszawa</City>
      <PostalCode>01-012</PostalCode>
      <Country>Poland</Country>
      <Phone>(26) 642-7012</Phone>
      <Fax>(26) 642-7012</Fax>
    </CustTable>
  </NewDataSet>
  <diffgr:before>
    <CustTable diffgr:id="CustTable1" msdata:rowOrder="0" xmlns="">
      <CustomerID>ALFKI</CustomerID>
      <CompanyName>TechnicalLead</CompanyName>
      <ContactName>Bob Tabor</ContactName>
```

LISTING 15.9   Continued

```
            <ContactTitle>Sales Representative</ContactTitle>
            <Address>Obere Str. 57</Address>
            <City>Berlin</City>
            <PostalCode>12209</PostalCode>
            <Country>Germany</Country>
            <Phone>030-0074321</Phone>
            <Fax>030-0076545</Fax>
          </CustTable>
        </diffgr:before>
      </diffgr:diffgram>
    </workDS>
  </SaveCustomers>
 </soap:Body>
</soap:Envelope>
```

Notice that this SOAP message contains two versions of the same row of data: the modified version of the row and the original value of the row. This is what's referred to as a DiffGram.

Understanding DiffGrams

A *DiffGram* is an XML serialization format that includes the original and current data of an element as well as a unique identifier that associates the original and current versions with one another. In this case, the `CustTable1` ID identifies the original row's data (in the `<diffgr:before>` element near the bottom of Listing 15.9) and the current data (in the `<NewDataSet>` element near the top of Listing 15.9).

After this DiffGram is received by the `SaveCustomers` Web method, the DiffGram XML is deserialized back into a DataSet (complete with the `RowState` information and multiple versions of the data rows,) and the `Update` method can perform the appropriate action on each row.

Although it's not illustrated in Listings 15.5 and 15.6, the `Update` method can raise exceptions when a concurrency or update collision occurs. Although this process is not handled completely by ADO.NET, it does much of the dirty work by determining how the changes affect the current state of the data in relation to its original state. For example, if Consumer A obtains the DataSet, and Consumer B obtains the same DataSet, makes changes, and submits them back before Consumer A does, Consumer A's `DataAdapter.Update` command will not affect any records and a `DBConcurrencyException` will be thrown. If you want the `Update` to finish regardless of original values, you need to explicitly set the `UpdateCommand` for the `DataAdapter`, not rely on automatic command generation.

15

Summary

ADO.NET DataSets were engineered for the needs of a disconnected Web Service environment. DataSets are serialized into XML for easy transport to both Microsoft and non-Microsoft consumers. Data that is modified in a disconnected result set can be merged back to the original data source by using the `DataAdapter` and the DataSet. The DataSet keeps track of the changes that were made, and the `DataAdapter` dutifully commits those changes back when its `Update` method is called.

DataSets are extremely powerful and have a great deal of flexibility. You can construct them manually, from an XSD, from a relational database, or from any other data source. You can relate them together and enforce those relational constraints even while disconnected from their original data sources.

Using the Web Services Designer in Visual Studio .NET

IN THIS CHAPTER

When developing ASP.NET Web Forms in Visual Studio .NET, the importance of the designer surface is apparent. It allows visual and nonvisual components to be added easily to the Web Form. Ultimately, what happens is that references and settings are added and hidden from the developer by default in the Web Form's Code Behind module in a code section contained in the Web Form Designer Generated Code region. When the Web Form is run, those references are instanced into objects, properties are set on those objects, and visual and nonvisual elements on the Web Form come alive and perform their duties.

However, when developing ASP.NET Web Services in Visual Studio .NET, the importance of the designer surface is less obvious. Ultimately the Web Service has no visual elements, but nonvisual elements can be added to the designer, providing a RAD-like (Rapid Application Development) approach to creating instances and setting properties of objects in Server Explorer and the Toolbox. The designer surface also takes care of the sometimes gory behind-the-scenes details of creating an instance of certain resources. Certainly, you could do all this yourself if you were so inclined, but many developers will opt to become familiar with and use this aspect of Visual Studio .NET.

In this brief chapter, you will see how to use the Web Services Designer by creating a simple EventLog reader. The Web Services Designer makes creating an instance of the `EventLog` classes and their initial settings a snap, and will allow you to easily monitor the server event logs from any machine where a network trust relationship is established. The following example can be the beginnings of a Web Service that monitors the health of servers in your server farm.

The `EventLogService` Class

To see how the Web Services Designer works, you'll be working with a new project called Chapter16VB (for VB .NET code) or Chapter16CSharp (for C# code). In this project, the default Service1.asmx file is renamed as EventLogService.asmx. If you double-click the surface of the Web Services Designer, you can access the Code Behind module. This is where you change any references from the default `Service1` class to the new `EventLogService` class to match the new name of the Web Service project.

> **NOTE**
>
> For step-by-step instructions of how to create a Web Service project, rename the Web Service, and access the Code Behind module, see the examples in previous chapters of this book.

Switch back to the Web Services Designer tab and open Server Explorer, which is next to the Toolbox on the left-hand side of the screen. Navigate through Server Explorer to find the tree node that represents your machine (in my case, it's "taborr"), and then expand that node to find the Event Logs resource. It's listed along with the rest of the resources available on your computer, such as Message Queues, Databases, and System Performance information (note that the node entries in your window will no doubt look different from the ones you see in this chapter's figures).

Server Explorer serves two purposes. It allows you to drag and drop elements from the resources it contains to the designer surface of your Web Service or Web Form. This is an easy shortcut to creating references and setting properties to access that resource in code. This use is the one you're examining in this chapter. Another use of Server Explorer is to manage your machine, or other machines in your environment that you need to manage. For example, you could use Server Explorer instead of SQL Server's Enterprise Manager to manage databases on your network or on the Internet. (At the time of this writing, that feature will be available only with the Enterprise version of Visual Studio .NET.) Other management tasks include monitoring system resources or event logs.

Next, you click to select the Application child of the Event Logs node and drop it on the designer surface. Doing so automatically sets the `Application` property of the Event Logs component on your designer surface and, therefore, in code. When you're finished, the designer surface should look like Figure 16.1.

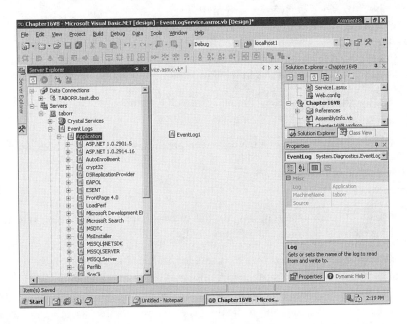

FIGURE 16.1

Dragging and dropping from Server Explorer to the designer surface.

NOTE

Objects under the Application node will vary from what you see in Figure 16.1, based on your machine configuration.

If you click to select the EventLog1 icon on the designer surface, you can review its properties in the Properties window. Because this icon was dragged and dropped from Server Explorer, several of the settings have already been made for you, a common feature of many items in Server Explorer. This feature is especially helpful when you're creating ADO.NET Connections, Commands, DataAdapters, and DataSets from Server Explorer. Although explaining how to create all those items is beyond the scope of Chapter 15, "Passing ADO.NET DataSets via Web Services," keep in mind that this is a good shortcut to writing all the code necessary to connect and work with databases.

NOTE

Note that you could use Server Explorer as I'm demonstrating in this example *or* the Toolbox's Data or Components sections to add elements to the Web Service's designer surface. The difference between these methods is that you can navigate to an actual instance of what you want to interact with when using Server Explorer and you get one or more properties filled in automatically for you when you add an item to the designer surface. Still, using the Toolbox's version of the components yields some benefit; it allows you to enter values in the Properties window instead of having to code them yourself.

In the Properties window, notice that the following properties have already been set for you:

- `Log`   Application
- `MachineName`   taborr

Next you need to set the `Source` property; for this example, it's set to BROWSER. When finished, the Properties window should look like Figure 16.2.

Now you're ready to add code to access the event log and send it back to a Web Services consumer. Double-click the designer surface to access the Code Behind module. The lines formatted in bold in Listings 16.1 and 16.2 show the code to be entered for VB .NET or C#, respectively. Much of the code is automatically generated for you by Visual Studio .NET, but the entire code is presented here for context as you enter the examples yourself.

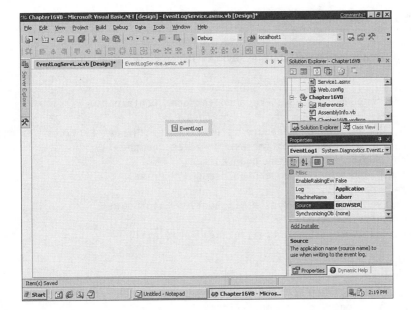

FIGURE 16.2

Setting the Source property in the Properties window.

LISTING 16.1   EventLogService.asmx.vb in VB .NET

```vb
Imports System.Web.Services
Public Class EventLogService
    Inherits System.Web.Services.WebService

    Public Class EventLogEntry
        Public Message As String
        Public EventID As Integer
    End Class

#Region " Web Services Designer Generated Code "

    Public Sub New()
        MyBase.New()

        'This call is required by the Web Services Designer.
        InitializeComponent()

        'Add your own initialization code after the InitializeComponent() call
```

LISTING 16.1   Continued

```vb
    End Sub
    Friend WithEvents EventLog1 As System.Diagnostics.EventLog

    'Required by the Web Services Designer
    Private components As System.ComponentModel.Container

    'NOTE: The following procedure is required by the Web Services Designer
    'It can be modified using the Web Services Designer.
    'Do not modify it using the code editor.
    <System.Diagnostics.DebuggerStepThrough()> Private Sub
InitializeComponent()
        Me.EventLog1 = New System.Diagnostics.EventLog()
        CType(Me.EventLog1,
System.ComponentModel.ISupportInitialize).BeginInit()
        '
        'EventLog1
        '
        Me.EventLog1.Log = "Application"
        Me.EventLog1.MachineName = "taborr"
        Me.EventLog1.Source = "BROWSER"
        CType(Me.EventLog1, System.ComponentModel.ISupportInitialize).EndInit()

    End Sub

    Protected Overloads Overrides Sub Dispose(ByVal disposing As Boolean)
        'CODEGEN: This procedure is required by the Web Services Designer
        'Do not modify it using the code editor.
    End Sub

#End Region

    <WebMethod()> Public Function GetEventLog(ByVal iEventNumber As Integer) As _
EventLogEntry

        Dim eventlogentry As EventLogEntry = New EventLogEntry()

        eventlogentry.EventID = EventLog1.Entries.Item(iEventNumber).EventID
        eventlogentry.Message = EventLog1.Entries.Item(iEventNumber).Message

        GetEventLog = eventlogentry

    End Function

End Class
```

LISTING 16.2 EventLogService.asmx.cs in C#

```csharp
using System;
using System.Collections;
using System.ComponentModel;
using System.Data;
using System.Diagnostics;
using System.Web;
using System.Web.Services;

namespace Chapter16CSharp
{
    /// <summary>
    /// Summary description for Service1.
    /// </summary>
    public class EventLogService : System.Web.Services.WebService
    {
        private System.Diagnostics.EventLog eventLog1;

        public class EventLogEntry
        {
            public string Message;
            public int EventID;
        }


        public EventLogService()
        {
            //CODEGEN: This call is required by the ASP.NET Web Services
Designer
            InitializeComponent();
        }

        #region Component Designer generated code
        /// <summary>
        /// Required method for Designer support - do not modify
        /// the contents of this method with the code editor.
        /// </summary>
        private void InitializeComponent()
        {
            this.eventLog1 = new System.Diagnostics.EventLog();

((System.ComponentModel.ISupportInitialize)(this.eventLog1)).BeginInit();
            //
            // eventLog1
            //
```

LISTING 16.2 Continued

```
        this.eventLog1.Log = "Application";
        this.eventLog1.MachineName = "taborr";
        this.eventLog1.Source = "BROWSER";

((System.ComponentModel.ISupportInitialize)(this.eventLog1)).EndInit();

    }
    #endregion

    /// <summary>
    /// Clean up any resources being used.
    /// </summary>
    protected override void Dispose( bool disposing )
    {
    }


    [WebMethod]
    public EventLogEntry GetEventLog(int iEventNumber)
    {
        EventLogEntry eventlogentry = new EventLogEntry();

        eventlogentry.EventID = eventLog1.Entries[iEventNumber].EventID;
        eventlogentry.Message = eventLog1.Entries[iEventNumber].Message;

        return eventlogentry;
    }
  }
}
```

Next you need to create a new class structure to house the EventID and Message properties that you obtain from the EventLog class. In the EventLogEntry Web method, you accept an ordinal event number to select which event you want to access. Then take the event information from the EventLog1 object's properties and place them into an instance of the EventLogEntry class. The instance of the EventLogEntry class is returned to the consumer of the Web Service, where the class structure is serialized to XML.

Please note the code is generated for you by Visual Studio .NET in the InitializeComponent method. As a result of dragging and dropping the reference from the Event Logs node to the designer surface, the code to create an instance of the EventLog class and populate it with the necessary properties is completed for you. All you have to worry about is referencing the properties and methods of the instance of the class that was created from within your Web Service.

Instead of creating a client for this example, I decided to simply test it in the Web Services help page. In Solution Explorer, right-click EventLogService.asmx, and choose View in Browser on the pop-up menu. When the initial help page appears, select the lone Web Method made available by the Web Service (GetEventLog), and the test page appears. If you enter the numeric value 1 in the iEventValue text box and click the Invoke button, your screen should look similar to the one in Figure 16.3.

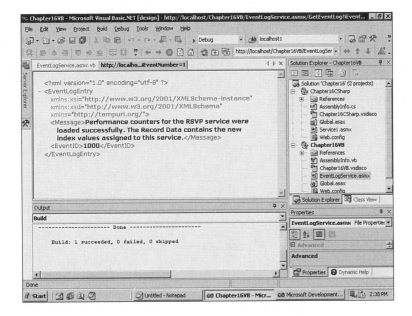

FIGURE 16.3
Result of testing the EventLogService.asmx.

As you can see, the Web Service returns a message and an event ID for the selected EventLog entry.

Summary

In this chapter you discovered a great shortcut for writing code and managing the resources within your environment. By dragging and dropping icons from Server Explorer (and the Toolbox) to the Web Services Designer surface, instances of classes that access system resources are created and code is generated to access those resources programmatically. This feature allows you to reference items in a more RAD-like fashion, thus reducing the time to develop Web Services.

COM Interoperability and Web Services

IN THIS CHAPTER

Developers have been creating COM components for years, so it was essential for Microsoft, while developing .NET, to provide interoperability between the COM world and the .NET world. This interoperability makes it easy for a .NET application to consume a COM component and a COM application to consume a .NET component.

Although it is not always a seamless transition between the two worlds (as you will soon find, data type differences, among other difficulties, must be conquered), interoperability does work and is a viable solution as companies migrate to building .NET applications.

It is fairly easy to write a wrapper around your existing COM components to make them available as Web Services, as illustrated in this chapter, and the underlying components can be replaced over time.

This chapter briefly discusses how interoperability works and highlights some issues you might encounter when trying to wrap a simple method call of a COM component with a .NET Web Service.

How Interoperability Works

When a COM DLL is imported into .NET, a *wrapper* object is created within .NET that you can use to reference the component. The wrapper object marshals data between COM and .NET each time a call is made to a property or method, and the wrapper performs data type conversion between the two environments, if necessary. This object becomes necessary if data types are used that are not common to both environments. Integer and floating point numbers are common to both the COM automation types and the Common Language Runtime (CLR) types in .NET. Dates and strings, however, sometimes require conversion, depending on the programming language used to create the component. Conversion is a costly process, so if performance is important to you, make sure you take data types into consideration when implementing interoperability.

This of course raises the question "Why not just leave them and settle on a half-and-half solution?" The answer is quite simple, in that marshaling data between the managed (.NET) and unmanaged (COM) code is expensive from a system-resource perspective. If you are seeking high performance, you would be well advised to migrate components over as soon as possible (perhaps starting by using Visual Studio .NET's Migration Wizard).

To better illustrate how to wrap method calls of a COM object using an ASP.NET Web Service, consider the following section, "Interoperability Example," that shows how methods utilizing different data types can be accessed using COM interoperability.

An Interoperability Example

To see how easy it is with VS .NET to use a legacy COM object in a .NET application, you'll work your way through an example that focuses on interoperability. The example shows how to use a COM component in an ASP.NET Web Service.

To begin, you need a simple COM component. This example uses a Visual Basic 6 component that has five functions. Each of the functions focuses on a different data type (integer, double, date, string, or variant). The goal is to see what data type problems crop up when calling a component via interoperability. The benefit of this exercise is twofold:

- To better understand the process of adding a reference to a COM component in an ASP.NET project.
- To realize the problems you might encounter when using COM in .NET.

The example, from start to finish, consists of the following steps:

1. Creating the COM component.
2. Registering the COM component in COM+ Services.
3. Creating a reference to the COM component in the ASP.NET Web Service project.
4. Accessing the COM component's methods and properties.

Creating the COM Component

For this example, you create a Visual Basic 6.0 project called InteropExample, with one class called `ExampleMethods`. Listing 17.1 shows the code entered into that class module.

LISTING 17.1   Visual Basic 6.0 Code Listing for ExampleMethods.cls
___

```
Public Function addIntegers(ByVal iFirstNumber As Integer, ByVal iSecondNumber
As Integer) As Integer

    addIntegers = iFirstNumber + iSecondNumber

End Function

Public Function addDoubles(ByVal dFirstNumber As Double, ByVal dSecondNumber As
Double) As Double

    addDoubles = dFirstNumber + dSecondNumber

End Function
```

LISTING 17.1   Continued

```
Public Function calculateDate(ByVal dDate As Date, ByVal iDays As Integer) As
Date

    calculateDate = DateAdd("d", iDays, dDate)

End Function

Public Function concatenateStrings(ByVal sFirstString As String, ByVal
sSecondString As String) As String

    concatenateStrings = sFirstString & sSecondString

End Function

Public Function concatenateVariants(ByVal sFirstVar As Variant, ByVal
sSecondVar As Variant) As Variant

    concatenateVariants = sFirstVar + sSecondVar

End Function
```

Registering the COM Component

These methods are simple, but provide a good proving ground for referencing a COM component in .NET. After compiling the DLL, you create a new empty package in COM+ Services
called InteropExample. In Windows Explorer, you can then drag and drop the COM component to the new COM+ package.

Creating a Reference to the COM Component in the Web Service

To create the Web Service, first create a new project in Visual Studio .NET called
Chapter17VB (or Chapter17CSharp, if you're using C#) and rename the default Service1.asmx
file as InteropExample.asmx. Next, change the references to Service1 in the Code Behind module to reflect the name change to InteropExample.

To add a reference to the COM object, follow these steps:

1. Right-click the project in Solution Explorer and choose Add Reference from the pop-up
   menu to open the Add Reference dialog box.

2. In the dialog box, click the COM tab, and select the COM component previously registered in COM+ Services. Click the Select button to add the component to the Selected
   Components list at the bottom of the dialog box (see Figure 17.1).

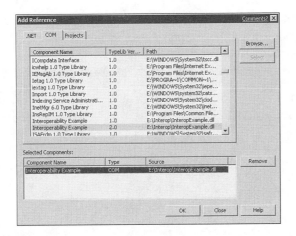

FIGURE 17.1

Adding a component in the Add Reference dialog box.

3. Click the OK button at the bottom of the dialog box, and you'll see a message box asking you to create a primary interop assembly (the wrapper) for the type library from the COM component (see Figure 17.2). Basically, Microsoft couldn't find the necessary wrapper already in the project or on disk and wants to make sure you intend to create the necessary .NET wrapper to facilitate marshaling data between .NET and COM. Of course, you should click the Yes button.

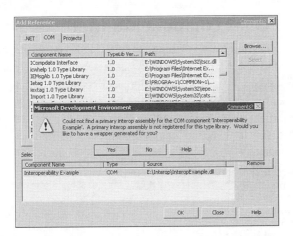

FIGURE 17.2

The interop assembly message box.

4. You should then see a new node for this project in the References section of Solution Explorer, indicating that the reference was successfully added (see Figure 17.3).

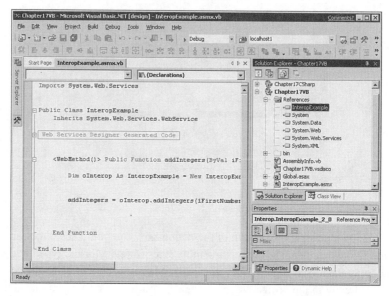

FIGURE 17.3
The project's reference in Solution Explorer.

Accessing the COM Component's Methods and Properties

Now it's time to add code. You want to wrap each of the COM component's existing methods with Web methods in the ASP.NET Web Service that match the COM component's method signature as closely as possible. Because of the differences between .NET and COM, plus variations in how data types are implemented in C# and VB.NET, this task is a little more challenging than you might think. Enter the code formatted in bold in Listing 17.2 (for VB .NET) or Listing 17.3 (for C#) into the Code Behind file for the InteropExample.asmx file.

LISTING 17.2 InteropExample.asmx.vb in VB .NET

```
Imports System.Web.Services
Imports InteropExample

Public Class InteropExample
    Inherits System.Web.Services.WebService

#Region " Web Services Designer Generated Code "
```

LISTING 17.2   Continued

```
Public Sub New()
    MyBase.New()

    'This call is required by the Web Services Designer.
    InitializeComponent()

    'Add your own initialization code after the InitializeComponent() call

End Sub

'Required by the Web Services Designer
Private components As System.ComponentModel.Container

'NOTE: The following procedure is required by the Web Services Designer
'It can be modified using the Web Services Designer.
'Do not modify it using the code editor.
<System.Diagnostics.DebuggerStepThrough()> Private Sub
InitializeComponent()
    components = New System.ComponentModel.Container()
End Sub

Protected Overloads Overrides Sub Dispose(ByVal disposing As Boolean)
    'CODEGEN: This procedure is required by the Web Services Designer
    'Do not modify it using the code editor.
End Sub

#End Region


    <WebMethod()> Public Function addIntegers(ByVal iFirstNumber As Integer, _
ByVal iSecondNumber As Integer) As Integer

        Dim oInterop As ExampleMethods = New ExampleMethods()

        addIntegers = oInterop.addIntegers(iFirstNumber, iSecondNumber)

    End Function

    <WebMethod()> Public Function addDoubles(ByVal iFirstNumber As Double, _
ByVal iSecondNumber As Double) As Double

        Dim oInterop As ExampleMethods = New ExampleMethods()

        addDoubles = oInterop.addDoubles(iFirstNumber, iSecondNumber)
```

LISTING 17.2   Continued

```vbnet
    End Function

    <WebMethod()> Public Function concatenateStrings(ByVal sFirstString As _
String, ByVal sSecondString As String) As String

        Dim oInterop As ExampleMethods = New ExampleMethods()

        concatenateStrings = oInterop.concatenateStrings(sFirstString, _
sSecondString)

    End Function

    <WebMethod()> Public Function calculateDate(ByVal dDate As Date, ByVal _
iDays As Integer) As Date

        Dim oInterop As ExampleMethods = New ExampleMethods()

        calculateDate = oInterop.calculateDate(dDate, iDays)

    End Function

    <WebMethod()> Public Function concatenateVariants(ByVal vFirstVar As _
Integer, ByVal vSecondVar As Integer) As String

        Dim oInterop As ExampleMethods = New ExampleMethods()

        concatenateVariants = oInterop.concatenateVariants(vFirstVar, _
vSecondVar)

    End Function

End Class
```

LISTING 17.3   InteropExample.asmx.cs in C#

```csharp
using System;
using System.Collections;
using System.ComponentModel;
using System.Data;
using System.Diagnostics;
using System.Web;
using System.Web.Services;
using InteropExample;
```

LISTING 17.3   Continued

```csharp
namespace Chapter17CSharp
{
    /// <summary>
    /// Summary description for Service1.
    /// </summary>
    public class InteropExample : System.Web.Services.WebService
    {
        public InteropExample()
        {
            //CODEGEN: This call is required by the ASP.NET Web Services
Designer
            InitializeComponent();
        }

        #region Component Designer generated code
        /// <summary>
        /// Required method for Designer support - do not modify
        /// the contents of this method with the code editor.
        /// </summary>
        private void InitializeComponent()
        {
        }
        #endregion

        /// <summary>
        /// Clean up any resources being used.
        /// </summary>
        protected override void Dispose( bool disposing )
        {
        }

        [WebMethod]
        public int addIntegers(short iFirstNumber, short iSecondNumber)
        {
            ExampleMethods oInterop = new ExampleMethods();

            return oInterop.addIntegers(iFirstNumber, iSecondNumber);
        }

        [WebMethod]
        public double addDoubles(double dFirstNumber, double dSecondNumber)
        {
            ExampleMethods oInterop = new ExampleMethods();
```

LISTING 17.3 Continued

```
            return oInterop.addDoubles(dFirstNumber, dSecondNumber);
        }

        [WebMethod]
        public string concatenateStrings(string sFirstString, string
sSecondString)
        {
            ExampleMethods oInterop = new ExampleMethods();

            return oInterop.concatenateStrings(sFirstString, sSecondString);
        }

        [WebMethod]
        public System.DateTime calculateDate(System.DateTime dDate, short
iDays)
        {
            ExampleMethods oInterop = new ExampleMethods();

            return oInterop.calculateDate(dDate, iDays);
        }

        [WebMethod]
        public object concatenateVariants(object vFirstVar, object vSecondVar)
        {
            ExampleMethods oInterop = new ExampleMethods();

            return oInterop.concatenateVariants(vFirstVar, vSecondVar);
        }

    }
}
```

The first statements in the code—the Imports statement for VB .NET or the using statement for C#—create a reference to the COM component. These statements allow you to reference the ExampleMethods class without prefixing it with the InteropExample component name.

Notice the wrapper that's created as you add the reference. When the IntelliSense pop-up is displayed for the ExampleMethods calls, note that the method signature displayed is not the actual method signature on your COM component, but the data types necessary in each parameter for that specific language to call the COM component's methods. Most notable were the differences between the VB 6.0 integer and the C# short data types.

The variant data type poses the biggest challenge because the wrapper turns the variant input parameters to object types, as shown in Figure 17.4.

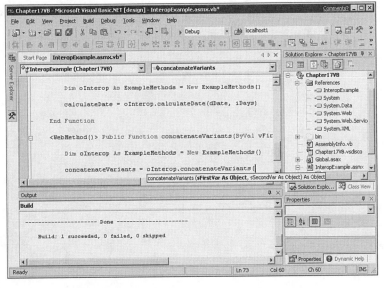

FIGURE 17.4
IntelliSense help on a variant method represented by the object type in .NET.

The final step is to test the Web Service wrapper methods in the Web Service test page to see whether you get the results you expected.

Summary

COM components can be used in the .NET environment because Microsoft developed interoperability wrappers that mask the complexity of translating data types and marshaling the data for method calls. Although there is a performance hit and some data type issues in conversion between managed (.NET) and unmanaged (COM) environments, interoperability offers a way to achieve a homogenous environment until you can completely migrate to .NET.

Using Transactions in Web Services

When developing business applications, often there is a need to call multiple components and/or manipulate data in multiple databases. When all the operations in your code must complete or recover cleanly (if a single operation fails), you need to use transactions. The most popular example for using transactions is in a banking environment. When you take $40 dollars out of an ATM, two things must happen. First, money must be debited from your account, and second, cash must be available to be dispensed from the cash machine. If either of these operations fails, one party will make out quite well, albeit unfairly. If there is not enough money in your account or in the machine, the transaction must halt, and the process must be set back (or rolled back) to its original status (that is, money should not be debited from your account).

You can implement transactions in your Web Services to coordinate a series of steps (calls to components or the database) that must all happen or must all fail. This chapter will briefly review the technologies that work behind the scenes to facilitate transactions and the limitations of using transactions in Web Services. You will also see an example that demonstrates how to implement a transaction in your Web Service that will roll back if problems occur. Finally, you'll take a look at the future of transactions for Web Services.

Understanding Transactions

Transactions are a set of operations that all succeed or all fail as a single unit. As explained in the introduction, if one operation within that unit fails, the entire unit fails. The Distributed Transaction Coordinator (DTC), a Windows service that coordinates transactions across components and is used with programmatic interfaces and other services supplied by COM+, facilitates the use of transactions with relatively little effort required on your part. You will learn more about the DTC in the following section.

How Transactions Work

Transactions are one facet of a larger set of services called COM+ Services. These services include the following:

- **Transaction support:** Allows multiple operations to be committed or to be rolled back as one complete unit of work.

- **Object pooling:** Keeps multiple instances of objects around to avoid the overhead of instancing and initializing components.

- **Just-In-Time (JIT) object activation:** Enables a developer to create an instance of a class at any time, but the resources are not allocated to that object until it is actually used. This allows fewer instances to service more requests.

- **Security:** Based on users' roles, they may or may not be allowed to perform certain business tasks.

- **Event support:** Allows components or applications to request notification when certain events are raised by other components.

- **Component message queuing:** Allows requests to components to be queued when the server can't keep up with all the requests made to it. The request is "thrown over the wall," and clients can continue processing, knowing that the request will be processed in the order it was received.

- **Component load balancing:** Can route a request to the component server in a server farm that can best handle the spillover load one server is currently experiencing.

These services provide a great deal of "plumbing" code that developers used to have to create for each application. They also ensure higher levels of consistency, stability, security, and scalability. These topics are outside the scope of this book on Web Services, but *Deploying and Managing Microsoft .NET Web Farms*, by Barry Bloom (Sams Publishing, 2001), is an excellent source to help you understand the practical use of COM+ Services in your server farm architecture.

Transaction support is facilitated by the Distributed Transaction Coordinator (DTC), which is a Windows service in charge of managing all operations that make up a transaction. By implementing certain programmatic interfaces, components can be enlisted to work within the context of a calling application's existing transaction. Alternatively, the component can start a new transaction or can decide to operate without transactions, options that are set by using the Component Services Administration tool. If a component is set to support or use a transaction, it allows the DTC to query its state and to issue commands. In a sense, the component relinquishes control and allows the DTC to tell it what to do and when to do it. The components have an important responsibility to report back to the DTC if they encounter problems.

The DTC uses a process called a *two-phased commit* to coordinate the separate actions of each component. It first issues the call to each component as a request that the component reports back with a vote on whether it can carry out the request. This is not majority rule; the collection of votes from the components must form a consensus. If even one component can't fulfill the request (or if it times out), the DTC takes charge and issues a command to all participating components to abort and roll back to their previous states. That means updates, inserts, or deletes to a database should be aborted or not committed, and any variables should be set back to their original values. On the other hand, if each component votes to continue, the DTC issues another round of messages to the components to complete the transaction.

In practical terms, you use an instance of a component (representing a transaction *context*) to complete or abort the transaction. This process will be clearer when you view the code example in "The Transaction Example," later in this chapter.

Transactions, COM+ Services, and .NET

COM+ Services are COM-based and, therefore, "unmanaged" code, so a little extra effort is required to make use of these services from within your .NET assemblies. This extra effort is necessary because of the intricacies of the inherent differences between COM+ and .NET components and the Interop layer provided by .NET that enables them to work together. How much effort is involved? Well, it includes adding several attributes to your classes such as running a couple of utilities that will load and register the .NET assembly, creating a type library for the assembly, importing the type library into a COM+ Services application, and configuring the application's properties. Fortunately, when you're using ASP.NET, much of the complexity of adding transaction support to your ASP.NET Web Service is hidden through the use of a single property of the WebMethod attribute.

> **NOTE**
>
> If you are curious about how to use COM+ Services in your .NET assemblies (outside ASP.NET), please refer to the help for the System.EnterpriseServices class as well as the sn.exe, al.exe, and RegSvcs.exe utilities.

Limitations of Transactions in ASP.NET Web Services

Although it is true that much of the complexity of adding transaction support to your Web Services is encapsulated by using a single property of a single attribute (discussed in the following sections), there is a limit to what you can do with transactions in your Web Services.

The limitation is that Web Services can participate in a transaction only as the root of a new transaction. In other words, a Web Service can't be just one operation among others within the unit. Instead, it is the operation that creates a new context containing other operations, which all operate as a unit. The Web Service is simply the "calling application" that kicks off the transaction because it uses HTTP, which is stateless by nature, so it doesn't lend itself to voting and rolling back—not yet, at least. (Read more about how this might change in "Transactions Across Web Services," at the end of the chapter.)

Attributes and Properties for Transactions in Web Services

As mentioned, to use transactions, you simply set a single property of the WebMethod attribute: the TransactionOption property. There is also an attribute called AutoComplete that is very useful as well. Both are discussed in the following sections before you see how they're used in the this chapter's example.

The `TransactionOption` Property

To indicate that your Web Service should be the root of a transaction, you set the `TransactionOption` property of the `WebMethod` attribute that you apply to any Web methods that will trigger a transaction. The following lines show how this property is set in VB .NET and in C#:

VB .NET

```
<WebMethod(TransactionOption:=(TransactionOption))>
```

C#

```
[WebMethod(TransactionOption=(TransactionOption))]
```

You must replace the *(TransactionOption)* text in the preceding line with an enumerated value from the `TransactionOptionEnum` class. There are five possible values, but for the purpose of Web Services, because they are limited to being only the root of a transaction, they basically break down into two options, as shown in Table 18.1.

TABLE 18.1 Possible Values from the *TransactionOptionEnum* Class

Value	Description
`Disabled, NotSupported, Supported`	Indicates that the Web Service method does not run within the scope of a transaction. When a request is processed, the Web method is executed without a transaction. Basically, these settings turn off the Web Service's ability to participate in a transaction. By default, `TransactionOption` is set to `Disabled`.
`Required, RequiresNew`	Indicates that the Web Service method requires a transaction. Web methods can participate only as the root object in a transaction, so a new transaction will be created for the Web method. You can use either value, but your code should be self-documenting, so use `RequiresNew` because it's more indicative of what actually occurs.

18

USING TRANSACTIONS IN WEB SERVICES

Therefore, when you add specific values to the previous examples, the code for setting the `TransactionOption` property looks like this:

VB .NET

```
<WebMethod(TransactionOption:=TransactionOption.RequiresNew)>
```

C#

```
[WebMethod(TransactionOption=TransactionOption.RequiresNew)]
```

The `AutoComplete` Attribute

When managing the unit of work that composes a transaction in your Web Services, you need to work with the `ContextUtil` object, which is provided by the `System.EnterpriseServices` class to programmatically tell the DTC when to send the `Commit` or `Rollback` statement. You will see how this happens in the transaction example, later in this chapter.

However, you can tell the DTC to go ahead and commit as soon as you determine that everything worked fine by applying the `AutoComplete` attribute to the Web method. It is used as follows for VB .NET or C#:

VB .NET

```
<AutoComplete(), WebMethod(TransactionOption:=TransactionOption.RequiresNew)>
```

C#

```
[AutoComplete]
[WebMethod(TransactionOption=TransactionOption.RequiresNew)]
```

As you can see, multiple attributes can be applied to a single class to accommodate both the `WebMethod` and `AutoComplete` attributes.

The Transaction Example

The following sample Web Service has two methods: `TransactionExample1` and `TransactionExample2`. Each of these methods manages a series of SQL Server (or Microsoft Data Engine, MSDE) database commands to update or delete data from the Pubs database that ships with the default installation of SQL Server.

`TransactionExample1` is doomed for failure because it issues a `Delete` command on the Authors table that conflicts with a foreign key constraint. When this occurs, the other statement, an update, gets rolled back.

`TransactionExample2` should succeed, unless the rows are missing in your database because of other exercises you might have tried in other training material. After both update statements successfully vote (that is, indicate to the DTC that they have succeeded), they are both committed to the database.

Unlike other Web Services created throughout this book, this example focuses less on the outcome than on the exact sequence of events that determine whether the transaction should finish or be rolled back. To help delineate the outline of events, breakpoints were set on the Web Service. In the section "Examining the Web Service in Debug Mode," following the code example, these breakpoints are stepped through in Debug mode so that you can clearly see what happened.

Building the Web Service

To follow along, please take the following steps:

1. In Visual Studio .NET, choose File | New on the menu to open the New Project dialog box.

2. Select your language in the Project Types list box on the left (Visual Basic Projects or Visual C# Projects), and then select ASP.NET Web Service in the Templates list box on the right.

3. In the Name text box, type **Chapter18VB** (for VB .NET) or **Chapter18CSharp** (for C#).

4. Accept the default location in the Location field.

5. Click the OK button. Visual Studio .NET will create a new project based on the language and template you selected.

The next step is to create a reference to the System.EnterpriseServices class. Because it's a vital step in the process, the following section goes into more depth on why you must create this reference.

Creating a Reference to the System.EnterpriseServices Class

Remember that you *must* create a reference to the System.EnterpriseServices class for transactions to work. If you are using Visual Studio .NET, you'll notice complaints (threatening little blue and red squiggly lines) in the code window if you use the TransactionOption enumeration class, the AutoComplete attribute, or the ContextUtil object without first creating a reference to the System.EnterpriseServices class. Furthermore, you will be unable to compile the Web Service without this reference.

To create the reference, follow these steps:

1. Right-click your project in Solution Explorer, and choose Add References from the pop-up menu.

2. In the Add References dialog box, click the .NET Assemblies tab if the dialog box didn't open to that tab. Click to select System.EnterpriseServices in the list of components. (You might have to scroll down to find it.)

3. Click the Select button to move your selection to the Selected list box. Now click the OK button.

4. Click the OK button to accept your changes and close the dialog box.

Continuing to Build the Transaction Example

Now that you have added a reference to the System.EnterpriseServices class, please continue with the following steps:

1. Unlike the exercises in previous chapters, you will not rename the the Web Service (.asmx) file.

2. Click the Show All Files icon at the top of the Solution Explorer window to display all the hidden files, including the Code Behind file for the Service1.asmx.

3. Click the + next to the Service1.asmx file to reveal the Service1.asmx.vb (for VB .NET) or Service1.asmx.cs (for C#) file.

4. Select the Service1.asmx.vb or Service1.asmx.cs file in Solution Explorer, and then click the View Code button at the top of the Solution Explorer window to display the Code Behind file in the main area of Visual Studio .NET. This is where you'll edit the Code Behind file. As you can see, Visual Studio .NET has already generated code in this file for you.

5. Type the code formatted in bold in Listing 18.1 for VB .NET or Listing 18.2 for C# into the Code Behind file that's currently open. As is the convention throughout this book, the code not formatted in bold is included as context to help you determine where to enter your code.

> **NOTE**
>
> Make sure you substitute the text REPLACEWITHYOURSERVERNAME with the name of your SQL Server machine in the following listings.
>
> If you experience a permissions problem caused by the settings of the connection string in the following listings, try a trusted connection instead by using the following connection string:
>
> ```
> "server=(local);database=pubs;Trusted_Connection=yes"
> ```

LISTING 18.1   Service1.asmx.vb for VB .NET

```
Imports System.Web.Services
Imports System.EnterpriseServices
Imports System.Data.SqlClient
```

LISTING 18.1   Continued

```
Public Class Service1
    Inherits System.Web.Services.WebService

#Region " Web Services Designer Generated Code "

    Public Sub New()
        MyBase.New()

        'This call is required by the Web Services Designer.
        InitializeComponent()

        'Add your own initialization code after the InitializeComponent() call

    End Sub

    'Required by the Web Services Designer
    Private components As System.ComponentModel.Container

    'NOTE: The following procedure is required by the Web Services Designer
    'It can be modified using the Web Services Designer.
    'Do not modify it using the code editor.
    <System.Diagnostics.DebuggerStepThrough()> Private Sub
InitializeComponent()
        components = New System.ComponentModel.Container()
    End Sub

    Protected Overloads Overrides Sub Dispose(ByVal disposing As Boolean)
        'CODEGEN: This procedure is required by the Web Services Designer
        'Do not modify it using the code editor.
    End Sub

#End Region

    <WebMethod(TransactionOption:=TransactionOption.RequiresNew)> _
    Public Function TransactionExample1(ByVal lastName As String) As Boolean

Try
            Dim sqlConn As SqlConnection = _
                New SqlConnection("user id=sa;" & _
                "database=pubs;" & _
                "server=REPLACEWITHYOURSERVERNAME")
            sqlConn.Open()

            ' The first statement
            Dim sUpdate As String = "UPDATE authors " & _
                "SET au_lname = 'Nowitski' " & _
                "WHERE au_id = '724-08-9931'"
```

LISTING 18.1 Continued

```
            Dim cmdUpdate As SqlCommand = New SqlCommand(sUpdate, sqlConn)
            cmdUpdate.ExecuteNonQuery()


            ' The second statement.
            Dim sDelete As String = "DELETE FROM authors where au_lname='" + _
    lastName + "'"
            Dim cmdDelete As SqlCommand = New SqlCommand(sDelete, sqlConn)
            cmdDelete.ExecuteNonQuery()

            ContextUtil.SetComplete()
            TransactionExample1 = True

        Catch e As Exception

            ContextUtil.SetAbort()
            TransactionExample1 = False

        End Try

    End Function

<AutoComplete(), _
    WebMethod(TransactionOption:=TransactionOption.RequiresNew)> _
        Public Function TransactionExample2() as Boolean

            Try

                Dim sqlConn As SqlConnection = _
                    New SqlConnection("user id=sa;" & _
                    database=pubs;server=REPLACEWITHYOURSERVERNAME")
                sqlConn.Open()

                ' The first statement
                Dim sUpdate1 as String = "UPDATE authors " & _
                    "SET au_lname = 'Nowitski' " & _
                    "WHERE au_id='724-08-9931'"
                Dim cmdUpdate1 As SqlCommand = _
                    New SqlCommand(sUpdate1, sqlConn)
                cmdUpdate1.ExecuteNonQuery()

                ' The second statement
                Dim sUpdate2 As String = "UPDATE authors " & _
                    "SET au_lname='Grant', au_fname='Conrad' " & _
                    "WHERE au_id='998-72-3567'"

                Dim cmdUpdate2 As SqlCommand = _
                    New SqlCommand(sUpdate2, sqlConn)
                cmdUpdate2.ExecuteNonQuery()
```

LISTING 18.1   Continued

```
TransactionExample2 = True

        Catch e As Exception

            ContextUtil.SetAbort()
            TransactionExample2 = False

        End Try

    End Function


End Class
```

LISTING 18.2   Service1.asmx.cs for C#

```csharp
using System;
using System.Collections;
using System.ComponentModel;
using System.Data;
using System.Diagnostics;
using System.Web;
using System.Web.Services;
using System.EnterpriseServices;
using System.Data.SqlClient;

namespace Chapter18CSharp
{
    /// <summary>
    /// Summary description for Service1.
    /// </summary>
    public class Service1 : System.Web.Services.WebService
    {
        public Service1()
        {
            //CODEGEN: This call is required by the ASP.NET Web Services
Designer
            InitializeComponent();
        }

        #region Component Designer generated code
        /// <summary>
        /// Required method for Designer support - do not modify
        /// the contents of this method with the code editor.
```

LISTING 18.2   Continued

```
/// </summary>
private void InitializeComponent()
{
}
#endregion

/// <summary>
/// Clean up any resources being used.
/// </summary>
protected override void Dispose( bool disposing )
{
}

[WebMethod(TransactionOption=TransactionOption.RequiresNew)]
public bool TransactionExample1(string lastName)
{

    try
    {
        SqlConnection sqlConn = new SqlConnection("user
id=sa;database=pubs;server=REPLACEWITHYOURSERVERNAME");
        sqlConn.Open();

        // The first statement
        String sUpdate = "UPDATE authors SET au_lname = 'Nowitski'
WHERE au_id='724-08-9931'";
        SqlCommand cmdUpdate = new SqlCommand(sUpdate, sqlConn);
        cmdUpdate.ExecuteNonQuery();


        // The second statement.
        String sDelete = "DELETE FROM authors where au_lname='" +
lastName + "'" ;
        SqlCommand cmdDelete = new SqlCommand(sDelete,sqlConn);
        cmdDelete.ExecuteNonQuery();

        ContextUtil.SetComplete();
        return true;

    }
    catch (Exception e)
    {
        ContextUtil.SetAbort();
        return false;
```

LISTING 18.2   Continued

```
            }

        }

        [AutoComplete]
        [WebMethod(TransactionOption=TransactionOption.RequiresNew)]
        public bool TransactionExample2()
        {

            try
            {
                SqlConnection sqlConn = new SqlConnection("user
id=sa;database=pubs;server= REPLACEWITHYOURSERVERNAME ");
                sqlConn.Open();

                // The first statement
                String sUpdate1 = "UPDATE authors SET au_lname = 'Nowitski'
WHERE au_id='724-08-9931'";
                SqlCommand cmdUpdate1 = new SqlCommand(sUpdate1, sqlConn);
                cmdUpdate1.ExecuteNonQuery();


                // The second statement.
                String sUpdate2 = "UPDATE authors SET au_lname = 'Grant',
au_fname = 'Conrad' WHERE au_id='998-72-3567'";
                SqlCommand cmdUpdate2 = new SqlCommand(sUpdate2, sqlConn);
                cmdUpdate2.ExecuteNonQuery();

                return true;

            }
            catch (Exception e)
            {
                ContextUtil.SetAbort();
                return false;
            }

        }

    }
}
```

Compile the Web Service by choosing Build | Build Solution on the menu. If there were any problems during the build, make sure you typed the code exactly as it appears in the code listing—and remember that many things are case sensitive in .NET.

After compiling the Web Service, you initially test it by using the Web Service help page. For `TransactionExample1`, enter **White** for the `lastName` argument, which should be one of the Authors in the Pubs database. This test should return the value `false`.

For `TransactionExample2`, you can simply start the Web Service, and if all goes well (in other words, as long as the two rows selected in the Pubs database match two rows from your Pubs database), it should return the value `true`.

However, *how* you get those values is more interesting that *what* the values are. The following section explains how to walk through a Web Service in Visual Studio.NET's Debug mode, using the various built-in tools that assist in developing and debugging your Web Services.

Examining the Web Service in Debug Mode

Although you may have had experience with debugging applications in the past, Visual Studio .NET offers new debugging features, and debugging a Web Service has some small nuances that makes the process a little different than in other types of applications. To walk through a Web Service, you must follow these steps:

1. Set a breakpoint in your code. You can do this by clicking to the left of the code line you want to stop on, or selecting the line and pressing Ctrl+B on your keyboard. A breakpoint is indicated with a red dot to the left side, and the entire line of code is highlighted in red (unless you have changed your default colors).

2. If your solution has multiple projects, you must select one project to be the startup project. In Solution Explorer, it's the project in bold text. Right-click on the project you want to start debugging, and choose Set as Startup Project on the pop-up menu.

3. Press F5 on the keyboard, or click the arrow button on the toolbar (it looks like a left-pointing stereo button).

4. If the project you are debugging is a Web Service, after a few seconds a new browser will open to the Web Service help page.

5. Select the method you want to test in the Web Service help page, and click the Invoke button to start it.

6. The Visual Studio .NET IDE then gains focus and displays new windows (especially the Locals window) and toolbars for the purpose of viewing the values of variables and objects, information about the threads being used, and so forth (see Figure 18.1). At this point, the code stops running, but the application is still "alive." To step through the code one line at a time, walking over calls to other methods, press F10 repeatedly. Each time

you step to a new line of code, the Locals window is refreshed with the values of new variables and reflects the changes to existing variables and properties of objects. The current line of code is indicated with a yellow highlight.

7. You can review the variables and the values of objects and their properties in the Locals window or by "hovering" your mouse over the variable in the code window.

8. After you are finished debugging, you can press F5 or click the run arrow to continue running the code, or click the Stop button on the Debug toolbar to end.

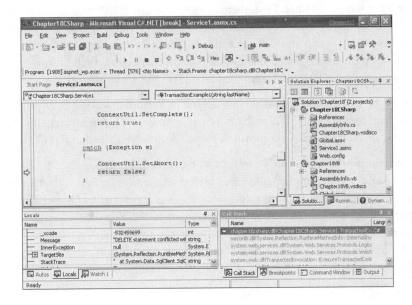

18

USING
TRANSACTIONS IN
WEB SERVICES

FIGURE 18.1
The Visual Studio .NET IDE in Debug mode.

Use the previous steps to set a breakpoint in the `TransactionExample1` method, and use the name `White` as the input when testing the method in the Web Service help page. As you step through the code, you'll notice that the first statement, the update, works fine. However, as the execute statement is called on the delete method, the `Catch` exception handler is triggered. You'll notice that a new value called `e` appears in the Locals window; this value is the instance of the `Exception` object in the `Catch` statement. If you expand the `e` value, you'll see many properties and values. Scroll down until you see the `message` property. It should have the following value:

```
"DELETE statement conflicted with COLUMN REFERENCE constraint
'FK__titleauth__au_id__0519C6AF'. The conflict occurred in database 'pubs',
table 'titleauthor', column 'au_id'.  The statement has been terminated."
```

This message indicates that the transaction was rolled back because the delete statement would have violated a table constraint. The update statement, although you were able to step through it in the code and everything seemed fine, was rolled back and the row was not updated.

Transactions Across Web Services

Currently, there is no mechanism for managing transactions in multiple Web Services residing across the Internet. However, some things lead me to believe that this mechanism will be created in the not-too-distant future. First, there is no reason that SOAP messages cannot contain the information necessary to accommodate the two-phased commit approach to transactions. SOAP headers could contain all the data needed to handle information about a transaction context (if one was present) and about other services in the transaction, such as supporting special interfaces to vote, commit, or roll back based on a DTC-like piece of software.

Second, there has been some discussion in newsgroups and articles about homegrown approaches to accomplish this. The problem is that it removes the "discoverability" of the Web Services because no transaction coordinator can currently be described in DISCO or WSDL.

Third, a specification by Microsoft's competitors has already been suggested for this purpose. Transaction Authority Markup Language (XAML) is a specification in its infancy that seeks to facilitate transactions across Web Services. However, it is sponsored by Oracle, Sun, and IBM, and Microsoft's name is conspicuously not represented on the Web site (`http://www.xaml.org`). I would expect to see a competing specification for transactional Web Services from Microsoft as well as a tool to support this functionality, such as another version of the DTC and possibly an SDK or set of .NET classes that make implementing transactions across Web Services simple.

Summary

In this chapter, you learned about using transactions in your Web Services. Web Services can start transactions and can manage the process, but cannot be involved as part of the processes that compose the transactional unit of work.

Implementing transactions in ASP.NET Web Services is as simple as creating a reference to the `System.EnterpriseServices` class, adding the `TransactionOption` property to the `WebMethod` attribute, and then handling whether the transaction should be committed or rolled back, based on the success or failure of each process within the unit of work that forms a transaction. Alternatively, you can add the `AutoComplete` attribute, which automatically commits the transaction if there are no errors in each of the transaction's processes.

You have also seen an example of a transaction in action and learned to watch how it works by stepping through the Web Service code in Debug mode.

Calling Web Services Asynchronously

IN THIS CHAPTER

By default, when an ASP.NET Web Forms or a Windows Forms application calls a Web Service, it makes a *synchronous* call, meaning that the application comes to a grinding halt while it waits for a response from the Web Service. This process can definitely affect the performance of your applications, especially when calling several Web Services. However, you could potentially enjoy performance gains by calling the Web Service, and then continuing to address other business logic or processing needs, such as giving the user control of the application. When the Web Service response is returned, the application then responds accordingly. This process is referred to as calling Web Services *asynchronously*.

In this chapter, you'll learn how to call Web Services asynchronously from ASP.NET and Windows Forms. You'll also review an example that exercises all the different methods of calling asynchronously and learn where each method is useful.

How Asynchronous Calls Work

How do you build an asynchronous Web Service? You don't. That's right—there is nothing special you have to do to create a Web Service that can be called asynchronously. Actually, when you create a Web reference in your consuming application, a proxy is created for the call to the Web Service. If you've cracked open the proxy code and looked at it, you'll notice an additional method that enables you to issue a call, but not wait for its response (Begin<WebMethodName>), and another method that allows you to return to the response and retrieve the results (End<WebMethodName>). So there are no asynchronous Web Services—just asynchronous calls to Web Services.

Callbacks Versus WaitHandles

There are two basic methods for calling Web Services asynchronously. Each one has a purpose and a setting in which it excels, as described in the following sections.

Understanding Callbacks

A *callback* is a function that waits in readiness to process the response from the Web Service. A reference to that function is passed into the initial call to the Web Service's Begin<WebMethodName> method and is managed by the AsyncCallback object. This object knows how to reference a function designated as the callback function and coordinate that information with the IAsyncResult object, which knows how to take the incoming results and route them to the AsyncCallback's function.

The callback function has a reference to the instance of the IAsyncResult object containing information on the specific results from a specific call, and can use properties from it to retrieve a reference back to the AsyncCallback object. From here, the End<WebMethodName> method is called and the results can be parsed.

The benefit of callbacks is that they enable you to return control of the application to the user. When the function that initially makes the call goes out of scope, the user can then continue to interact with the application. When the results are returned to the `AsyncCallback`'s function, the application briefly takes over and refreshes the screen with the new data. Therefore, callbacks are ideal when you want quick response on a Windows Forms application.

The reason callbacks are not ideal for Web Forms is that the Web Forms could finish processing and deliver the page to the user before the results from the Web Service come in. At this point, it is too late; the page has finished processing and there is no way to tell the Web page now residing on the user's browser that some new information has been received that might be pertinent. Of course, you could have the browser refresh itself to determine whether the results of the Web Service have arrived, but it would be messy. There is a better way to handle asynchronous calls to ASP.NET Web Forms, discussed in the next section.

Understanding `WaitHandle` Functions

The `IAsyncResult` interface implements the functionality that holds a pointer to a callback function, which runs when the Web Service returns with the response. Alternatively, the `WaitHandle` function waits for the response to finish before it allows processing to continue. Calls to the Web Service can be made and other processing can continue, but ultimately the function handles processing the results of the Web Service on its own without the aid of an additional function.

Although `WaitHandle` can definitely be used by Windows Forms applications (as the following example in this chapter attests), it is a better fit for ASP.NET Web Forms that need to finish all processing before sending a completely processed page back to the user's browser.

There are three varieties of `WaitHandle` functions:

- **WaitAll**   This method waits until all Web Services have finished before allowing the function to continue processing. Using this approach, you could handle the Web Service calls very early, perform other processing, and then wait until all the Web Services return with results before continuing with more processing, possibly even with the results of the Web Services.

- **WaitAny**   This method waits until the first (of potentially many) Web Service returns a result before allowing the function to continue processing. With this approach, you could use multiple service providers who offer similar Web Services, and pick the service that comes back the quickest with results. This is a little tricky, however, because it's the nature of Web Services to eventually complete all requests. Therefore, if you are trying to locate the fastest of two or more providers, and each charges a service fee, you might be getting double-charged for two calls for essentially the same service.

19

- **WaitOne**   This method is the equivalent of callbacks in that it is concerned with only one Web Service, not multiples like the other `WaitHandle` methods. After the Web Service is called, processing can continue until the `WaitOne` method is satisfied with the results from the Web Service call. Then, processing can resume.

The Asynchronous Web Services Example

In this example, two identical Web Services take in the number of milliseconds to sleep (using the `System.Threading.Thread.Sleep()` method) and return a message at the end of the sleep cycle. A Windows Form project then consumes the Web Services to exercise the different methods of asynchronous calls.

Building the Web Services

You'll take a slightly different approach in this chapter's exercise by creating a blank solution, and then adding new projects to that solution. To follow along, please perform the following steps:

1. In Visual Studio .NET, choose File | New | Blank Solution on the menu to open the New Project dialog box.

2. Select Visual Studio Solutions in the Project Types pane and Blank Solution in the Templates pane.

3. In the Name text box, enter **Chapter19**.

4. Accept the default location in the Location field.

5. Click the OK button. Visual Studio .NET will create a new Blank Solution.

6. Right-click the Chapter19 solution icon in Solution Explorer, and choose Add | New Project on the pop-up menu.

7. Select your language in the Project Types list box on the left (Visual Basic Projects or Visual C# Projects), and then select ASP.NET Web Service in the Templates list box on the right.

8. In the Name text box, type **Chapter19VB** (for VB .NET) or **Chapter19CSharp** (for C#).

9. Accept the default location in the Location field.

10. Click the OK button. Visual Studio .NET will create a new project based on the language and template you selected.

11. In Solution Explorer, rename the Service1.asmx file as SleepService1.asmx by right-clicking the file, and then choosing Rename on the pop-up menu. Type the new name of the file in the text box, and then press Enter.

Now you will add a second project to this solution in the steps that follow:

1. Right-click the Chapter19 solution icon in Solution Explorer, and choose Add | New Project on the pop-up menu.

2. Select your language in the Project Types list box on the left (Visual Basic Projects or Visual C# Projects), and then select ASP.NET Web Service in the Templates list box on the right.

3. In the Name text box, type **Chapter19VB2** (for VB .NET) or **Chapter19CSharp2** (for C#).

4. Accept the default location in the Location field.

5. Click the OK button. Visual Studio .NET will create a new project based on the language and template you selected.

6. In Solution Explorer, rename Service1.asmx as SleepService2.asmx by right-clicking the file, and then choosing Rename. Type the new name of the file in the text box, and press Enter.

Next, you will open the Code Behind file for both SleepService1.asmx and SleepService2.asmx to add code. The functions are practically identical, with the exception of their function name. Therefore, please note that I've supplied the code only once for brevity, but you should add this code for each Web Service, changing references from SleepService1 to SleepService2 and the Web method name from SleepServiceA to SleepServiceB. Don't forget to alter the return string to reflect A or B.

1. Click the Show All Files icon at the top of the Solution Explorer window to display all the hidden files, including the Code Behind file for SleepService1.asmx and SleepService2.asmx.

2. Click the + sign next to SleepService1.asmx to reveal the SleepService1.asmx.vb (for VB .NET) or SleepService1.asmx.cs (for C#). Do the same for the SleepService2.asmx file.

3. Select the SleepService1.asmx.vb or SleepService1.asmx.cs file in Solution Explorer, and then click the View Code button at the top of the Solution Explorer window to display the Code Behind file in the main area of Visual Studio .NET. This is where you'll edit the Code Behind file. As you can see, Visual Studio.NET has already generated code in this file.

4. Type the code formatted in bold in Listing 19.1 for VB.NET or Listing 19.2 for C# into the Code Behind file that's currently open. The code not formatted in bold is included to help you determine where to enter your code.

5. Repeat steps 3 and 4 for the SleepService2.asmx version of the function. Remember to change SleepService1 to SleepService2 and the Web method SleepServiceA to SleepServiceB in the following code listings. Also, don't forget to alter the return string to use B.

LISTING 19.1   SleepService1.asmx.vb for VB .NET

```vb
Imports System.Web.Services
Imports System.Threading

Public Class SleepService1
    Inherits System.Web.Services.WebService

#Region " Web Services Designer Generated Code "

    Public Sub New()
        MyBase.New()

        'This call is required by the Web Services Designer.
        InitializeComponent()

        'Add your own initialization code after the InitializeComponent() call

    End Sub


    'Required by the Web Services Designer
    Private components As System.ComponentModel.Container

    'NOTE: The following procedure is required by the Web Services Designer
    'It can be modified using the Web Services Designer.
    'Do not modify it using the code editor.
    <System.Diagnostics.DebuggerStepThrough()> Private Sub
InitializeComponent()
        components = New System.ComponentModel.Container()
    End Sub

    Protected Overloads Overrides Sub Dispose(ByVal disposing As Boolean)
        'CODEGEN: This procedure is required by the Web Services Designer
        'Do not modify it using the code editor.
    End Sub

#End Region

    <WebMethod()> Public Function SleepServiceA(ByVal iSleepDuration As _
Integer) As String

        Thread.Sleep(iSleepDuration)

        SleepServiceA = "A Finished"

    End Function

End Class
```

LISTING 19.2 SleepService1.asmx.cs for C#

```csharp
using System;
using System.Collections;
using System.ComponentModel;
using System.Data;
using System.Diagnostics;
using System.Web;
using System.Web.Services;
using System.Threading;

namespace Chapter19CSharp
{
    /// <summary>
    /// Summary description for SleepService1.
    /// </summary>
    public class SleepService1 : System.Web.Services.WebService
    {
        public SleepService1()
        {
            //CODEGEN: This call is required by the ASP.NET Web Services
Designer
            InitializeComponent();
        }

        #region Component Designer generated code
        /// <summary>
        /// Required method for Designer support - do not modify
        /// the contents of this method with the code editor.
        /// </summary>
        private void InitializeComponent()
        {
        }
        #endregion

        /// <summary>
        /// Clean up any resources being used.
        /// </summary>
        protected override void Dispose( bool disposing )
        {
        }

        [WebMethod]
        public string SleepServiceA(int iSleepDuration)
        {
            Thread.Sleep(iSleepDuration);
```

LISTING 19.2 Continued

```
            return "A Finished";
        }
    }
}
```

As explained earlier, these Web Services have a simple task: to cause the thread to sleep for the number of milliseconds passed by the consumer into the Web method `SleepServiceA`. When finished, a simple message is sent back to the consuming application. This helps simulate the latency often encountered when calling Web Services across the world or calling processor-intensive Web Services.

Compile the Web Services by choosing Build | Build on the menu. If there were any problems during the build, make sure you typed the code exactly as it appears in the code listing (keeping in mind to check for case sensitivity in code elements).

Building the Client

The client is where you begin to see how asynchronous calls to Web Services work. This example uses a Windows Form application to call the Web Services asynchronously. To continue following along, perform these steps:

1. Right-click on the Chapter19 solution icon, and choose Add | New Project on the pop-up menu.

2. Select your language in the Project Types list box on the left (Visual Basic Projects or Visual C# Projects), and then select Windows Application in the Templates list box on the right.

3. In the Name text box, type **Chapter19VBClient** (for VB .NET) or **Chapter19CSharpClient** (for C#).

4. Accept the default location in the Location field.

5. Click the OK button. Visual Studio .NET will create a new Windows Form project based on the language and template you selected.

6. In Solution Explorer, rename Form1.vb (or Form1.cs) as AsyncClient.vb (or AsyncClient.cs) by right-clicking the file, and then choosing Rename. Type the new name of the file in the text box, and press Enter.

7. In the main area, the Windows Form designer should be open. Drag and drop four command buttons from the Toolbox to the designer surface. Select each of these command buttons, and modify the `Text` property to reflect the operation they will perform in the code, as follows:

- Using Callback
- Using WaitHandle (All)
- Using WaitHandle (Any)
- Using WaitHandle (One)

8. Drag and drop three text boxes to the designer surface. Set the names of the text boxes to txtA, txtB, and txtResult (respectively), and remove any values in the Text properties.

9. Drag and drop two labels on the designer surface. The text of these controls is changed to A and B, and the font size is modified to 18 point.

10. Arrange each of the objects on the Windows Form designer to resemble Figure 19.1.

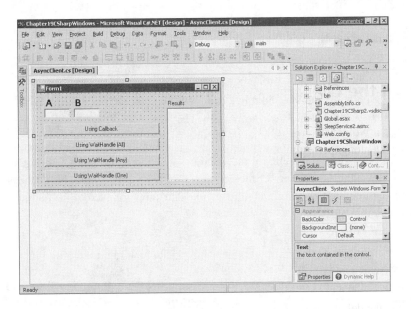

FIGURE 19.1
The AsyncClient Windows Form.

Before continuing on to the code examples, remember that you must create a Web reference to each of the two Web Services created earlier in this chapter. To do that, follow these steps:

1. Right-click the Chapter19VB (or Chapter19CSharp) project file in Solution Explorer, and choose Add Web Reference on the pop-up menu to open the Add Web Reference dialog box.

2. In this dialog box, click the Web References on Local Web Server link at the bottom of the window to refresh the Available References list box. Select the Chapter19VB (or Chapter19CSharp) entry to refresh the list again.

3. In the Available References list, SleepService1.asmx should appear alone. Click the Add Reference button at the bottom. The dialog box closes, and the new Web reference is displayed in Solution Explorer.

4. Repeat steps 1 to 3, this time creating a Web reference to the Chapter19VB2 (or Chapter19CSharp2) project.

5. In Solution Explorer, the Chapter19VBClient (or Chapter19CSharpClient) will have two Web references: one for localhost and another for localhost1. Even though both Web references come from the same machine, Visual Studio .NET simply creates a second Web reference object. To rectify this, expand the localhost1 object, right-click the SleepService2.wsdl, and choose Cut on the pop-up menu.

6. Right-click the localhost icon in Solution Explorer, and choose Paste to place the SleepService2.wsdl and its proxy class, the SleepService2.vb or SleepService2.cs file, as a child to the localhost object.

7. Double-click the SleepService2.vb (or SleepService2.cs) file to access the proxy class for this Web reference, and change any reference from `locahost1` to `localhost`.

8. Type the code formatted in bold in Listing 19.3 for VB.NET or Listing 19.4 for C# into the Code Behind file that's currently open. The code not formatted in bold is included to help you determine where to enter your code.

To access the Code Behind module for the Windows Form, double-click one of the buttons on the form's designer surface, using the tabs at the top of the Visual Studio .NET IDE. In fact, you should do this repeatedly to create the method signatures for each of the button's `click` event handlers.

NOTE

In the following code examples, the Visual Studio .NET IDE generates more code than usual because of the number of Windows controls added to the designer surface. Therefore, to spare you from code that is not germane to this discussion, I've used vertical ellipses, like so:

```
#Region " Windows Form Designer generated code "
    .
    .
    .
#End Region
```

These ellipses indicate a lot of code in that region that you should not modify, and it has no relevance to the tasks you're performing in these examples. If you would like to see this code example in its entirety, you can download it from the location mentioned in this book's "Introduction."

LISTING 19.3   AsyncClient.vb for VB .NET

```
Imports System.Threading

Public Class AsyncClient
    Inherits System.Windows.Forms.Form

#Region " Windows Form Designer generated code "

 .

 .

 .
#End Region

    Private Sub button1_Click(ByVal sender As System.Object, ByVal e As
System.EventArgs) Handles button1.Click
        Dim cService As localhost.SleepService1 = New localhost.SleepService1()

        ' cb is essentially a function pointer to ServiceCallback
        Dim cb As AsyncCallback = New AsyncCallback(AddressOf ServiceCallback)

        ' Call the Begin method of the proxy class to initiate the
        ' asynchronous call to the Web Service method.
        cService.BeginSleepServiceA(Integer.Parse(txtA.Text), cb, cService)

    End Sub

    Public Sub ServiceCallback(ByVal ar As IAsyncResult)
        ' Retrieve the original state for the proxy
        Dim cService As localhost.SleepService1 = ar.AsyncState

        ' Retrieve the results by calling the End method of the proxy class
        txtResult.Text = cService.EndSleepServiceA(ar)
    End Sub

    Private Sub button2_Click(ByVal sender As System.Object, ByVal e As
System.EventArgs) Handles button2.Click

        Dim cServiceA As localhost.SleepService1 = New _
localhost.SleepService1()
        Dim cServiceB As localhost.SleepService2 = New _
localhost.SleepService2()

        Dim arA As IAsyncResult = _
cServiceA.BeginSleepServiceA(Integer.Parse(txtA.Text), Nothing, Nothing)
        Dim arB As IAsyncResult = _
cServiceB.BeginSleepServiceB(Integer.Parse(txtB.Text), Nothing, Nothing)
```

LISTING 19.3   Continued

```vbnet
        Dim wh() As WaitHandle = {arA.AsyncWaitHandle, arB.AsyncWaitHandle}

        ' Wait for both async Web Service calls to finish
        WaitHandle.WaitAll(wh)

        ' Retrieve the results by calling the End method of the proxy class
        txtResult.Text = cServiceA.EndSleepServiceA(arA)
        txtResult.Text += "\r\n" + cServiceB.EndSleepServiceB(arB)

    End Sub

    Private Sub button3_Click(ByVal sender As System.Object, ByVal e As _
System.EventArgs) Handles button3.Click

        Dim cServiceA As localhost.SleepService1 = New _
localhost.SleepService1()
        Dim cServiceB As localhost.SleepService2 = New _
localhost.SleepService2()

        Dim arA As IAsyncResult = _
cServiceA.BeginSleepServiceA(Integer.Parse(txtA.Text), Nothing, Nothing)
        Dim arB As IAsyncResult = _
cServiceB.BeginSleepServiceB(Integer.Parse(txtB.Text), Nothing, Nothing)

        Dim wh() As WaitHandle = {arA.AsyncWaitHandle, arB.AsyncWaitHandle}

        ' Wait for the first Web Service to finish, then process
        Dim iReturn As Integer = WaitHandle.WaitAny(wh)

        If arA.IsCompleted Then
            txtResult.Text = cServiceA.EndSleepServiceA(arA)
        ElseIf arB.IsCompleted Then
            txtResult.Text = cServiceB.EndSleepServiceB(arB)
        End If

    End Sub

    Private Sub button4_Click(ByVal sender As System.Object, ByVal e As _
System.EventArgs) Handles button4.Click

        Dim cServiceA As localhost.SleepService1 = New _
localhost.SleepService1()
```

LISTING 19.3   Continued

```
        Dim arA As IAsyncResult = _
cServiceA.BeginSleepServiceA(Integer.Parse(txtA.Text), Nothing, Nothing)

        ' Perform as much work as possible, then wait to see if Web Service
        ' is finished.
        txtResult.Text = "Please wait ..."
        AsyncClient.ActiveForm.Refresh()

        arA.AsyncWaitHandle.WaitOne()

        txtResult.Text = cServiceA.EndSleepServiceA(arA)

    End Sub

End Class
```

LISTING 19.4   AsyncClient.cs for C#

```
using System;
using System.Drawing;
using System.Collections;
using System.ComponentModel;
using System.Windows.Forms;
using System.Data;
using System.Threading;

namespace Chapter19CSharpWindows
{
    /// <summary>
    /// Summary description for Form1.
    /// </summary>
    ///
    public class AsyncClient : System.Windows.Forms.Form
    {
        private System.Windows.Forms.Button button1;
        private System.Windows.Forms.Button button2;
        private System.Windows.Forms.Button button3;
        private System.Windows.Forms.Button button4;
        private System.Windows.Forms.Label label1;
        private System.Windows.Forms.Label B;
        private System.Windows.Forms.TextBox txtA;
        private System.Windows.Forms.TextBox txtB;
        private System.Windows.Forms.TextBox txtResult;
        private System.Windows.Forms.Label label2;
```

LISTING 19.4   Continued

```csharp
/// <summary>
/// Required designer variable.
/// </summary>
private System.ComponentModel.Container components = null;

public AsyncClient()
{
    //
    // Required for Windows Form Designer support
    //
    InitializeComponent();

    //
    // TODO: Add any constructor code after InitializeComponent call
    //
}

/// <summary>
/// Clean up any resources being used.
/// </summary>
protected override void Dispose( bool disposing )
{
    if( disposing )
    {
        if (components != null)
        {
            components.Dispose();
        }
    }
    base.Dispose( disposing );
}

#region Windows Form Designer generated code
        .
        .
        .

#endregion

/// <summary>
/// The main entry point for the application.
/// </summary>
[MTAThread]
static void Main()
{
```

LISTING 19.4 Continued

```csharp
        Application.Run(new AsyncClient());
    }

    private void button1_Click(object sender, System.EventArgs e)
    {
        localhost.SleepService1 cService = new localhost.SleepService1();

        // cb is a function pointer to ServiceCallback
        AsyncCallback cb = new AsyncCallback(ServiceCallback);

        // Call the Begin method of the proxy class to initiate the
        // asynchronous call to the Web Service method.
        cService.BeginSleepServiceA(int.Parse(txtA.Text), cb, cService);
    }

    public void ServiceCallback(IAsyncResult ar)
    {
        // Retrieve the original state for the proxy
        localhost.SleepService1 cService =
(localhost.SleepService1)ar.AsyncState;

        // Retrieve the results by calling the End method of the proxy
class
        txtResult.Text = cService.EndSleepServiceA(ar);
    }

    private void button2_Click(object sender, System.EventArgs e)
    {
        localhost.SleepService1 cServiceA = new localhost.SleepService1();
        localhost.SleepService2 cServiceB = new localhost.SleepService2();

        IAsyncResult arA =
cServiceA.BeginSleepServiceA(int.Parse(txtA.Text), null, null);
        IAsyncResult arB =
cServiceB.BeginSleepServiceB(int.Parse(txtB.Text), null, null);

        WaitHandle[] wh = {arA.AsyncWaitHandle, arB.AsyncWaitHandle};

        // Wait for both async Web Service calls to finish
        WaitHandle.WaitAll(wh);

        // Retrieve the results by calling the End method of the proxy
class
        txtResult.Text = cServiceA.EndSleepServiceA(arA);
```

19

LISTING 19.4 Continued

```csharp
                txtResult.Text += "\r\n" + cServiceB.EndSleepServiceB(arB);
        }

        private void button3_Click(object sender, System.EventArgs e)
        {

            localhost.SleepService1 cServiceA = new localhost.SleepService1();
            localhost.SleepService2 cServiceB = new localhost.SleepService2();

            IAsyncResult arA =
cServiceA.BeginSleepServiceA(int.Parse(txtA.Text), null, null);
            IAsyncResult arB =
cServiceB.BeginSleepServiceB(int.Parse(txtB.Text), null, null);

            WaitHandle[] wh = {arA.AsyncWaitHandle, arB.AsyncWaitHandle};

            // Wait for the first Web Service to finish, then process
            int iReturn = WaitHandle.WaitAny(wh);

            if (arA.IsCompleted)
            {
                txtResult.Text = cServiceA.EndSleepServiceA(arA);
            }
            else if (arB.IsCompleted)
            {
                txtResult.Text = cServiceB.EndSleepServiceB(arB);
            }
        }

        private void button4_Click(object sender, System.EventArgs e)
        {
            localhost.SleepService1 cServiceA = new localhost.SleepService1();

            IAsyncResult arA =
cServiceA.BeginSleepServiceA(int.Parse(txtA.Text), null, null);

            // Perform as much work as possible, then wait to see if Web
Service
            // is finished.
            txtResult.Text = "Please wait ...";
            AsyncClient.ActiveForm.Refresh();

            arA.AsyncWaitHandle.WaitOne();

            txtResult.Text = cServiceA.EndSleepServiceA(arA);
```

LISTING 19.4   Continued

```
        }
    }
}
```

The `button1_Click` event (for the Using Callback button) calls the SleepService Web Service by using the callback approach. This approach entails creating an `AsyncCallback` object, passing in the name of the function (the `ServiceCallback` function) that should be called when the Web Service results are returned. Next, a call is made to the proxy's `Begin<WebServiceMethod>` method (`BeginSleepServiceA`), passing in an instance of the `AsyncCallback` object and the input parameters for the Web Service. After this line of code, the function ends, and users are free to interact with the application as they choose.

After the SleepService returns results, the `ServiceCallback` function is alerted and passed an instance of `IAsyncResult`, the object that along with the `AsyncCallback` object, facilitates the asynchronous return of the correct information to the appropriate client call. The `ServiceCallback` function is where the results of the Web Service are retrieved and displayed.

The `button2_Click` event (for the Using WaitHandle (All) button) calls both SleepService Web Services by using the `WaitHandle.WaitAll` approach. An instance of the `IAsyncResult` object is returned from both `Begin<WebServiceMethod>` calls to the Web Service. An array of `WaitHandle` objects are created by passing in the two instances of the `IAsyncResult` object, and that array (`wh`) is instructed to wait for both Web Services to conclude before continuing on with the `WaitAll` method. After both Web Services return with their results, the function continues processing by displaying the results to the form.

The `button3_Click` event (for the Using WaitHandle (Any) button) operates much in the same way as the `button2_Click` event, except that it uses the `WaitHandle.WaitAny` approach. After the array of `WaitHandle` objects is created, the client application is instructed to wait for the first Web Service to finish before continuing to process the rest of the function. The results of the lagging Web Service are ignored if it has not yet finished (determined by using the `IsCompleted` property of the particular `IAsyncResult` instance.)

Although the `button4_Click` event (for the Using WaitHandle (One) button) is akin to the other `WaitHandle` approaches, it's actually more similar to the callback approach. This `click` event uses the `WaitOne` method of the `WaitHandle` object, which effectively creates a callback that runs within the same function. With this approach, you can call the Web Service at the very beginning of the function, and then continue to perform other processing. In this example, a "Please wait" message is written to the screen, but conceivably you could have queried other objects or databases and performed a calculation or two—whatever business logic was necessary—until the last possible moment when you need the result of the Web Service before it can continue. The distinction between this approach and a callback is that no additional method is required. The difference between this and the other `WaitHandle` methods is that it involves only one Web Service, not multiple ones. Although it is entirely possible to use multiple Web Services that all use the `WaitOne` approach, you might be better served using one of the other `WaitHandle` approaches.

Testing the Callbacks and `WaitHandle` Functions

To test this application, follow these steps:

1. Set the Windows Form application to the default startup project by right-clicking it in Solution Explorer, and then choosing Set as Startup Project on the pop-up menu.

2. Compile the entire solution by choosing Build | Build Solution on the menu. If there were any problems during the build, make sure you typed the code exactly as it appears in the code listing, and remember that many code elements are case sensitive in .NET.

3. Press F5 or choose Debug | Run on the menu to run the application.

To test the callback approach, enter a numeric value that represents milliseconds in the text box labeled "A." I entered `10000` (that is, 10 seconds). Then click the Using Callback button. After a while—usually more than 10 seconds because of compilation and caching—the results appear in the Results text box: `A Finished`. Your AsyncClient Windows Form should look similar to Figure 19.2.

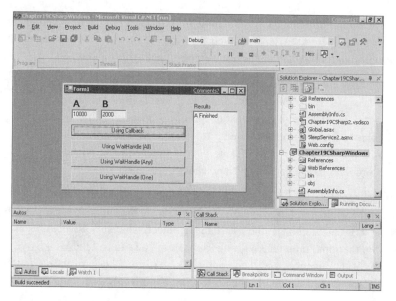

FIGURE 19.2

Results of using the callback approach in the AsyncClient Windows Form.

To test the `WaitHandle.WaitAll` and `WaitHandle.WaitAny` methods, enter a value in the B text box. I entered 2000 (2 seconds). This value is enough of a disparity that the B service should return faster than the A service. However, after clicking the `Using WaitHandle (All)` button, the process still takes a full 10 seconds (or more) because it must wait for both Web Services to return. Clicking the Using WaitHandle (Any) button takes much less time because it responds to the first Web Service that finishes.

Finally, to test the `WaitHandle.WaitOne` method, leave the values in the A and B text boxes alone and click the Using WaitHandle (One) button. The message in the Results text box changes to `Please wait...` before displaying the text A `Finished` some 10 seconds (or so) later.

Summary

An effective way to improve the performance of your applications that use Web Services is to consider calling those Web Services asynchronously. Most Web Services live on the Internet, where latency caused by network traffic and distance can be a factor in diminishing performance. Through strategic coding, you can make calls to Web Services, and then allow the user to regain control of the application (for Windows Forms application) or continue processing by calling other components or databases or performing other processor-intensive calculations (for ASP.NET Web Forms).

Calling Web Services asynchronously has little to do with the Web Service itself, but everything to do with the application that calls it. In other words, there is nothing special you must do when creating Web Services for them to be called asynchronously.

In this chapter, you have seen the use of four different approaches to calling Web Services asynchronously. The callback method is a good approach when you need to make a call and then return control of the application to the user until the call has finished. This method is ideal for a Windows Forms application. The `WaitHandle` approaches enable you to call a Web Service and then wait for the first one to return (`WaitAny`), wait for all the Web Services to return (`WaitAll`), or implement an in-function alternative to callbacks (`WaitOne`). Because the `WaitHandle` approach makes the call and returns the values—all within the same function—it is the preferred approach for Web Forms applications.

Consuming Web Services in
Office XP

IN THIS CHAPTER

In the spirit of showing how to consume Web Services from many different types of clients, I've created an example of consuming two Web methods from an Excel 2002 (Office XP) client. As you'll soon discover, this approach demonstrates the ability to create VBA-based Excel applications that respond to events and to retrieve information and write it to a spreadsheet, and the ability of the MSXML 3.0 object to call Web Services and return the SOAP XML that can then be processed.

The MSXML 3.0 object's HTTP object enables you to call a Web Service using HTTP-GET, HTTP-POST, or SOAP. In this chapter, you'll see how to call Web Services by using the HTTP-GET and SOAP methods. When using the SOAP method, you set the header information and the body of the request, and send it to an HTTP endpoint. If successful, the object returns the SOAP response as a parsed XML DOM, ready to be accessed in a hierarchical object. If unsuccessful, the object returns information about why the call failed.

> **NOTE**
>
> The title of this chapter is a slight misnomer. In actuality, this chapter describes how to use the MSXML 3.0 object to call a Web Service, and works perfectly with Office 2000, too. Additionally, the concepts and example can be modified to work with Visual Basic 6.0 and earlier versions as well as classic Active Server Pages and other applications that can make calls to the MSXML 3.0 component. This component is installed with Internet Explorer 5.0 and later, or can be downloaded independently from the http://msdn.microsoft.com Web site.

The Office Web Service Example

Many companies use Excel every week to calculate timesheets for departmental billing and fax them to their accounting departments. You can imagine the work required to take all the faxes and manually enter the numbers from the faxed Excel spreadsheet to the payroll application these companies use. By using Web Services, many of these companies could have employees log their time via Excel spreadsheets, or any other software that could consume the service, to enter and submit their hours. Additionally, employees could see the exact amount of taxes, insurance payments, and so forth that are deducted from the amount entered in their bank accounts at the end of the pay period.

Creating the Web Service

To follow along, please perform the following steps:

1. In Visual Studio .NET, choose File | New | Project on the menu to open the New Project dialog box.

2. Select your language in the Project Types list box on the left (Visual Basic Projects or Visual C# Projects), and then select ASP.NET Web Service in the Templates list box on the right.

3. In the Name text box, type **Chapter20VB** if you are creating this project using VB .NET, or type **Chapter20CSharp** if you are creating it using C#.

4. Accept the default location in the Location field.

5. Click the OK button. Visual Studio .NET will create a new project based on the language and template you selected.

6. In Solution Explorer, rename Service1.asmx as OfficeService.asmx by right-clicking the file, and then choosing Rename on the pop-up menu. Type the new name of the file in the text box with the Service1.asmx filename highlighted, and press Enter to accept the name change.

7. Click the Show All Files icon at the top of the Solution Explorer window to display all the hidden files, including the Code Behind file for OfficeService.asmx.

8. Click the + next to the OfficeService.asmx file to reveal OfficeService.asmx.vb (for VB .NET) or OfficeService.asmx.cs (for C#).

9. Select the OfficeService.asmx.vb or OfficeService.asmx.cs file in Solution Explorer, and then click the View Code button at the top of the Solution Explorer window to display the Code Behind file in the main area of Visual Studio .NET. This is where you'll edit the Code Behind file. As you can see, Visual Studio .NET has already generated code in this file for you.

10. Type the code formatted in bold in Listing 20.1 for VB .NET or Listing 20.2 for C# into the Code Behind file that is currently open. As is the convention throughout this book, the code not formatted in bold is included as context to help you determine where to enter your code.

LISTING 20.1 OfficeService.asmx.vb in VB .NET Code

```
Imports System.Web.Services

Public Class OfficeService
    Inherits System.Web.Services.WebService

    Public Class WeeklySummary
        Public ConsultantRate As Double
        Public TotalHours As Double
        Public GrossEarnings As Double
        Public Taxes As Double
        Public MedicalDeducation As Double
```

LISTING 20.1 Continued

```
        Public NetEarnings As Double
        Public Approval As String
    End Class

#Region " Web Services Designer Generated Code "

    Public Sub New()
        MyBase.New()

        'This call is required by the Web Services Designer.
        InitializeComponent()

        'Add your own initialization code after the InitializeComponent() call

    End Sub

    'Required by the Web Services Designer
    Private components As System.ComponentModel.Container

    'NOTE: The following procedure is required by the Web Services Designer
    'It can be modified using the Web Services Designer.
    'Do not modify it using the code editor.
    <System.Diagnostics.DebuggerStepThrough()> Private Sub
InitializeComponent()
        components = New System.ComponentModel.Container()
    End Sub

    Protected Overloads Overrides Sub Dispose(ByVal disposing As Boolean)
        'CODEGEN: This procedure is required by the Web Services Designer
        'Do not modify it using the code editor.
    End Sub

#End Region

    <WebMethod()> Public Function PostHours(ByVal sConsultantID As String, _
        ByVal dHours As Double) As String

        'Save hours for Consultant
        'Return approval code
        PostHours = "A12301"
    End Function

    <WebMethod()> Public Function PostWeek(ByVal sConsultantID As String, _
        ByVal dMonday As Double, ByVal dTuesday As Double, _
```

LISTING 20.1   Continued

```
        ByVal dWednesday As Double, ByVal dThursday As Double, _
        ByVal dFriday As Double) As WeeklySummary

        Dim myWS As WeeklySummary = New WeeklySummary()

        ' We'll assume we use the sConsultantID for a database lookup
        ' to get the ConsultantRate and the MedicalDeduction.
        myWS.ConsultantRate = 45
        myWS.TotalHours = dMonday + dTuesday + dWednesday + dThursday + dFriday
        myWS.GrossEarnings = myWS.ConsultantRate * myWS.TotalHours
        myWS.Taxes = myWS.GrossEarnings * 0.3
        myWS.MedicalDeduction = 300
        myWS.NetEarnings = myWS.GrossEarnings - (myWS.Taxes + _
myWS.MedicalDeduction)

        ' Again, assume we are calculating this and storing it off.
        myWS.Approval = "Q00009"

        PostWeek = myWS

    End Function

End Class
```

LISTING 20.2   OfficeService.asmx.cs in C# Code

```csharp
using System;
using System.Collections;
using System.ComponentModel;
using System.Data;
using System.Diagnostics;
using System.Web;
using System.Web.Services;

namespace Chapter20CSharp
{
    /// <summary>
    /// Summary description for Service1.
    /// </summary>
    public class OfficeService : System.Web.Services.WebService
    {

        public class WeeklySummary
        {
```

LISTING 20.2 Continued

```csharp
        public double ConsultantRate;
        public double TotalHours;
        public double GrossEarnings;
        public double Taxes;
        public double MedicalDeduction;
        public double NetEarnings;
        public string Approval;
    }

public OfficeService()
{
    //CODEGEN: This call is required by the
    //ASP.NET Web Services Designer
    InitializeComponent();
}

#region Component Designer generated code
/// <summary>
/// Required method for Designer support - do not modify
/// the contents of this method with the code editor.
/// </summary>
private void InitializeComponent()
{
}
#endregion

/// <summary>
/// Clean up any resources being used.
/// </summary>
protected override void Dispose( bool disposing )
{
}

[WebMethod]
public string PostHours(string sConsultantID, double dHours)
{

    // Save hours for Consultant
    // Return approval code
    return "A12301";
}

[WebMethod]
public WeeklySummary PostWeek(string sConsultantID, double dMonday,
```

LISTING 20.2 Continued

```
            double dTuesday, double dWednesday, double dThursday,
            double dFriday)
    {

        WeeklySummary myWS = new WeeklySummary();

        // We'll assume we use the sConsultantID for a database lookup
        // to get the ConsultantRate and the MedicalDeduction.
        myWS.ConsultantRate = 45;
        myWS.TotalHours =
            dMonday + dTuesday + dWednesday + dThursday + dFriday;
        myWS.GrossEarnings = myWS.ConsultantRate * myWS.TotalHours;
        myWS.Taxes = myWS.GrossEarnings * .3;
        myWS.MedicalDeduction = 300;
        myWS.NetEarnings = myWS.GrossEarnings -
            (myWS.Taxes + myWS.MedicalDeduction);

        // Again, assume we are calculating this and storing it off.
        myWS.Approval = "Q00009";

        return myWS;
    }
  }
}
```

Compile the Web Service by choosing Build | Build on the menu. If there were any problems during the build, make sure you typed the code exactly as it appears in the code listing, and remember, many things are case sensitive in .NET.

Test the Web Services in the Web Service help page by right-clicking the OfficeService.asmx file in Solution Explorer, and then choosing View in Browser on the pop-up menu.

Creating the Excel Spreadsheet: Part 1

Now you will create a spreadsheet with interactive form elements that will invoke and display the results of the Web Service. In the first part of this exercise, you add a button that enables users to submit their consultant IDs and hours to the PostHours() Web method. To continue, perform the following steps:

1. Open Excel, and save a new spreadsheet as OfficeTest.xls.
2. Add text to two cells in A1 and A4 (as shown in Figure 20.1) to indicate labels for the input you need. Click the Button icon on the Forms toolbar and draw a button on the right side of the window.

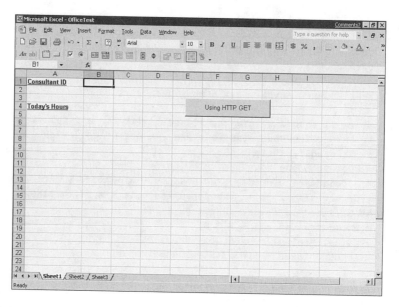

FIGURE 20.1
The initial OfficeTest spreadsheet.

3. When the Assign Macro dialog box opens, click the New button to open the Visual Basic for Applications (VBA) development window. Figure 20.2 shows the VBA IDE, with the button event handler Sub Button1_Click() as the only code onscreen.

> **NOTE**
>
> If you are creating this example using Excel 2000, the event name will actually be commandButton1_Click1(). Please keep this in mind as you type in the Excel code listing.

> **NOTE**
>
> If the Forms toolbar does not appear, right-click an empty area of the toolbar near the top of the window and choose Forms on the pop-up menu. If the Forms toolbar does not dock with the rest of the toolbars, you can drag it into place near the other toolbars.

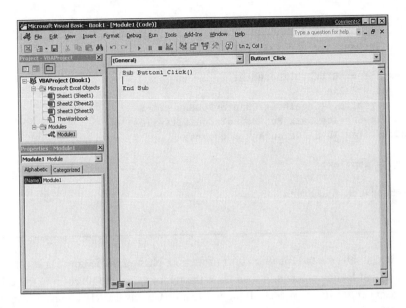

FIGURE 20.2

The VBA IDE for the Sub Button1_Click() *event handler.*

4. Next, add a reference to the MSXML 3.0 object. To do this, choose Tools | References on the VBA menu. In the References dialog box, scroll down and click the Microsoft XML 3.0 check box, and then click the OK button. Now you will be able to reference this object in your code.

5. Add the code in Listing 20.3. This code handles the Button1_Click() event and also adds the CallWebService() function, which takes care of calling the Web Service and returning the values from it.

LISTING 20.3   Excel VBA Code Listing

```
Dim dom As MSXML2.DOMDocument

Sub Button1_Click()

    Dim sReturn
    sReturn = CallWebservice(ActiveSheet.Range("B1").Value, _
        ActiveSheet.Range("B4").Value)

    Range("C4").Select
    ActiveCell.Value = sReturn

End Sub
```

LISTING 20.3   Continued

```
Function CallWebservice(sConsultantID, dHours)

    Set dom = New MSXML2.DOMDocument
    dom.async = False
    dom.Load ("http://localhost/Chapter20CSharp/" & _
        "OfficeService.asmx/PostHours?sConsultantID=" & _
        sConsultantID & "&dHours=" & dHours)

    sReturn = dom.Text

    CallWebservice = sReturn

End Function
```

Button1_Click() calls the CallWebService() function, passing in the ConsultantID (cell B1) and the Hours (cell B4) parameters. It then takes the return value and places it in the C4 cell. The CallWebService() function does all the work. It constructs a URL, complete with the name of the Web Service, the Web method, and the input parameters for the Web method, and loads the result into an XML DOM object. Because only one value is returned, the dom.Text property is supplied without the accompanying XML.

Testing the Spreadsheet

To test the spreadsheet, save the code and return the spreadsheet in Excel. Enter a value in the B1 cell (a fictitious ConsultantID, such as "A12301") and the number of hours worked in the B4 cell (such as 8). Then click Button1 on the spreadsheet, and the results should look similar to Figure 20.3.

NOTE

If you weren't able to test the application because you got a message about macros and security, your security settings might be set too high to work with macros. For the purpose of development, you should set the security setting to Medium, which asks each time a new Excel spreadsheet is opened whether you want to enable or disable macros. If you are not sure, select Disable, and then look at the code to see if it could be potentially harmful. To change the security settings, choose Tools | Options on the menu, select the Security tab, and click the Macro Security button to open the Security dialog box. On the Macro Security tab, make sure the Medium radio button is selected, and then click OK twice.

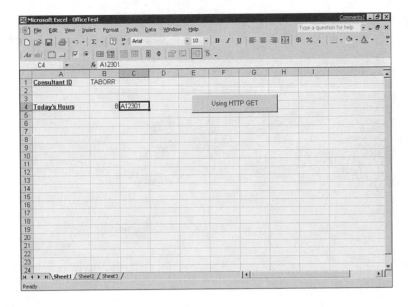

FIGURE 20.3
Results of clicking Button1.

Creating the Excel Spreadsheet: Part 2

In this part of the example, you'll create another section of the same spreadsheet that submits an entire week of hours at a time. Additionally, it retrieves multiple values from the Web Service and displays them onscreen. You will also see how to call the Web Service by using SOAP instead of HTTP-GET. The drawback of this approach is that you must construct the SOAP message by hand, including the appropriate HTTP request headers. (See the note following Listing 20.4 for a hint on how to ensure that your SOAP and HTTP requests are properly formed.) If the message is malformed even slightly, the call to the Web Service will not function. The advantage of this approach, however, is that it uses SOAP. Although the code doesn't check for errors, this approach returns a SOAP fault if an error occurs, so you can determine exactly what went wrong. To continue, follow these steps:

1. In the OfficeTest spreadsheet, add text in cells A25 to A30 of the existing spreadsheet to represent labels for the input values (as shown in Figure 20.4).

2. Click the Button icon on the Forms toolbar and draw a button for calling your SOAP-driven Web method.

3. When the Assign Macro dialog box opens, click the New button to open the VBA development window. Next, add the code in Listing 20.4. This new button is referenced as Button2 in Excel 2002 or commandButton2 in Excel 2000.

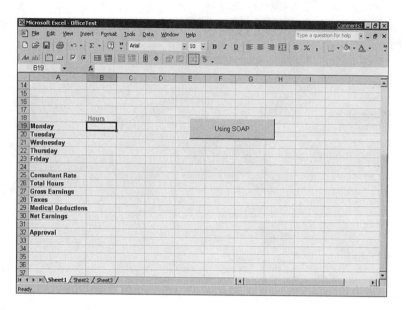

FIGURE 20.4

Setting up the spreadsheet for the second example.

LISTING 20.4   Excel VBA Code Listing (Continued)

```
Sub Button2_Click()

    Dim sConsID
    Dim dMon, dTues, dWed, dThurs, dFri

    sConsID = ActiveSheet.Range("B1").Value
    dMon = ActiveSheet.Range("B19").Value
    dTues = ActiveSheet.Range("B20").Value
    dWed = ActiveSheet.Range("B21").Value
    dThurs = ActiveSheet.Range("B22").Value
    dFri = ActiveSheet.Range("B23").Value

    Set node = GetWeeklySummary(sConsID, dMon, dTues, dWed, dThurs, dFri)
    If (Not node Is Nothing) Then

        With ActiveSheet
            .Range("B25").Value = _
                node.selectSingleNode("//ConsultantRate").Text
            .Range("B26").Value = _
                node.selectSingleNode("//TotalHours").Text
            .Range("B27").Value = _
```

LISTING 20.4   Continued

```
                    node.selectSingleNode("//GrossEarnings").Text
                .Range("B28").Value = _
                    node.selectSingleNode("//Taxes").Text
                .Range("B29").Value = _
                    node.selectSingleNode("//MedicalDeduction").Text
                .Range("B30").Value = _
                    node.selectSingleNode("//NetEarnings").Text
                .Range("B32").Value = _
                    node.selectSingleNode("//Approval").Text
        End With
    End If


End Sub

Function CallSOAPWebService(sRequest)

    Dim doc As MSXML2.DOMDocument
    Set doc = New MSXML2.DOMDocument
    doc.validateOnParse = False
    If (Not doc.loadXML(sRequest)) Then
        MsgBox "Problem: " & doc.parseError.reason & _
            " on line: " & doc.parseError.Line
        Exit Function
    End If

    Dim http As MSXML2.XMLHTTP
    Set http = New MSXML2.XMLHTTP

    http.Open "POST", _
        "http://localhost/Chapter20CSharp/OfficeService.asmx", False

    http.setRequestHeader "Host", "localhost"
    http.setRequestHeader "Content-Type", "text/xml; charset=utf-8"
    http.setRequestHeader "Content-Length", CStr(Len(doc.xml))
    http.setRequestHeader "SOAPAction", "http://tempuri.org/PostWeek"
    http.send (doc.xml)

    If (http.statusText <> "OK") Then
        MsgBox http.Status
        MsgBox http.readyState
    End If
```

LISTING 20.4   Continued

```
    Set CallSOAPWebService = http.responseXML

End Function


Private Function GetWeeklySummary(sConsID, dMon, dTues, dWed, dThurs, dFri)

    sRequest = "<PostWeek xmlns='http://tempuri.org/'>" & Chr(13) & _
        "<sConsultantID>" & sConsID & "</sConsultantID>" & Chr(13) & _
        "<dMonday>" & dMon & "</dMonday>" & Chr(13) & _
        "<dTuesday>" & dTues & "</dTuesday>" & Chr(13) & _
        "<dWednesday>" & dWed & "</dWednesday>" & Chr(13) & _
        "<dThursday>" & dThurs & "</dThursday>" & Chr(13) & _
        "<dFriday>" & dFri & "</dFriday>" & Chr(13) & _
        "</PostWeek>"

    sRequest = FormatSoapRequest(sRequest)

    Set GetWeeklySummary = CallSOAPWebService(sRequest)

End Function


Function FormatSoapRequest(sRequest)

    FormatSoapRequest = "<?xml version='1.0' encoding='UTF-8'?>" & Chr(13) & _
        "<soap:Envelope " & _
         "xmlns:xsi='http://www.w3.org/2001/XMLSchema-instance' " & _
         "xmlns:xsd='http://www.w3.org/2001/XMLSchema' " & _
         "xmlns:soap='http://schemas.xmlsoap.org/soap/envelope/'>" & _
         Chr(13) & "<soap:Body>" & Chr(13) & sRequest & _
         Chr(13) & "</soap:Body>" & Chr(13) & _
        "</soap:Envelope>"

End Function
```

The code in Listing 20.4 creates three functions in addition to the Sub Button2_Click() handler. The responsibility of the Button2_Click() function is to get values from the spreadsheet, submit them to the GetWeeklySummary() function, and then use the returned XML DOM (and an XPath query) to extract and display the return values in the appropriate cells of the spreadsheet.

These are the three functions created:

- **GetWeeklySummary()**   Formats the SOAP body
- **FormatSOAPRequest()**   Formats the SOAP envelope
- **CallSOAPWebService()**   Loads the SOAP message created by the other functions into an MSXML object to make sure the XML SOAP message is properly formatted. This function creates the MSXML2.XMLHTTP object, sets the Open and setRequestHeader methods, and then sends the SOAP message to the OfficeService.asmx Web method PostWeek. If it's unsuccessful, a message box reports the nature of the problem. Otherwise, the response SOAP XML stream is returned as an XML DOM to the Button2_Click() function.

NOTE

I relied heavily on the Web Service's help page to assist me in determining the correct format of the SOAP envelope, the SOAP body, and the HTTP request headers. Until I paid close attention to the sample SOAP call, shown in Figure 20.5, I had several unsuccessful attempts.

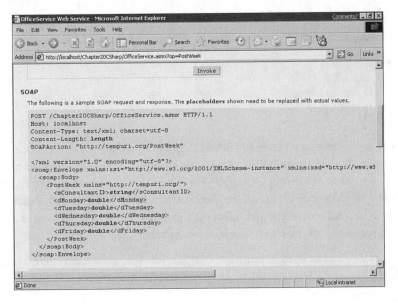

FIGURE 20.5

The sample SOAP call on the Web Service help page.

Testing the Spreadsheet

To test the spreadsheet, fill cells B19 through B23 with numeric values that represent the hours a consultant worked each day, and then click Button2. After a moment, you should see results similar to those in Figure 20.6.

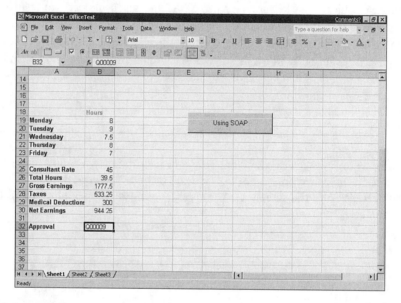

FIGURE 20.6
Results of clicking Button2.

Summary

Web Services can be consumed by many different applications, especially those that are script- or VBA-based, such as Microsoft Office XP. In this chapter, you have learned the process of calling Web Services to make your Office XP–based applications more versatile and interactive. The actual mechanism used to call the Web Services is the MSXML 3.0 object. This object can post an XML document and offers the flexibility to return the results in an XML DOM, which parses the results into a usable object hierarchy.

This same approach can be used to integrate Web Services into almost any application, including ASP pages, Visual Basic Windows applications, and COM+ objects.

Web Service Behaviors

IN THIS CHAPTER

Until now, you have seen only examples in which Web Services are consumed at the Web server or within another middle-tier component or application. In other words, you have created Web Services that are consumed by an ASP.NET Web Form that renders the information somehow on a Web page, which then sends that information to a Web browser. However, by using Web Service Behaviors, your Web pages can call Web Services from the client Web browser (as long as it is Internet Explorer 5.0 or higher) and render that data on the page using client-side JScript and Dynamic HTML (DHTML).

There are some advantages to using Web Service Behaviors, such as separating the content or data from the presentation layer. The client Web browser does not need to reload the page to get its latest version. It can simply call the Web Service and represent the new data dynamically, thus reducing the amount of network traffic and the perceived speed of your Web application.

However, there are some limitations and drawbacks, too. First, you must have a good deal of familiarity with client-side scripting techniques, including JScript and DHTML, to take advantage of this approach. Second, it works only on the newer generation of Internet Explorer, thus leaving out older IE versions and every other browser (Netscape, for example).The biggest limitation for some people is that, for security reasons, the current implementation of Web Service Behaviors works only with Web Services hosted in the same domain as the client Web page that makes the request. In other words, if you go to a Web page hosted on `http://www.technicallead.com`, and it is using a Web Service Behavior, it can call only the Web Services hosted on that same site. To work around this limitation, the documentation suggests that you consume the Web Services hosted elsewhere with a Web Service wrapper on your servers. The client Web page can then call your Web Service, which in turn calls the Web Service from, say, `http://www.soapwebservices.com`. Security is certainly a valid concern, but this limitation lessens the usefulness of Web Service Behaviors just a little.

For all of its disadvantages and limitations, however, this technology still makes sense in some situations. In this chapter, you learn more about DHTML Behaviors, see how the Web Service Behavior works behind the scenes, and step through an example that allows you to see the Web Service in action.

Understanding DHTML Behaviors

DHTML Behaviors are simple lightweight components encapsulating functionality or behaviors that can then be applied to Web page elements to enhance the page's default behavior. They work in Internet Explorer 5.0 and above and are typically used to facilitate dynamic features on Web pages, such as tree views and rollovers.

Behaviors are saved into HTC files (short for "HTML Control") and attached to elements by using `<style>` tags in the HTML document's `<head>` section (known as the CSS Behavior

Attribute approach) or inline by using the `style` attribute. The following example shows the use of a DHTML Behavior attached to a specific `<div>` tag:

```
<DIV STYLE="behavior:url(myBehavior.htc)">Conrad</DIV>
```

This Behavior could, for example, change the text color as the user's mouse passes over it, or it could make the text fly off the page if the user clicks a certain button on the page. Any DHTML or JScript magic you can think of can be encapsulated in a Behavior (an HTC file) and reused on multiple pages.

The benefits of Behaviors include the following:

- JScript developers can create the hard-core functionality, and HTML developers or graphic artists can easily apply them to the page elements they create without needing an in-depth understanding of the implementation.

- Pages created with DHTML Behaviors are cleaner and more manageable because the JScript is encapsulated in the HTC file.

- Code reuse can be realized by referencing the source code residing in a single file rather than cutting and pasting the code each time it's needed into every Web page that uses the Behavior.

For more information on DHTML Behaviors in general, go to:

```
http://msdn.microsoft.com/workshop/author/behaviors/overview.asp
```

How the Web Service Behavior Works

The Web Service Behavior is implemented as an HTML Control (HTC) file. The complexity of the following tasks and features are encapsulated and hidden from developers who implement Web Service Behaviors in their pages:

- Understanding the Web Service's WSDL

- Knowing how to format a SOAP request based on the WSDL

- Knowing how to communicate with the source of the Web Service

- Translating a SOAP response

- Translating a SOAP fault

Because the HTC file is merely a text file, you can open it to see the actual implementation of these features, if you like. After viewing the file, these steps are all that's left to do:

- Attach to the Web Service Behavior

- Identify the Web Service that will be used

- Call methods on the Web Service

- Handle results from the Web Service calls

Attaching to the Web Service Behavior

This step is analogous to creating a reference to the behavior and creating a new instance. To attach a Web Service Behavior to an HTML Web page, use the following syntax:

```
<body>
  <div id="Services" style="behavior:url(webservice.htc)"></div>
</body>
```

The `style` attribute is similar to the one used for the DHTML Behavior example, with the exception that the *behavior* being attached to is the Web Service Behavior's HTC file that resides on your Web site. To avoid relative path problems, you should keep the HTC file in the same directory as the page that calls it.

Also, an `ID` attribute is added that's used to reference this Behavior, as opposed to other Behaviors used on the page.

Identifying the Web Service

Next, you must identify the Web Service on the server that you will use. The following syntax creates a reference to the Web Service you'll use later in this chapter:

```
Services.useService("WSBehavior.asmx?WSDL", "WSBehavior");
```

The `Services` component is from the `ID` attribute in the `<div>` tag that was used to attach to the Web Service in the preceding section. The `useService` method, contained in the webservice.htc file, obtains the WSDL file (with ASP.NET Web Services, it's generated automatically by using the Web Service's filename and appending the `?WSDL` query string) and a "friendly" name ("WSBehavior," in this example) that is used to reference this Web Service in the rest of the code.

You can reference and use multiple Web Services in code as long as each is identified with a different "friendly name." This action downloads the Service Contract (WSDL) for the Web Service, which is used to construct the appropriate SOAP request message when the `callService` method is called.

Calling Web Service Methods

To actually perform the act of calling the Web Service, you use the `callService` method in one of two ways. You can create a custom event to handle the results of the Web Service, or use the built-in event to handle the result. With the first option, the `callService` method has an optional parameter—`handleWSBehavior`, in this example—that accepts the name of a callback function you create and implement for each `callService` method you perform, as shown in the following line:

```
iCallID = Services.WSBehavior.callService(handleWSBehavior, "myMethod", 5, 6)
```

The preceding line of code calls the WSBehavior's `myMethod` function, passing 5 and 6 as input parameters. By default, Web Service Behaviors are asynchronous, so this line of code completes immediately, setting an `iCallID` identifier for referencing that specific call to the Web Service. The code also sets the optional callback function, `handleWSBehavior`. When the Web Service asynchronously returns a result to your client, the Behavior expects a function called `handleWSBehavior` in the code. Callbacks are useful when you must handle the results from two or more Web Services differently, and this approach gives you fine-grained control over how each Web Service call is handled.

The second option is not setting the optional callback function, but using the `onWSresult` event handler function instead. This event is fired every time a Web Service is called and no callback is specified. This approach enables you to handle all Web Service calls in the same handler function. This event handler function works much the same way as the callback, with a result object passed into it when the Web Service completes.

Before you move on, notice the input parameters at the end of the `callService` method. This is an expanding set of parameters that allows you to set as many parameters as the particular Web Service needs. For example, here is the same call if three string properties are needed to satisfy the WSBehavior Web Service:

```
iCallID = Services.WSBehavior.callService(handleWSBehavior,

    "myMethod", "first", "second", "third")
```

Handling Results from the Web Service

The callback function (or `onWSresult` event) is passed a result object that contains the values resulting from the Web Service call. The following code shows an example of the `handleWSBehavior` callback function:

```
function handleWSBehavior(results)
{
    if (results.error)
    {
        var sFaultCode = results.errorDetail.code;
        var sFaultString = results.errorDetail.string;
        var sFaultSOAP = results.errorDetail.raw;
    }
    else
    {
        alert(results.value);
    }
}
```

The `results` object can return the actual SOAP response if the `raw` property is used. It can be loaded into the MSXML object for processing. Otherwise, using the `value` property returns the data in a more usable format because it is parsed and available through a more object-based structure. The `results` object has an `error` property that, if true, can alert your code to an existing problem. You can examine the `errorDetail` object (as shown in the preceding code example) to discover the error code (the `code` property), the message (`string` property), and the actual SOAP fault (`raw` property).

The WSBehavior Example

This example contains three Web Services that are called from client-side JScript to display the returned results on the Web page without reloading it. First, you create the ASP.NET Web Service, which has the following three Web methods:

- **GetHello()**   This Web method takes a string, appends `"Hello, "` to it, and returns it to the client. This procedure helps illustrate using a simple data type in the Web Service Behavior and displaying the result by using the `result.value` property.

- **List()**   This Web method takes a directory from the web server's hard drive and displays each child directory and the files in each directory for what could turn out to be a very complex XML document. This method illustrates using complex data types in the Web Service Behavior.

- **GetAuthors()**   This Web method uses the pubs database that is installed with SQL Server. It obtains a dataset of the Authors table, which is serialized and returned to the browser. This method could be the beginning of a series of dataset-bound client-side controls that allow the user to edit data, and then the dataset—complete with DiffGrams—to the Web Service to be persisted back to the data store. This is quite a bit of work, however, and way beyond the scope of this book.

Building the WSBehavior Web Service

First, create a new project called Chapter21VB (or Chapter21CSharp), and rename the default Service1.asmx file as WSBehavior.asmx in Solution Explorer. Open the Code Behind file for these pages and add the code formatted in bold in Listing 21.1 (for VB .NET) or Listing 21.2 (for C#). The code not formatted in bold was generated by Visual Studio .NET and was left in the listings as context to help you determine where to enter the code.

> **NOTE**
>
> For detailed step-by-step instructions to create a new Web Services project, rename the file, and access the Code Behind module, please refer to one of the previous chapters in this book.

LISTING 21.1 WSBehavior.asmx.vb in VB.NET

```vbnet
Imports System.Web.Services
Imports System.Data.SqlClient
Imports System.Collections
Imports System.Xml.Serialization

Public Class WSBehavior
    Inherits System.Web.Services.WebService

    Public Class Dir

Public Class Dir
        Public Name As String

        <XmlArray("SubDirs"), XmlArrayItem("Dir", GetType(Dir))> _
        Public SubDirs As New ArrayList()

        <XmlArray("Files"), XmlArrayItem(GetType(String))> _
        Public Files As New ArrayList()
    End Class

#Region " Web Services Designer Generated Code "

    Public Sub New()
        MyBase.New()

        'This call is required by the Web Services Designer.
        InitializeComponent()
        'Add your own initialization code after the InitializeComponent() call
    End Sub

    'Required by the Web Services Designer
    Private components As System.ComponentModel.Container

    'NOTE: The following procedure is required by the Web Services Designer
    'It can be modified using the Web Services Designer.
    'Do not modify it using the code editor.
    <System.Diagnostics.DebuggerStepThrough()> Private Sub
InitializeComponent()
        components = New System.ComponentModel.Container()
    End Sub

    Protected Overloads Overrides Sub Dispose(ByVal disposing As Boolean)
        'CODEGEN: This procedure is required by the Web Services Designer
        'Do not modify it using the code editor.
    End Sub

#End Region
```

LISTING 21.1   Continued

```
<WebMethod()> Public Function GetHello(ByVal name As String) As String
    GetHello = "Hello, " & name
End Function


<WebMethod()> Public Function List(ByVal sPath As String) As Dir

    Dim i As Integer
    Dim j As Integer

    Dim info As System.IO.DirectoryInfo = New _
System.IO.DirectoryInfo(sPath)
    Dim d As New Dir()
    d.Name = info.Name

    Dim files As System.IO.FileInfo() = info.GetFiles()
    If files.Length > 0 Then
        For i = 0 To files.Length - 1
            d.Files.Add(files(i).Name)
        Next i
    End If

    Dim dirs As System.IO.DirectoryInfo() = info.GetDirectories()
    If dirs.Length > 0 Then
        For j = 0 To dirs.Length - 1
            d.SubDirs.Add(List(dirs(j).FullName))
        Next j
    End If

    List = d

End Function

<WebMethod()> Public Function GetAuthors() As DataSet

    Dim con As SqlConnection = New _
SqlConnection("server=localhost;database=pubs;uid=sa;pwd=;")
    Dim adp As SqlDataAdapter = New SqlDataAdapter("SELECT * FROM Authors", _
con)
    Dim ds As DataSet = New DataSet("Pubs")

    con.Open()
    Try
        adp.Fill(ds, "Authors")
    Finally
```

LISTING 21.1   Continued

```
            con.Close()
        End Try
        GetAuthors = ds
    End Function
End Class
```

LISTING 21.2   WSBehavior.asmx.cs in C#

```csharp
using System;
using System.Collections;
using System.ComponentModel;
using System.Data;
using System.Diagnostics;
using System.Web;
using System.Web.Services;
using System.Data.SqlClient;
using System.Xml.Serialization;

namespace Chapter21CSharp
{
    public class Dir
    {
        public string Name;
        public Dir[] SubDirs;
        public string[] Files;
    }

    public class WSBehavior : System.Web.Services.WebService
    {
        public WSBehavior()
        {
            //CODEGEN: This call is required by the ASP.NET Web Services
Designer
            InitializeComponent();
        }

        #region Component Designer generated code
        /// <summary>
        /// Required method for Designer support - do not modify
        /// the contents of this method with the code editor.
        /// </summary>
        private void InitializeComponent()
        {
```

LISTING 21.2   Continued

```
    }
    #endregion

    /// <summary>
    /// Clean up any resources being used.
    /// </summary>
    public override void Dispose()
    {
    }

    [WebMethod]
    public string GetHello(string name)
    {
        return "Hello, " + name;
    }

    [WebMethod]
    public Dir List(string sPath)
    {
        //sPath = Server.MapPath(sPath);
        System.IO.DirectoryInfo info = new System.IO.DirectoryInfo(sPath);

        Dir d = new Dir();
        d.Name = info.Name;

        System.IO.FileInfo[] files = info.GetFiles();
        d.Files = new string[files.Length];
        for (int i=0; i<files.Length; i++)
        {
            d.Files[i] = files[i].Name;
        }

        System.IO.DirectoryInfo[] dirs = info.GetDirectories();
        d.SubDirs = new Dir[dirs.Length];
        for (int i=0; i<dirs.Length; i++)
        {
            d.SubDirs[i] = List(dirs[i].FullName);
        }

        return d;
    }

    [WebMethod]
    public DataSet GetAuthors()
    {
```

LISTING 21.2 Continued

```
        SqlConnection con = new
SqlConnection("server=localhost;database=pubs;uid=sa;pwd=;");
        SqlDataAdapter adp = new SqlDataAdapter("SELECT * FROM Authors",
con);
        DataSet ds = new DataSet("Pubs");

        con.Open();
        try
        {
            adp.Fill(ds, "Authors");
        }
        finally
        {
            con.Close();
        }

        return ds;
        }
    }
}
```

> **NOTE**
>
> Please be aware of the use of the connection string in the preceding examples. You might need to change it to accommodate the settings on your machine or in your environment. Additionally, you can try the following snippet, or some derivation, to assist in connecting if the code in the listings does not work:
>
> ```
> SqlConnection myConnection = new
> SqlConnection("server=(local);database=pubs;Trusted_Connection=yes");
> ```

The implementations for these Web methods are fairly straightforward, so instead of explaining them in detail, the following section focuses on the Web Service Behavior.

Downloading the WebService.htc

Make sure you download the latest WebService.htc control from the Microsoft site:

```
http://msdn.microsoft.com/workshop/author/webservice/webservice.htc
```

NOTE

If this link for the WebService.htc control does not work, you can search MSDN for the term "Web Service Behavior."

Having the most recent Web Service Behavior ensures that your application will work with the latest changes to Visual Studio .NET.

After you download the file to your computer, copy it into your project (that is, the same physical directory as the Web Service files you have created). You can open it if you like, although in my experience, Visual Studio .NET has a difficult time parsing through it and representing the syntax highlighting correctly.

Building the WSBehavior Client with the Web Service Behavior

Next, add a new Web page (HTML page) to the project (right-click on the project in Solution Explorer and choose Add | Add HTML Web Page on the pop-up menu), name the page WSBehaviorClient.htm, and type in the code in Listing 21.3.

LISTING 21.3   HTML Code for WSBehaviorClient.htm

```
<!DOCTYPE HTML PUBLIC "-//W3C//DTD HTML 4.0 Transitional//EN" >
<HTML>
<HEAD>
<TITLE>Web Service Behavior Sample</TITLE>
<script>
function window_onLoad()
{
    Services.useService("WSBehavior.asmx?WSDL", "WSBehavior");
}

function SimpleTypeResult(result)
{
    if(result.error)
    {
        Output.value = result.errorDetail.raw;
    }
    else
    {
        Output.value = result.value;
    }
}
```

LISTING 21.3 Continued

```
function showDir(dir)
{
    for (var i=0; i<dir.SubDirs.length; i++)
    {
        Output.value += dir.SubDirs[i].Name + "\r\n";
    }

    for (var i=0; i<dir.Files.length; i++)
    {
        Output.value += dir.Files[i] + "\r\n";
    }
}

function ComplexTypeResult(result)
{
    if(result.error)
    {
        Output.value = result.errorDetail.raw.xml;
    }
    else
    {
        // the result is an object hierarchy
        // that is the same as the object hierarchy
        // that was serialized from the server
        var d = result.value;
        Output.value = "";
        showDir(d);
    }
}

function DataSetResult(result)
{
    if(result.error)
    {
        Output.value = result.errorDetail.raw;
    }
    else
    {
        // the result is an XML DOM document
        // containing the XSD schema and the
        // XML data
        Output.value = result.value.xml;
    }
}
```

LISTING 21.3   Continued

```
function btnSimpleType_onClick()
{
    var name = prompt('Enter your name:', '');
    if (name != null && name != "")
    Services.WSBehavior.call(SimpleTypeResult, "GetHello", name);
}
function btnComplexType_onClick()
{
    var name = prompt('Enter directory path:', '');
    if (name != null && name != "")
        Services.WSBehavior.callService(ComplexTypeResult, "List", name);
}
function btnDataSet_onClick()
{
    Services.WSBehavior.call(DataSetResult, "GetAuthors");
}
</script>
</HEAD>
<BODY onload="window_onLoad()">
<INPUT type="button" value="Simple Type" onclick="btnSimpleType_onClick()">
<INPUT type="button" value="Complex Type" onclick="btnComplexType_onClick()">
<INPUT type="button" value="DataSet" onclick="btnDataSet_onClick()">
<textarea id="Output"
    style="width:100%;height:400px;border:solid black 1px;">
</textarea>
<div id="Services" showprogress="true"
    style="behavior:url(webservice.htc);display:none;">
</div>
</BODY>
</HTML>
```

When the Web page loads, the window_onLoad() event is fired. The handler for this event references the Web Service's WSDL and sets the "friendly name." When the user clicks each of the buttons, the appropriate event is fired (as designated in the onclick property of each button), which sets the callService method in motion. Each of the callService methods designates a callback function to receive the results. The results are then displayed in the text area control on the Web page. If you want to expand this example on your own, you could perform additional processing on the results, load them into the MSXML object, and display them in a tree, among other possibilities.

NOTE

It is imperative that you use the latest webservice.htc from Microsoft (it might not necessarily be the one that ships with Visual Studio .NET or the .NET Framework) and that you follow the instructions, especially about the folder the file must reside in, for this example to work.

To test the Web Service Behavior in action, right-click on the WSBehaviorClient.htm file in Solution Explorer and choose View in Browser. The results should be similar to Figure 21.1.

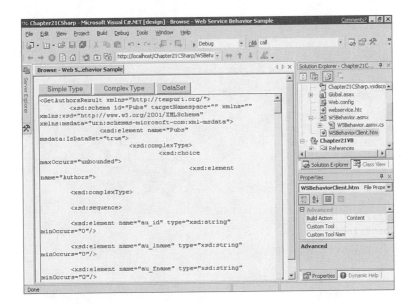

FIGURE 21.1
The results of the WSBehaviorClient.htm Web Service Behavior.

One last note: In the <div> tag where you specify the webservice.htc as the DHTML Behavior of choice, you also set the showprogress property; when set to true, it displays a blue bar in the upper-left area of the Web browser with scrolling text that states "In progress." During development, this is a great way to make sure your pages are working correctly, but should probably be set to false when you make the Web page available to the world.

Summary

Web Service Behaviors enable Internet Explorer 5.0 and higher to call Web Services and display or modify the results by using DHTML and client-side JScript. This allows the Web page to be updated without a full refresh of the entire page, thus saving time and bandwidth. In this chapter, you learned how to create an instance of the Web Service Behavior in your Web page, how to reference a Web Service, call it, and display the results.

For more information on Web Service Behaviors, I would encourage you to take a look at this site:

```
http://msdn.microsoft.com/workshop/author/webservice/overview.asp
```

Manipulating SOAP Headers in Web Services

IN THIS CHAPTER

In this chapter you will learn how to utilize the header section of the SOAP messages that are sent to and received from Web Services. The .NET Framework provides easy-to-use interfaces that allow you to append and read the information in the SOAP header.

As you may recall from Chapter 7, "Examining SOAP," the SOAP header is an optional part of the SOAP message. It is intended for additional information that's not part of the method call, but might be important contextually to processing the method call—for example, an account ID, a date/time stamp, a transactional vote, or even an encryption key. Here is an example of a SOAP message with a properly formatted SOAP header that is passing account ID information:

```
<SOAP-ENV:Envelope xmlns:SOAP- ENV="http://schemas.cmlsoap.org/soap/envelope/">
  <SOAP-ENV:Header>
    <ACCT:AccountID
      xmlns:ACCT="urn:schemas-myurl-com:accountid"
      SOAP-ENV:root="1">
      T120769
    </ACCT>
  </SOAP-ENV:Header>

  <SOAP-ENV:Body>

    <!-- The rest of the SOAP body goes here -->

  </SOAP-ENV:Body>
</SOAP-ENV:Envelope>
```

The .NET Framework classes allow full control of every aspect of the SOAP header and prevent developers from creating improperly formatted header messages.

Creating a Sample SOAP Header Web Service

In the remainder of this chapter, you'll see how to create a Web Service and a client ASP.NET Web page that uses the Web Service to send and receive information through the SOAP header. This type of information could just as easily have been sent in the SOAP message body, but the intent of this example is to exercise the .NET Framework classes so that you can interact with the SOAP header.

In the following example, the user of an ASP.NET Web page enters a name, and the Web Service appends it to the string "Hello,". Also, the Web Service takes a numeric value (a call counter), adds one to it, and returns it to the client. The data being sent to and retrieved from the Web Service will be passed in the SOAP header, instead of the SOAP message body. Figure 22.1 illustrates the end result of the exercise for this chapter.

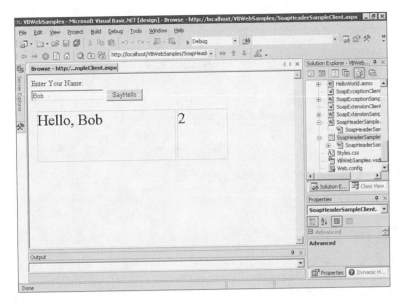

FIGURE 22.1
End result of the SOAP header example.

Building the Sample SOAP Header Web Service

If you want to follow along with the example in this chapter, you can simply add another Web Service file to your existing C# or VB .NET Web Services projects. Rename the new Web Service as SoapHeaderSample.asmx in Solution Explorer. Open the Code Behind file, and add the code formatted in bold in Listing 22.1 (for VB .NET) or Listing 22.2 (for C#). The code not formatted in bold was generated by Visual Studio .NET, and was left in the listings as context to help you determine where to enter the code.

Note that in the section following the listings, I'll point out lines of code you need to add. Make sure the end result of your modifications looks exactly like the code in the listings so that it works properly.

LISTING 22.1 SoapHeaderSample.asmx.vb in VB .NET

```
Imports System.Web.Services
Imports System.Web.Services.Protocols

' we create a custom header by deriving
' a class from System.Web.Services.Protocols.SoapHeader
Public Class MyHeader
    Inherits SoapHeader
```

LISTING 22.1   Continued

```
      Public UserName As String
      Public CallCounter As Integer
End Class

Public Class SoapHeaderSample
      Inherits System.Web.Services.WebService

#Region " Web Services Designer Generated Code "

      'Required by the WebServices Designer
      Private components As System.ComponentModel.Container

      Public Sub New()
          MyBase.New()

          'CODEGEN: This procedure is required by the WebServices Designer
          'Do not modify it using the code editor.
          InitializeComponent()

          'Add your own initialization code after the InitializeComponent call
      End Sub

      Private Sub InitializeComponent()
          'CODEGEN: This procedure is required by the WebServices Designer
          'Do not modify it using the code editor.
          components = New System.ComponentModel.Container()
      End Sub

      Overloads Overrides Sub Dispose()
          'CODEGEN: This procedure is required by the WebServices Designer
          'Do not modify it using the code editor.
      End Sub

#End Region

      Private Shared _callCounter As Integer = 0

      ' declare an instance of our custom SOAP header
      Public header As New MyHeader()

      <WebMethod(), SoapHeader("header", Required:=True,
  Direction:=SoapHeaderDirection.InOut)> _
      Public Function SayHello() As String
          ' if no header was passed in this call then create one
```

LISTING 22.1   Continued

```
        ' we could throw an exception here if we cannot perform
        ' our task without the header
        If header Is Nothing Then
            header = New MyHeader()
        End If

        ' increment the call counter
        _callCounter = _callCounter + 1
        header.CallCounter = _callCounter

        ' return a custom hello message based on the header information
        SayHello = "Hello, " + header.UserName
    End Function

End Class
```

LISTING 22.2   SoapHeaderSample.asmx.cx in C#

```csharp
namespace Chapter22CSharp
{
    using System;
    using System.Collections;
    using System.ComponentModel;
    using System.Data;
    using System.Diagnostics;
    using System.Web;
    using System.Web.Services;
    using System.Web.Services.Protocols;

    public class MyHeader : SoapHeader
    {
        public string UserName;
        public int CallCounter;
    }

    /// <summary>
    ///    Summary description for SoapHeaderSample.
    /// </summary>
    public class SoapHeaderSample : System.Web.Services.WebService
    {
        public SoapHeaderSample()
        {
            //CODEGEN: This call is required by the ASP.NET Web Services
Designer
```

LISTING 22.2   Continued

```
            InitializeComponent();
        }

    #region Component Designer generated code
        /// <summary>
        ///     Required method for Designer support - do not modify
        ///     the contents of this method with the code editor.
        /// </summary>
        private void InitializeComponent()
        {
        }
    #endregion

    /// <summary>
    ///     Clean up any resources being used.
    /// </summary>
    public override void Dispose()
    {
    }

    private static int _callCounter = 0;

    public MyHeader header;

    [
    WebMethod(),
    SoapHeader("header", Required=true, Direction=SoapHeaderDirection.InOut)
    ]
    public string SayHello()
    {
        _callCounter++;
        header.CallCounter = _callCounter;
        return "Hello " + header.UserName;
    }
  }
}
```

Explanation of the SoapHeaderSample.asmx Code

In the preceding listings, you create a public class called MyHeader that inherits from
SoapHeader (shortened from System.Web.Services.Protocol.SoapHeader because of the
using statement at the top of the code), and then create two properties called UserName and
CallCounter. An instance of the MyHeader class will be used when the actual Web Service is
created later in the code example.

Preceding the `MyHeader` class is code that Visual Studio .NET created for the `SoapHeaderSample` class. There is no need to modify the constructor (`public SoapHeaderSample()`), `InitializeComponent()`, or `Dispose()` methods. At the bottom of the code example, an instance of the `MyHeader` class is created, which is simply called `header`.

Also at the bottom of the code example is the `SayHello()` Web Service as designated by the `WebMethod` attribute of the class. Notice that an additional attribute is supplied, called `SoapHeader`, which specifies that the `SayHello()` Web Service will use the header section of the SOAP message returned from this Web Service. In fact, the SOAP message's header section is a requirement (`Required=true` property), and is accepted and returned from the Web Service (`Direction=SoapHeaderDirection.InOut` property). The first property of the `SoapHeader` attribute is a reference to the instance of the `MyHeader` class. This property of the `SoapHeader` attribute instructs the compiler to include two elements—`UserName` and `CallCounter`—in both the request and response SOAP messages to and from the client. As a result, the SOAP request message for this Web Service will look something like this:

```xml
<?xml version="1.0" encoding="utf-8"?>
<soap:Envelope xmlns:soap="http://schemas.xmlsoap.org/soap/envelope/"
xmlns:xsi="http://www.w3.org/2001/XMLSchema-instance"
xmlns:xsd="http://www.w3.org/2001/XMLSchema">
  <soap:Header>
    <MyHeader xmlns="http://tempuri.org/">
      <UserName>Steve</UserName>
      <CallCounter>1</CallCounter>
    </MyHeader>
  </soap:Header>
  <soap:Body>
    <SayHello xmlns="http://tempuri.org/" />
  </soap:Body>
</soap:Envelope>
```

And the response looks like this:

```xml
<?xml version="1.0" encoding="utf-8"?>
<soap:Envelope xmlns:soap="http://schemas.xmlsoap.org/soap/envelope/"
xmlns:xsi="http://www.w3.org/2001/XMLSchema-instance"
xmlns:xsd="http://www.w3.org/2001/XMLSchema">
  <soap:Header>
    <MyHeader xmlns="http://tempuri.org/">
      <UserName>Steve</UserName>
      <CallCounter>2</CallCounter>
    </MyHeader>
  </soap:Header>
  <soap:Body>
    <SayHelloResponse xmlns="http://tempuri.org/">
```

```
      <SayHelloResult>Hello Steve</SayHelloResult>
    </SayHelloResponse>
  </soap:Body>
</soap:Envelope>
```

Understanding the SoapHeader Attribute

Before creating the client that will consume this Web Service, let's briefly explore some other aspects of the SoapHeader attribute and its associated properties.

The SoapHeader attribute connects a definition of a class derived from the SoapHeader class (in the preceding example, it was the MyHeader class) with the Web Service method—the SayHello() method, in this case. You can derive many different classes from SoapHeader and associate all of them with the Web Service method by simply appending more SoapHeader attributes above the Web Service method body, as shown here:

```
[WebMethod(Description="A simple Hello World Web Service.")]
[SoapHeader("FirstHeader", Direction=SoapHeaderDirection.InOut,Required=true)]
[SoapHeader("SecondHeader", Direction=SoapHeaderDirection.In,Required=true)]
[SoapHeader("ThirdHeader", Direction=SoapHeaderDirection.Out,Required=false)]
public void Hello() { ... }
```

The first property of the SoapHeader attribute is the MethodName, which is a reference to the name of the instantiated SoapHeader class. For example, if you derive the MyFirstHeader class from SoapHeader and create an instance of MyFirstHeader called FirstHeader, then FirstHeader would be the MethodName, like so:

```
[SoapHeader("FirstHeader", Direction=SoapHeaderDirection.InOut,Required=true)]
```

The second property is the Direction, which dictates how the SoapHeader will be used. There are three possibilities, as specified in the SoapHeaderDirection enumeration:

- **In**   This SoapHeader is sent from the client to the Web Service only
- **Out**   This SoapHeader is sent from the Web Service to the client only
- **InOut**   This SoapHeader is sent back and forth between the Web Service and client

The third property of the SoapHeader attribute is the Required flag, indicating whether the SoapHeader must exist when the message is sent. Failure to do so results in a SoapHeaderException.

CAUTION

The .NET runtime throws an error if you forget to set the Direction and the Required properties.

Building the Sample SOAP Header Client

To continue with this chapter's example, you can build an ASP.NET Web Form that calls the Web Service by sending a `CallCounter` and the `UserName` in the SOAP header and then retrieves and displays those values from the Web Service's SOAP header, after the Web Service has a chance to process the values.

If you are attempting to build this example yourself, first create a Web reference to the Web Service you built in the previous section. This Web reference creates a proxy for you and allows you to refer to your Web Service by using `localhost` or the name of your computer. For instructions on creating a Web reference, see Chapter 5, "Consuming a Simple Web Service in Visual Studio .NET."

Next, you should add a new file called SoapHeaderSampleClient.aspx to the project. Open the file in Visual Studio, and drag HTML controls from the Toolbox to the designer surface. When you're finished, it should look similar to Figure 22.2.

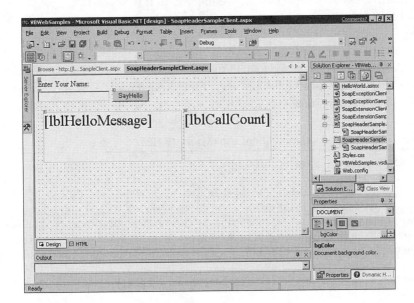

FIGURE 22.2
The designer surface for the SOAP header client.

The properties of the six controls are listed in Table 22.1.

TABLE 22.1   Controls for the SOAP Header Client

Control Type	Control Name	Other Properties
Label	Label1	Set the Text property to Enter Your Name:
Text Box	txtUserName	
Label	lblCallCount	
Label	lblHelloMessage	
Button	btnSayHello	Set the Text property to SayHello

> **NOTE**
>
> The placement and size of the controls on the designer surface is not as important as the control types and the names you give them so that the code in the following listings will reference the control instances you created.

Double-click the btnSayHello button to open the SoapHeaderSampleClient.aspx.cs (or SoapHeaderSampleClient.aspx.vb for VB .NET) Code Behind module. Modify the code by entering the lines formatted in bold in Listing 22.3 (for VB .NET) or Listing 22.4 (for C#).

LISTING 22.3   SoapHeaderSampleClient.aspx.vb in VB.NET

```
Public Class SoapHeaderSampleClient
    Inherits System.Web.UI.Page
    Protected WithEvents Label1 As System.Web.UI.WebControls.Label
    Protected WithEvents lblCallCount As System.Web.UI.WebControls.Label
    Protected WithEvents lblHelloMessage As System.Web.UI.WebControls.Label
    Protected WithEvents btnSayHello As System.Web.UI.WebControls.Button
    Protected WithEvents txtUserName As System.Web.UI.WebControls.TextBox

    Protected sample As New localhost.SoapHeaderSample()

#Region " Web Form Designer Generated Code "

    'This call is required by the Web Form Designer.
    <System.Diagnostics.DebuggerStepThrough()> Private Sub
InitializeComponent()

    End Sub
```

LISTING 22.3 Continued

```
    Private Sub Page_Init(ByVal sender As System.Object, ByVal e As
System.EventArgs) Handles MyBase.Init
          'CODEGEN: This method call is required by the Web Form Designer
          'Do not modify it using the code editor.
          InitializeComponent()
    End Sub

#End Region

    Private Sub Page_Load(ByVal sender As System.Object, ByVal e As
System.EventArgs) Handles MyBase.Load

        If sample.MyHeaderValue Is Nothing Then
            sample.MyHeaderValue = New taborr.MyHeader()
        End If

    End Sub

    Private Sub btnSayHello_Click(ByVal sender As System.Object, ByVal e As
System.EventArgs) Handles btnSayHello.Click

        sample.MyHeaderValue.UserName = txtUserName.Text
        lblHelloMessage.Text = sample.SayHello
        lblCallCount.Text = sample.MyHeaderValue.CallCounter.ToString

    End Sub

End Class
```

LISTING 22.4 SoapHeaderSampleClient.aspx.cs in C#

```csharp
namespace Chapter22CSharp
{
    using System;
    using System.Collections;
    using System.ComponentModel;
    using System.Data;
    using System.Drawing;
    using System.Web;
    using System.Web.SessionState;
    using System.Web.UI;
    using System.Web.UI.WebControls;
    using System.Web.UI.HtmlControls;
```

LISTING 22.4 Continued

```
/// <summary>
///          Summary description for SoapHeaderSampleClient.
/// </summary>
public class SoapHeaderSampleClient : System.Web.UI.Page
{
    protected System.Web.UI.WebControls.TextBox txtUserName;
    protected System.Web.UI.WebControls.Button btnSayHello;
    protected System.Web.UI.WebControls.Label Label1;
    protected System.Web.UI.WebControls.Label lblHelloMessage;
    protected System.Web.UI.WebControls.Label lblCallCount;

    // create an instance of the web service proxy
    protected static localhost.SoapHeaderSample sample =
        new localhost.SoapHeaderSample();

    public SoapHeaderSampleClient()
    {
        Page.Init += new System.EventHandler(Page_Init);
    }

    protected void Page_Load(object sender, System.EventArgs e)
    {
        if (sample.MyHeaderValue == null)
            sample.MyHeaderValue = new localhost.MyHeader();
    }

    protected void Page_Init(object sender, EventArgs e)
    {
        //
        // CODEGEN: This call is required by the ASP.NET Windows Form
Designer.
        //
        InitializeComponent();
    }

    #region Web Form Designer generated code
    /// <summary>
    ///     Required method for Designer support - do not modify
    ///     the contents of this method with the code editor.
    /// </summary>
    private void InitializeComponent()
    {
        this.btnSayHello.Click += new
System.EventHandler(this.btnSayHello_Click);
```

LISTING 22.4 Continued

```
            this.Load += new System.EventHandler(this.Page_Load);
        }
        #endregion

        protected void btnSayHello_Click(object sender, System.EventArgs e)
        {
            sample.MyHeaderValue.UserName = txtUserName.Text;
            lblHelloMessage.Text = sample.SayHello();
            lblCallCount.Text = sample.MyHeaderValue.CallCounter.ToString();
        }
    }
}
```

Besides wrapping the entire Code Behind module in your namespace, you need to make two modifications to the file. First, add the following line to the SoapHeaderSampleClient class:

```
protected static localhost.SoapHeaderSample sample =
    new localhost.SoapHeaderSample();
```

This line creates an instance of the Web Service proxy, which enables you to refer to the Web Service simply as sample.

Next, perform the following check in the Page_Load event:

```
if (sample.MyHeaderValue == null)
    sample.MyHeaderValue = new localhost.MyHeader();
```

This code creates a new instance of the MyHeader class, if one doesn't already exist. This step is necessary because the MyHeader class definition holds information about the two properties, CallCounter and UserName, that the client must use to send and retrieve the values from the SOAP header.

Finally, add the following code to the btnSayHello_Click event:

```
            sample.MyHeaderValue.UserName = txtUserName.Text;
            lblHelloMessage.Text = sample.SayHello();
            lblCallCount.Text = sample.MyHeaderValue.CallCounter.ToString();
```

When the user clicks the btnSayHello button, this code sets the UserName header value to the value the user enters in the txtUserName text box. The request is submitted to the Web method SayHello(), and the result of the Web Service is returned to the lblHelloMessage label. Finally, retrieve the CallCount value from the SOAP header and place it in the lblCallCount text box.

Viewing the Results

If all goes well, you should see the results displayed in Figure 22.3.

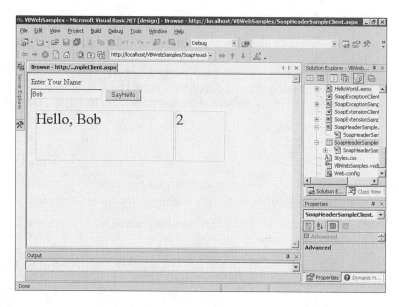

FIGURE 22.3
Results of the SOAP header client and Web Service.

Upon repeated use, the CallCount value will increment.

How It Works

By adding a SOAP extension to view the underlying SOAP messages, you can see the exchange between the SoapHeaderSampleClient.aspx and the SoapHeaderSample.asmx Web Service, as demonstrated in the following code snippets.

When the Web Service is requested the first time, you set the UserName (in this case, Bob) and the CallCounter is automatically set to 0; the proxy class initializes this value for you because you did not set it in code. You could have just as easily set the initial value of the CallCounter to a specific number. The following is the SOAP message that is sent to the Web Service:

```
<?xml version="1.0" encoding="utf-8"?>
<soap:Envelope xmlns:soap="http://schemas.xmlsoap.org/soap/envelope/"
xmlns:xsi="http://www.w3.org/2001/XMLSchema-instance"
xmlns:xsd="http://www.w3.org/2001/XMLSchema">
  <soap:Header>
    <MyHeader xmlns="http://tempuri.org/">
```

```
        <UserName>Bob</UserName>
        <CallCounter>0</CallCounter>
      </MyHeader>
    </soap:Header>
    <soap:Body>
      <SayHello xmlns="http://tempuri.org/" />
    </soap:Body>
</soap:Envelope>
```

After the Web Service processes the values from the Soap header, it prepares a value to be returned in the SOAP body section (in this case, the <SayHelloResult> value is Hello Bob) and the <CallCounter> in the header is incremented by 1.

```
<?xml version="1.0" encoding="utf-8"?>
<soap:Envelope xmlns:soap="http://schemas.xmlsoap.org/soap/envelope/"
xmlns:xsi="http://www.w3.org/2001/XMLSchema-instance"
xmlns:xsd="http://www.w3.org/2001/XMLSchema">
  <soap:Header>
    <MyHeader xmlns="http://tempuri.org/">
      <UserName>Bob</UserName>
      <CallCounter>1</CallCounter>
    </MyHeader>
  </soap:Header>
  <soap:Body>
    <SayHelloResponse xmlns="http://tempuri.org/">
      <SayHelloResult>Hello Bob</SayHelloResult>
    </SayHelloResponse>
  </soap:Body>
</soap:Envelope>
```

Handling Unknown Headers

According to the SOAP specification, SOAP headers can be sent to your Web Service, even though your Web Service hasn't defined them and is not expecting to receive them. This feature makes two procedures possible.

First, a Web Service could call other Web Services in an orchestrated manner. In this situation, your Web Service would be responsible for passing along any SOAP headers to the next Web Service, which would pluck off the parts it needs to process correctly, and continue to potentially call the next Web Service in the chain. In fact, the Actor property of the SoapHeader enables a client to set the intended recipient of the header information.

Second, an industry could define certain standard Web Service interfaces that include optional header information. Your particular implementation might not need this optional information to perform its job, so it could ignore that header information. The .NET Framework's Web Services classes give Web Service creators and consumers some control over how headers should be processed.

When a SOAP message is deserialized and converted into objects, a special collection of SOAP headers, called SoapUnknownHeaders, is created and made accessible to the Web Service. Developers of the Web Service can choose to look through the SoapUnknownHeaders collection to determine what to do with each header. The developer can programmatically set the DidUnderstand property on each SOAP header. By default, however, the DidUnderstand property is set to true by the Web Service's handler. The client can check the DidUnderstand property after the call to the Web Service to determine which headers the Web Service processed. Therefore, if clients of your Web Services might pass header information that is outside what you have defined in your Web Service (and what's defined in your WSDL), you need to pay special attention to this property so that the client receives feedback about to the success or failure of the Web Service to understand the header.

Before calling the Web Service, the client can set a MustUnderstand property on the header, which tells the Web Service to return an error (a SOAP fault) in case the Web Service sets that header's DidUnderstand property to false.

CAUTION

I'd like to add the following caveat about SOAPUnknownHeaders and .NET Web Services. When creating a client for Web Services in .NET, the creation of a Web reference creates the proxy and the necessary type information for creating a SOAP header and sending it to the Web Service. This makes it extremely difficult to send an "unknown header" from a .NET Web Service consumer to a .NET Web Service. Although you could conceivably tap into the Web reference–generated classes on the client and extend the code to send an unknown header, it would be a lot of work. Therefore, you should ask yourself if you really need to include headers in your code that a Web Service does not support.

Summary

In this chapter, you have seen the purpose of SOAP headers and explored how to use them with the .NET Framework classes. First, you created a Web Service that accepted method arguments via the SOAP headers. Next, you created an ASP.NET client that called the Web Service and displayed the results. As you worked through the example, you also learned about the purpose and the function of the SoapHeader attribute.

You also learned that the SoapUnknownHeaders collection is a way of retrieving and sending headers that fall outside the defined SOAP headers by the Web Service. This collection is useful when your Web Service is not the intended recipient of the header information, but is expected to send that information along a call stack of Web Services.

Manipulating SOAP Messages Using XML Attributes

IN THIS CHAPTER

When developing Web Services for consumption outside your own company, you might need to modify the default Web Service interface/WSDL to conform to an industry standard or a trading partner's request. In such cases, you can use XML attributes to change the way the SOAP/XML message bodies are structured to accommodate these requirements. In this chapter, you'll learn what XML attributes are and see how to modify the SOAP/XML messages in your Web Services by using those attributes.

The purpose of XML attributes is to allow the developer to control how the XML representing a class is serialized for storage (to disk) or transport (for Web Services). Making the return value of a Web Service an actual class offers greater flexibility in returning much more to the user than a single return value, as demonstrated in examples earlier in this book. Left alone, the XMLSerializer class, which is responsible for the serialization process, would send all the values back as XML elements. Although this might be adequate in many cases, other external requirements (for example, industry standards or trading partner restrictions) might demand a certain XML structure encoded in the return values. For these situations, XML attributes fill the bill.

The System.XML.Serialization.XMLSerializer class gives you several ways to control how the serialization happens. Primarily, you control three of these aspects using three attributes:

- **XMLElement**   Forces the property of the class to be serialized as an XML element
- **XMLAttribute**   Forces the property of the class to be serialized as an XML attribute
- **XMLIgnore**   Forces the property of the class to be omitted from the serialization process

These attributes are applied to the properties of the class just as any other .NET attribute is, as shown in the following example:

VB.NET

```
Public Class myClass
    <XmlAttribute()> Public myProperty As String
End Class
```

In C#:

```
public class myClass
{
    [XmlAttribute]
    public string myProperty;
}
```

Example of Manipulating SOAP Messages in Web Services

The rest of this chapter is devoted to a sample application that illustrates how to add XML attributes in order to change the SOAP messages (as well as the HTTP-GET and HTTP-POST messages). To see this procedure in action, you'll create two classes that are returned by two Web Services. The first Web Service, GetAuthorInfo, returns an instance of the AuthorInfo class, which has no XML attributes to affect the serialization. The second Web Service, GetCoAuthorInfo, returns an instance of the CoAuthorInfo class, which demonstrates what happens when each of the XML attributes listed earlier are used.

If you want to follow along, perform these steps:

1. In Visual Studio .NET, choose File | New | Project from the menu to open the New Project dialog box.

2. Select your language in the Project Types list box on the left (Visual Basic Projects or Visual C# Projects), and then select ASP.NET Web Service in the Templates list box on the right.

3. In the Name text box, type **Chapter23VB** for VB .NET) or **Chapter23CSharp** (for C#).

4. Accept the default location in the Location field.

5. Click the OK button. Visual Studio .NET will create a new project based on the language and template you selected.

6. In Solution Explorer, rename Service1.asmx as CustomSOAPFormat.asmx by right clicking the file and choosing Rename. Type the new name of the file, and press Enter.

7. Click the Show All Files icon at the top of the Solution Explorer window to display all the hidden files, including the Code Behind file for CustomSOAPFormat.asmx.

8. Click the + sign next to the ComplexTypesSample.asmx file to reveal the CustomSOAPFormat.asmx.vb (VB .NET) or CustomSOAPFormat.asmx.cs (C#) file.

9. Select the CustomSOAPFormat.asmx.vb or CustomSOAPFormat.asmx.cs file in Solution Explorer, and then click the View Code button at the top of the Solution Explorer window to open the Code Behind file in the main area of Visual Studio .NET. This is where you'll edit the Code Behind file. As you can see, Visual Studio .NET has already generated code in this file.

10. Type the code formatted in bold in Listing 23.1 for VB.NET or Listing 23.2 for C# into the Code Behind file that's currently open. As is the convention throughout this book, the code not formatted in bold is included to help you determine where to enter your code.

LISTING 23.1   CustomSOAPFormat.asmx.vb for VB .NET

```vb
Imports System.Web.Services
Imports System.Xml.Serialization

Public Class AuthorInfo
    Public FirstName As String
    Public LastName As String
    Public Email As String
End Class

Public Class CoAuthorInfo
    <XmlAttribute()> _
    Public FirstName As String

    <XmlElement()> _
    Public LastName As String

    <XmlIgnore()> _
    Public Email As String
End Class

Public Class CustomSoapFormat
    Inherits System.Web.Services.WebService

    <WebMethod()> _
    Public Function GetAuthorInfo() As AuthorInfo
        Dim info As New AuthorInfo()
        info.FirstName = "Bob"
        info.LastName = "Tabor"
        info.Email = "bob@technicallead.com"
        GetAuthorInfo = info
    End Function

    <WebMethod()> _
    Public Function GetCoAuthorInfo() As CoAuthorInfo
        Dim info As New CoAuthorInfo()
        info.FirstName = "David"
        info.LastName = "Findley"
        info.Email = "david@technicallead.com"
        GetCoAuthorInfo = info
    End Function

End Class
```

LISTING 23.2   CustomSOAPFormat.asmx.cs for C#

```csharp
namespace CSharpWebSamples
{
    using System;
    using System.Collections;
    using System.ComponentModel;
    using System.Data;
    using System.Diagnostics;
    using System.Web;
    using System.Web.Services;
    using System.Xml.Serialization;

    public class AuthorInfo
    {
        public string FirstName;
        public string LastName;
        public string Email;
    }

    public class CoAuthorInfo
    {
        [XmlAttribute]
        public string FirstName;

        [XmlElement]
        public string LastName;

        [XmlIgnore]
        public string Email;
    }

    public class CustomSoapFormat : System.Web.Services.WebService
    {
        [WebMethod]
        public AuthorInfo GetAuthorInfo()
        {
            AuthorInfo info = new AuthorInfo();
            info.FirstName = "Bob";
            info.LastName = "Tabor";
            info.Email = "bob@technicallead.com";
            return info;
        }

        [WebMethod]
        public CoAuthorInfo GetCoAuthorInfo()
        {
```

LISTING 23.2 Continued

```
        CoAuthorInfo info = new CoAuthorInfo();
        info.FirstName = "David";
        info.LastName = "Findley";
        info.Email = "david@technicallead.com";
        return info;
    }

    public override void Dispose()
    {
    }
}
}
```

Examining the Results

Compile the Web Service by choosing Build | Build Solution on the menu, and if any errors occur during the build, double-check that you typed the code exactly as it appears in the code listing. Remember, many things are case sensitive in .NET.

Right-click the CustomSOAPFormat.aspx file in Solution Explorer, and choose View In Browser on the pop-up menu.

When you open the CustomSOAPFormat.asmx file in your Web browser, you see the trusty Web Services help file display both Web Services. First, click the GetAuthorInfo Web Service link. Scrolling down to the SOAP message entry, you will see something very similar to the following:

```
HTTP/1.1 200 OK
Content-Type: text/xml; charset=utf-8
Content-Length: length

<?xml version="1.0"?>
<soap:Envelope xmlns:xsi="http://www.w3.org/2000/10/XMLSchema-instance"
xmlns:xsd="http://www.w3.org/2000/10/XMLSchema"
xmlns:soap="http://schemas.xmlsoap.org/soap/envelope">
  <soap:Body>
    <GetAuthorInfoResponse xmlns="http://tempuri.org/">
      <GetAuthorInfoResult>
        <FirstName>string</FirstName>
        <LastName>string</LastName>
        <Email>string</Email>
      </GetAuthorInfoResult>
    </GetAuthorInfoResponse>
  </soap:Body>
</soap:Envelope>
```

Notice that each of the properties of the class are serialized as XML elements.

Now click the `GetCoAuthorInfo` Web Service link on the help page. Scrolling down to the SOAP message entry, you will again see something very similar to the following:

```
HTTP/1.1 200 OK
Content-Type: text/xml; charset=utf-8
Content-Length: length

<?xml version="1.0"?>
<soap:Envelope xmlns:xsi="http://www.w3.org/2000/10/XMLSchema-instance"
xmlns:xsd="http://www.w3.org/2000/10/XMLSchema"
xmlns:soap="http://schemas.xmlsoap.org/soap/envelope">
  <soap:Body>
    <GetCoAuthorInfoResponse xmlns="http://tempuri.org/">
      <GetCoAuthorInfoResult FirstName="string">
        <LastName>string</LastName>
      </GetCoAuthorInfoResult>
    </GetCoAuthorInfoResponse>
  </soap:Body>
</soap:Envelope>
```

Notice that the `FirstName` property is serialized as an XML attribute (because of the `<XmlAttribute>` attribute you applied to it), the `LastName` property is serialized as an XML element (because of the `<XmlElement>` attribute), and, as you would expect, the `Email` property is not serialized at all (because of the `<XmlIgnore>` attribute).

It is worth noting that the `HTTP-GET` and `HTTP-POST` messages had similar results. The output from these Web Service calls were affected by adding the XML serialization attributes, too.

Summary

In this chapter, you reviewed how to manipulate the serialization process for the purpose of modifying your SOAP message's structure. By adorning the properties of a class with serialization attributes and returning an instance of the class in your Web Service, you changed how the SOAP message (and the `HTTP-GET` and `HTTP-POST` messages) appears. This method is useful when the message output must conform to some predefined XML structure.

Using SOAP Extensions

IN THIS CHAPTER

SOAP extensions allow you to plug into .NET Framework's SOAP architecture to perform some pre- or post-processing on SOAP messages. When a SOAP message is received by the Web Service's HTTP Handler, the SOAP message is deserialized into objects (for example, `SoapHeader` objects or `SoapMessage` objects) and eventually passed into your Web method. Then, after your Web method has finished, the result, as well as any `SoapHeaders` objects or `SoapException` objects, are serialized into a SOAP message and sent back up the chain and to the client.

However, you can hook into the request chain before and after the SOAP message is deserialized into objects to be processed by the Web method, and after the Web method has finished processing and the objects are serialized back into SOAP messages.

When working with extensions, there are four "stages":

- **BeforeDeserialize** This stage occurs before the SOAP message is deserialized into objects and sent to the requested Web Service. Therefore, you still have access to the actual SOAP message.

- **AfterDeserialize** This stage occurs after the SOAP message is deserialized into objects and sent to the requested Web Services, so you now have access only to the objects that represent the SOAP message.

- **BeforeSerialize** This stage occurs after the Web Service has finished processing and before the returned objects are serialized back into a SOAP message and sent to the client. Therefore, you still have access to all the objects that will ultimately be serialized into a SOAP message.

- **AfterSerialize** This stage occurs after the Web Service has finished processing and after the returned objects are serialized back into a SOAP message and sent to the client, so you now have access to the SOAP message being sent back to the client.

You might be wondering how SOAP extensions differ from HTTP Modules. First, you can selectively place extensions on certain Web methods, and ignore other ones, which is much more difficult to do with HTTP Modules. Second, you can access the deserialized objects in the `AfterDeserialize` and `BeforeSerialize` stages, but you cannot access these objects in HTTP Modules; HTTP Modules allow you to see only the `SoapMessage` object, and little else. Third, it is easier to modify values before and after the Web method has processed the request by using extensions instead of HTTP Modules. HTTP Modules still serve a purpose, however. It is just a matter of selecting the right tool for the job, so it's important to understand when to use each tool.

What Can You Do with SOAP Extensions?

In this chapter, you'll use SOAP extensions to log the actual SOAP message sent in the request and response to a text file. SOAP extensions could also be used to set an encryption/decryption algorithm on Web Service calls, to compress/decompress SOAP messages before they are processed, to gather diagnostic information or calculate the execution time of a Web Service. This supports old Web Service interfaces by intercepting the SOAP request and modifying its values to reflect the new interface, or even to extend the functionality to accept SOAP attachments. There are many exciting things you can do with SOAP extensions.

The SoapLogger Extension Example

As mentioned, this example will show you how to create a SOAP extension to capture the actual SOAP messages being sent to and from the Web Services. In fact, many of the SOAP messages listed in this book were captured by using this technique so that you could get a look at what goes on behind the scenes. After working through this example, try using this tool to trace the health of your Web Services when consumers begin to use them and (inevitably) call with questions or complaints.

To exercise the SOAP extension, you'll create a Web Service that returns book and author information in a series of related classes. The ultimate goal, however, is not the result of the Web Service itself, but the result of the extension. The SOAP messages sent to and returned by the Web Service will be logged into a text file.

As a general roadmap, the following list describes the classes you'll be creating. Two classes are part of the SOAP extension, and three classes are Web Service classes used to exercise the extension. The classes are as follows:

- **SoapLoggerAttribute class:** This class derives from the `SoapExtensionAttribute` class, and is a custom attribute for the purpose of attaching to your Web Service class. This class associates, or applies, the extension to a particular Web Service class. It also defines any additional properties that can be set within the attribute. In this example, you allow the user of the extension to specify a location for the log file to be written to, or the user can just accept the default location of C:\soap.log.

- **SoapLogger class:** This class derives from the `SoapExtension` class and overrides many of the methods that the .NET Framework's extension infrastructure depends on. It is used to include your extension in the call chain, including the `ProcessMessage` method, which is called each time .NET encounters a new stage. This is where you perform the actual processing that makes this example different from, say, an example that implements encryption or compression.

- **ExtensionSample class:** This class is a Web Service that simply returns an author's information when requested.

- **Author and Book classes:** An instance of these classes will be returned by your Web Service.

To follow along with this example, create a Web Service project in Visual Studio .NET called Chapter24VB (or Chapter24CSharp), rename the WebService1.asmx file as ExtensionSample.asmx, and in the Code Behind file for this Web Service (ExtensionSample.asmx.cs for C# or ExtensionSample.asmx.vb for VB .NET), type in the code formatted in bold in Listing 24.1 for C# or Listing 24.2 for VB .NET. Although this example is somewhat lengthy, SOAP extensions are an advanced use of the .NET Framework and demand this amount of code to implement them. The sections after the listings break up the code and explain each part as you go along.

> **NOTE**
>
> For step-by-step instructions on creating a Web Service project in Visual Studio .NET, renaming the files, and accessing the Code Behind modules, please refer to examples earlier in this book.

LISTING 24.1 ExtensionSample.asmx.cs in C#

```csharp
namespace Chapter24CSharp
{
    using System;
    using System.Collections;
    using System.ComponentModel;
    using System.Data;
    using System.Diagnostics;
    using System.Web;
    using System.Web.Services;
    using System.Web.Services.Protocols;
    using System.IO;
    using System.Xml;
    using System.Xml.Serialization;

    [AttributeUsage(AttributeTargets.Method)]
    public class SoapLoggerAttribute : SoapExtensionAttribute
    {
        private int _priority = 0;
        private string _logFile = @"C:\soap.log";
        public SoapLoggerAttribute() {}
        public SoapLoggerAttribute(string logFile) {_logFile = logFile;}
        public string LogFile {get{return _logFile;}}
        public override Type ExtensionType {get{return typeof(SoapLogger);}}
        public override int Priority {
            get {return _priority;}
            set{_priority = value;}
        }
    }
```

LISTING 24.2   ExtensionSample.asmx.vb in VB.NET

```vb
Imports System.Web.Services
Imports System.Web.Services.Protocols
Imports System.IO
Imports System.Xml

' Create a new custom attribute that will allow
' users to configure the log file. This attribute
' will also tell the ASP.NET system which type to
' load for our extension
<AttributeUsage(AttributeTargets.Method)> Public Class SoapLoggerAttribute
    Inherits SoapExtensionAttribute

#Region "Private Member Variables"
    Private _priority As Integer = 0
    Private _logFile As String = "C:\soap.log"
#End Region

#Region "Contructors"
    Public Sub New()
    End Sub

    Public Sub New(ByVal logFile As String)
        _logFile = logFile
    End Sub
#End Region

#Region "Public Properties"
    Public ReadOnly Property LogFile()
        Get
            LogFile = _logFile
        End Get
    End Property

    Public Overrides ReadOnly Property ExtensionType() As Type
        Get
            ExtensionType = Type.GetType("VBWebSamples.SoapLogger")
        End Get
    End Property

    Public Overrides Property Priority() As Integer
        Get
            Priority = _priority
        End Get
        Set(ByVal Value As Integer)
            _priority = Value
```

LISTING 24.2   Continued

```
        End Set
    End Property
#End Region

End Class
```

As mentioned, the `SoapLoggerAttribute` class is what applies the extension (`SoapLogger`) to a Web Service. Creating a custom attribute is an advanced feature of .NET, so this chapter doesn't go into much depth on creating custom attributes outside the context of Web Services. However, the preceding code has several important features that you should examine.

The most important property is `ExtensionType`, which defines the type as `SoapLogger`. This is what the .NET Framework's extension architecture uses to determine the class that implements the `SoapExtension`. Notice that the class is set to return `typeof(SoapLogger)`, which points to the `SoapLogger` class (discussed in a moment). You must override the `ExtensionType` property because the class derives from `SoapExtensionAttribute`—its value is expected by the .NET Framework's extension architecture.

The next most important property is `LogFile`. Notice that a private version of the `LogFile` property (`_logFile`) is set to the default location `c:\soap.log`. When users apply the `SoapLoggerAttribute` to their Web methods, they can override this default value by setting the `LogFile` property. The `SoapLogger` class uses the value of this property to determine where to write the file stream to.

This brings you to the `SoapLoggerAttribute` method, which is an overloaded constructor method that supports two distinct interfaces. The `SoapLoggerAttribute` can be called by supplying the `LogFile` or by not supplying the `LogFile`, in which case a default location is used.

Finally, the `Priority` property has a private version (`_priority`) that is set with a default value of `0`. The `Priority` property specifies the order in which this `SoapExtension` should be executed in relation to other `SoapExtensions` that are applied to a given Web Service. Yes, that is right—you can apply multiple `SoapExtensions` that you create to any given Web Service. A value of `0` tells the .NET Framework's extension architecture to give this `SoapExtension` the highest priority. A `SoapExtension` with a `Priority` value of `1`, `2`, `3`, and so forth would be given lower priority. This is important when considering *when* your extensions are performed and could potentially be a place to look when problems occur in your Web Services. You must override the `Priority` property because your class derives from `SoapExtensionAttribute`—its value is expected by the .NET Framework's extension architecture.

Continue this example by typing the code in Listing 24.3 for C# or 24.4 for VB .NET into the Code Behind module.

LISTING 24.3   ExtensionSample.asmx.cs in C# (Continued)

```csharp
public class SoapLogger : SoapExtension
{
    private string LogFile = "";
    private Stream SoapStream;
    private Stream TempStream;

    public override object GetInitializer(Type serviceType)
    {
        return null;
    }

    public override object GetInitializer(LogicalMethodInfo methodInfo, _
        SoapExtensionAttribute attribute)
    {
        return ((SoapLoggerAttribute)attribute).LogFile;
    }
    public override void Initialize(object initializer)
    {
        LogFile = (string)initializer;
    }
}
```

LISTING 24.4   ExtensionSample.asmx.vb in VB.NET (Continued)

```vbnet
' Create a new SoapExtension class. When users
' apply the above attribute to a method of their
' web service, this class will be instantiated
' by the ASP.NET system
Public Class SoapLogger
    Inherits SoapExtension

#Region "Private Member Variables"
    Private LogFile As String = ""
    Private SoapStream As Stream
    Private TempStream As Stream
#End Region

#Region "Public Overrides"
    Public Overloads Overrides Function GetInitializer( _
        ByVal serviceType As Type) As Object
        ' we need to read some service configuration from the attribute
        ' so differ creating an initializer
        GetInitializer = Nothing
```

LISTING 24.4   Continued

```
End Function
Public Overloads Overrides Function GetInitializer( _
    ByVal methodInfo As LogicalMethodInfo, _
    ByVal attribute As SoapExtensionAttribute) As Object
    ' whatever we return here will be passed back to
    ' our initialize method every time the ASP.NET system
    ' needs to create a new instance of this extension class
    Dim loggerAttr As SoapLoggerAttribute = attribute
    GetInitializer = loggerAttr.LogFile
End Function
Public Overrides Sub Initialize(ByVal initializer As Object)
    ' grab the logfile name that we returned in
    ' GetInitializer
    LogFile = initializer
End Sub
```

In this section of the code, you create a new SoapExtension class. When users apply the SoapLoggerAttribute to a method of their Web Services, this class will be instantiated by the .NET Framework extension architecture.

Notice that there are two versions of the GetInitializer method, one for each of the initializers for the SoapLoggerAttribute. If you supply a LogFile location when you apply the SoapLoggerAttribute to a Web Service, the GetInitializer method gets that value and returns it to the extension architecture. Eventually, that value makes its way to the Initialize method of the SoapLogger class every time the extension architecture needs to create a new instance of this extension class. The Initialize method saves the value returned from the GetInitializer method into a private variable for later use (LogFile).

Continue this example by typing the code in Listing 24.5 for C# or 24.6 for VB .NET into the Code Behind module.

LISTING 24.5   ExtensionSample.asmx.cs in C# (Continued)

```
public override Stream ChainStream(Stream stream)
{
    SoapStream = stream;
    TempStream = new MemoryStream();
    return TempStream;
}
```

LISTING 24.6   ExtensionSample.asmx.vb in VB.NET (Continued)

```
Public Overrides Function ChainStream(ByVal stream As Stream) As Stream
    ' by overriding ChainStream we can
    ' cause the ASP.NET system to use
    ' our stream for buffering SOAP messages
    ' rather than the default stream.
    ' we will store off the original stream
    ' so we can pass the data back down to the ASP.NET system
    ' in original stream that it created.
    SoapStream = stream
    TempStream = New MemoryStream()
    ChainStream = TempStream
End Function
```

The `ChainStream` function gives a SOAP extension access to the memory buffer (stream) that contains the SOAP request or response. It ensures that the SOAP extension with the highest priority has first access to the actual message sent to or from the Web Service. You override the `ChainStream` function to save a copy of that memory buffer so that you can read it, modify it, and so forth. Initially, the stream is copied to the `SoapStream` object (a memory stream object created to hold a temporary copy of the SOAP message), and a new blank stream object called `TempStream` is returned. Next, the `ProcessMessage` function uses the `CopyTextStream` function to do the following:

- Copy the contents of `SoapStream` into `TempStream` if the `message.Stage` is `BeforeDeserialize`
- Use the `StreamWriter` to write the `TempStream` to a log file.

The reference to the `Stream` object passed into the `ChainStream` function contains the serialized SOAP request at the `BeforeDeserialize SoapMessageStage` if the SOAP extension is applied to a Web Service method. The `Stream` reference returned from `ChainStream` is written to when the serialization occurs, and thus contains the serialized SOAP response in the `AfterSerialize SoapMessageStage` when the SOAP extension is applied to a Web Service method.

Continue this example by typing the code in Listing 24.7 for C# or 24.8 for VB .NET into the Code Behind module.

24

USING SOAP EXTENSIONS

LISTING 24.7   ExtensionSample.asmx.cs in C# (Continued)

```
public void CopyTextStream(Stream src, Stream dest)
{
    TextReader reader = new StreamReader(src);
    TextWriter writer = new StreamWriter(dest);
    writer.WriteLine(reader.ReadToEnd());
    writer.Flush();
}
```

LISTING 24.8   ExtensionSample.asmx.vb in VB.NET (Continued)

```vb
#Region "Private Utility Functions"
    Public Sub CopyTextStream(ByVal src As Stream, _
        ByVal dest As Stream)
        Dim reader As New StreamReader(src)
        Dim writer As New StreamWriter(dest)
        writer.WriteLine(reader.ReadToEnd())
        writer.Flush()
    End Sub
#End Region
```

CopyTextStream is a helper function you create to perform the chore of actually taking whatever is in the src argument (which is a MemoryStream object containing a SOAP message) and
writing it to a MemoryStream object called dest (which will be your own memory buffer that
you can play with).

Continue this example by typing the code in Listing 24.9 for C# or 24.10 for VB .NET into the
Code Behind module.

LISTING 24.9   ExtensionSample.asmx.cs in C# (Continued)

```csharp
public override void ProcessMessage(SoapMessage message)
{
    switch (message.Stage)
    {
        case SoapMessageStage.BeforeDeserialize:
        {
            // copy the SOAP request from the network stream
            // into our memory buffer
            CopyTextStream(SoapStream, TempStream);
            FileStream fs = new FileStream(LogFile, FileMode.Append,
                FileAccess.Write);
            StreamWriter sw = new StreamWriter(fs);
            sw.WriteLine("** BEGIN SOAP REQUEST: {0}", DateTime.Now);
            sw.Flush();
            // copy the mem buffer stream to the log file
            TempStream.Position = 0;
            CopyTextStream(TempStream, fs);
            sw.WriteLine("** END SOAP REQUEST");
            sw.Flush();
            fs.Close();

            // reset the memory buffer position
            // so the ASP.NET system can parse and
            // decode the message
```

LISTING 24.9   Continued

```csharp
                    TempStream.Position = 0;
            }
            break;
            case SoapMessageStage.AfterSerialize:
            {
                FileStream fs = new FileStream(LogFile, FileMode.Append,
                    FileAccess.Write);
                StreamWriter sw = new StreamWriter(fs);
                sw.WriteLine("** BEGIN SOAP RESPONSE: {0}", DateTime.Now);
                sw.Flush();
                TempStream.Position = 0;
                CopyTextStream(TempStream, fs);
                sw.WriteLine("** END SOAP RESPONSE");
                sw.Flush();

                // copy the memory beffered response
                // to the network stream
                TempStream.Position = 0;
                CopyTextStream(TempStream, SoapStream);
                fs.Close();
            }
            break;
        }
        return;
    }
}
```

LISTING 24.10   ExtensionSample.asmx.vb in VB.NET Continued

```vbnet
Public Overrides Sub ProcessMessage(ByVal message As SoapMessage)
    ' this method will be called several times during
    ' the processing of a SOAP request. The ASP.NET system
    ' tells us which stage the SOAP request is at with the
    ' Stage property of the SoapMessage class
    Select Case message.Stage
        Case SoapMessageStage.BeforeDeserialize
            ' copy the SOAP request from the network stream
            ' into our memory buffer
            CopyTextStream(SoapStream, TempStream)
            Dim fs As New FileStream(LogFile, FileMode.Append, _
                FileAccess.Write)
            Dim sw As New StreamWriter(fs)
            sw.WriteLine("** BEGIN SOAP REQUEST: {0}", DateTime.Now)
            sw.Flush()
```

LISTING 24.10 Continued

```
                     ' copy the mem buffer stream to the log file
                     TempStream.Position = 0
                     CopyTextStream(TempStream, fs)
                     sw.WriteLine("** END SOAP REQUEST")
                     sw.Flush()
                     fs.Close()

                     ' reset the memory buffer position
                     ' so the ASP.NET system can parse and
                     ' decode the message
                     TempStream.Position = 0
                Case SoapMessageStage.AfterSerialize
                     Dim fs As New FileStream(LogFile, FileMode.Append, _
                         FileAccess.Write)
                     Dim sw As New StreamWriter(fs)
                     sw.WriteLine("** BEGIN SOAP RESPONSE: {0}", DateTime.Now)
                     sw.Flush()
                     TempStream.Position = 0
                     CopyTextStream(TempStream, fs)
                     sw.WriteLine("** END SOAP RESPONSE")
                     sw.Flush()

                     ' copy the memory beffered response
                     ' to the network stream
                     TempStream.Position = 0
                     CopyTextStream(TempStream, SoapStream)

                     fs.Close()
            End Select
        End Sub
#End Region

End Class
```

This is the actual meat of the code. The `ProcessMessage` method is called by the .NET Framework's extension architecture each time a stage event is fired. The `Stage` property of the `SoapMessage` that is passed into the `ProcessMessage` method contains the current stage to be processed. You can perform different operations, depending on the stage, as shown in the preceding listings.

When implementing your own code while working in the `ProcessMessage`, you will have access to the `SoapStream` as illustrated in the previous code (it's simply written to a file) when working in the `BeforeDeserialize` and `AfterSerialize` stages. When you are working with the `AfterDeserialize` and `BeforeSerialize` methods, you will be able to work with the `SoapMessage` object and all its child objects and methods, including the following:

- **Headers**   A collection of all the `SoapHeaders`
- **MethodName**   The name of the Web method that was requested
- **ParamNames**   An array of strings representing the names of the parameter in the request or response
- **ParamTypes**   An array of types representing the types of the parameters in the request or response
- **ParamValues**   An array of objects representing the values in the request or response
- **XmlNamespace**   The XML namespace where the object that contains the called method is located

Because you can read from and write to all these objects, you could change the content of any of these aspects of the message before it is sent to the actual Web Service. This is where the power of extensions resides.

Most of the code in this implementation of the `ProcessMessage` method involves writing the message streams to the log file, although serializing a stream to a file is beyond the scope of this chapter. For more information about `MemoryStreams`, `FileStreams`, `StreamWriters`, and `StreamReaders`, please consult the .NET Framework's MSDN Library that comes with both Visual Studio .NET and the .NET Framework.

Listings 24.11 (for C#) and 24.12 (for VB .NET) illustrate how to use the `SoapLogger` extension by applying `SoapLoggerAttribute` to a Web method you create. Although you have used one .asmx file to contain both the extension and the Web Service, you could keep the previous code in one file and the following code in a separate file. As long as they are in the same namespace, you can easily use the extension in a Web Service that resides in another file.

Continue this example by typing the code in Listing 24.11 for C# or 24.12 for VB .NET into the Code Behind module. As mentioned earlier, be sure to type in only the code formatted in bold.

24

LISTING 24.11   ExtensionSample.asmx.cs in C# (Continued)

```
public class Author
{
    public string FirstName;
    public string LastName;
    public string Email;
    [XmlArray]
    public Book[] Books;
}
```

LISTING 24.11   Continued

```
public class Book
{
    public string Title;
    public string Publisher;
}


/// <summary>
///     Summary description for ExtensionSample.
/// </summary>
///
[WebService(Namespace="http://technicallead.com/csharpwebsamples")]
public class ExtensionSample : System.Web.Services.WebService
{
    public ExtensionSample()
    {
        //CODEGEN: This call is required by the
        //ASP.NET Web Services Designer
        InitializeComponent();
    }

#region Component Designer generated code
    /// <summary>
    ///     Required method for Designer support - do not modify
    ///     the contents of this method with the code editor.
    /// </summary>
    private void InitializeComponent()
    {
    }
#endregion

    /// <summary>
    ///     Clean up any resources being used.
    /// </summary>
    public override void Dispose()
    {
    }


    [
    WebMethod,
    SoapLogger
    ]
    public Author GetAuthorInfo()
    {
        Author author = new Author();
```

LISTING 24.11 Continued

```csharp
            author.FirstName = "Bob";
            author.LastName = "Tabor";
            author.Email = "bob@technicallead.com";
            author.Books = new Book[2];
            author.Books[0] = new Book();
            author.Books[0].Title = "Microsoft .NET WebServices";
            author.Books[0].Publisher = "SAMS Publishing";
            author.Books[1] = new Book();
            author.Books[1].Title = "Microsoft .NET WebServices 2nd Edition";
            author.Books[1].Publisher = "SAMS Publishing";

            return author;
        }

        [
        WebMethod,
        SoapLogger
        ]
        public Author SaveAuthorInfo(Author a)
        {
            return a;
        }
    }
}
```

LISTING 24.12 ExtensionSample.asmx.vb in VB.NET (Continued)

```vbnet
Public Class Author
    Public FirstName As String
    Public LastName As String
    Public Email As String
    Public Books As Book()
End Class

Public Class Book
    Public Title As String
    Public Publisher As String
End Class


Public Class SoapExtensionSample
    Inherits System.Web.Services.WebService

#Region " Web Services Designer Generated Code "
```

24

USING SOAP
EXTENSIONS

LISTING 24.12   Continued

```
    Public Sub New()
        MyBase.New()

        'This call is required by the Web Services Designer.
        InitializeComponent()

        'Add your own initialization code after the InitializeComponent() call

    End Sub

    'Required by the Web Services Designer
    Private components As System.ComponentModel.Container

    'NOTE: The following procedure is required by the Web Services Designer
    'It can be modified using the Web Services Designer.
    'Do not modify it using the code editor.
    <System.Diagnostics.DebuggerStepThroughAttribute()>
    Private Sub InitializeComponent()
        components = New System.ComponentModel.Container()
    End Sub

    Overloads Overrides Sub Dispose()
        'CODEGEN: This procedure is required by the Web Services Designer
        'Do not modify it using the code editor.
    End Sub

#End Region

#Region "Web Methods"

    <WebMethod(), SoapLogger("C:\vbsoap.log")>
    Public Function GetAuthorInfo() As Author
        Dim info As New Author()
        info.FirstName = "Bob"
        info.LastName = "Tabor"
        info.Email = "bob@technicallead.com"
        ReDim info.Books(2)
        info.Books(0) = New Book()
        info.Books(0).Title = "Microsoft .NET WebServices"
        info.Books(0).Publisher = "SAMS Publishing"
        info.Books(1) = New Book()
        info.Books(1).Title = "Microsoft .NET WebServices 2nd Edition"
        info.Books(1).Publisher = "SAMS Publishing"
```

LISTING 24.12 Continued

```
        GetAuthorInfo = info
    End Function

#End Region

End Class
```

First, you create two classes, Author and Book, which are used by the ExtensionSample Web Service. ExtensionSample has two methods: GetAuthorInfo and SaveAuthorInfo. The most important aspect of this code is applying the SoapLogger attribute to these two Web methods. You then perform some processing (filling up an instance of the Author class) and return.

Creating a Client

You need to create a client to consume the ExtensionSample Web Service. The code used to do this doesn't attempt to display the information that is returned; it simply calls the GetAuthorInfo Web method so that you can see the SOAP message logged to the file.

Be sure to create a Web reference to the ExtensionSample Web Service you created.

> **NOTE**
>
> Refer to the step-by-step instructions in a previous chapter (especially Chapter 5) for details on how to create a Web reference and compile the Web Service.

Create a new aspx Web Form file called ExtensionSampleClient.aspx and place a single button (Button1) on the designer surface. Double-click the button to add code to its Click event. Type in the code formatted in bold in Listing 24.13 (for C#) or 24.14 (for VB .NET) (pay attention particularly to the Button1_Click function and the declaration of mySample and myAuthor) to handle the Click event and call your Web Service. Visual Studio .NET generates much of the following code, which has been included to help you determine where to enter your code.

LISTING 24.13 ExtensionSampleClient.aspx.cs in C#

```
using System;
using System.Collections;
using System.ComponentModel;
using System.Data;
using System.Drawing;
using System.Web;
```

LISTING 24.13 Continued

```csharp
using System.Web.SessionState;
using System.Web.UI;
using System.Web.UI.WebControls;
using System.Web.UI.HtmlControls;

namespace Chapter24CSharp

{
    /// <summary>
    /// Summary description for ExtensionSampleClient.
    /// </summary>
    public class ExtensionSampleClient : System.Web.UI.Page
    {
        protected System.Web.UI.WebControls.Button Button1;

        public localhost.ExtensionSample mySample =
            new localhost.ExtensionSample();
        public localhost.Author myAuthor = new localhost.Author();

        public ExtensionSampleClient()
        {
            Page.Init += new System.EventHandler(Page_Init);
        }
        private void Page_Load(object sender, System.EventArgs e)
        {
            // Put user code to initialize the page here
        }
        private void Page_Init(object sender, EventArgs e)
        {
            //
            // CODEGEN: This call is required by the ASP.NET Windows Form
Designer.
            //
            InitializeComponent();
        }
        #region Web Form Designer generated code
        /// <summary>
        /// Required method for Designer support - do not modify
        /// the contents of this method with the code editor.
        /// </summary>
        private void InitializeComponent()
        {
            this.Button1.Click += new
System.EventHandler(this.Button1_Click);
            this.Load += new System.EventHandler(this.Page_Load);
```

LISTING 24.13   Continued

```
        }
    #endregion

    private void Button1_Click(object sender, System.EventArgs e)
    {
        myAuthor = mySample.GetAuthorInfo();
    }
  }
}
```

LISTING 24.14   ExtensionSampleClient.aspx.vb in VB.NET

```
Public Class ExtensionSampleClient
    Inherits System.Web.UI.Page
    Protected WithEvents Button1 As System.Web.UI.WebControls.Button

    Protected mySample As New localhost.SoapExtensionSample()
    Protected myAuthor As New localhost.Author()


#Region " Web Form Designer Generated Code "

    'This call is required by the Web Form Designer.
    <System.Diagnostics.DebuggerStepThrough()>
    Private Sub InitializeComponent()

    End Sub

    Private Sub Page_Init(ByVal sender As System.Object, _
        ByVal e As System.EventArgs) Handles MyBase.Init
        'CODEGEN: This method call is required by the Web Form Designer
        'Do not modify it using the code editor.
        InitializeComponent()
    End Sub

#End Region

    Private Sub Page_Load(ByVal sender As System.Object, _
        ByVal e As System.EventArgs) Handles MyBase.Load
        'Put user code to initialize the page here
    End Sub
```

LISTING 24.14   Continued

```
    Private Sub Button1_Click(ByVal sender As System.Object, _
        ByVal e As System.EventArgs) Handles Button1.Click
        myAuthor = mySample.GetAuthorInfo()
    End Sub
End Class
```

What's most important in this code is the creation of the public myAuthor and mySample properties, which are instances of classes created in the Web reference. Also, the code includes a
line to call the GetAuthorInfo Web method in the Button1 Click event. The rest of the code is
generated by Visual Studio .NET.

Results of Running the Extension

After you have compiled the code and opened the SoapExtensionClient.aspx file in a browser,
click the lone button on the form. Your page should look similar to Figure 24.1.

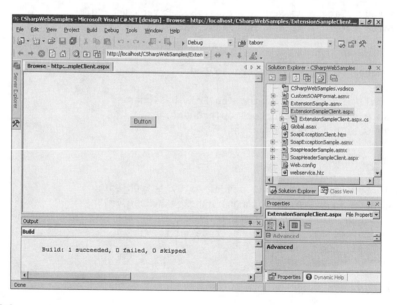

FIGURE 24.1
The SoapExtensionClient Web page.

Although the page's appearance doesn't change when you click the button, check the root
directory of your C:\ drive and you'll find a file called soap.log. Open it in Windows Notepad
to see results similar to this:

```
** BEGIN SOAP REQUEST: 5/18/2001 1:21:12 PM
<?xml version="1.0" encoding="utf-8"?>
```

```
<soap:Envelope
xmlns:soap="http://schemas.xmlsoap.org/soap/envelope/"xmlns:xsi="http://www.w3.
org/2001/XMLSchema-instance"
xmlns:xsd="http://www.w3.org/2001/XMLSchema">
  <soap:Body>
    <GetAuthorInfo xmlns="http://technicallead.com/csharpwebsamples" />
  </soap:Body>
</soap:Envelope>
** END SOAP REQUEST

** BEGIN SOAP RESPONSE: 5/18/2001 1:21:12 PM
<?xml version="1.0" encoding="utf-8"?>
<soap:Envelope xmlns:soap="http://schemas.xmlsoap.org/soap/envelope/"
xmlns:xsi="http://www.w3.org/2001/XMLSchema-instance"
xmlns:xsd="http://www.w3.org/2001/XMLSchema">
  <soap:Body>
    <GetAuthorInfoResponse xmlns="http://technicallead.com/csharpwebsamples">
      <GetAuthorInfoResult>
        <FirstName>Bob</FirstName>
        <LastName>Tabor</LastName>
        <Email>bob@technicallead.com</Email>
        <Books>
          <Book>
            <Title>Microsoft .NET WebServices</Title>
            <Publisher>SAMS Publishing</Publisher>
          </Book>
          <Book>
            <Title>Microsoft .NET WebServices 2nd Edition</Title>
            <Publisher>SAMS Publishing</Publisher>
          </Book>
        </Books>
      </GetAuthorInfoResult>
    </GetAuthorInfoResponse>
  </soap:Body>
</soap:Envelope>
** END SOAP RESPONSE
```

24

USING SOAP
EXTENSIONS

NOTE

You could experience problems if your current permission settings do not allow you to write to the designated path specified in the code listing. If you encounter unexpected results, you might want to check your settings.

You'll notice that there are two distinct sections: the SOAP REQUEST section that contains the SOAP Request message, and the SOAP RESPONSE section, which contains a serialized version of a class you instanced and sent back via the Web Service. Each of these sections are tagged with ** BEGIN and ** END and contain the date and time.

Summary

SOAP extensions are a valuable plug-in to .NET's SOAP handling framework. They allow you to selectively intercept SOAP messages before or after they are deserialized into objects for processing or serialized back into a SOAP messages for a return trip to the server. As a result, you can create powerful add-ins that inspect the actual SOAP messages and perform operations on that data at critical points in the message's trip from the client to the Web Service.

Understanding UDDI

IN THIS CHAPTER

Perhaps you have built a series of Web Services so that your trading partners can create orders and check on inventory levels in your company. Your trading partners are availing themselves of this new functionality and because there are only a dozen of them, you can walk their development team through the process of finding the Web Services residing on your server. However, you realize that there are other trading partners who would be interested in the products and services you supply. How do you notify the world that you exist and that you can take orders electronically? How do you support potentially hundreds of new trading partners as they begin to develop systems that use your Web Services without making it your full-time job? These are the very questions that a new technology called UDDI seeks to address.

This chapter introduces UDDI from a business and a technical perspective. From a business perspective, you'll examine several scenarios that use UDDI and learn about the available categorizations for targeting your Web Services to customers. You'll also see how UDDI can solve real-world problems of finding businesses that want to conduct business electronically. From a technical perspective, you'll learn about the different data entities and the relationship between them as well as the UDDI site operators and how they replicate data. You'll also get an overview of the Programmer's API for working programmatically with UDDI so that you can automate the process of finding trading partners and submitting your own Web Services for discovery.

What Is UDDI?

In its most basic form, Universal Discovery, Description, and Integration (UDDI) is a Web site (http://www.uddi.org) you can visit to look for trading partners who sell products or services you might be interested in. Generally, UDDI is a set of specifications and technologies that act as a search engine for Web Services. You can search by the type of product or service you are looking for, the location of the company, or other combinations of search criteria. As a provider of Web Services, you can also register your Web Service with the UDDI registry and tell the world that your company and its Web Services exist.

UDDI is more than just a simple search engine, however. It also contains descriptions of how to interact with those Web Services programmatically. More specifically, it enables companies to find electronic trading partners and then facilitates the electronic exchange of data by making it possible for trading partners' public interfaces to be discovered automatically through programming.

Examining each word that makes up the acronym *UDDI* helps clarify what it does. *Universal* indicates that UDDI is a global resource available to trading partners around the world. *Description* suggests that your business or programmatic interface can be described in a way that enables others to search for and discover it. Using the UDDI specification, you can describe your business and Web Services in textual descriptions as well as other popular categorization methods: known identifiers, standard taxonomies, and business service types (discussed in "UDDI Registry Data" later in this chapter).

Discovery has a two-fold meaning: the traditional way in which businesses find other businesses to trade with (for example, making contacts in person, doing research on a company), and the programmatic and automatic discovery described in Chapter 9, "Understanding DISCO." .

Finally, *integration* refers to acquiring knowledge dynamically about the exact method calls, data types, and return types used when calling the trading partner's Web Service.

UDDI: A Business Perspective

UDDI is not just about discovering the technical details of a Web Service; it is also about finding businesses that supply or consume the products and services your organization provides. In this respect, it is similar to many existing Web sites that offer a searchable index of businesses as well as a categorization of those businesses. It transcends those types of sites by also allowing a search based on a service type. Service types are discussed in more detail in the following scenario sections, but basically they are programmatic Web Service interfaces that businesses use to describe what they support. The actual implementation of the Web Service is not important—what's important is that they have the same method of calling the Web Service. Service types differ from other methods of searching for trading partners by providing an industry-supported standard or a means of finding other companies that use the same software your company uses. Being able to find these companies makes integrating with them that much more automated.

In an effort to better understand UDDI, take a moment to look at several scenarios in the following sections that better describe its function and promise. All of these scenarios will soon be commonplace with the adoption of UDDI.

Scenario 1: Manually Querying UDDI

In this scenario, your company is searching for a supplier of widgets. Although you could look in your local yellow pages and communicate via fax and telephone, management wants to take a less time-consuming, and therefore less expensive, approach to finding pricing and availability information as well as ordering widgets. Because widgets are a commodity, management wants to find out which supplier is selling widgets at the lowest price on any given day. Grant, a member of the management team, searches the UDDI registry for widgets and locates several companies that supply them. In fact, most of the suppliers use a common API (service type) for providing pricing, availability, ordering, and checking order status. Grant forwards the companies' unique identifiers to you, and you use that information to find more detailed technical information about interacting electronically with them by using the UDDI directory.

Scenario 2: Programmatically Querying UDDI

With your new accounting software package, you can search a UDDI directory and find all the possible trading partners who use the same accounting software. You all use the same service type for general purchasing, shipping, and inventory data, so knowing which trading partners you can automatically interact with is valuable information. During setup of the accounting program, you are required to include, for example, your business name, contact information, and categorization information. The accounting software's setup program automatically contacts the UDDI registry, creates a entry for your company, and then locates all other companies that use a special service type unique to that accounting software. The accounting software's setup shows you these companies and reports that you can seamlessly trade with them if you want.

Scenario 3: UDDI as a Search Engine Resource

In this scenario, a popular business directory search engine rewrites its software to make finding a business that fits your search criteria more accurate. It does this by crawling through the UDDI registry and learning about companies and their products, services, management team, and the types of services they offer for electronic commerce. The business directory takes this information and uses its own special algorithms to sort and link this information into its own repository. When Web surfers browse the search engine's updated listings, they will find a closer match with the types of products and services they are looking for because they have used the UDDI registry as an added resource.

Scenario 4: UDDI as an e-Marketplace Resource

Vertical marketplaces crawl the UDDI registry to find companies that provide products and services within a narrow vertical market. For example, WidgetNet is a vertical marketplace for widgets. Suppliers can offer their wares through this marketplace, and anyone searching for various makes and models of widgets can come to this marketplace to find the best widget provider that's geographically closest to them. WidgetNet also provides a Web-based order form for customer orders and, for a small fee, handles filling the end customer's order. WidgetNet offers customers huge value because they have to go to only one place to find the best deal on widgets. WidgetNet has established a well-known presence in the marketplace, so it also gives suppliers the opportunity to sell to end customers who might never have heard of them otherwise. WidgetNet searches the UDDI registry constantly, looking for new companies that supply widgets. It then works with them to support a whole series of Web Services based on the WidgetNet service type.

UDDI Registry Data

UDDI represents three distinct types of registry data, discussed in the following sections.

White Pages

White pages contain basic business information, such as the name of the business, a textual description (possibly in multiple languages), and contact information, including names, phone numbers, e-mail addresses, fax numbers, and Web sites that belong to those businesses. Additionally, white page information includes known identifiers for businesses, such as Thomas Registry or Data Universal Numbering System (DUNS) identifiers.

Yellow Pages

Yellow pages categorize the business information by taxonomies. In the first version of UDDI, this taxonomy includes categorizing by industry, product or service, and location.

To categorize by industry, UDDI uses the North American Industry Classification System (NAICS). This system was created in 1997 by government agencies from the United States, Mexico, and Canada to facilitate collecting, tabulating, presenting, and analyzing data on companies throughout North America. NAICS was an effort to promote uniformity and comparability in the presentation and analysis of statistical data describing the participating countries' economy.

To categorize by product or service, UDDI uses the UNSPSC standard of classifying the actual products and services each company produces. It is an eight-digit hierarchical classification system based on the merger of the United Nations' Common Coding System (UNCCS) and Dun & Bradstreet's Standard Products and Services Classification (SPCS). Visa and Dun & Bradstreet spearheaded the effort by seeking a method for classifying each line of a credit card's expenditures to generate improved analysis of consumer behavior trends.

To categorize by location, UDDI uses simple geographical information, such as country and state or province.

Green Pages

The green pages include information that describes how to interact electronically with the business, including the business processes (that is, the multiple Web Services needed to create an order, check inventory, and so forth), the service descriptions (the individual Web Services and what they are used for), and the binding information explaining how to call a given Web Service through programming. The binding information typically has a link to a resource, such as a DISCO or WSDL file, and possibly an informational HTML page that explains the nuances of the Web Service.

Additionally, Web Services can be categorized just as businesses can, which makes it easier to create a search for a Web Service that might fall outside the description of the business it belongs to.

UDDI: A Technical Perspective

UDDI will ultimately have many operator sites, but currently three sites support UDDI: Microsoft, IBM, and Ariba. Consequently, they are the three major contributors to UDDI. You can find UDDI implementations at the following addresses:

```
http://uddi.ariba.com
http://www.ibm.com/services/uddi
http://uddi.microsoft.com
```

In the future, there will be more operator sites. Why not provide just one centralized site instead of three (or more) distributed sites? Having multiple sites allows for better load distribution. Also, each operator site can combine the UDDI data with other value-added data, products, and services to distinguish it from the other operator sites. The three current sites are an example of how many sites can be created to conform to the standard and work together, despite using different tools, hardware, and software platforms.

The operator sites stay in sync by using replication. Details on replication are made available only for approved site operators, however. For more information about becoming a site operator, you should visit `http://www.uddi.org`.

The Web Services Interface to UDDI

You can programmatically interface with UDDI via its Web Services. This collection of Web Services allows you to do just about anything with Web Services programmatically that you might do manually through the existing UDDI Web sites—creating UDDI registration records, updating or deleting records, and searching for UDDI entries of other companies. These interfaces are described in depth in the Programmer's API Guide to UDDI (available at `http://www.uddi.org`), but an overview is given in "The UDDI Programmer's API Specification," later in this chapter. Any software that can send and receive a SOAP message can interact with UDDI.

UDDI and Other Types of Web Services

As mentioned earlier, the UDDI registry's green pages has a link to information about the Web Service. The Web Service does not necessarily have to be a SOAP-based Web Service, such as the ones you have built in this book. In the foreseeable future, companies are much more likely to use SOAP to exchange information as its prevalence in the marketplace grows. However, it is conceivable that a different protocol will gain attention and soon be the vogue of electronic data exchange. If that should happen, UDDI will be flexible enough so that those new types of Web Services can be discovered, described, and interrogated.

Authorization and Security

Each site operator node is responsible for implementing security and authorization in its own way. Microsoft chooses to authorize people via their Passport services, for example. Authorization and security are necessary when companies need to update or delete their service descriptions. You can imagine the havoc that could be wreaked if no limits were set on who had permission to update information! For this reason, company information does not get transferred between operator sites, and login names and passwords cannot be transferred from one operator site to another.

The UDDI Invocation and Recovery Model

The UDDI specification outlines a model for most applications and users interacting with a UDDI registry. This model provides a step-by-step recipe for using Web Services that are discovered by using UDDI.

As you develop your application over time, you will likely find a trading partner by using UDDI; you can then find more information about the services this trading partner offers by drilling down into the UDDI registry for this data. ("The UDDI Data Structures" explains the businessEntity, businessService, and bindingTemplate information later in the chapter.) Your application should save the technical information about binding to the Web Service in a configuration file or database. This "technical information" (the bindingTemplate) is then used when your code must consume the Web Service to find and make the appropriate call. When your application calls the Web Service, the Web Service returns a successful piece of data or an error message. If the Web Service is down or has moved, your application should be robust enough to recover by querying the UDDI registry to see whether the address has changed. If it has, your application can recover gracefully by rerouting to the new address and saving this new configuration data. If there is still a problem, your application can notify the user, and a more manual process can be initiated to find the cause of the problem.

This model is supported by the UDDI specification as a design pattern that all applications using UDDI programmatically should follow. Be cognizant of this model as you set out to use UDDI programmatically from your applications.

UDDI Data Structures

Now that you've seen an overview of UDDI, it's time to plunge in and look at its major components , including the main data entities, and to understand what type of data is stored in the registry. Then, you can look at the relationships between those data entities.

There are four different data structures in UDDI:

- **businessEntity**   The data structure for the white pages described earlier
- **businessService**   The data structure for the yellow pages described earlier
- **bindingTemplate**   The data structure for the green pages described earlier
- **tModel**   A pointer to a technical specification that one or more Web Services can adhere to

These data structures are explained in more detail in the following sections, which describe the main data elements used in each one. However, if you're interested in a more detailed look at additional data elements for these data structures, check the UDDI Data Structures Reference at http://www.uddi.org. Each data structure also has an associated identifierBag and/or categoryBag, which are discussed later in "The categoryBag and identifierBag Elements."

The businessEntity Structure

The businessEntity structure includes data elements that describe the business, its contacts, addresses, and URLs where you can find additional information (such as discovery information). Most important, it has a collection of businessService structures (Web Services) associated with it. The data elements for businessEntity are described in Table 25.1.

TABLE 25.1   Data Elements for `businessEntity`

Data Element	Descriptio
BusinessKey	A unique identifier for the business.
DiscoveryURLs	A collection of URLs that provide some form of discovery (that is, DISCO or WSDL files).
Name	Searchable element.
Description	Optional (one for each language is allowed).
BusinessServices	A collection of `businessService` structures (see "The `businessService` Structure").
Contacts	A collection of contacts (a structure themselves, with name, phone, e-mail, and address information).

The `businessService` Structure

The `businesService` structure is a distinct Web Service provided by a specific `businessEntity`. The `businessService` structure has the data elements described in Table 25.2.

TABLE 25.2   Data Elements for `businessService`

Data Element	Description
businessKey	A "foreign key" identifier to the `businessEntity` that provides the Web Service.
serviceKey	A unique identifier for the service.
name	Searchable name.
description	Optional (one for each language is allowed).
bindingTemplates	A collection of `bindingTemplate` structures (see "The `bindingTemplate` Structure").

The `bindingTemplate` Structure

The `bindingTemplate` structure represents technical descriptions of Web Services. It includes a URI and other links to information that could be important while implementing a Web Service in your application. Technical people and software applications use the data in this structure to actually consume the Web Service. Table 25.3 describes the data elements in the `bindingTemplate` structure.

TABLE 25.3   Data Elements for `bindingTemplate`

Data Element	Description
bindingKey	A unique identifier.
businessKey	A "foreign key" that associates the `bindingTemplate` to a `businessEntity`.
serviceKey	A "foreign key" that associates the `bindingTemplate` to a `businesService`.
accessPoint	A URI, an e-mail address, a telephone number, and so on that points to an entry point for the Web Service (see the paragraph following this table).
hostingRedirector	If no `accessPoint` is found, this element must be present. It represents a `bindingTemplate` structure that should be used in place of the current `bindingTemplate`. This element could be useful in recovery after a Web Service call fails (see "The UDDI Invocation and Recovery Model" earlier in this chapter).
tModelInstanceDetails	List of `tModelInfo` structures (see text following this table).

The `accessPoint` is attribute-qualified, meaning it must be prefixed by a valid `URLType`, such as `mailto:`, `http:`, `https:`, `ftp:`, `fax:`, or `phone:`.

The `tModelInstanceDetails` field of the `bindingTemplate` contains a collection of one or more `tModelInstanceInfo` structures. Each of these structures in turn references a collection of `tModel` structures. Yes, that's right—one `bindingTemplate` can be associated with many `tModels`. (See Figure 25.1 for a visual representation of this concept.) In other words, a Web Service (as defined in the `bindingTemplate`) can implement zero to many interfaces (`tModels`) that are defined in UDDI. The collection of all the `tModel` structures implemented by a `bindingTemplate` is sometimes referred to as the Web Service's "digital fingerprint."

The `tModel` Structure

A `tModel` entry is a straightforward concept: It is a "technical fingerprint" that describes a common interface that one or more Web Services can adhere to. The `tModel` includes the data elements described in Table 25.4.

Business Entry

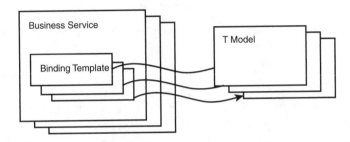

FIGURE 25.1

Relationship between tModelInstanceDetail, bindingTemplate, tModelInstanceInfo, *and* tModel *data structures.*

TABLE 25.4   Data Elements for tModel

Data Element	Description
tModelKey	A unique identifier for the tModel.
name	Searchable name of the tModel.
description	A description of the tModel.
overviewDoc	Contains references to descriptions and other information on the tModel.

The categoryBag and identifierBag Elements

The identifierBag element allows certain structures (businessEntity and tModel) to be located via common forms of identification, such as a tax ID or Dun & Bradstreet number. This information is stored as name/value pairs and can be searched by using the find_xxx method call using certain search parameters (as explained in the following section "Search Qualifiers").

The categoryBag elements allow certain structures (such as businessService) to be categorized according to any available taxonomy or classification systems, including the UNSPSC and NAICS systems discussed previously (see "Yellow Pages" earlier in this chapter). This information is stored as name/value pairs and can be searched by using search parameters.

The UDDI Programmer's API Specification

The UDDI Programmer's API Specification is a document that outlines the public SOAP-callable method interfaces to perform every operation on a UDDI site operator. It is composed of two parts: the Inquiry API for querying and browsing through the UDDI registry to find businesses and services the end user is searching for, and the Publishers API for adding, updating, and deleting business and service information in the UDDI registry.

This section of the chapter will outline the two prominent APIs and their general purpose for building applications that implement UDDI functionality.

Inquiry API

Each UDDI data structure (`businessEntity`, `businessService`, `bindingTemplate`, and `tModel`) has a `find_xxx` and a `get_xxx` function. These eight functions make up the Inquiry API, which allows the user to search for keywords or values in the registry on a given data entity, and then get all the data associated with that entry. This API is used primarily as a means of locating and displaying businesses, services, and so forth that the end user is trying to locate.

Search Qualifiers

Each of the four `find_xxx` functions can be enhanced with search qualifiers. A typical leftmost name search, used by default, looks similar to this example (notice the body in particular):

```
<?xml version='1.0' encoding='UTF-8' ?>
<Envelope xmlns='http://schemas.xmlsoap.org/soap/envelope/'>
<Body>
  <find_business generic='1.0' xmlns='urn:uddi-org:api'>
    <name>TechnicalLead</name>
  </find_business>
</Body>
</Envelope>
```

This search will look for only those company names that begin with "TechnicalLead," which could include companies named Technicalleader, Technicalleadership, and so forth. Using the search qualifiers, you can specify multiple search criteria and broaden or narrow the search, as shown in this example:

```
<?xml version='1.0' encoding='UTF-8' ?>
<Envelope xmlns='http://schemas.xmlsoap.org/soap/envelope/'>
<Body>
  <find_business generic='1.0' xmlns='urn:uddi-org:api'>
    <findQualifiers>
      <caseSensitiveMatch>TechnicalLead</ caseSensitiveMatch>
      <sortByDateAsc />
```

```
    </findQualifiers>
  </find_business>
</Body>
</Envelope>
```

When this search runs, it will perform a leftmost search to look for only those entries with the proper case, and will then sort the results by the date they were submitted to the registry. There are six search qualifiers:

```
ExactNameMatch

CaseSensitiveMatch

SortByNameAsc

SortByNameDesc

SortByDateAsc

SortByDateDesc
```

Publishers API

Each UDDI data structure (`businessEntity`, `businessService`, `bindingTemplate`, and `tModel`) has a `save_xxx` and a `delete_xxxx` function. These eight functions (as well as three other functions that control security) form the Publication API, which enables the user to modify existing entries in the registry (only those entries they are authorized to modify, however) and create new ones by using the `save_xxx` functions. The `delete_xxx` functions completely remove the given data structure. This API is used primarily as a means of creating and updating business and service information that the end user is authorized to modify.

The Future of UDDI

UDDI has a planned evolution into 2002. The goal of the first phase, which began in September 2000, was to provide a fundamental implementation of the specification and thereby build support for this technology. Three taxonomies were supplied to categorize businesses and services, and the focus was on describing services.

The second phase started in March 2001 and moved from a business unit focus to an enterprise focus, allowing larger companies to register more of their business units and the services they support. More taxonomies were added, and the focus turned from describing individual Web Services to describing "layered" Web Services, groups that work together to accomplish a business process.

The third phase is slated to begin in December 2001 and will move from an enterprise focus to an association focus, emphasizing a common set of service types for entire industries. It promises to support custom taxonomies and offer a way to describe workflows that contain multiple business processes, each made up of multiple Web Services.

The most important aspect of UDDI's future is its eventual submission to a standards organization (perhaps ECMA), ensuring that it will be developed by many different interested parties and will not serve the interests of any one business or organization. Visit the UDDI Frequently Asked Questions page at `http://www.uddi.org/faqs.html` for more information about submission to a standards body.

The Promise of Universal Discovery

UDDI seeks to facilitate a world in which all businesses and their public programmatic interfaces can be dynamically discovered and used. UDDI will facilitate the type of exchanges discussed in Chapter 1, "Introducing Web Services." It hopes to make integrating business processes between companies transparent and automatic.

UDDI also has value within an enterprise. As noted throughout this book, large enterprises with many departments that are geographically dispersed can benefit from reusing code through Web Services. Web Services also enable departments within large organizations to exchange information, even though they might use different operating systems. But how do these departments learn about the work that other companies are doing? What's needed is a large searchable database of departments and programmatic interfaces so that other departments can make the most of investments the enterprise has made in information technology. UDDI could potentially fill the bill for this purpose in a more private capacity. In other words, the organization might not want to make these interfaces available to the entire world, just to other departments and subsidiaries within the enterprise. A private tailored version of UDDI could be created for this purpose.

Summary

UDDI is a specification that enables trading partners to discover and interrogate each other's Web Services. Think "search engine for Web Services" that makes it possible for end users to find products and services they need by searching a business listing, business categorizations, or programmatic description of the actual Web Services. There are three basic types of data in UDDI: white pages (general business information), yellow pages (business categorizations), and green pages (descriptions of Web Services supported by companies).

Microsoft, Ariba, and IBM maintain their own UDDI registries by using their technologies, software, and hardware. The three implementations of UDDI synchronize the entries made into their databases on a nightly basis. Over time, other companies will likely be allowed to be site operators.

A UDDI registry makes a set of APIs available in the form of SOAP Web Services so that applications and users can query and administer Web Services that are registered in the database. Currently, several sites allow users to view the registry, desktop applications, search engines, and business directories, and e-marketplaces can programmatically crawl through the UDDI registry to find products and services for end users.

Configuring, Deploying, and Securing Web Services

IN THIS CHAPTER

In this chapter you'll learn about the steps you must take to get your Web Services ready for real-world use. This includes making the settings such as database connection strings configurable so that as you move your Web Service from a development environment to a staging and production environment, you can easily switch the target environment in an XML file. The steps also include creating a deployment project in Visual Studio .NET to compile and include the necessary distribution files to other servers in your environment. This chapter also covers issues related to securing your Web Services so that only authorized individuals or organizations can use the Web Services, and so that the messages themselves can not be easily intercepted and read when traveling across the Internet.

Configuration

This section seeks to answer the question, "How can I make my Web Service configurable so that I can change the settings without recompiling the Web Service?" The answer is relatively straightforward, if you know where to look for it, because behind the scenes, ASP.NET provides the web.config file, which can be used to store configuration settings specific to your application. Having this file in your Web application (it's not there by default unless you are using Visual Studio .NET, which provides the file as well as a template for its use) enables you to add settings to it that could require manual changes over time, such as when you are moving the application to a different server environment. An example of the items you might choose to configure via the web.config file could include the following:

- Connection strings to data sources
- File paths that are used in the application
- Security settings (as explained in the section "Security" later in this chapter)
- Flags or application settings that affect program flow

In the following sections, you'll see two methods for using and modifying the web.config configuration settings: through code and in the Visual Studio .NET IDE.

The web.config File

The web.config file is an XML file that usually consists of a series of settings, although it is acceptable to have no settings in this file at all. If you create a new Web Service project in Visual Studio .NET and open the web.config file that's generated automatically and added to the project, you will see a number of empty settings with text explaining each section and its proper use. To configure settings in your application, you need to add a new section to the web.config file called `<appSettings />` section, which Visual Studio .NET does not provide by default. In the `<appSettings />` section, you can add as many configurable settings as you like, using the `<add key="somekey" value="somevalue" />` XML element as a child to the `<appSettings />` element. You use the `key` attribute to identify the setting, and the `value` attribute contains the configurable setting. The following is an example of a web.config file with unnecessary settings left out:

```
<?xml version="1.0" encoding="utf-8" ?>
<configuration>
...
    <appSettings>
        <add key="YourKey" value="YourValue" />
    </appSettings>
...
</configuration>
```

In the preceding code, the section, <appSettings /> section is formatted in bold text, and ellipses denote that there are a dozen or so other elements you will probably find in this file that are used to configure other aspects of the application.

Using the web.config File Programmatically

The <appSettings> values are useful only if you can access them from your application to dynamically configure the flow or other path and connection attributes. Fortunately, the .NET Framework provides the System.Configuration.ConfigurationSettings class with the AppSettings() method. Assume that you have a web.config configuration file with the following <appSettings> section:

```
<configuration>
    <appSettings>
        <add key="SomeSetting" value="Booter" />
    </appSettings>
</configuration>
```

You can use the following line of code to retrieve the "SomeSetting" key value programmatically:

VB .NET Code Snippet

```
Imports System.Configuration
.
.
.
sValue = ConfigurationSettings.AppSettings("SomeSetting")
```

C# Code Snippet

```
Using System.Configuration;
.
.
.
sValue = ConfigurationSettings.AppSettings("SomeSetting");
```

Additionally, the ConfigurationSettings class supplies a GetConfig() method that enables you to access any of the sections of the web.config file to use its settings.

Using the web.config File via Visual Studio .NET

Many of the objects that can be dragged and dropped from the Server Explorer and Toolbox onto your Web Service's designer surface have dynamic properties, which can obtain their values from settings in the web.config file without you having to write any code (actually, code is written for you in the Code Behind file for the Web Service). For example, by dragging and dropping an OLE DB `Connection` object from the Server Explorer onto your Web Service's designer surface, you can access its dynamic properties in the Properties window by expanding the (Dynamic Properties) entry. As you can see in Figure 26.1, for a `SqlConnection` component, there is only one dynamic property: `ConnectionString`.

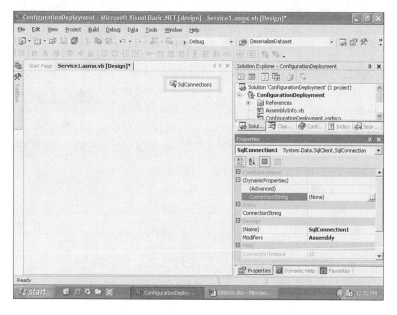

FIGURE 26.1
Dynamic Properties in the Properties window.

When you select the `ConnectionString` entry that by default contains (None) in the property setting, an ellipsis button appears to the right of that entry. Click that button to open the Dynamic Property: 'SqlConnection1.ConnectionString' dialog box (see Figure 26.2).

Select the Map Property to a Key in a Configuration File check box to enable the Key drop-down list box, where you can select a different `<appSetting>` key if one exists in the web.config file. When you click the OK button, the dialog box closes and a small blue icon appears next to the `ConnectionString` property, indicating that the value for this property is bound to the web.config file (see Figure 26.3).

FIGURE 26.2
Dynamic Property dialog box.

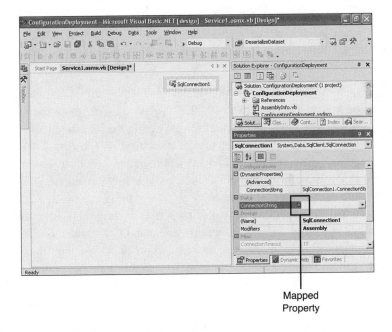

Mapped
Property

FIGURE 26.3
The Mapped Property icon for the ConnectionString *property.*

If you click the drop-down list arrow next to the ConnectionString property to select an existing database connection or create a new one, the settings will be saved in the web.config file. After making a selection, you can attempt to open the web.config file in Solution Explorer. When you do, you will be prompted with an odd message box that says the web.config file is already open, and asks if you want to close it.

When a change is made to the ConnectionString property (or any dynamic property bound to the web.config file), behind the scenes, an instance of the web.config file is opened and must be saved before it can be displayed. Clicking Yes in the message box opens a dialog box requesting that you save the .asmx file you made the modification to. Click the Yes button again, and when the web.config appears, it should contain a setting similar to the following:

```
<configuration>
  <appSettings>
```

```
<!-- User application and configured property settings go here.-->
<!-- Example: <add key="settingName" value="settingValue"/> -->
<add key="SqlConnection1.ConnectionString"
     value="data source=YOURSOURCE;
     initial catalog=YOURDB;
     integrated security=SSPI;
     persist security info=False;
     workstation id=YOURID;packet size=4096" />
  </appSettings>
</configuration>
```

The `<add key="SqlConnection1.ConnectionString" />` setting can now be changed manually in a text editor, or you can continue to modify it by using Visual Studio .NET as needed.

Using the Configuration Manager

The Configuration Manager in Visual Studio .NET allows you to define solution configurations containing information about whether each of the projects in the solution should be rebuilt and what the target platform should be for each project (typically .NET, but potentially could be others in the future). You can also select a project configuration (a collection of properties about the project). By using this tool, you can have a single solution with multiple projects that are configured differently and could be deployed for many different scenarios. Each project configuration can include settings for dozens of properties, including the start page to use for debugging (for ASP.NET Web Form applications), command-line arguments, compilation optimizations, the output path when building assemblies, information to display during compilation, and more. A project configuration also allows you to select a configuration file that will replace the web.config file in your project to target different settings for different solution configurations.

In other words, if you create three solution configurations—Development, Staging, and Production—your ASP.NET Web Service project will have three new project configurations, each with a different configuration file assigned to each, if needed. Therefore, you can add new configuration files called Development.config, Staging.config, and Production.config to your project and configure their application settings appropriately. (These filenames are merely examples; you can name the files anything you like.) When you build or debug your solution to target the Staging environment, for example, Visual Studio .NET dynamically renames the Staging.config file so that the settings come from the renamed Staging.config instead of the existing web.config file. This becomes important when you create a deployment project that will use this project configuration information to include the proper files for distribution to your target environment.

To create project and solution configurations that use different properties and configuration files for each type of environment, follow these steps:

1. Select your ASP.NET Web Service project name in Solution Explorer.

2. Choose Build | Configuration Manager on the menu, which displays the Configuration Manager dialog box, shown in Figure 26.4.

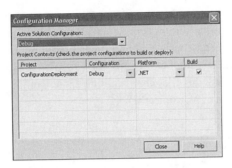

FIGURE 26.4

The Configuration Manager dialog box.

3. Select <New> in the Active Solution Configuration list box. The New Solution Configuration dialog box opens (see Figure 26.5).

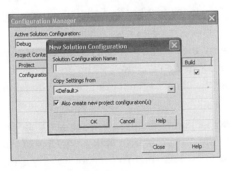

FIGURE 26.5

The New Solution Configuration dialog box.

4. Type in **Staging** in the Solution Configuration Name text box. Leave the <Default> value displayed in the Copy Settings From list box, and leave the Also Create New Project Configuration(s) check box selected. This check box indicates that a new project configuration by the same name will be created, too. Click the OK button to close this dialog box.

5. In the Configuration Manager dialog box, the Active Solution Configuration has changed to Staging. In the Project Contexts section is a list of projects in the current solution, where you can select the project configuration (you'll understand what this does in just a moment), the platform (currently just .NET, but could be other platforms in the future), and whether to build this project in the solution when this solution configuration is selected. In this case, just leave the default settings, and click the Close button.

Now you'll modify the properties of the project configuration that you just created. In particular, when you select the Staging solution configuration to be built and deployed, each project in the solution defers to its project configuration settings, which in this case is also named Staging. First, you'll create a second web.config file called Staging.config, and then you will tell Visual Studio .NET to use this file when building and compiling your solution in the Staging solution and project configurations.

> **NOTE**
>
> Currently, C# projects in Visual Studio .NET do not offer the capability of setting the OverRide File property.

1. Rename the existing web.config file as Staging.config by right-clicking its entry in Solution Explorer, and then choosing Rename on the pop-up menu. Type the new filename, **Staging.config**, in the text box in Solution Explorer. Press Enter when you are finished.

2. Open the Staging.config file and make changes to the file's `section, web.config file> <appSettings />` section that are specific to the Staging environment. For example, you could change the `ConnectionString` property to connect to the Staging environment's database.

3. Right-click the project name in Solution Explorer, and choose Add | New Item on the pop-up menu to open the Add New Item dialog box. Select Web Configuration File in the Templates pane, and click Open. (You cannot name this file. That is why you were instructed to rename the existing web.config file in your project.)

4. Open the new web.config file and make changes in the file's `<appSettings />` section `section, web.config file>`that are specific to the Debug environment (or your development environment).

5. Select the project name in Solution Explorer, and then choose Project | Properties on the menu to open the Property Pages dialog box, shown in Figure 26.6.

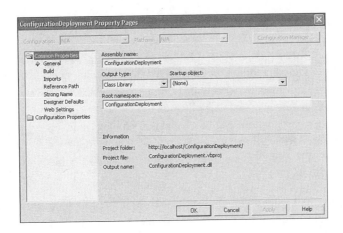

FIGURE 26.6
The Property Pages dialog box.

6. Expand the Configuration Properties node in the left-hand pane. Select Staging in the Configuration list box at the top of the dialog box. Now select the Deployment node in the left-hand pane (see Figure 26.7). The Configuration property page is displayed in the right-hand pane.

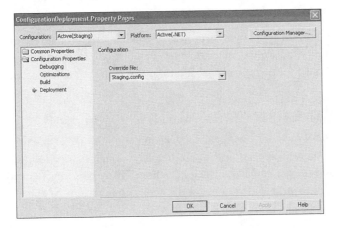

FIGURE 26.7
Expanding the Deployment node.

7. Select Staging.config in the Override File drop-down list box, and click the OK button.

Now when you create a deployment project using Visual Studio .NET, you can specify which solution configuration to build and deploy. The Staging.config file will be copied into the installation file and renamed as web.config so that your Staging settings in the file's `<appSettings />` section, section are used in that environment.

Deployment

In most enterprises, the development box is rarely the production box. In other words, you typically don't develop an application on the same box it will be running on (although this is sometimes a popular choice for "down and dirty" applications or smaller organizations). Therefore, moving your finished, tested application to another environment (from development to staging, or staging to production) can be a logistical problem unless the proper tools and processes are in place. ASP.NET and Visual Studio .NET make deployment easier than in the "classic" ASP days. This section answers the question, "How do I publish my ASP.NET Web Service to the environment I want?"

There are three ways to deploy a Web project, discussed in the following sections. However, only one of these ways offers a complete picture of the deployment process, including properly configuring IIS and copying the files to their respective locations.

Using XCopy Deployment

.NET does not require that you register your components or add them to a COM+ package, so you can simply copy the files to their correct location in a target environment, and the application will work—at least, in theory it works. In reality, the files are just one part of deploying a project. When it comes to ASP.NET Web Services, you also need to create a site and modify its settings in IIS, and possibly change configurations for a given server in the web.config file.

However, a simple method for copying a project or application from one environment to another is to use the DOS Xcopy command. Open a command-prompt window and type in a command similar to the following one (substituting your source and destination folders for the ones provided here):

```
Xcopy c:\source c:\destination /E
```

This is a simple use of the Xcopy command, appending only the /E argument, which instructs Xcopy to copy the source folder as well as all subfolders to the destination. There are dozens of additional arguments you can add to customize how Xcopy performs the copy command. To see the command-line syntax and options for the Xcopy command, type **Xcopy /?** in a command-prompt window.

Using the Copy Project Command in Visual Studio .NET

A step up from the DOS Xcopy command is the Visual Studio .NET's Copy Project command. However, this approach is similar to XCopy in that it simply copies files. It does not modify IIS on the target environment or copy the correct version of the web.config file that is specific for that environment.

These are the typical steps for copying a project to a server:

1. Choose Project | Copy Project on the menu to open the Copy Project dialog box.

2. Enter the destination project folder (you can click the browse button to find it). For the Web access method, select the FrontPage radio button. In the Copy section at the bottom, select the Only Files Needed to Run This Application radio button (see Figure 26.8).

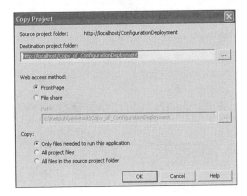

FIGURE 26.8

The Copy Project dialog box.

3. Click the OK button. Visual Studio .NET attempts to copy the project to the destination you selected in step 2.

Before this application can be used, however, you will need to make sure the web.config file and IIS are configured correctly.

The next method is more complicated, but vastly more precise in ensuring a consisting build and deployment strategy.

Creating a Deployment Project in Visual Studio .NET

This option creates a project in your solution configuration that also contains your Web Service project. The result of the project is an .msi file that runs within the Windows Installer built into Windows 2000 and XP. The .msi file contains all the dependency files and knows how to automatically configure IIS virtual directory settings. The .msi file registers and verifies the location of assemblies and takes caution when potentially overwriting newer versions of files that would cause your application to break. After the .msi file is created, you can copy it to the target Web Server and run it. The result should be a Web application that is correctly configured and ready to be used by your clients.

To add a deployment project to your current Web Service project's solution, perform the following steps:

1. Right-click on the Solution icon in Solution Explorer, and choose Add | New Project on the pop-up menu.

2. When the Add New Project dialog box opens, select the setup and deployment projects in the Project Types pane. Select Web Setup Project in the Templates pane, and type in a name for the new project. Optionally, adjust the Location setting where the project will be created. Click the OK button.

3. The File System editor appears in the main area of Visual Studio .NET. Select the Web Application Folder in the right-hand pane, shown in Figure 26.9.

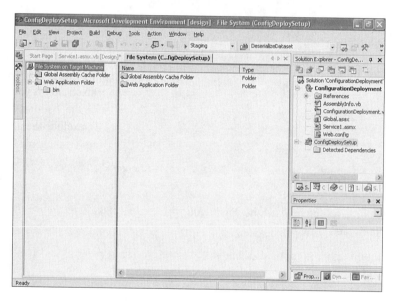

FIGURE 26.9
The File System editor.

4. Choose Action | Add | Project Output on the menu to open the Add Project Output Group dialog box (see Figure 26.10). For each project in the solution, make sure to select Primary Output in the list, and select a solution configuration for this deployment project. If you managed your solution and project configuration settings correctly (as outlined in the earlier section "Using the Configuration Manager"), you should see all the solution configurations you added, such as Staging, in this list. Click the OK button.

FIGURE 26.10
The Add Project Output Group dialog box.

5. In Solution Explorer, select the Web setup project name you created in step 2 and expand it. Then expand the Detected Dependencies folder. Two files typically appear: the .NET distributable file (dotnetfxredist_x86_enu.msm) and the mscorlib.dll file. If you are targeting a machine known to have .NET installed on it, you can make the .msi installation file much smaller by excluding these files from the setup project. To exclude them, right-click on each file in Solution Explorer, and choose Exclude on the pop-up menu. A little gray circle with a line through it appears over each of the files you excluded (see Figure 26.11).

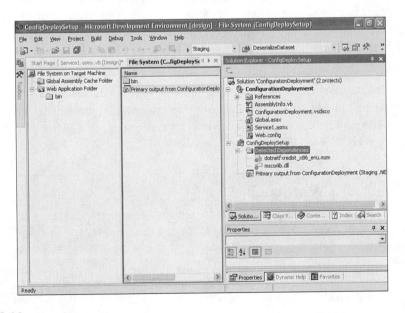

FIGURE 26.11
Excluded files in the Web setup project.

6. To create the .msi file, choose Build | Build Solution (to build the entire solution) or just Build | Build *SetupProjectName* on the menu. The .msi file by default will be created at this pathname:

```
C:\Documents and Settings\yourmachine\My Documents\Visual Studio Projects\
yourSolutionName\YourWebSetupProjectName\Release\YourWebSetupProjectName.msi
```

7. To install this .msi file in the target environment, copy it to the correct Web server, and then double-click the file. The Windows Installer processes the instructions compiled into the .msi file, copies the files, and then copies the appropriate settings into IIS. Additionally, if you modified the web.config file through the solution and project configuration settings, it will have the settings you placed in the Staging.config file.

Configuration and deployment are large topics in .NET and deserve an entire book devoted to just that subject matter. However, these instructions should get you thinking in the right direction for deploying your Web Services. Additionally, you might want to consider using the Microsoft App Center for deploying Web Services to a server farm. Consult *Deploying and Managing Microsoft .NET Web Farms* by Barry Bloom (Sams Publishing, ISBN 0-672-32057-6, specifically Chapters 11 through 13) for more information about server farms and the App Center for .NET applications.

Security

Securing your Web Services is perhaps one of the most important considerations when deploying them publicly on the Internet. You could risk exposure, intellectual theft, and potential loss of data integrity if you put your Web Services on the Internet and just hope no one finds them. This feeble attempt at security is known as "security via obscurity." You need to be more proactive if you want to prevent unauthorized use of your Web Services.

However, not every Web Service requires the same type of security, or any security at all. Understanding how Web Services are typically used in real business environments helps you determine the best type of security to apply in a given situation. Sometimes no security (outside the built-in Internet Information Services security) is necessary, such as when you're creating free public domain Web Services.

THE VALUE OF A WEB SERVICE

When free public domain Web Services began to appear on the Internet, they included calculations such as metric conversions, Celsius to Fahrenheit conversions, screen scrapers, chats, and discussion boards. Before using these services, you must consider the following:

- You could create on your own the functionality you seek to consume from a publicly available Web Service, or you could purchase software that performs many of these operations. Why do I encourage you to not use Web Services in this scenario? Because each time you make a call to a Web Service, your end users must wait while the initial request is made to your Web server, then they must wait as your application makes a second request to a Web Service potentially across the world before a Web page can be served back to the user. This method creates slower sites and wastes bandwidth. As a general rule, if you can do it yourself, then do it yourself. If you need information from a trading partner, or information that you cannot generate on your own because of a lack of subject matter expertise, then call a Web Service to supply that information.

- For Web Services that your site relies on to manage and save data, such as a private discussion board, a third-party e-commerce solution, or a customer management system, you should ask yourself "Do I really want an organization/individual I've never met to handle my or my users' data?"

- Finally, can you rely on free Web Services with no "service level agreements"? If their Web Service is unavailable, or is removed from their site, how will that affect your site? I had a nasty experience with the Microsoft bCentral service, which decided to change directions and no longer support the e-mail list management services it had provided to my site for a year. I was left scrambling to find another service provider to handle my needs.

When exposing Web Services that provide sensitive data, such as customer records transferred between companies in a partner relationship management application, purchase orders in a supply chain management application, or affiliate marketing information, keeping the data secure and providing these services only to authorized users and companies becomes critical. Some situations are in the middle of the two extremes, such as a Web Service used for interdepartmental communication in a large organization.

There are three issues of importance in securing Web Services. They deal with the three potential "holes" or vulnerabilities of this technology.

First, there's the open nature of the Internet. Although you might decide to rely on your Web Service being covert and undiscoverable (by having no entry in UDDI and no DISCO file or excluding the Web Service from the dynamic discovery file), chances are that someone will find the Web Service. Therefore, you must ensure that when users do find the Web Service, only authorized ones can access the data and perform tasks or retrieve data. This issue deals with the topic of authorization.

Second, there's the anonymous nature of the Internet. How do you *really* know someone is who he or she claims to be? Typically, you rely on a password matched to a username or user ID to determine the claim's validity. However, this is usually not a reliable way to verify a user's credentials because usernames and passwords are often shared. This issue deals with the topic of authentication.

26

Third, there's the open format of the SOAP message. Because it is simply ASCII text, the data can be intercepted or sniffed while traveling across a network. If the data is a customer record, a credit card number, or a patient's social security number followed by a medical history, for example, developers must take every safeguard to ensure that data cannot be read easily and that it cannot be modified during transmission. This issue deals with the topic of encryption.

There are other issues, such as Web server security, physical security, database security, file security, and network security, that can affect how secure a Web Service and the entire enterprise really are. However, these issues are usually out of the typical developer's control, so you must rely on the services of database administrators, network administrators and other security professionals to ensure a fundamental security infrastructure. The issues discussed in this section deal with what developers can do to protect organizational resources when creating a public interface to a company's business logic.

> **NOTE**
>
> This section gives you an overview of securing your Web Services, not step-by-step instructions to configuring Internet Information Services, which is beyond the scope of this book. For more information, consult the IIS documentation or *Microsoft IIS 5 Administration* by Gerry O'Brien (Sams Publishing, ISBN: 0-672-31964-0) for detailed explanations of security techniques and settings based on the general principles laid out in this section. Additionally, you should work with the relevant people in your organization to determine the best security policy for Web Services.

Authentication and Authorization

The issues of authorization and authentication raise two critical questions: "How can I ensure that only certain users have access to certain Web Services?" and "How can I make sure users are who they say they are?" It is difficult to authorize users without first authenticating them, and there is little point in authenticating users unless you intend to authorize them to use something on the site. Therefore, these two topics are covered simultaneously.

When users make requests to a secured Web Service, they must supply some credentials to prove they are who they claim to be. This is an easy and well-understood operation in the world of Web pages. In a Web page, the browser handles this interaction by sending the user's initial request to a resource on a Web server. The Web server detects that the requested resource has been secured pending authentication and authorization, and sends a message back to the client's browser. This could take the form of an HTTP message that pops open a logon dialog box or a Web page that requests the user's ID and password. The user supplies credentials, and is then allowed or denied access based on the login, the state of the user account, and the authorization business rules.

However, in the Web Service arena, pop-up boxes and logon Web page forms are not an option because by default, Web Services do not have visual representations; they are simply programmatic interfaces. This is not to say that user ID and password information can no longer be used as a method of authentication. The following sections explain some methods that can be used to authenticate Web Service consumers.

Managing Authentication with Logon Credentials

Using the logon credentials approach, an account ID and password are sent via an HTTP header, a SOAP header, or other means to the Web Service to authenticate the user. After credential information is sent to Internet Information Services (IIS), it validates the account and determines its permissions to resources on the site.

Integrated Windows Authentication

Integrated Windows authentication—also known as NTLM, or *challenge response*—requires that the client application send Windows account credentials in an encrypted format (a hash algorithm) to IIS. The caveat with this type of authentication is that it requires a Windows client (such as Internet Explorer or a Web Service consumer running on a Windows machine) to send the hashed credentials in the appropriate format. This makes it ideal for intranet applications, but diminishes its usefulness on the Internet.

Basic Authentication

Basic authentication, also known as clear-text authentication, allows the user ID and password to be sent from the consumer to the Web Service in the header of the HTTP message. However, the data is sent as base64-encoded data, which can be easily converted to human-readable text. Although the lack of encryption makes this method seem like the worst possible solution, it is actually quite useful when combined with an encryption method such as Secure Socket Layer (discussed in the section "Encryption" later in this chapter). Also, it is more "open" than Integrated Windows authentication, thus allowing non-Windows platforms to send credential information.

Forms-Based Authentication

In forms-based authentication, a Web Service is requested by a consumer, and IIS checks whether the consumer has been authenticated by searching for a HTTP cookie. If the credentials are not in the cookie, IIS redirects the consumer to a Web Page to enter the logon ID and password. Obviously, this is a problem because Web Services by their very nature cannot be used by a Web browser. Consumers might be expecting a SOAP message, but they receive HTML (the logon Web Form) back from IIS. Although it is possible to make this method work with Web Services by using the SetAuthCookie() method of the System.Web.Security. FormsAuthentication class, it's not the best way to accomplish authentication and should be overlooked in favor of the other methods described here.

Managing Authentication with IIS Address Restrictions

Using the address restriction approach lends a great deal of security without a lot of software development effort. This approach can take two forms, as described in the next sections.

IIS IP Address or Domain Name Restrictions

In this method, you configure IIS to refuse connections that do not originate from certain IP addresses or certain domain names. This is a fairly simple way to add security to your Web Services without a great deal of effort. However, this method assumes that you know the exact IP address or domain name your users will come from and that there are a limited number of users. Managing more than a few dozen consumers could become laborious unless you are working with fixed ranges of IP addresses.

Managing Authentication with Client-Side Certificates

Client-side certificates are provided by a trusted third party to ensure that Web Service consumers are who they claim to be. You can configure IIS to accept or require client certificates and use the certificate information sent by clients along with the SOAP request to determine who they are, and then authorize them accordingly. If you want to enable your application to use client certificates, you must install a server certificate first, and require that all transmissions be encrypted through HTTPS (more about HTTPS and SSL in the "Authorization" section). This method is clearly the best solution for Web Services that deliver sensitive information over the Internet.

Managing Authentication Without IIS

There are other ways to manage authentication that do not involve IIS, described in the following sections.

Custom SOAP Header Authentication

In this method, the Web Service provider develops an authentication scheme that requires consumers to send their logon IDs and passwords within the SOAP message. Anyone can access the Web Service, but the credentials are authenticated against an XML file, a database, or some other list of valid user IDs and passwords. The Web Service itself, not IIS, would then be responsible for validating users and returning a SOAP fault if the account is invalid. The ID and password should be sent in the SOAP header because they are not pertinent to the Web Service's actual call signature. Also, a SOAP extension should be used to strip off and validate the ID and password information because it could be applied to multiple Web Services on the same server instead of having to embed this logic in every Web Service you create. Obviously, to protect the IDs and passwords, the SOAP message should be encrypted. Care must be taken when using this approach that security holes are not exposed, so it's a less desirable approach for Web Services that need a higher degree of security. However, this approach does offer a high degree of flexibility in where and how accounts are managed.

Passport

Passport is an authentication service from Microsoft that allows consumers to supply their authentication credentials to Microsoft, and Microsoft then supplies this information to its clients (Web sites or Web Service providers) via a secure cookie or in the request's query string. Your site or Web Service would look for the cookie or query string, and if it exists, the user can then be further authorized to use services on the site. However, if the cookie does not exist, the user is instructed (manually for a Web site, or programmatically for a Web Service) to log on to the Microsoft Passport service. Passport is a good idea in theory, enabling users to manage one account instead of having a different logon ID and password for each site or Web Service. It also allows organizations that host sites and services to outsource their authentication needs to a third party, potentially reducing costs.

Authorization

After you know who the user is, you can move on to answer the question, "How can I ensure that only certain users have access to certain Web Services?" There are three basic approaches to authorization, described in the following sections.

Windows Access Control Lists

A Windows user account can be associated with one or more groups. Even when IIS authentication is disabled and anonymous access is allowed, behind the scenes IIS assigns the request to a special account called IUSR_machinename through the *impersonation* process. Both users and groups can have permissions to access information, such as files, directories, machines, or Web Services. Conversely, users and groups can be denied access to these resources. The managed list of what a particular group or user can access is referred to as the *access control list* (*ACL*). When users authenticate themselves to IIS, based on their Windows account, they can be granted or denied access to a Web Service based on the ACL. This is a low-effort approach to adding authorization to your Web Service application, but it does have some minor limitations, such as requiring that accounts be administered through Windows.

ASP.NET Authorization

In this authorization model, ASP.NET manages which resources are available to a particular consumer. The web.config file generated automatically by Visual Studio .NET (or added manually in the SDK) in each ASP.NET application can be configured to provide a second layer of protection for resources, beyond what IIS provides with ACLs. Based on authenticated user or group roles, the ASP.NET application permits or denies requests to ASP.NET resources according to the <authorization> section of the web.config file.

Custom Authorization Solution

An organization might want to create its own custom authorization mechanism that manages user IDs and passwords and the permissions granted to users. Although this approach offers much more flexibility, it does extend the development time and risks being less secure that what Microsoft has provided to developers and administrators through ACLs and ASP.NET authorization. This type of authorization is supported in ASP.NET through a series of security classes and can be added in via an HTTP Module or a SOAP extension, or built right into the Web Service.

Encryption

SOAP messages are inherently text messages, so they are subject to being captured and read by a third party when being transmitted between the provider and consumer. Encryption answers the question "How can I make sure no one can see the contents of the SOAP message?" Encryption uses mathematical formulas to transform a message into an unintelligible format. Both parties—the sender and the receiver—have a key to unravel the message that allows only them to be able to read it. Because SOAP messages are typically transmitted on port 80, you can borrow from the success of a proven technology to encrypt messages: Secure Socket Layer (SSL). During a communication session using SSL, the Web browser issues a request for a secure connection to the server by using the `https://` protocol heading, instead of the normal `http://`. The client and the server negotiate the encryption strength (that is, how many bits are used to secure the message; the more bits, the more secure your message is), and then a public key is sent to the client. The client uses this key to decrypt and encrypt data sent to and from the server during the current session. When the session is over, the key is no longer valid, and a new one must be issued for the next session.

How do you enable encryption? You obtain a server certificate from a trusted certificate provider. You can find certificate vendors at `http://backoffice.microsoft.com/security-partners/`. You can also get a trial certificate from the VeriSign corporation for development and education purposes at `http://www.verisign.com`. Next, you install the certificate in IIS. For more information, please refer to a resource such as *Microsoft IIS 5 Administration* by Gerry O'Brien (Sams Publishing, ISBN: 0-672-31964-0, specifically Chapter 8, "Security").

> **NOTE**
>
> When you use SSL encryption, your dynamically generated WSDL file will reflect the fact that consumers must call the Web Service by using HTTPS instead of HTTP.

Authentication and Authorization Scenarios

To show how the various technologies described in these sections can be used together, I've outlined five possible scenarios that will address most security needs. Many more combinations of technologies could be added to this list, but the objective is to help you synthesize the strengths and weaknesses of each approach to find the solution that suits your application the best.

Scenario 1

Authentication: Client-side certificates

Authorization: IIS configured to require client certificates, ASP.NET web.config file (`<authorization>` section) used to grant permissions to users or groups

Encryption: SSL required

Advantages: Very secure because of client-side certificates; non-platform specific

Disadvantages: Initial setup for new consumers can be laborious because they must acquire client certificates, administrators must create an account for them in Windows, and settings must be added in the web.config file.

Uses: Good for low number of consumers and/or highly sensitive information

Scenario 2

Authentication: Custom (credentials sent via the SOAP header)

Authorization: Custom (SOAP extension evaluates SOAP header contents and compares credentials to a database table)

Encryption: SSL highly recommended

Advantages: Highly flexible architecture allowing for unique security needs; low barrier to entry for the consumer

Disadvantages: Potential security concerns; depends on the diligence of the developer and whether SSL is used

Uses: Good for potentially high numbers of consumers or for unique authentication requirements

Scenario 3

Authentication: Integrated Windows authentication

Authorization: Access control lists

Encryption: SSL not required

Advantages: Somewhat secure because of the hash algorithm Windows uses to encode credentials; short development time

Disadvantages: Windows consumers only

Uses: A corporate intranet

Scenario 4

Authentication: IIS IP address or domain name restrictions

Authorization: None (uses impersonation for the default IUSER_machinename account)

Encryption: Highly recommended

Advantages: Very secure because only certain IP addresses or domain names are allowed; non-platform specific; shorter development cycle because IIS handles most of the complexity of refusing requests

26

CONFIGURING, DEPLOYING, AND SECURING WEB SERVICES

Disadvantages: Accommodates fewer users because of the amount of administration necessary in IIS; less control over specific account available because no authorization is used

Uses: An "all you can eat for one low price" subscription service

Scenario 5

Authentication: Anonymous

Authorization: None (uses impersonation for the default IUSR_machinename account)

Encryption: None

Advantages: Lowest barrier to use

Disadvantages: Least secure

Usage: Good for a public service

If you have decided that a custom authorization and authentication scheme is the approach you want to pursue, the next section will give you some direction to help you along the way.

Programmatic Authorization

The examples in the following sections will give you the general principles for accessing security information captured from the current context the ASP.NET Web Services are running in. The System.Web.HttpContext.User object supplies properties (described in Table 26.1) to help you determine information about the identity and roles of the current Web Service consumer.

TABLE 26.1   The System.Web.HttpContext.User Object's Properties

Property or Method Name	Description
Identity property	Returns an instance of the Identity object, as defined in Table 26.2.
IsInRole() method	For security reasons, you are not allowed to iterate through all the roles a particular user is privy to. Therefore, this method allows you to determine whether the user is in a specific role you want to programmatically check. Returns true if the user is in the specified role or false if the user is not. Roles are typically entered as *accountGroup*\group. The *accountGroup* could actually be a network domain, the name of the local machine, or the keyword BUILTIN to access specific groups such as Users and Administrators.

TABLE 26.2   The `System.Web.HttpContext.User.Identity` Object's Properties

Property Name	Description
AuthenticationType	Obtains the method of authentication used to authenticate the user, such as Basic authentication, NTLM, Kerberos, and Passport authentication, to name a few.
IsAuthenticated	Returns `true` is the user was authenticated or `false` if the user was not. The user will not be authenticated if the Web Service's site is configured to allow Anonymous access and if .NET authorization is not configured.
Name	Obtains the name of the current user.

The code examples that follow are provided to help you understand the basics of sending and retrieving authentication information in your Web Service and its consumers. You could create an HTTP Module or a SOAP extension, or hard-code the check for user information and roles supplied by .NET to allow or deny access to your Web Services. There are a number of different directions in which you could go, so I've provided code snippets of accessing this information to help get you started.

Sending Authentication Information to the Web Service

Use the code in Listings 26.1 and 26.2 in an ASP.NET Web Service consumer's Code Behind file to send the necessary credential information to the Web Service that requires consumers to authenticate themselves.

LISTING 26.1   VB.NET Snippet to Send Authentication Information via Web Services

```
Private Sub Button1_Click(ByVal sender As System.Object, _
    ByVal e As System.EventArgs) Handles Button1.Click
    Dim oWebService As New localhost.Service1()

    ' Pass the UserName, Password, and Domain information
    ' via the NetworkCredential constructor.
    Dim oCredential As New NetworkCredential("yourUserName", _
        "yourPassword", "yourDomain")

    ' Alternatively, you can set the UserName, Password,
    ' and Domain as individual properties of the
    ' oCredential object.
    ' oCredential.UserName = "yourUserName"
    ' oCredential.Password = "yourPassword"
    ' oCredential.Domain = "yourDomain"
```

LISTING 26.1 Continued

```
' Now, set the Credential property of the Web Service
' proxy to the oCredential instance.
oWebService.Credentials = oCredential

Response.Write(oWebService.HelloWorld())

End Sub
```

LISTING 26.2 C# Snippet to send Authentication Information via Web Services

```csharp
private void Button1_Click(object sender, System.EventArgs e)
    {
        localhost.Service1 oWebService = new localhost.Service1();

        // Pass the UserName, Password, and Domain information
        // via the NetworkCredential constructor.

        NetworkCredential oCredential = new
            NetworkCredential("yourUserName",
                "yourPassword", "yourDomain");

        // Alternatively, you can set the UserName, Password,
        // and Domain as individual properties of the
        // oCredential object.
        // oCredential.UserName = "yourUserName"
        // oCredential.Password = "yourPassword"
        // oCredential.Domain = "yourDomain"

        // Now, set the Credential property of the Web Service
        // proxy to the oCredential instance.
        oWebService.Credentials = oCredential;

        Response.Write(oWebService.HelloWorld());

    }
```

Obtaining Authentication Information from the Consumer

The code in Listings 26.3 and 26.4 demonstrates how to retrieve the settings sent by .NET that were used during authentication.

LISTING 26.3 VB.NET Code Snippet to Obtain Authentication Information via Web Services

```
<WebMethod()> Public Function HelloWorld() As String

    Dim sAuthType As String
    Dim sAuthName As String
    Dim bIsAuthenticated As Boolean
    Dim bIsInRole As Boolean

    sAuthType = User.Identity.AuthenticationType
    sAuthName = User.Identity.Name
    bIsAuthenticated = User.Identity.IsAuthenticated

    bIsInRole = User.IsInRole("BUILTIN\User")

    HelloWorld = "Hello, " & sAuthName

End Function
```

LISTING 26.4 C# Code Snippet to Obtain Authentication Information via Web Services

```
[WebMethod]
public string HelloWorld()
{

    string sAuthType;
    string sAuthName;
    bool bIsAuthenticated;
    bool bIsInRole;

    sAuthType = User.Identity.AuthenticationType();
    sAuthName = User.Identity.Name();
    bIsAuthenticated = User.Identity.IsAuthenticated();

    bIsInRole = User.IsInRole("BUILTIN\\User");

    return "Hello, " & sAuthName;

}
```

From here, you could check for the UserName in a database or perform other operations based on the business rules for different roles.

Summary

Visual Studio .NET makes configuring, deploying, and securing Web Services simple. Configuration is managed through a simple XML file called web.config that can contain a series of elements and attributes that define custom settings for your application. Multiple versions of this file can be created and used during deployment to target a specific environment's settings (database connection strings, file paths, and so forth).

Deploying a Web Service project can be as simple as copying the necessary files into their IIS folders on the target Web server, or you can use a more sophisticated approach by adding a Web setup project that manages which files to copy as well as setting the appropriate IIS properties and using the correct configuration file for the target environment.

Security addresses the inherent risks associated with exposing programmatic interfaces on the Internet and transmitting text-based messages that could potentially be intercepted and hacked. By addressing authentication (are the users who they claim to be?), authorization (does this user have the necessary permissions to use the Web Service?), and encryption (scrambling and descrambling the SOAP message), you can address most of the problems that are likely to occur. This chapter has outlined the possible combinations of authorization, authentication, and encryption options to create a security solution for your organization based on the target technologies, risks, and audience that will consume the Web Service. Additionally, this chapter has shown you brief examples of how to programmatically set and retrieve user identity settings that are fundamental to building a custom authentication solution.

Introducing .NET My Services

IN THIS CHAPTER

This last chapter discusses a new set of Web Services and a Web Service platform that will be hosted by Microsoft. These Web Services, named .NET My Services, will allow individuals to save their personal information, such as their contacts, payment information, and calendar, in a "digital safety deposit box." Companies can request to "see" certain parts of that data (via Web Services), and that request will be communicated to the users (via Web Services), who can then make decisions on what information companies should be able to access and for how long. This technology solves a series of problems for both the end user and companies that adopt .NET My Services. However, there will be huge obstacles to the adoption of .NET My Services, as noted at the end of this chapter.

> **NOTE**
>
> You might have heard of this technology by its original codename, Hailstorm.

.NET Building Block Services

When the .NET vision was revealed in the summer of 2000, "Building Block Services" were alluded to as a key component of the "programmable web" concept. These Building Block Services (also referred to early on as "MegaServices") would allow Microsoft to provide Web Services to consumers to help them securely manage their personal information online while offering authentication and data management services to companies. Think of the building blocks as "plumbing," much like the plumbing services of COM+: transaction support, message queuing, and component and connection pooling. Developers could build these services on their own, but it would extend the development time of projects that need these services, make their implementation inconsistent with every other implementation, and possibly be riddled with bugs because of their complexity.

.NET My Services has become one of these "Building Block Services" and provides the plumbing for user authentication, data security, and data management.

What Is .NET My Services?

At the time of this writing, .NET My Services is in early development. However, some details on its composition are available and have been outlined in the following sections.

.NET My Services in a Box

The first available technology preview for .NET My Services is .NET My Services in a Box (or, possibly, Hailstorm in a Box; this could not be confirmed at the time of this writing). This product allows developers to get a feel for how to request .NET My Services data and how to build applications that use .NET My Services in the future. Four services will be available to use during this time to get your feet wet:

- **myAddress:** Allows end users to store all forms of physical and virtual address information (such as e-mail or a Web site).
- **myContacts:** Allows end users to store relationships such as those you might find in an address book, a buddy list, and so forth.
- **myProfile:** Allows end users to store personal information, including name, picture locations, identification numbers, and work-related information.
- **myServices:** Can be queried to determine which services a specific end user has subscribed to.

Microsoft Passport

As discussed in Chapter 26, "Configuring, Deploying, and Securing Web Services," Microsoft Passport will become the cornerstone of authenticating users to access their data and authenticating companies to access users' information. Passport features a single sign-on service that requires users to remember only one username/password set for all sites that use Passport to authenticate their members. If you use Passport on your site, users log on to Passport on Microsoft's site, and then your application can identify specific users by their Passport User ID; users have the benefit of keeping their logon information secure and protected by encryption. Ultimately, .NET My Services forces the use of Passport to securely authenticate users and companies to make sure they are who they claim to be.

Future Versions of .NET My Services

By mid-2002, .NET My Services is expected to release more services and become a live resource. At that time, the following .NET My Services services are expected to go live:

myLocation

myNotifications

myInbox

myCalendar

myDocuments

myApplicationSettings

myFavoriteWebSites

myDevices

myWallet

How .NET My Services Works

Microsoft will host the services on multiple server farms across the world to provide redundancy in case of malfunctions or severe network outages. Next, companies that use .NET My Services will have already established an account and have agreed to the strict terms of how the data retrieved from .NET My Services can be used. Developers will use the Client Runtime to makes calls to .NET My Services, which provides a security layer to encryption/decryption services to the SOAP messages passed between .NET My Services and the consuming company's servers.

In some cases, the data will be immediately available for use. In other cases, .NET My Services will notify the company when data becomes available through a special Notification Web Service. Whether the data is immediately available depends on end users' security settings on the requested data and whether they have acknowledged and allowed the company access to this data.

Companies can also request that whenever users' information changes (`changeNotification()` method), such as their address or calendar, they receive a notification so that they can update their own data store. Companies can scrub their databases to ensure that they always have the latest information about their customers. Although companies could access .NET My Services every time they needed information about an individual, this would be expensive in terms of network traffic and time. Some might object to companies storing this data locally and not using .NET My Services each time to access the information, but Microsoft will enforce strict guidelines on the accepted use and storage of an end user's personal data. Non-compliance could result in the company's .NET My Services access being revoked.

Companies will form SOAP messages to request information from .NET My Services, which is the codename for a set of XML Message Interface (XMI) methods that define the formation, or interfaces, of SOAP messages that will be required to obtain information from .NET My Services. The XMI includes specific SOAP elements and attributes to identify a specific end user, the version of the data about this individual (`ChangeNumber()` method), and the language used to query .NET My Services for the appropriate user or collection of users' information. Most of the body of a .NET My Services SOAP message is formed using a new specification called Hailstorm Data Manipulation Language (HSDL). Although the details on how to use HSDL are beyond the scope of this book, it allows you to query for specific information about a particular end user or set of end users, and return only the results that are based on certain criteria, such as the number of occurrences for a particular node. HSDL is a subset of XPath, allowing you to query XML nodes for specific information.

Usage Scenarios

The following scenarios will help spark your imagination as to what .NET My Services will help accomplish.

Online Travel Agency

Using .NET My Services, an online travel agency, could notify users when travel deals are made available for certain dates (based on the myCalendar service) or locations (based on the user's current location from the myLocation service). The online travel agency could use the myWallet service to expedite the purchasing process, schedule the event on your calendar (again, using myCalendar), and provide information, based on your preferences, to offer additional services such as car rental and hotels. As the date arrives, the agency could notify you that the price has dropped or the plane has been delayed, for example, and adjust your schedule accordingly.

Groupware for Geographically Dispersed Teams

As groupware, .NET My Services can coordinate locations and meeting times for an entire outside sales organization's calendars, allowing them to retrieve their mail from any PC and receive important sales and client updates via their cellphones or PDAs.

Online Auctions

eBay has agreed to be an early adopter of .NET My Services and will implement it to notify users that they have been outbid on a particular item. It will also authenticate users to eBay and keep payment and shipping information current.

Benefits to End Users

.NET My Services offers some significant benefits for end users.

Digital Safety Deposit Box

Users can keep their data securely in a digital safety deposit box. The data is encrypted and stored and can be changed or accessed only by the data's owner or by an organization that has been allowed access by the owner of that information. This feature reduces the need to repeatedly type in user information on each of the sites you do business with on the Web.

Full Fidelity Access Control

Users can establish who can see specific elements of information in their digital safety deposit box. Entities that request information are given a role, such as "friend" or "associate," or they are not allowed access. This role is determined by the end user who owns the data being requested.

Device Independent

Notifications and access to the data can be accomplished from any computing device on any operating system (because the interface is SOAP). This device independence allows notifications to be sent to phone, pagers, PDAs, or desktop computers. It also enables companies to access .NET My Services data regardless of their operating systems or platforms, allowing ubiquitous access and convenience for the end user.

Seamless Web Experience

.NET My Services and Passport can make the Web a more seamless experience, with sites offering more personalized services to consumers based on regional settings or other preferences.

Benefits to Businesses

Businesses can also benefit from .NET My Services in the following ways.

Freshest User Data

.NET My Services enables businesses to always have access to the most up-to-date information about the users that have agreed to allow the company access to their data. This feature allows companies to "scrub" their databases to remove old entries about contact or payment information and ensures that their efforts to contact users are more successful.

Outsourcing Authentication Services

.NET My Services allows businesses to outsource their authentication needs to Microsoft, freeing them from development and maintenance expenses associated with authentication, including personnel, software, and hardware costs.

Reduced Purchase Friction

.NET My Services makes the buying process easier to navigate for the end user, allowing for a "friction-less" purchasing experience. Users can simply indicate that they want to purchase certain items and sign on to Passport, without needing to enter any other information. This feature is a benefit to companies as well because streamlining the purchasing process reduces the number of abandoned shopping carts.

From a Technical Perspective

.NET My Services offers IT departments and developers some benefits in terms of providing authentication plumbing and outsourcing authentication needs. These features are described in more depth in the following sections.

Authentication Plumbing Reduces Development Time

Just as developers have used plumbing such as COM+ Services and Microsoft Message Queue (MSMQ), they could rely on .NET My Services for their authentication needs for Web users.

Instead of devising a homegrown authentication solution or using LDAP or Active Directory (which, in my estimation, is more complex and expensive than .NET My Services for this purpose), developers could simply make calls to Microsoft .NET My Services.

Delivers on Promise of Programmable Web

.NET My Services enables developers to create applications that allow end users to enjoy a more personalized experience on Web sites. These personalized features could include writing reminders to the user's calendar, allowing quicker checkout when purchasing items, notification of friends' birthdays, suggestions for birthday gifts, and so on.

Outsourced Authentication Means Less to Support

.NET My Services not only provides developers with a set of plumbing to make authentication easier, but it also gives IT managers the option of outsourcing authentication. By outsourcing, companies can save money by reducing the number of staff members needed for authentication, or at least free up existing IT staff to focus on other critical tasks.

Hurdles to Passport/.NET My Services Adoption

.NET My Services is not without its challenges—and its detractors.

Opposition from the Usual Suspects

Before .NET My Services can be rolled out, Microsoft might have to prove to U.S. lawmakers and courts (at the request of AOL and SUN Microsystems) that it is not abusing its position as the leader in the desktop operating system market to force .NET My Services on consumers or to prevent competitors from offering similar services. Additionally, in October 2001, privacy organizations and other industry groups were petitioning the Federal Trade Commission (FTC) about how Passport is being presented to users of Windows XP and its ability to share information between Microsoft properties. They are asking the government to force Microsoft to provide a way to use the Microsoft sites without disclosing their identity and allow users to make use of non-Microsoft payment services.

Reluctance to Support Microsoft

Although Passport is open and can be used by any operating system, many times the use of a technology becomes a "religious war," with one side refusing to even consider what the other side is offering. In this case, it's probably not likely that non-Microsoft developers and development shops will opt to use a Microsoft technology when competing services (such as AOL's MagicCarpet and unannounced services from other vendors) will soon be introduced with similar offerings.

Cost

Typically, everyone wants security, but no one (except the government) is willing to pay for it. In the Microsoft model, consumers will be charged to store their information "in the cloud" (in other words, on an Internet server operated by Microsoft). Microsoft will spend a lot of time and money marketing this concept, but ultimately it will come down to how much the service costs and whether it could be bundled with other useful services, similar to how the phone company packages caller ID, call waiting, and other features for one low monthly charge.

Currently, in the Microsoft pricing model, companies will have to pay to use .NET My Services. They will have to decide how cost-effective is it to outsource all the authentication services that they typically have to build and maintain to a service provider such as Microsoft.

There's also a catch-22: Companies might be reluctant to implement .NET My Services unless enough people are using it, and consumers could be reluctant to pay for .NET My Services unless there are enough companies accepting it. Charging both the end consumers and the consuming corporate client is tricky because it seems that a "critical mass" must be reached for both simultaneously.

Security

At the time of this writing, the exact security model for .NET My Services data encryption has not been completely outlined, although it will be based on the Microsoft brand of Kerberos. Regardless of the type of data encryption used, other security holes will need to be adequately plugged. Security advocates warn that .NET My Services is exactly the type of Web resource that attracts hackers: high profile, a challenge (Microsoft says it can't be done), and chock full of personal data. A vulnerability has already been exposed in Passport's authentication system that enables an attacker to view a user's cookie and gain access to personal information. Other experts describe a scenario similar to what recently happened to AOL: Hackers could create a fake site that looks like the sign-on page to get usernames and passwords. Another potential problem is that anyone can create an account for anyone else without any verification of identities. Microsoft is looking for ways to combat these potential problems to make its logon page distinct and address initial identification concerns by showing personalized information unique to each user.

Privacy

Obviously, a breach in security is one way that privacy is compromised. Additionally, privacy advocates complain that the .NET My Services process of redirecting a browser from one Web site to the Passport site, verifying the use, and then redirecting the user back to the site is inherently flawed and could enable Microsoft and partner sites to exchange information about users. Many large portal sites currently have this ability, but this problem is exacerbated the more the portal knows about its users. Microsoft pledges that the data is stored encrypted and not even employees will be able to view the information in individual records. It is also enforcing contracts with corporate users that they adhere to a code of ethics for the data that .NET My Services supplies to them. Non-compliance could result in the offending company's exclusion from using .NET My Services.

Big Brother Complex

Consider a large organization that…

- Keeps your personal data in a digital safety deposit box, and everything that makes you "you" could potentially be saved there, including medical records, employment information, and other permanent records.

- Has the ability (whether it chooses to use this ability is another issue) to aggregate the information collected from many of the Web's most popular destinations.

- Creates the world's most popular operating system (and its new reliance on Web integration).

- Creates the world's most popular office suite of applications (and their new reliance on Web integration).

- Has the ability to monitor your television viewing habits via UltimateTV's Personal Video Recorder feature (whether it chooses to use this ability is, again, another issue, although I suspect my TiVo does monitor my viewing habits).

…and you have the makings for a cause of concern for many privacy advocates. They would suggest that Microsoft could potentially track everything about everyone. Although such an Orwellian belief seems rather paranoid (consider the complexity of such a feat), it is not out of the realm of possibility, and could be perceived by the general public as Big Brother watching them—a view that is no doubt a strike against the .NET My Services effort.

Summary

.NET My Services offers authentication services that allow end users to keep all their personal information stored securely and provide access to it on a limited basis to companies and organizations. Organizations can use .NET My Services to outsource their authentication needs, perform data scrubbing to keep their data more current, and give their users a richer environment.

.NET My Services has its critics, even though it has not yet been fully developed or released. Criticisms generally are aimed at concerns about security and privacy of user data. Microsoft has promised to take steps to ensure a high degree of security and is formulating a code of ethics and contracts that enforce the proper use of the data among its partners.

27

INTRODUCING
.NET MY
SERVICES

SOAP, Web Services, and .NET Links on the Internet

W3C SOAP Version 1.2 Second Working Draft (October, 2001)

http://www.w3.org/TR/soap12-part1/

http://www.w3.org/TR/soap12-part2/

W3C Web Service Description Language (WSDL) 1.1

http://www.w3.org/TR/wsdl

UDDI

http://www.uddi.org

http://uddi.microsoft.com

.NET Web Services

http://www.soapwebservices.com

http://www.learnvisualstudio.net

http://msdn.microsoft.com

http://www.dotnetjunkies.com

http://www.dotnetwire.com

http://www.gotdotnet.com/playground/services/

http://www.411asp.net

.NET My Services (Hailstorm) and Passport

`http://www.microsoft.com/NET/netmyservices_snapshot.asp`

`http://www.passport.com`

Other Great References

`http://www.salcentral.com` (Web Services brokerage)

Many Good Links

`http://www.xmethods.com` (list of free Web Services)

`http://www.perfectxml.com/soap.asp` (good tutorials)

`http://www.soap-wrc.com`

`http://www.soaprpc.com`

`http://www.soapware.org`

`http://www.lucin.com`

`http://www.xmlwebservices.com`

`http://www.xmltrustcenter.org/index.htm` (interesting Web Services and security concepts)

INDEX

A

M